ENGLISH FOR THE COLLEGE BOARDS

HENRY I. CHRIST

Dedicated to serving
our nation's youth

Amsco School Publications, Inc.
315 Hudson Street/New York, N.Y. 10013

Grateful acknowledgment is made to Dr. Stephen
Sparacio, Baldwin Public Schools, Baldwin, New York,
for his helpful suggestions on the manuscript.

When ordering this book, please specify:
either **R 436 W** or ENGLISH FOR THE COLLEGE BOARDS.

ISBN 0-87720-687-2

Printed in the United States of America

CONTENTS

ACKNOWLEDGMENTS

Page 283: From *Art and Ardor,* by Cynthia Ozick, by permission of Alfred A. Knopf, Inc.

Page 286: From "The Long Loneliness," *The Star Thrower,* by Loren Eisely, by permission of Times Books, a Division of Random House, Inc.

Page 304: From *The Mathematical Experience,* by Philip J. Davis and Reuben Hersh, pp. 6–7, copyright 1982, by permission of Birkhauser Boston, Inc., published by Houghton Mifflin.

Page 305: From *The Cosmic Mind-Boggling Book,* by Neil McAleer, page 134, copyright 1982, by permission of Warner Books, New York.

Page 306: *From Teaching A Stone To Talk: Expeditions and Encounters,* by Annie Dillard, copyright 1982 by Annie Dillard, reprinted by permission of Harper & Row, Publishers, Inc.

Page 306: From "Microbiological Mining" by Carole L. Brierley, in *Scientific American,* August 1982, p. 44, by permission of Scientific American, Inc.

Page 308: From *Innocents Abroad* by Mark Twain.

Page 309: From "Structuralism in Reverse" by J. Randall Curtis, reprinted from *Et cetera,* Vol. 40, No. 4, by permission of the International Society for General Semantics.

Page 314: From *The Birth of Britain,* by Winston Churchill, copyright 1956, by permission of Dodd, Mead & Company, Inc. (U.S. rights) and McClelland & Stewart Ltd. (Canadian rights).

Page 315: From "The King of Ragtime," by Brian McGinty, May 1984, *American History Illustrated,* reprinted courtesy of Historical Times, Inc., 1984.

Page 315: From "Let's Stop Farming the System," by Rexford A. Resler, May 1984, *American Forests,* by permission of American Forestry Association, Washington, D.C.

Page 316: From "The Metropolitan Museum of Art Bulletin," Winter 1981–82, page 58, copyright © 1982, The Metropolitan Museum of Art, by permission of The Metropolitan Museum of Art, New York.

Page 322: From *The Fabulous Originals,* by Irving Wallace, published by Alfred A. Knopf, Inc., 1955, by permission from Irving Wallace.

Page 323: From *The Works of Robert Louis Stevenson in One Volume,* R. L. Stevenson.

Page 329: From Walter Pater, "Postscript," from *Appreciations, with an Essay on Style.*

Page 330: From *A Foot in England,* by W. H. Hudson.

Page 330: From *The Elements of Style,* Third Edition, by William Strunk, Jr. and E. B. White, copyright 1979 by Macmillan Publishing Company by permission of Macmillan, New York.

Page 331: From "Acres and Pains" from *The Most of S. J. Perelman,* copyright © 1930, 1931, 1932, 1933, 1935, 1936–1953, 1955, 1956, 1958, by S. J. Perelman, reprinted by permission of Simon & Schuster, Inc.

Page 335: From "A Cup of Tea," from *The Dove's Nest,* by Katherine Mansfield.

Page 336: From *Obiter Dicta,* by Augustine Birrell.

Page 342: From *Revolution in Our Time,* by David J. Landes, copyright © 1983 by the President and Fellows of Harvard College, reprinted by permission of Harvard University Press, Cambridge, Massachusetts.

Page 343: From "The Well-Tempered Robot" by Howard Rheingold, December 1983, *Psychology Today,* p. 38, reprinted by permission from Psychology Today Magazine, copyright © 1983. (APA).

Page 344: From *The Flowering of New England,* by Van Wyck Brooks, copyright © 1936, 1952 by E. P. Dutton, Inc.; renewed 1964 by Gladys Brooks. Reprinted by permission of the publisher.

Page 345: From *The Mind in the Making: The Relation of Intelligence to Social Reform,* by James Harvey Robinson, copyright © 1921, by Harper & Row, Publishers, Inc.; renewed, 1949, by Bankers Trust Co. Reprinted by permission of Harper & Row Publishers, Inc.

Page 349: Excerpted from *Look Homeward, Angel.* Copyright 1929 Charles Scribner's Sons; copyright renewed 1957 Edward C. Aswell, Administrator C.T.A. Estate of Thomas Wolfe and/or Fred W. Wolf. Reprinted with permission of Charles Scribner's Sons.

Page 350: From *Levels of Knowing and Existence,* by Harry L. Weinberg, published by Harper & Row. Copyright 1959 by Harry L. Weinberg. Reprinted with permission.

Page 356: From *Extraterrestrial Civilizations,* by Isaac Asimov; copyright © 1979 by Isaac Asimov. Used by permission of Crown Publishers, Inc.

Page 357: From *Crosbie's Dictionary of Puns,* by John S. Crosbie; copyright © 1977 by John S. Crosbie; used by permission of Harmony Books, a division of Crown Publishers, Inc.

Page 358: From Giles St. Aubyn, excerpt from *The Year of Three Kings.* Copyright © 1983 Giles St. Aubyn. Reprinted with the permission of Atheneum Publishers, Inc.

Page 359: From *The Micro Millennium,* by Christopher Evans. Copyright © 1979 by Christopher Evans. Reprinted by permission of Viking Penguin, Inc.

Page 362: From "What Is Evidence," from the *Historian As Detective,* by Carl L. Becker.

Page 363: From *The Bedside, Bathtub, and Armchair Companion to Agatha Christie,* edited by Dick Riley and Pam McAllister, 1979, from the Introduction by Julian Symons. Reprinted by permission of Frederick Ungar Publishing Co.

Page 364: From "Sophisticated Man Is Not Superstitious?" from *The Prevalence of Nonsense* by Ashley Montague and Edward Darling. Copyright © 1967 by M. F. Ashley Montague and Edward Darling, reprinted by permission of Harper & Row, Publishers, Inc.

Page 365: From Philip French's review of "James Agee," by Laurence Bergreen, July 8, 1984, *Book Review.* Copyright © 1984 by The New York Times Company. Reprinted by permission.

Page 369: From *David Copperfield* by Charles Dickens.

Page 370: From *Under the Sea Wind* by Rachel Carson. Copyright © 1941 by Rachel Carson. Renewed 1969 by Roger Christie. Reprinted by permission of Oxford University Press, Inc.

Page 376: From *The Magic of Walking* by Aaron Sussman and Ruth Goode. Copyright © 1967 by Aaron Sussman and Ruth Goode. Reprinted by permission of Simon & Schuster, Inc.

Page 377: Excerpt from *The Conduct of Life,* copyright 1951 by Lewis Mumford. Reprinted by permission of Harcourt Brace Jovanovich, Inc.

Page 378: From *The Living Clocks,* by Ritchie R. Ward. Copyright © 1971 by Ritchie R. Ward. Reprinted by permission of Alfred A. Knopf, Inc.

Page 379: From *The Complete Greek Drama,* edited by Whitney J. Oates and Eugene O'Neill, Jr. Copyright 1938 and renewed 1966 by Random House, Inc. Reprinted by permission of the publisher.

Page 383: Excerpt from *The Dancing Wu Li Masters* by Gary Zukav. Copyright © 1979 by Gary Zukav. By permission of William Morrow & Company.

Page 384: From *Names on the Land* by George R. Stewart. Copyright © 1945, 1958, 1967 by George R. Stewart. Copyright © renewed by George R. Stewart. Reprinted by permission of Houghton Mifflin Company.

SAT questions selected from *6 SATs.* College Entrance Examination Board, 1982. Reprinted by permission of Educational Testing Service, the copyright owner of the sample questions.

Permission to reprint the above material does not constitute review or endorsement by Educational Testing Service or the College Board, of this publication as a whole or of any other testing information it may contain.

INTRODUCTION

Can You Improve Your Score?

You are consulting this book because you are planning to take the SAT. You may be wondering how to go about preparing for the test or hoping that some magic formula may be found here for obtaining a high score.

When the Pharaoh Ptolemy I asked the philosopher Euclid whether there might be some easy way to learn geometry, Euclid is reported to have told him, "There is no royal road to geometry."

Neither is there a royal road to success on the SAT either. What can you do? How can you prepare for so formidable a challenge? With so little time and so much at stake, how should you go about preparing for the SAT? Can any book provide the crucial help you need for this task?

"How Can I Raise My SAT Scores?," a booklet published by the College Entrance Examination Board, answers this question like this: "Quickly and immediately, probably not much. Over longer periods, it depends upon how much time, effort, and concentration go into the preparation." But you have not lived your life in a scholastic and cultural vacuum. You have been developing many skills throughout your life. The SAT booklet goes on to say, "The best preparation for the SAT is to have had varied opportunities of this kind and to have made the most of them."

English for the College Boards accepts the point of view that a crash course in amassing knowledge is impractical preparation. What *is* practical, however, is learning how to use the resources you already have and to develop certain key concepts and insights that will be helpful when you sit down to take the SAT.

English for the College Boards is NOT a cram course. It is, instead, a program with specific major goals:

1. To explain test strategy in general and the SAT strategy in particular.
2. To demonstrate how you can put this strategy to good use.
3. To show you how to reach into your experiences for insights and answers.
4. To provide certain organizing principles that will help you to handle SAT questions.
5. To supply key information, like a detailed study of contexts and roots, that will repay a hundred times over the time you spend on mastery.
6. To build language power, not merely amass bits of knowledge.
7. To be useful beyond the SAT, providing a source book and reference volume for the years ahead.

Doing well on the SAT is one goal. Doing well in later life is another. *English for the College Boards* helps you do both.

What Is the SAT?

The Scholastic Aptitude Test (SAT) is an objective (multiple-choice) test of abilities needed in college-level courses. As its name suggests, it is a test of *aptitude*. You are asked to use ideas and facts in questions requiring you to think. You are <u>not</u> asked to repeat memorized information from different school subject courses.

In all, there are six separate tests of 30 minutes each. Two of these tests are verbal, two are mathematical, one is grammar and usage (and not included in your final score), and one is experimental (and not scored at all).

English for the College Boards prepares you for the two verbal tests of 30 minutes each. Together, the two tests consist of 85 multiple-choice questions—45 questions in one test and 40 in the other.

There are four different kinds of questions in the verbal tests:

25 antonyms
15 sentence completions
20 word relationships (often called "analogies")
25 reading comprehensions, based on reading passages

How Does This Book Help?

1. It has as its major goal the building of language power, not the amassing of bits of knowledge—soon to be forgotten.
2. It analyzes in detail the four kinds of questions on the SAT verbal sections and provides detailed explanations of strategy.
3. It provides an extensive study of analogies; for example, the discussion breaks down the various types of analogies, explains each type, and provides examples and drill.
4. It provides direct and specific help in handling questions involving vocabulary power. It develops strategies that will help you to approach new and unfamiliar words intelligently.
5. It stresses important matters like figurative language and allusions. It reviews and amplifies the subject matter, with abundant examples.
6. It provides extensive help in the area of roots, prefixes, and suffixes, with sample words, reviews, applications, and summaries.
7. The structure of the book is pedagogically sound. It is a self-teaching text. Trial tests, examples, explanations, reviews, and summaries develop sound strategies for approaching SAT questions. A glance at the contents will give some idea of the book's teaching strategy.
8. The diagnostic tests and the facsimile tests have cross references to text pages where help can be found in answering the questions.
9. The book is organized into three major *Divisions:*
   Division A: Vocabulary
   Division B: Reading Comprehension
   Division C: Facsimile Tests
   Divisions A and B are subdivided into *Sections* and *Parts*, specializing in the specific concepts and skills needed for the SAT.

10. Answers are provided for all questions in the book. The answers and analysis for the *Trial Tests* appear immediately after the exercises. The answers for the *Time Out for Review* exercises are found on pages 388–390. The answers for all diagnostic tests and *Facsimile Tests 1, 2,* and *3* are completely analyzed on pages 391–424. Answers for *Facsimile Tests 3* and *4* appear on page 425.

How Is Each Kind of Question Handled?

Sentence Completions   Sections I, II, and III (Division A) all provide help here, but Section I is especially useful. Since the answers to sentence-completion questions depend primarily upon context clues, Section I provides a detailed analysis of various kinds of context clues.

Sections are subdivided into parts. Each part follows a sound procedure:

1. The topic is introduced and explained.
2. A *Trial Test* gives immediate practice in trying out the skill. Answers and analysis of the Trial Test provide immediate helps.
3. A typical SAT question is introduced—called *Problem* in the text.
4. The problem is analyzed and a *Strategy* outlined to solve it.
5. *Time Out for Review* provides additional drill and application.
6. A *Summary* pulls together the teaching points and reviews the information.

Antonyms   Sections II and III of Division A are especially helpful in preparing for the antonym questions. These sections have two purposes: to help you retrieve information you already have and to provide an intelligent approach to meeting new words.

Analogies (Word Relationships)   Section IV of Division A is devoted wholly to analogies. By breaking the analogies questions into 25 different types, this section provides insight into how analogies questions are constructed. It shows how putting the analogy into statement form takes away much of its mystery and dread. The five facsimile tests provide much help for this question—too often handled poorly by candidates. As always, page numbers with the answers identify each analogy type and provide further drill in recognition.

Reading Comprehension Questions   Since reading depends upon vocabulary—which is essential for all SAT questions—the entire book provides preparation for the reading tests. Division B deals specifically with reading skills. This division analyzes the reading skills tested in the SAT. Since these skills provide an admirable cross section of reading skills in general, they also provide help in improving reading for purposes other than the SAT. In six sections, each with subsections, called parts, *English for the College Boards* provides a complete review of major reading skills.

Again, the procedure is sound.

1. The topic is introduced and explained.
2. A reading passage and *Trial Test* enable you to try your skill.
3. Another reading passage (a *Problem*) is presented.
4. A detailed analysis (a *Strategy*) explains the skills tested in the problem.
5. *Time Out for Review* provides still another passage. The test accompanying this passage tests skills just taught and reviews other skills taught earlier in the section.
6. A *Summary* pulls the main points together.

Preparing for the SAT

1. Set up a schedule of preparation, with some time devoted each day to the project.
2. Before the test, review key strategies as outlined in the book. Go over the types of questions asked on the SAT. Be sure you are familiar with the test's structure.
3. Keep yourself in good physical condition. Get a good night's sleep before the test. Don't fret about last-minute cramming. By the time of the test, you will have done all you can. Worrying will be counterproductive.
4. Become familiar with the way in which answers are recorded.
5. Arrive in plenty of time.
6. Have a watch with you to gauge your allotment of time. Don't spend too much time on any one question. If you are stumped, go on to the next question. If you have time, go back for another look.
7. Here is a rule of thumb on timing. On antonym, analogy, and sentence-completion questions, try not to spend more than 30 seconds on any one question. Just go on to the next question. If you have extra time at the end of the test, go back to the unfinished questions. On reading comprehension questions, you are asked to read a passage and answer questions about it. First, notice the number of questions for a passage. For a 3-question passage, allow yourself 4 minutes to read the passage and answer the questions. For a 4-question passage, allow yourself 5 minutes, and so on. Use this add-a-minute formula, but try not to go beyond 8 minutes for any passage and set of questions.
8. Read the directions carefully and follow them.
9. Since you will be penalized a fraction for incorrect answers, don't guess if you have *no* clue to the correct answer. An educated guess, however, is probably strategically wise.
10. Don't panic if you don't know an answer. You are not expected to know all the answers. Do the best you can with the resources you have. That's all you can be expected to do.

DIVISION A

Vocabulary

Remember . . .
When preparing for the SAT

■ Rely upon your built-in knowledge of words, the experiences you have already had with language. *English for the College Boards* will show you how to use this built-in knowledge and how to expand your current vocabulary.

■ Do not rely on studying long lists of difficult words. Unless you use the words soon afterward, you will probably forget them. Besides, the word lists you study may not contain any of the words on the test you will take.

■ Master the skills of test-taking. This book will show you how.

Section I: Context Clues

How did you learn that a **lane** is a narrow road, that a **platter** is a kind of dish, and that a **glove** is a hand covering? You probably never looked these words up in a dictionary. You learned them through experience, through hearing the words in a certain situation, a *context*.

"Here, put on these **gloves** when you go out. It's cold outside."

You learned the word **glove** without having it defined for you. Nearly all common words are learned through the context of experience. Even words like **hope**, **love**, **friendship**, and **justice** are mastered in much the same way.

Here is another example.

"That's not **fair**."

If you hear that expression applied to certain situations, you soon decide what is fair and what is unfair.

You have learned new words in your reading, too. Consider this sentence.

"The sailors caught a dozen **pompano** and made a beach fire for a fish fry at sunset."

Even if you had never seen the word **pompano** before, you would know, from the context, that the pompano is a fish. The words surrounding **pompano**, the word's context, provide all the clues you need.

Each time you use a word in a new context, you sharpen your understanding of the word. One reading will often provide enough clues to learn a new word. The image created will also help you remember the word.

How will learning to use context clues help you in taking the SAT? One section of the test, the sentence-completion question, relies heavily on context clues for deriving the correct answer, but context helps elsewhere as well. First, let's sample a few easier sentences to familiarize you with the context clues in action and to analyze techniques for handling words. Next you will examine some actual test questions.

PART 1

Context Clue: The Entire Sentence

This clue is a common one, but it sometimes requires some thought and ingenuity to make an intelligent guess with word meanings.

> **A.** The **incessant** traffic noise outside my hotel window, though not loud, gave me scarcely a moment's sleep throughout the night.

What kind of noise would keep someone from sleeping? A loud noise would present a problem, but the sentence specifically says "not loud." What other quality of noise would interfere with sleep? Some kind of persistent noise. Is the noise in the quoted sentence occasional, or steady and continuous? "Gave me scarcely a moment's sleep" suggests that the noise is steady. It never stops. If the sentence had said the noise "interrupted my sleep," we might infer that the sound comes and goes. But the sentence tells us the noise "gave me scarcely a moment's sleep."

Obviously, **incessant** means "never stopping." As you will see later, the spelling of **incessant** provides some other clues to meaning, clues that help you to nail down the meaning.

> **B.** As a result of the new owner's surprisingly **indolent** ways, the formerly flourishing farm sank into neglect and failure.

What ways would cause a farm to sink into "neglect and failure"? Certainly not careful, energetic, or efficient ways. A neglected farm is not worked enough. If it is not worked enough, the owner must be either lazy or physically unable to do the work. What is the best guess here? The word "surprisingly" suggests that everyone expected the new owner to do a good job. Apparently, the owner was not ill or physically incapacitated in any way. Therefore, he or she must be lazy. **Indolent** means "lazy."

Trial Test

Take the following short test to make sure you understand this kind of context clue. Write the letter of the word or words that have the same meaning as the boldfaced word.

EXAMPLE

After the flood the policyholders took some comfort in knowing that they would be **compensated** for their losses.

   (A) charged   (D) called
   (B) forgiven   (E) repaid
   (C) prepared   __E__

If the policyholders were comforted, then the correct choice is (E).

1. Through the binoculars we could **discern** two hikers on the ridge of Mt. Jefferson.
   (A) call to   (D) report
   (B) see clearly   (E) wave to
   (C) photograph   1 ___

2. Because the plan seemed **feasible**, the explorers put it into operation.
   (A) detailed   (D) workable
   (B) exciting   (E) commonplace
   (C) premeditated   2 ___

3. After the **cessation** of hostilities, an unaccustomed calm settled over the city.
   (A) stopping   (D) description
   (B) expansion   (E) denunciation
   (C) eruption   3 ___

4. The medication **assuaged** the pain and permitted Charles a few hours of sleep.
   - (A) localized
   - (B) varied
   - (C) inflamed
   - (D) recalled
   - (E) lessened

   4 ___

5. Bonnie made a **grimace** when she sipped the vinegar instead of the cider.
   - (A) curtsy
   - (B) prepared speech
   - (C) distorted face
   - (D) backbend
   - (E) agitated dance step

   5 ___

6. In the tennis tournament, Jeanne slapped a hard volley to the corner, and Linda quickly **retaliated** with a smash down the line.
   - (A) struck quietly
   - (B) exclaimed bitterly
   - (C) objected strenuously
   - (D) found excuses
   - (E) returned like for like

   6 ___

7. Mel couldn't conceal his **chagrin** when he tripped awkwardly in front of Betty.
   - (A) embarrassment
   - (B) sense of humor
   - (C) delight
   - (D) expression
   - (E) curiosity

   7 ___

8. The March robin has always been the traditional **harbinger** of spring.
   - (A) bird
   - (B) forerunner
   - (C) lover
   - (D) friend
   - (E) latecomer

   8 ___

9. Pru worked **assiduously** throughout the night and completed her term report in time for morning class.
   - (A) cheerfully
   - (B) thoughtlessly
   - (C) frequently
   - (D) industriously
   - (E) prayerfully

   9 ___

10. In a relatively brief career, Jesse James **perpetrated** many crimes.
    - (A) committed
    - (B) solved
    - (C) reported
    - (D) permitted
    - (E) witnessed

    10 ___

Answers to Trial Test

1. (B) Since binoculars are being used, the answer must have something to do with seeing. The only answer that deals with seeing is *see clearly*.

2. (D) If the explorers put the plan into operation, the answer must show that the plan is practical. The only answer that deals with this point is *workable*.

3. (A) If "calm settled over the city," hostilities must have stopped. The correct answer is *stopping*.

4. (E) If Charles was permitted "a few hours of sleep," the pain must have lessened. The correct answer is *lessened*.

5. (C) Since vinegar is sharp and sour, Bonnie's expression must have shown her unhappy surprise. The correct answer is *distorted face*.

6. (E) The back-and-forth nature of a tennis match provides the clue here. Linda returned the volley. The correct answer is *returned like for like*.

7. (A) If Mel "tripped awkwardly in front of Betty," he must have been embarrassed. The correct answer is *embarrassment*.

8. (B) Robins announce the coming of spring. Therefore a *harbinger* must be some kind of early messenger. The word that best suggests this definition is *forerunner*.

9. (D) If Pru worked throughout the night and finished her report in time, she must have worked hard. The correct answer is *industriously*.

10. (A) Jesse James is a famous outlaw who was involved in only one side of the battle against crime: the wrong side. The correct answer is *committed*.

Now examine an actual test question. The question requires the applicant to select the word or set of words that *best* completes the sentence.

Problem

Susan did not resent the arduous work, for she believed that every --- that demands thought, attention, and independent judgment --- the quality of daily life.

    (A) task . . heightens
    (B) profession . . belittles
    (C) hobby . . undercuts
    (D) folly . . exalts
    (E) diversion . . disrupts

Strategy

Here is a helpful first step. Finish the sentence with your own words before looking at the answers suggested. Taking this first step gives you some feeling for the structure of the completed sentence and helps with judging possible alternatives. Then evaluate the alternatives provided.

If you are unfamiliar with a word in the sentence, examine the context and make an intelligent guess. If, for example, you don't know the word "arduous," you will find a lot of help in the context, or the other words, in the sentence. The sentence suggests that arduous work might be resented, for a special point is made of the fact that Susan did <u>not</u> resent it. What kind of work might be resented? A good guess is *hard work*. "Arduous" probably means "hard to do." But even if you did not determine the meaning of "arduous" exactly, you could still figure out that arduous work might be considered unpleasant. This judgment would assist in choosing the correct answer.

How do the various alternatives fit?

Choice (A) Try out the first pair.

Susan did not resent the arduous work, for she believed that every *task* that demands thought, attention, and independent judgment *heightens* the quality of daily life.

Task is obviously a good choice, for it is clearly related to "work" in the preceding clause. How does *heightens* also fit into the scheme? Sometimes in questions of this kind the first alternative may work, but the second one may not. Or the reverse may be true. If *heightens* is an unfamiliar word to you, the word within it is a clue. The word *height* is associated with intensity. The height of indignation, for example, is an intense form of indignation. *Heightens* probably means "make more intense." Does the word make sense in the completed sentence? Obviously it does. A demanding task improves the quality of everyday living.

Notice that now the entire sentence makes sense. Susan did not resent hard work because she realized that challenging tasks make living richer. These two words (task and heightens) fit admirably well. But the directions say to select the words that best complete the sentence. Perhaps there are other words that do an even better job.

Choice (*B*)   If you insert *profession* and *belittles*, you run into problems. *Profession* isn't as good a word as *task*, but it does make sense. However, what of *belittles*? *Belittles* destroys the meaning of the sentence. *Belittle*, clearly meaning "make little," makes nonsense of Susan's attitude. Choice (*B*) then is incorrect.

Choice (*C*)   If you insert *hobby* into the first blank, you have a barely possible answer but not so good an answer as that in (*A*). The required word should involve arduous work. A task certainly involves arduous work, as does a profession. A *hobby* might involve arduous work, but *hobby* is a leisure-time activity. Go on to *undercuts*. This presents the same problem as *belittles* in (*B*). Even if you are not precisely sure of the meaning of *undercut* ("to make less effective"), you can still be sure the idea is negative. The barely possible *hobby* and the unsuitable *undercuts* make this choice a poor one.

Choice (*D*)   If you insert *folly* into the first blank, you run into trouble immediately. *Folly* runs counter to the idea of work. Susan accepts work but not folly. Besides, *folly* doesn't demand "thought, attention, and independent judgment." You can reject this choice immediately, but just to be sure, you ought to try out the second word in the second blank. If you know that *exalts* means "raise up," "glorify," you have verified your guess that (*D*) is incorrect. If you do not know the meaning of *exalts*, you have still rejected (*D*) because *folly* doesn't make sense. Thus far no alternative is as good as (*A*).

Choice (*E*)   The first choice in (*E*) is *diversion*, a hard word. You can guess at the meaning by looking at the little word within the bigger one and noting related words (divert, diverse, diversity). A strategy for handling this skill is discussed later (page 74). Fortunately, however, you don't have to waste too much time, for if one alternative in the pair is incorrect, the answer is incorrect. Look at *disrupts*. *Disrupts* (meaning "breaks up, disturbs") is a fairly common word, but even if it is unfamiliar to you, you can guess that a word beginning with *dis* may well be a negative word. *Dislike*, *displease*, and *disloyal* are all negative words. The context of the entire sentence requires a positive word here. Why else would Susan not resent the arduous work? A *diversion* that disturbs or lessens the quality of everyday life would not be Susan's choice.

The preceding analysis shows certain things.

1. You don't have to know every word to get the answer correct.
2. By a process of elimination, you can often find the best answer. Quite often it is enough to guess intelligently at only one of the choices.
3. The context of the sentence AS A WHOLE is the crucial element in the answer. Just ask: "What words make best sense when inserted into the blanks?"

Although we have taken a lot of time to analyze each choice carefully, you will not need to spend as much time in deciding upon your answer. Trying out all alternatives rapidly and in succession often gives the applicant a feeling for the sentence as a whole. Quite often the correct answer will jump from the page. At other times, a little more careful evaluation will be necessary.

Time Out For Review

Write the letter of the word or words that have the same meaning as the boldfaced word.

1. No one knew the reason for the sudden, **prodigious** increase in real estate values in so short a time.
   (A) small
   (B) enormous
   (C) average
   (D) disappointing
   (E) expected
   1 ___

2. The play "**Blithe** Spirit" is about a non-threatening, fun-loving ghost.
   (A) ghostly
   (B) athletic
   (C) deteriorated
   (D) cheerful
   (E) flexible
   2 ___

3. Totally absorbed in the computer program, the students were **oblivious to** the hallway noises.
   (A) unaware of
   (B) antagonistic toward
   (C) concerned about
   (D) absorbed in
   (E) distracted by
   3 ___

4. The group of **ornithologists** went on lengthy bird-watching hikes.
   (A) dental specialists
   (B) spellers
   (C) bird experts
   (D) story collectors
   (E) bone doctors
   4 ___

5. A victim is doomed because there is no known **antidote** for the rare snakebite.
   (A) amusing story
   (B) appetizer
   (C) old furniture
   (D) remedy
   (E) deer
   5 ___

6. The audience was shrieking with laughter, but no one could discover the reason for such **levity**.
   (A) frivolity
   (B) tax
   (C) riverbank
   (D) floating in air
   (E) controlling device
   6 ___

7. The press club did a hilarious **parody** of the President's address, called "The State of the Household."
   (A) talking bird
   (B) abnormal distrust
   (C) contradictory statement
   (D) one-celled creature
   (E) humorous imitation
   7 ___

8. At its **apogee** the satellite reached its maximum distance of 480 miles from earth.
   (A) words of regret
   (B) attack
   (C) farthest point
   (D) lack of interest
   (E) window opening
   8 ___

9. The job is too much responsibility for a **callow** youngster, hardly out of school.
   (A) thick-skinned
   (B) immature
   (C) lily-like
   (D) rich in food energy
   (E) experienced
   9 ___

10. Because of the **plethora** of jobs and housing in the area, everyone was well off.
    (A) curse
    (B) plentiful supply
    (C) lack
    (D) lung disease
    (E) feeling of well-being
    10 ___

SUMMARY PART 1

Context Clue: The Entire Sentence

When you deal with the problems in an SAT question, there are strategies to use. Often the entire sentence provides clues to the meaning of a word in that sentence.

1. Complete the sentence with *your own words* before looking at the choices.
2. Then go ahead and work with the choices provided.
3. If you are not familiar with a word, examine the word's context. Then make an intelligent choice.

PART 2

Context Clue: Pairing

Since writers often repeat themselves slightly to make a point, watch out for paired words. If you don't know the first word, you'll probably know the second.

Pauline was an **ardent,** enthusiastic collector of old Roman coins.

Since the words **ardent** and "enthusiastic" are paired and obviously descriptive of the same person, you have good reason to believe they are related. "Enthusiastic," a common word, provides a substantial clue to the less common word **ardent.**

Trial Test

Take the following trial test to make sure you understand this type of context clue. Underline the word or words that are paired with the word in boldface. Write the letter of your answer in the space at the right.

EXAMPLE

Benedict Arnold at last was **perfidious,** faithless to the ideals he once professed.

(A) fastidious   (D) egotistical
(B) talented   (E) treacherous
(C) relentless

                       E

"Faithless" is paired with **perfidious** and should be underlined. It makes clear that **perfidious** means *treacherous* (*E*).

1. Perry has a colorful, **flamboyant** style of dress that sets him apart.
   (A) drab   (D) happy
   (B) showy   (E) irritating
   (C) conservative

                 1 ___

2. The audience's **acclamation** gratified the soloist, who liked the obvious approval of her performance.
   (A) interest   (D) applause
   (B) participation   (E) coolness
   (C) evaluation

                 2 ___

3. Scrooge's actions were mean and **despicable.**
   (A) aware   (D) desperate
   (B) unpredictable   (E) unkind
   (C) generous

                 3 ___

4. The lawyer **demurred,** disapproving the suggested settlement.
   (A) objected   (D) orated
   (B) chuckled   (E) sat down
   (C) consented

                 4 ___

5. It is not unusual for a young child to live in **reveries** and daydreams.
   (A) nurseries   (D) prayers
   (B) realities   (E) misgivings
   (C) fantasies

                 5 ___

6. The treasurer's reports were always **concise** and to the point.
   (A) elaborate   (D) brief
   (B) uninformative   (E) labored
   (C) funny

                 6 ___

7. The mountain climb proved too **arduous** and difficult for the inexperienced members of the party.
   (A) monotonous   (D) chilly
   (B) strenuous   (E) rocky
   (C) unexpected

                 7 ___

8. To **malign** someone, to tell an evil lie about him, might lay the speaker open to charges of slander.
   (A) wrong   (D) irritate
   (B) advertise   (E) discuss
   (C) report

                 8 ___

9. The inhabitants of the besieged city endured **privation** and hardship unknown in peacetime.

(A) fury   (D) experiences
(B) want   (E) repetition
(C) excitement

9 ___

10. Ever since he failed the math test, Greg has been **morose** and ill-tempered.

(A) excitable   (D) speechless
(B) resigned   (E) gloomy
(C) vicious

10 ___

Answers to Trial Test

1. (*B*) The word **flamboyant** is paired with "colorful." The word closest in meaning to both words in the pair is *showy*.

2. (*D*) **Acclamation** is paired with "obvious approval." The correct answer is *applause*.

3. (*E*) **Despicable** is paired with "mean." The correct answer is *unkind*.

4. (*A*) **Demurred** is paired with "disapproving." To demur is to disapprove. The correct answer is *objected*.

5. (*C*) **Reveries** is paired with "daydreams." Daydreams are *fantasies*.

6. (*D*) **Concise** is paired with "to the point." Something to the point is *brief*, not wordy.

7. (*B*) **Arduous** and "difficult" are paired. *Strenuous* means about the same.

8. (*A*) **Malign** is paired with "to tell an evil lie." The idea of evil suggests that the correct answer is *wrong*.

9. (*B*) **Privation** and "hardship" are paired. The correct answer is *want*. Here *want* is used as a noun.

10. (*E*) **Morose** and "ill-tempered" are paired. The word closest to describing such a state of mind is *gloomy*.

Examine another actual test question.

Problem

Ms. Wilton urged patience and --- in dealing with the protesters rather than the unyielding attitude the administration had adopted.

(A) obstinacy   (D) compromise
(B) desperation   (E) retaliation
(C) arrogance

Strategy

Here "patience" is obviously being paired with the word needed in the blank. How does each of the alternatives fit as a possible member of the pair?

Choice (*A*) *Obstinacy* doesn't fit the blank too well. *Obstinacy* (remember the adjective *obstinate*) means "stubbornness." Stubbornness does not go well with patience.

Choice (*B*) *Desperation* is a poor match as well. *Desperation* (remember *desperate*), like *obstinacy*, does not go well with patience.

Choice (*C*) *Arrogance* clashes with patience. Arrogant persons are rarely patient, for they want their way—immediately.

Choice (*D*) *Compromise* is a good match. Patient people are not overbearing or in a hurry. They are willing to take time, to see other sides, to make adjustments in their own viewpoints. *Compromise* seems like the answer, but make sure by looking at the last possibility.

Choice (*E*) *Retaliation* conflicts directly with patience. To *retaliate*, to "strike back," may come after patience has been exhausted, but it does not match patience.

Compromise (*D*) is obviously the right answer. Notice that this sentence also provides other clues. The sentence as a whole calls for a positive word in the blank.

As you work with context clues, you will often find several in one sentence, all helping you to learn the unfamiliar word.

Time Out for Review

Write the letter of the word or words that have the same meaning as the boldfaced word.

1. It isn't worth all the trouble to get a measly, **paltry** 20-cent refund.
   - (A) small
   - (B) pale
   - (C) unexpected
   - (D) trembling
   - (E) warm

   1 ___

2. The house in the expensive new neighborhood seemed showy and **ostentatious.**
   - (A) swinging to and fro
   - (B) banished; shut out
   - (C) modest
   - (D) pretentious; done to attract attention
   - (E) absorbent

   2 ___

3. After the business failed, the owner was **destitute,** without a penny to his name.
   - (A) very sad
   - (B) deserted
   - (C) very poor
   - (D) dried out
   - (E) like a tyrant

   3 ___

4. The news of the fare increase was received with **vituperation** and abusive remarks.
   - (A) a sense of humor
   - (B) a healthful food element
   - (C) bitter scolding
   - (D) surgery
   - (E) approval

   4 ___

5. There was an unspoken, **tacit** agreement that all expenses would be shared.
   - (A) diplomatic
   - (B) silent; understood
   - (C) maneuverable
   - (D) touching
   - (E) debatable

   5 ___

6. Money has not been a problem for Gale since she came into the bequest, or **legacy,** from her aunt.
   - (A) old tale
   - (B) inheritance
   - (C) veteran's group
   - (D) lawsuit
   - (E) readable writing

   6 ___

7. With the sandals, gym shorts, and cap, the white shirt and tie were indeed **incongruous,** hopelessly out of place.

(A) without ability   (D) disrespectful
(B) without a name   (E) colorful
(C) inappropriate   7 ___

8. One warning of an earthquake is a display of uncommon, **unwonted** behavior by animals.

(A) brilliant   (D) irreverent
(B) unusual   (E) colorful
(C) angered   8 ___

9. The combination of high inflation and low employment was a **paradox,** a pairing of opposite conditions.

(A) heavenly place   (D) contradiction
(B) example   (E) illustrative
(C) established   story
     custom   9 ___

10. The Delmarva Peninsula **comprises,** or includes, parts of three states: Delaware, Maryland, and Virginia.

(A) agrees to   (D) promises
(B) contains   (E) understands
(C) obeys; follows
                             10 ___

SUMMARY PART 2

Context Clue: Pairing

1. Be on the lookout for paired words or ideas. (Writers often repeat themselves to make a point.)
2. If you don't know one of the words or ideas, you may know the other.

PART 3

Context Clue: Direct Explanation

Surprisingly often, a tricky word will actually be explained in the same sentence in which it appears.

Greg was so **avaricious** he refused to spend money even for necessities and almost starved among his collection of gold coins.

The sentence provides the explanation for **avaricious.** Someone who hoards money unwisely, who refuses to spend even for necessities, is ''greedy to the point of sickness.'' There you have the definition of avaricious.

Sometimes an appositive provides the direct explanation you need.

Hedonism, the pursuit of pleasure at all costs, may lead to misery.

The appositive phrase, ''the pursuit of pleasure at all costs,'' clearly tells the meaning of **hedonism.** It defines the word in context.

Sometimes a participial phrase provides helpful clues to the meaning of a word.

Gazelles are **herbivorous,** eating only grasses and other vegetation.

The participial phrase, ''eating only grasses and other vegetation,'' tells the meaning of **herbivorous.** It, too, defines the word in context.

Trial Test

Take the following trial test to make sure you understand this type of context clue. Underline the word or words that explain the boldfaced word. Write the letter of your answer in the space at the right.

EXAMPLE

Jud's remarks served to **exacerbate** the problem, <u>making a solution more remote than ever.</u>

(A) slightly ease   (D) cleverly
(B) make worse   explain
(C) clearly reveal   (E) repeat

                     B

''Making a solution more remote than ever'' explains **exacerbate** and should be underlined. The correct answer is *make worse (B).*

1. Jody lived a **sedentary** life, rarely engaging in exercise or even leaving the house for a walk along the colorful streets near his home.
   (A) lively   (D) inactive
   (B) varied   (E) interesting
   (C) puzzling   1 ___

2. Each wave of frantic buying and selling in the stock market tends to **subside,** or settle down, after a short time.
   (A) calm down   (D) explode
   (B) whirl about   (E) recover
   (C) stir up   2 ___

3. In carpentry, Chuck is a model of **ineptitude,** hitting a finger with a hammer and sawing a crooked line.
   (A) humor   (D) surprise
   (B) clumsiness   (E) discontent
   (C) failure to plan   3 ___

4. A 20-degree day can feel like ten below zero, depending on the wind **velocity,** the speed at which it is blowing.

   (A) heat   (D) good fortune
   (B) unpredictability (E) rapidity
   (C) agreement   4 ___

5. Among the high-risk group are fairly inactive adults with a **predilection,** or taste, for cholesterol-rich foods.

   (A) amusement (D) preference
   (B) necessity (E) portion
   (C) accuracy   5 ___

6. Senator Fogg launched into his usual **harangue,** an endless lecture on the frightful conditions everywhere.

   (A) long, ranting   (D) obvious lie
       speech   (E) dessert
   (B) exclamation of   6 ___
       pleasure
   (C) humorous
       comment

7. When they heard the Prime Minister's proposals, the members were **derisive,** hooting and howling their displeasure.

   (A) violent   (D) silent
   (B) scornful (E) secure
   (C) joyous   7 ___

8. A portion of the sign **protrudes** beyond the corner of the building, presenting an obstacle for every passerby.

   (A) becomes   (D) sticks out
       visible   (E) reappears
   (B) is being
       constructed
   (C) twists   8 ___

9. The assassination of the Archduke Ferdinand **precluded** a peaceful solution, making unavoidable the mass slaughter of World War I.

   (A) foretold   (D) presented
   (B) unfolded   (E) suggested
   (C) prevented   9 ___

10. Mr. Allen was **parsimonious** by nature, miserly and thrifty to the point of excess.

   (A) thoughtful (D) small
   (B) clever   (E) suspicious
   (C) stingy   10 ___

Answers to Trial Test

1. (*D*) "Rarely engaging in exercise" provides a definition of **sedentary.** Therefore the correct answer is *inactive*.

2. (*A*) **Subside** is explained by its appositive, "settle down." The correct answer is *calm down*.

3. (*B*) "Hitting a finger" and "sawing a crooked line" are given as examples of **ineptitude.** Since those activities show a lack of skill, the correct answer is *clumsiness*.

4. (*E*) **Velocity** is explained by its appositive, "speed." The correct answer is *rapidity*.

5. (*D*) **Predilection** is explained by its appositive, "taste." The correct answer is *preference*.

6. (*A*) **Harangue** is explained by its appositive, "endless lecture." The correct answer is *long, ranting speech*.

7. (*B*) If the **derisive** members ''hooted and howled,'' we can assume the correct answer is *scornful*.

8. (*D*) ''Presenting an obstacle'' explains **protrudes.** The correct answer is *sticks out*.

9. (*C*) ''Making unavoidable the mass slaughter'' tells us that **precluded** means ''made a peaceful solution impossible.'' The correct answer is *prevented*.

10. (*C*) ''Miserly and thrifty to the point of excess'' tells us what **parsimonious** means. The correct answer is *stingy*.

Study another actual test question.

Problem

Meteors become --- only after they enter the
atmosphere, for it is then that they begin to
burn and leave their luminous trails.

    (A) incandescent   (D) reflective
    (B) invisible   (E) elemental
    (C) illusionary

Strategy

Quite often, a clause beginning with ''for'' actually explains the point of the previous clause.

    I screamed, for the pain was intense.

Similarly, in the test sentence, the ''for'' clause says specifically that meteors ''burn and leave luminous trails.'' If the word ''luminous'' is new to you, you have the word *illuminate* to fall back on. Also, when something burns, it is usually bright.

Choice (*A*) *Incandescent* is probably a familiar word to you because of the incandescent electric light bulb. This seems like a good answer because the ''for'' clause has just told you that the meteors burn and leave bright trails. Just to be sure check the other alternatives.

Choice (*B*) *Invisible* is clearly inappropriate. If the meteors burn brightly, they cannot be invisible.

Choice (*C*) *Illusionary* suggests trickery or deception, from the word *illusion*. But there's nothing tricky or deceptive about the meteor's bright trail.

Choice (*D*) *Reflective* doesn't make sense in the sentence. *Reflective* means ''thoughtful,'' a meaning without relevance here.

Choice (*E*) *Elemental* is wide of the mark. The word has obviously nothing to do with brightness.

Note that the sense of the entire sentence is also a clue to meaning here. Having more than one clue to fall back on guarantees accuracy.

Quite often a subordinate clause actually explains the point of the main clause.

The Watergate committee sought to investigate **covert actions,** which had been concealed illegally from the American public.

This time the "which" clause explains that **covert actions** deal with illegal concealment.

Time Out for Review

Write the letter for the word or words that have the same meaning as the boldfaced word in each sentence.

1. In the 14th century, the Black Death was **rampant** in Europe, raging unchecked through the crowded cities.
   - (A) unrestrained
   - (B) unfortunate
   - (C) unexpected
   - (D) unforced
   - (E) unpopular

   1 ___

2. John Paul entered with his hat **askew,** for it perched at an impossible angle on his head.
   - (A) colorful
   - (B) upside down
   - (C) reversed
   - (D) crooked
   - (E) untouched

   2 ___

3. The counsel for the defense took strong exception to the prosecutor's **derogatory** comments, which humiliated the defendant and prejudiced the case against him.
   - (A) unfavorable and disparaging
   - (B) generous but sarcastic
   - (C) fierce and cruel
   - (D) unexpected and partial
   - (E) thoughtless and indefinite

   3 ___

4. Only a trained eye can **discern,** or tell the difference between, a high and low quality diamond.
   - (A) disagree
   - (B) recognize
   - (C) rule out
   - (D) control; train
   - (E) throw away

   4 ___

5. The entire school was run by a small, **arrogant** group, who lorded it over the rest of the students.
   - (A) well-spoken
   - (B) aromatic
   - (C) haughty; scornful
   - (D) romantic
   - (E) disorderly

   5 ___

6. Wherever the terrorist went, he was a **firebrand,** who stirred up the people to revolt and strike.
   - (A) good speaker
   - (B) messenger
   - (C) friend
   - (D) newscaster
   - (E) troublemaker

   6 ___

7. A book jacket often gives a **synopsis** of the plot, summarizing the major events.
   - (A) grammatical system
   - (B) condensation
   - (C) combination
   - (D) artificiality
   - (E) simultaneous event

   7 ___

8. Some citizens continue to live in **abject** poverty, with no way to escape from it.
   - (A) conforming
   - (B) hopeless
   - (C) sudden
   - (D) forgiven
   - (E) attention-getting

   8 ___

9. "Waste not, want not" is an old **maxim,** a tried and true bit of advice.
   - (A) wise saying
   - (B) greatest amount
   - (C) person who knows everything
   - (D) woman in charge
   - (E) grown-up person

   9 ___

10. In combat, a large tent may house an **infirmary,** a hospital for the injured.
    - (A) shaky place
    - (B) kind of tent
    - (C) treatment place
    - (D) illness
    - (E) endless distance

    10 ___

SUMMARY PART 3

Context Clue: Direct Explanation

For help with this kind of context clue, look for:

1. An appositive: an explanatory word or phrase set off by commas.
2. A participial phrase explaining the meaning of the key word.
3. An explanation beginning with *for*.
4. An explanation provided by a subordinate clause.

PART 4

Context Clue: Comparison

Sometimes a sentence will reveal the meaning of an unfamiliar word by including a helpful comparison.

In attacking the problem, Sandy was as **diligent** as a bee gathering honey.

A characteristic of a "bee gathering honey" is single-minded devotion to the task. The comparison tells us Sandy was hard-working and industrious.

Trial Test

Take the following trial test to make sure you understand this type of context clue. Underline the word or words that state the comparison to the boldfaced word. Write the letter of your answer in the space at the right.

EXAMPLE

After the hostage was **liberated** he felt as free as a bird.

  (A) embarrassed   (D) changed
  (B) let go   (E) understood
  (C) educated   **B**

"As free as a bird" should be underlined because it tells how a hostage that is "liberated" will feel if he is *let go*. (*B*)

1. Dundee often displays the **irascibility** of a wasp whose nest has been disturbed.
  (A) subtle charm   (D) inventive genius
  (B) cowardly behavior   (E) sweetness
  (C) quickness to anger   1 ___

2. With the sublety of a hammer smashing an eggshell, Frank **bludgeoned** everyone to agree.
  (A) asked   (D) destroyed
  (B) elected   (E) bullied
  (C) calmed   2 ___

3. The interior of the building was as **murky** as winter twilight with an overcast sky.
  (A) brilliant   (D) colorful
  (B) cold   (E) odorous
  (C) gloomy   3 ___

4. Pete's **incessant** interruptions had all the qualities of endless drops from a leaky faucet.
  (A) irrelevant   (D) exaggerated
  (B) sharp   (E) ill-tempered
  (C) continuing   4 ___

5. When the dinner bell is sounded, Carl moves with the **alacrity** of a startled lizard.
  (A) quick motion   (D) resourcefulness
  (B) intelligence   (E) body language
  (C) grace   5 ___

6. Jan's costume was as **incongruous** as an evening dress at a picnic.
  (A) dazzling   (D) indecisive
  (B) pleasing   (E) unavailing
  (C) unsuitable   6 ___

7. Maz's retorts had all the **caustic** charm of a corrosive acid.
  (A) biting   (D) bewildering
  (B) witty   (E) immortal
  (C) delightful   7 ___

8. The moped's tracks in the sand were as **sinuous** as a snake's trail.
  (A) unpleasant   (D) loathsome
  (B) intriguing   (E) winding
  (C) easily read   8 ___

9. The senator's **tirade** in Congress was like a mother's scolding a naughty son.
  (A) stay   (D) absenteeism
  (B) denunciation   (E) explanation
  (C) filibuster   9 ___

10. After two weeks I was as **ravenous** as a
tiger on a starvation diet.

   (A) angry   (D) prepared
   (B) upset   (E) blissful
   (C) hungry

                       10 _____

Answers to Trial Test

1. (*C*) "A wasp whose nest has been disturbed" is not likely to be happy. The comparision suggests that **irascibility** means *quickness to anger*.

2. (*E*) "A hammer smashing an eggshell" shows no "subtlety." Therefore Frank overwhelmed everyone. The correct answer is *bullied*.

3. (*C*) "Winter twilight" and "overcast sky" suggest darkness and gloominess. The correct answer is *gloomy*.

4. (*C*) "Endless drops from a leaky faucet" suggest a steady, annoying sound. The correct answer is *continuing*.

5. (*A*) "A startled lizard" moves rapidly. Therefore **alacrity** must mean *quick motion*.

6. (*C*) "An evening dress" is out of place "at a picnic." Therefore **incongruous** must mean *unsuitable*.

7. (*A*) "A corrosive acid" eats away substances. **Caustic** means *biting*.

8. (*E*) "A snake's trail" winds. Therefore **sinuous** means *winding*.

9. (*B*) "Scolding" is disapproving speech. Therefore **tirade** must mean *denunciation*.

10. (*C*) "A tiger on a starvation diet" would be very hungry. Therefore **ravenous** must mean *hungry*.

    Study another actual test question.

Problem

Just as congestion plagues every important
highway, so it --- the streets of every city.

    (A) delimits   (D) obviates
    (B) delays   (E) destroys
    (C) clogs

Strategy

    The comparison with *as* helps determine the answer to this question. The sentence compares congestion on the rural highways and on the city streets. The second clause must follow the sense of the first clause. The word "plague" is obviously negative. It tells us that congestion slows traffic on highways. The second clause must suggest that congestion slows traffic on city streets. Look at the choices.

Choice (A) *Delimits* has nothing to do with "congestion" in a physical sense. It means "fix the limits of," but the meaning has little, if anything, to do with the sentence.

Choice (B) *Delays* has the right suggestion. Traffic does cause delays. But streets are not delayed. "Delaying the streets of every city" doesn't make sense.

Choice (C) *Clogs* strikes the right note at once. "Congestion" suggests clogging. This alternative fits perfectly.

Choice (D) *Obviates* has the right negative tone, but it doesn't fit into the sentence. We can *clog* streets, we cannot *obviate* ("get rid of") them.

Choice (E) *Destroys* is hopelessly overstated. "Congestion" doesn't destroy the streets. It may destroy the peace of mind of the drivers, but it doesn't destroy the streets. The correct answer, *clogs* (C), was suggested by the comparison in the two clauses.

Time Out For Review

Write the letter of the word or words that have the same meaning as the boldfaced word in each sentence.

1. On the hot, hazy afternoon, we felt as **torpid** as a cat snoozing in the sun.
   (A) hot
   (B) energetic
   (C) sluggish
   (D) punished
   (E) injured
   1 ___

2. With the **impartiality** of a computer following its program, a competent judge makes a decision based on clear-cut evidence and facts.
   (A) impatience
   (B) fairness; not favoring either side
   (C) disorderliness
   (D) slowness
   (E) joyfulness
   2 ___

3. The shop windows filled with merchandise were as **tantalizing** to us as rich, tasty foods are to a dieter.
   (A) confusing
   (B) actual
   (C) meddling
   (D) tempting
   (E) disgusting
   3 ___

4. Melissa served the luncheon with the **dexterity** of a professional magician.
   (A) clumsiness
   (B) skillfulness
   (C) slowness
   (D) foolishness
   (E) forgetfulness
   4 ___

5. The chain-reaction accident on the freeway threw everyone into a state of **consternation,** like the frenzied activity of ants when a shovel is thrust into an ant colony.
   (A) utter confusion
   (B) total calm
   (C) seeing stars
   (D) incompetence
   (E) preservation
   5 ___

6. If the transit authority raises fares any more, the public will become as **restive** as a crowd waiting for a fight to break out.
   (A) relaxed
   (B) highly amused
   (C) supportive
   (D) completely restored
   (E) restless
   6 ___

7. Craig's abruptly quitting the committee was an **impetuous** act, like a child throwing a tantrum.
   (A) thoughtful; careful
   (B) profitable
   (C) foolish; rash
   (D) mature
   (E) tiresome; boring
   7 ___

8. The Hollidays' response to the invitation was as **tentative** as a cat's sniffing some unfamiliar food.
   (A) keyed up
   (B) hesitant; uncertain
   (C) soft
   (D) decisive; sure
   (E) fast; quick
   8 ___

9. Old Mr. Scaggs is as **parsimonious** as a miser counting his pennies.

(A) generous   (D) happy
(B) exact   (E) outgoing
(C) stingy

9 ___

10. The speaker's opening remarks were as **trite** as a third-rate verse on a flowery greeting card.

(A) literate   (D) ordinary
(B) splendid   (E) memorable
(C) moving

10 ___

SUMMARY PART 4

Context Clue: Comparison

1. Comparisons can suggest meanings. If you don't know a word, you will probably know the compared word or meaning.
2. "As" or "like" often begins a comparison.

PART 5

Context Clue: Contrast

Another form of comparison—what might be called a *negative comparison*—is contrast. Contrast frequently provides a clue to meaning.

> The actions of the speaker served to **nullify** the effect of the suggestion, not to support it.

The contrast beginning with "not" tells what the key word **nullify** is not. "Support" is opposed to **nullify**. The speaker obviously did his best to oppose the suggestion.

> Though the firecracker looked **innocuous**, it contained enough powder to shatter a small building.

The contrast suggested by "though" tells us **innocuous** means "innocent, not dangerous."

Trial Test

Take the following trial test to make sure you understand this type of context clue. Underline the word or words that contrast with the bold-faced word. Write the letter of your answer in the space at the right.

EXAMPLE

At one moment Prue seems to be sunk in **melancholy**; the next moment she changes and becomes bright and cheerful.

(A) gloom   (D) argument
(B) wit   (E) sleep
(C) fierce
     discussion

        A

"Bright" and "cheerful" contrast with **melancholy** and should be underlined. The contrast makes clear that **melancholy** means *gloom* (A).

1. The relationship between the twins was **discordant**, not harmonious.
   (A) careless   (D) curious
   (B) conflicting   (E) interesting
   (C) musical
          1 ___

2. Carla did not make a **unilateral** decision; instead, she invited all participants to share in decision making.
   (A) one-sided   (D) universally
   (B) foolish   disapproved
   (C) single   (E) ill-considered
          2 ___

3. Hayes made a **ludicrous** suggestion, but the other members took the proposal seriously.
   (A) meaty   (D) solemn
   (B) vigorous   (E) pleasant
   (C) laughable
          3 ___

4. When Miss Webster gets hold of an idea, she is **tenacious**, never weak and changing.
   (A) offensive   (D) adaptable
   (B) fickle   (E) persistent
   (C) friendly
          4 ___

5. At times, Mr. Collins is **penurious**; at others, generous.
   (A) penny-wise   (D) contributory
   (B) stingy   (E) weary
   (C) helpful
          5 ___

6. Jeremy is not **infallible**; he makes many errors.
   (A) always right
   (B) sometimes uncertain
   (C) generally persuasive
   (D) optimistic
   (E) never arbitrary

   6 ___

7. In this uncertain weather, the bees may be either active or **dormant**.
   (A) irritable
   (B) quiet
   (C) frivolous
   (D) indecisive
   (E) unprofitable

   7 ___

8. Too often, fame is **ephemeral**, not lasting.
   (A) livelong
   (B) lively
   (C) short-lived
   (D) living
   (E) lifelike

   8 ___

9. Joella's efforts with a clarinet range from **cacophony** to a blissful blending of sounds.
   (A) ingenuity
   (B) improvisation
   (C) symphony
   (D) harsh sounds
   (E) surprise

   9 ___

10. Midge's explanation did not **placate** her partner; it angered him.
    (A) interest
    (B) trick
    (C) arouse
    (D) eliminate
    (E) soothe

    10 ___

Answers to Trial Test

1. (*B*) The opposite of "harmonious" is *conflicting*.

2. (*A*) When all participants share in decision making, the decision is not **unilateral** or *one-sided*.

3. (*C*) **Ludicrous** is opposed to "taking the proposal seriously." Therefore **ludicrous** must mean *laughable*.

4. (*E*) If "weak" and "changing" are opposites of **tenacious**, the correct answer is *persistent*.

5. (*B*) "Generous" is opposed to **penurious**. The alternative which means the opposite of "generous" is *stingy*.

6. (*A*) The word "not" attached to **infallible** tells us that **infallible** means "the opposite of making many errors." The correct answer is *always right*.

7. (*B*) "Active" is contrasted with **dormant**. Therefore the correct answer must be the opposite of "active" or *quiet*.

8. (*C*) **Ephemeral** is contrasted with "lasting." Therefore the correct answer must be the opposite of "lasting" or *short-lived*.

9. (*D*) The wording shows that **cacophony** is contasted with "blissful blending." Therefore the correct answer must be the opposite of "blissful blending" or *harsh sounds*.

10. (*E*) **Placate** is contrasted with "angered." Therefore the correct answer must be the opposite of "angered" or *soothe*.

Study another actual test question.

Problem

Alice was annoyed that, although Edgar
accepted the --- of her argument, he would
not --- that her conclusion was correct.

(A) logic . .
   concede

(B) absurdity . .
   require

(C) sequence . .
   predict

(D) existence . .
   preclude

(E) feasibility . .
   dispute

Strategy

The contrast suggested by the *although* clause is the key to answering this question. The contrast is between acceptance and rejection. Edgar accepted some aspect of Alice's argument, but he obviously rejected her conclusion. Sometimes it is easy to overlook important little words. The key word "not" plays an important part in the analysis.

Choice (*A*)   Try the sentence, substituting the alternatives suggested. Alice was annoyed that, although Edgar accepted the *logic* of her argument, he would not *concede* that her conclusion was correct.

That sounds good! Every now and then, the first choice seems the best. The contrast now makes sense. Edgar accepted the logic of Alice's argument, but he wouldn't accept her conclusion. This lack of consistency might well annoy someone! The contrast between acceptance and rejection is clear if we substitute the two words suggested. But examine the remaining choices.

Choice (*B*)   The first alternative, *absurdity*, tends to discredit this pair. One is unlikely to accept *absurdity*. The second alternative, *require*, doesn't make sense.

Choice (*C*)   The first alternative, *sequence*, is a possibility, though not nearly as good a choice as *logic* in (*A*). The second alternative, *predict*, is clearly inadequate. Why would Edgar make a prediction? The alternatives are clearly not as good as those in (*A*).

Choice (*D*)   *Existence* is a weak alternative, but *preclude* is even more unlikely.

Choice (*E*)   *Dispute* is the clue to this answer. If Edgar did not dispute the conclusion, Alice would not have been annoyed.

The correct answer, (*A*), was indicated by the contrast suggested by the two clauses.

Time Out for Review

Write the letter of the word or words that have the same meaning as the boldfaced word in each sentence.

1. The owner of the famous restaurant greeted every guest **cordially**; there was nothing unpleasant or unfriendly about the place.
   - (A) coldly
   - (B) huffily
   - (C) warmly
   - (D) hastily
   - (E) indifferently

   1 ___

2. Although the salespersons seemed honest, their "promises" about the product were **deceptive**.
   - (A) misleading
   - (B) straightforward
   - (C) deep; penetrating
   - (D) true
   - (E) clear

   2 ___

3. A cat can be loving and gentle, but it can attack an enemy with astonishing strength and **ferocity**.
   - (A) speed
   - (B) honesty
   - (C) perfection
   - (D) viciousness
   - (E) intelligence

   3 ___

4. Even though the picnic lunch was **sufficient**, everyone could have eaten more.
   - (A) bountiful
   - (B) adequate
   - (C) delicious
   - (D) healthful
   - (E) unbearable

   4 ___

5. Although you might not call Harvey **obese**, you wouldn't nominate him for the Thin Man award, either.
   - (A) skinny
   - (B) jolly
   - (C) fat
   - (D) athletic
   - (E) healthy

   5 ___

6. Jennifer has an unusual **aptitude** for playing the piano, but a total inability to play any other instrument.
   - (A) viewpoint
   - (B) height
   - (C) appreciation
   - (D) talent
   - (E) enjoyment

   6 ___

7. Although everyday folklore says that dogs and cats dislike one another, many of them are clearly **affectionate** toward one another.
   - (A) sweet
   - (B) catching
   - (C) loving
   - (D) candied
   - (E) harmful

   7 ___

8. They say that Robin Hood took from the **affluent** and gave to the poor.
   - (A) flowing
   - (B) sick
   - (C) engaged
   - (D) rich
   - (E) soaked

   8 ___

9. An organization that prevents cruelty to animals is a **benevolent** organization.
   - (A) kindly
   - (B) unkind
   - (C) neglectful
   - (D) neutral
   - (E) large

   9 ___

10. In a pressroom, the roar of machinery is **perpetual**, but the rumbling is easier to bear than an occasional sudden burst of sound.
   - (A) brief
   - (B) constant
   - (C) periodic
   - (D) harmful
   - (E) puzzling

   10 ___

SUMMARY PART 5

Context Clue: Contrast

1. A contrast is a *negative comparison*. It tells what something is *not*.
2. Look for contrast words: **not**, **although**, **though**, **never**, **instead**, **but**, **either-or**, etc.

PART 6

Context Clue: Sequence

Sometimes the way in which items are arranged in a sentence provides a clue to meaning. In the Gettysburg Address, Abraham Lincoln said, "We cannot dedicate—we cannot consecrate—we cannot hallow—this ground." The sequence of items clearly indicates a rise in intensity. "Dedicate" is a strong word to honor the ground where the soldiers are buried. "Consecrate" is stronger. "Hallow" is stronger still.

The article I read is weak, tasteless, really **insipid**.

The grouping of adjectives suggests a progression from the mild word "weak" to the stronger word **insipid**.

Trial Test

Take the following trial test to make sure you understand this type of context clue. Underline the words that show the sequence to the bold-faced word. Write the letter of your answer in the space at the right.

EXAMPLE

The Halloween costume looked eerie and strange enough by day; at night it was positively **grotesque**.

(A) handsome   (D) fantastic
(B) well made   (E) commonplace
(C) timely   **D**

The phrasing shows a sequence from "eerie" and "strange" to **grotesque**. **Grotesque** is apparently a stronger word than "eerie" and "strange," both of which should be underlined. **Grotesque** means *fantastic* (*D*).

1. When facing a math problem, Grover is slow, even **obtuse**.

   (A) witty   (D) dull
   (B) secure   (E) well-rounded
   (C) thorough   1 ___

2. Leora's creative style requires that she first **improvise** freely and later revise carefully.

   (A) write slowly   (D) copy slavishly
   (B) read intensively (E) carry
   (C) compose   homeward
       offhand

3. The prices of articles at the fair were much too high, ranging from steep to **exorbitant**.

   (A) modest   (D) surprising
   (B) reasonable (E) low
   (C) excessive   3 ___

4. At the party, Lon's behavior was at first merely irritating, but later it became **obnoxious**.

   (A) offensive   (D) positive
   (B) funny   (E) serious
   (C) cruel   4 ___

5. Climbing on the lower slopes of Everest was challenging, but crossing ice fields on the upper slopes was truly **arduous**.

   (A) satisfying   (D) improbable
   (B) strenuous   (E) simple
   (C) comical   5 ___

6. The characters in Dina's novel were more than dull; they were **stereotyped**.

   (A) composed in   (D) copied from
       haste   another novel
   (B) tried   (D) stamped from a
       beforehand   mold
   (C) painted from
       life   6 ___

2 ___

7. The inconveniences most travelers consider merely **irksome** Sam finds unbearable.

(A) annoying   (D) inevitable
(B) expected   (E) preventable
(C) enjoyable

7 ___

8. The visual effects in the average horror movie are no longer mildly frightening; they must be **gruesome**.

(A) unpleasant   (D) hideous
(B) interesting   (E) colorful
(C) bitter

8 ___

9. The approaches to the Grand Canyon are magnificent, but the Canyon itself is **unparalleled**.

(A) unexpected   (D) speechless
(B) incomparable   (E) incomprehensible
(C) deep

10. My day started wild and gradually became more and more **frenetic**.

(A) even   (D) normal
(B) frantic   (E) independent
(C) picturesque

10 ___

Answers to Trial Test

1. (*D*) The wording suggests a change in degree from "slow" to **obtuse**. It even tells us that **obtuse** is like "slow"—only more so. The correct answer is *dull*.

2. (*C*) The change from **improvise** to "revise" suggests that improvise is freer, more spontaneous. The correct answer is *compose offhand*.

3. (*C*) "Steep" is high, but **exorbitant** is higher. The correct answer is *excessive*.

4. (*A*) The change from "irritating" to **obnoxious** suggests a downward trend. **Obnoxious** must mean "worse than irritating." The correct answer is *offensive*.

5. (*B*) The sequence suggests that **arduous** is harder than "challenging." The correct answer is *strenuous*.

6. (*E*) **Stereotyped** is obviously worse than "dull." The correct answer is *stamped from a mold*.

7. (*A*) **Irksome** is a lesser degree of "unbearable." **Irksome** is unpleasant but not unendurable. The correct answer is *annoying*.

8. (*D*) The wording, with "frightening," suggests that **gruesome** is a stronger word than frightening. *Unpleasant* and *bitter* are negative words, but we need a very strong word here. The correct answer is *hideous*.

9. (*B*) The wording suggests that **unparalleled** is not merely "magnificent." It is something greater, without any possible comparison. The correct answer is *incomparable*.

10. (*B*) The progression is from "wild" to something more wild. The correct answer is *frantic*.

Look at another actual test question.

Problem

> In order to make the best use of available human resources, we must first --- and then --- human talents.

    (A) educate . .   (D) discover . .
           equalize   develop

    (B) decompose   (E) produce . .
           . . rebuild   accrue

    (C) revitalize . .
           discern

Strategy

The sequence suggested by "first" and "and then" is the key to this question. Obviously the second alternative is an outgrowth of the first. This is how the alternatives work.

Choice (*A*) *Educate* seems like a fairly good alternative until we notice that "talents" is probably the object of the verb. We don't educate "talents." We educate *people*. The second alternative, *equalize*, is impractical and out of keeping with the suggestion "to make the best use of available human resources."

Choice (*B*) Why would anyone wish to *decompose*, break down, human talents? What would be the point of breaking them down only to rebuild them? This pair is unsatisfactory.

Choice (*C*) *Revitalize* sounds acceptable, but *discern* is inappropriate. We want to do more than look at human talents after we've revitalized them.

Choice (*D*) The sequence here makes sense. We first *discover* the talents and then *develop* them. Steps 1 and 2 are logical and reasonable.

Choice (*E*) We don't *produce* human talents. We *discover* and *develop* them. Some students might choose *accrue* because they don't know its meaning and think it just might be the right answer. The word means "to grow," but it doesn't take an object. Besides, the first alternative, *produce*, is clearly incorrect.

Since (*D*) is so obviously correct, none of the other alternatives makes a strong showing. It is wise to check them anyway, even if rapidly. Here, the sequence is the clue to meaning.

Time Out For Review

Write the letter for the word or words that have the same meaning as the boldfaced word in each sentence.

1. A back injury is not just painful, it can be **excruciating**.
   - (A) left out
   - (B) unpleasant
   - (C) extremely painful
   - (D) forgiven; pardoned
   - (E) rejected

   1 ___

2. Taking inventory is a difficult, **onerous** task.
   - (A) one of a kind
   - (B) ongoing; continuous
   - (C) all-knowing
   - (D) burdensome; oppressive
   - (E) unrepeated

   2 ___

3. During the long hike, the youngsters quickly became hungry and eventually became **ravenous**.
   - (A) unstrung
   - (B) very hungry
   - (C) very beautiful
   - (D) eaten up
   - (E) destroyed

   3 ___

4. Forgetting to thank the participants was a bad mistake, but leaving their names out of the program was an **egregious** one.
   - (A) self-centered
   - (B) equalizing
   - (C) conceited
   - (D) sociable; outgoing
   - (E) outrageous

   4 ___

5. Most of the committee meetings were private ones, but one was so **clandestine** it was never revealed to the public.
   - (A) very secretive
   - (B) very quiet
   - (C) very noisy
   - (D) very unpleasant
   - (E) very clear

   5 ___

6. Scott may be lazy, but his brother is downright **lethargic**.
   - (A) leathery; tough
   - (B) very strong
   - (C) extremely sluggish
   - (D) very heavy
   - (E) deadly

   6 ___

7. The officials were stubbornly against changing any rules, but they were **adamantly** opposed to easing the entrance requirements.
   - (A) moderately
   - (B) addictively
   - (C) increasingly
   - (D) unyieldingly
   - (E) confusedly

   7 ___

8. The members of the reducing clinic ranged in size from plump to **corpulent**.
   - (A) very fat
   - (B) incorporated
   - (C) correctible
   - (D) proven
   - (E) very certain

   8 ___

9. A heavy, gas-guzzling sedan may be outdated, but a horse-and-buggy is **archaic**.
   - (A) very cold
   - (B) no longer used
   - (C) very difficult
   - (D) very enthusiastic
   - (E) more recent

   9 ___

10. First the accused asked the judge for a light sentence; then he **implored** him to be let free.
   - (A) detested completely
   - (B) suggested indirectly
   - (C) punished severely
   - (D) pleaded urgently
   - (E) placed firmly

   10 ___

SUMMARY PART 6

Context Clue: Sequence

Words arranged in sequence show an increase in intensity. If you know just one of the words, you can figure out the rest.

PART 7
Context Clue: Function Words

In English, nouns and verbs are heavyweight words. They carry the burden of meaning in most sentences. Even a simple sentence like "Wasps sting" shows how important nouns and verbs can be. Just two words tell volumes.

Adjectives and adverbs are also strong content words, as they describe, limit, and qualify the powerful nouns and verbs. "Angry wasps sting mercilessly" paints a strong picture.

Because these four content words (nouns, verbs, adjectives, and adverbs) are so overpowering, we sometimes overlook other important words, like prepositions and conjunctions, words that show connections and relationships. These other words provide the glue that holds the content words together. Without the important *function words*, as they are sometimes called, sentences would not hang together.

> **After** Claude had skied, he put his skis **in** the rack **near** the front door **and** went **inside** the lodge.

In the preceding sentence, the content words provide most of the essential information, but they do not tell when and where. Words like **after, in, near, and,** and **inside** are needed to convey the message.

Often the meaning of a sentence hangs on a simple word like **not, but,** or **then.**

The following sampling of these function words will suggest the extent of their influence in creating sentences.

CAUSE-EFFECT: **as, because, for, if, since, so that, yet**
DEGREE: **somewhat, too, very**
PLACE: **above, along, across, around, at, behind, beside, below, beyond**
 (and many others)
OPPOSITE DIRECTION: **although, but, however, nevertheless, otherwise, unless**
SAME DIRECTION: **and, also, as well, besides**
TIME: **after, before, during, meanwhile, then, when, while, till, until**
NUMBERS: **few, less, many, more, some, one** (and other numerals)

> Buddy's room was **chaotic.** It did have a certain informal charm.

These two sentences provide very little help in suggesting the meaning of **chaotic.** In the context provided, **chaotic** might mean almost anything favorable, from "masculine" to "beautiful." We cannot make an intelligent guess.

Notice what happens when two seemingly unimportant words, **somewhat** and **but,** are inserted into the sentence.

> Buddy's room was **somewhat chaotic, but** it did have a certain informal charm.

Now the meaning of **chaotic** can be guessed at. The word **but** suggests that the room's charm is unexpected. Therefore **chaotic** must be a negative word, but **somewhat** softens the blow. The room is not **chaotic;** it is **somewhat chaotic.**

If, in spite of everything, the room has "a certain informal charm," we might reasonably guess that **chaotic** means "upset, disordered." "Informal" becomes an important clue to the meaning of **chaotic**, but the two words **but** and **somewhat** put us on the right track.

Function words are crucially important. Review the importance of **rather than** in the problem for Context Clue #2 (page 14) and the importance of **first** and **and then** in the problem for Context Clue #6 (page 32).

Trial Test

Take the following trial test to make sure you understand this type of context clue. Underline the function word in each sentence. Write the letter of your answer on the line at the right.

EXAMPLE

Her knowledge <u>and</u> **expertise** in the field of computer science qualified her for the job.

(A) beauty   (D) acting ability
(B) wealth   (E) dress
(C) specialized skill   <u>C</u>

You should have underlined **and,** which shows that knowledge is related to expertise. Expertise must mean *specialized skill*, (C) since the other choices are not in the same direction as knowledge.

1. Because the father was **domineering,** the children rebelled and left home.
   (A) weak but pleasant   (D) humorously fanciful
   (B) indifferent   (E) strongly controlling
   (C) wittily charming   1 ___

2. If there is further **diminution** of club funds, we'll have to increase next year's dues.
   (A) advertising   (D) spread
   (B) decrease   (E) theft
   (C) expansion   2 ___

3. A long drought threatened the community water supply, but a series of heavy rains **replenished** much of the water in the reservoir.
   (A) drained   (D) refilled
   (B) polluted   (E) wasted
   (C) dissipated   3 ___

4. Because Ted is so **gullible,** his friends like to tell him wild stories and exaggerated anecdotes.
   (A) funny   (D) birdlike
   (B) agreeable   (E) excitable
   (C) believing   4 ___

5. The editor replaced many tired words and expressions in an attempt to make the report sound less **hackneyed.**
   (A) commonplace   (D) unsound
   (B) vivid   (E) grim
   (C) critical   5 ___

6. I'll be left in a **quandary** unless you give me more help in choosing the right course.
   (A) time of decision   (D) state of uncertainty
   (B) trick of fate   (E) call for action
   (C) expression of hope   6 ___

7. Although Barbara is **meticulous** in matters of personal grooming, she is careless in keeping her checkbook account.
   (A) somewhat slovenly   (D) occasionally gentle
   (B) too cowardly   (E) rather casual
   (C) very careful   7 ___

8. Since she had been caught in a heavy downpour, Beth looked **disheveled** when she came into the house.
   (A) angry   (D) adorned
   (B) puzzled   (E) tired
   (C) untidy   8 ___

9. Until the roof leaked rainwater onto the dirt floor of the barn, we had been able to keep the stables **immaculate.**

(A) spotless   (D) locked
(B) wide open   (E) colorful
(C) dressy

9 ___

10. If I cannot **rectify** my mistake, I'll resign as club president.

(A) explain   (D) clarify
(B) correct   (E) magnify
(C) conceal

10 ___

Answers to Trial Test

1. (E) "Because" suggests the reason for the children's rebellion. The first four alternatives suggest no reason for rebellion, but the fifth does. The correct answer is *strongly controlling.*

2. (B) "If" suggests the reason for next year's dues increase. If the funds are inadequate, dues must be raised. (A), (C), and (D) make little sense. (E) is a remote possibility but unlikely. *Decrease* is the best answer.

3. (D) "But" tells us the drought was reversed. The rains *refilled* the reservoir with water.

4. (C) "Because" is the clue. Ted's friends "like to tell him wild stories" because he believes everything. The correct answer is *believing.*

5. (A) The words "in an attempt to" tell us the editor is trying to change the tired words and expressions, to make the report less *commonplace.*

6. (D) The key word "unless" shows a way out of the difficulty: "giving more help." If the speaker is uncertain about "the right course," he or she must be in a *state of uncertainty.*

7. (C) "Although" tells us we have contrasting ideas: *meticulous* and "careless." We need an alternative that is opposed to "careless." The correct answer is *very careful.*

8. (C) "Since" ties up the idea of the downpour with Beth's appearance. Rain does spoil peoples' appearances. The correct answer is *untidy.*

9. (A) "Until" suggests that the stables had been clean before rainwater leaked onto the dirt floor. The correct answer is *spotless.*

10. (B) The wording suggests that the speaker would like to correct a mistake or else resign as president. The correct answer is *correct.*

Look at another actual test question.

Problem

Because even the briefest period of idleness bored and exasperated her, she worked --- at some project or activity.

(A) constantly   (D) cynically
(B) reluctantly   (E) languidly
(C) occasionally

Strategy

"Because" is the key to the answer. Cause and effect are at work. The way in which she works at a project or activity is a result of her boredom and exasperation.

Choice (A) *Constantly* seems to fit the sentence well. The "because" clause tells us she cannot stand even the briefest period of idleness. Therefore, when she works, she'll avoid even a brief period of idleness—in short, *constantly*, all the time.

Choice (B) *Reluctantly* is directly opposed to the sense of the sentence. If she is bored by idleness, she won't be reluctant to work. She'll be eager to do so.

Choice (C) *Occasionally* does consider the time problem, but boredom at even brief periods of idleness suggests occasional work will not be enough.

Choice (D) *Cynically* suggests an attitude, a bitter attitude, but there is nothing in the sentence to suggest such an attitude. She won't overcome her boredom by being cynical.

Choice (E) *Languidly* also suggests an attitude and a manner of weakness, sluggishness. But she is a dynamo of activity, as the "because" clause suggests.

Constantly is clearly the best answer, indeed the only answer possible.

Time Out for Review

Write the letter of the word or words that have the same meaning as the boldfaced word in each sentence.

1. Although the topic was **abstruse,** Stephanie was able to write about it simply and clearly.
   - (A) easy to understand
   - (B) hard to understand
   - (C) blunt; insensitive
   - (D) very simple
   - (E) badly treated

   1 ____

2. We wished the day of surprises would go on forever, but such pleasures are usually **ephemeral.**
   - (A) pleasurable
   - (B) lasting
   - (C) short-lived
   - (D) surprising
   - (E) elated

   2 ____

3. Even though the professor is **erudite** in his subject, he doesn't know the first thing about everyday matters like balancing a checkbook or driving a car.
   - (A) uninformed
   - (B) rude
   - (C) incorrect
   - (D) scholarly
   - (E) impractical

   3 ____

4. Because the fashion show displayed only the **quintessence** of the new styles, only the best designers could participate.
   - (A) finest
   - (B) worst
   - (C) fifth
   - (D) hint
   - (E) selection

   4 ____

5. The youngsters had only a **nebulous** understanding of the opera, but they did enjoy the lavish staging and costumes.
   - (A) complete
   - (B) vague
   - (C) lavish
   - (D) marvelous
   - (E) necessary

   5 ____

6. No one thought their intentions were **belli-cose** until their troops stormed the city.

   (A) peaceful   (D) beautiful
   (B) stormy   (E) warlike
   (C) heavy   6 ___

7. After the **sardonic** reviews in the news media, nobody bothered to see the movie.

   (A) fishy   (D) praising
   (B) scornful   (E) neutral
   (C) positive   7 ___

8. Because of the **salubrious** food and climate at the resort, everyone felt wonderful after staying there.

   (A) sloppy   (D) healthful
   (B) salty   (E) unpleasant
   (C) moist   8 ___

9. After Lincoln **emancipated** the slaves, many of them still stayed with their former masters.

   (A) underfed   (D) imprisoned
   (B) mistreated (E) employed
   (C) set free   9 ___

10. Because Stan is so **gregarious,** he always seems to be in the center of activity, surrounded by people.

   (A) very deceitful (D) tall
   (B) growing   (E) outrageous
   (C) sociable   10 ___

SUMMARY PART 7

Clues From Context: Function Words

Nouns, verbs, adjectives, and adverbs are heavyweight words, giving basic meanings.

Function words (**because, somewhat, above, although,** etc.) change, intensify, and redirect the basic meanings.

Often the meaning of a sentence depends on one function word.

Review Test
Context Clues

The sentences below provide context clues to word meanings. From the group of words below, select a word to replace each boldface word. Write the word on the line at the right.

deceit	hateful	overcrowding	soaked
equivalent	poisonous	overelaborate	timid
excessive	made poor	peculiarities	turned aside
fortress	nobody	pierced	wearing away
harsh	noisy speech	punishment	yellowish

1. They stormed the **citadel** with arrows.   1. _____
2. There was such **congestion** in the halls that members could scarcely move.   2. _____
3. The tax plan of the nobles **impoverished** the peasantry, draining away all wealth.   3. _____
4. Soil **erosion** stripped the topsoil from some of our richest land.   4. _____
5. Far from being **diffident,** he has boldly stepped into the limelight.   5. _____
6. The tips of the shoes were **perforated,** the holes being at regular intervals.   6. _____
7. To the newcomer, the northeast winters were **rigorous** and severe.   7. _____
8. After long confinement in the dungeon, he emerged with thin frame and **sallow** complexion. 8. _____
9. He rushed into the house from the storm, his clothing thoroughly **saturated.**   9. _____
10. The mob growled menacingly as they listened to the speaker's unrestrained **harangue.** 10. _____
11. The theft from the poor widow made the crime even more **heinous.**   11. _____
12. The escaping fumes were not **noxious** but actually beneficial to the animals in the laboratory. 12. _____
13. Despite Thomson's odd **quirks,** people are very fond of him.   13. _____
14. The carved ceiling was too **ornate,** displeasing in its lack of simplicity.   14. _____
15. Jonathan never once **deviated** from the course he had set for himself early in life.   15. _____
16. Because of his own high standards of morality, Murchison spurned the **duplicity** of his comrades. 16. _____
17. The trader had a virtual monopoly of salt, and he charged **exorbitant** prices for it. 17. _____
18. From a **nonentity,** Jackson rose to the highest honor America can grant.   18. _____
19. He feared **retribution** for his evil deeds.   19. _____
20. The terms were **tantamount** to complete surrender.   20. _____

Summary
Section I: Context Clues

Review these context clues from time to time. If you understand how context helps you learn new words, you'll do better on the vocabulary sections of the SAT. You'll also do better on the reading sections. As a special bonus, you'll become a more efficient general reader and student.

Clue 1 The Entire Sentence

Use your own words first to make an intelligent guess with word meanings; then examine the whole sentence as a context clue.

The first **tremor** of the earthquake rattled the dishes and bounced the pots together.

Clue 2 Pairing

If you don't know one word in a pair, you may know the other.

Jefferson is so **dogmatic** and opinionated, no one cares to discuss anything with him.

Clue 3 Direct Explanation

The test sentence may give an explanation directly, in an appositive, in a participial phrase, in an explanation beginning with **for,** or in one provided by a subordinate clause.

Pittsburgh is at the **confluence** of the Allegheny and Monongahela rivers, where the two flow together to form the Ohio.

Clue 4 Comparison

The compared word or meaning can be a clue; **as** or **like** are clue words.

When Doreen has a task to do, she is as **assiduous** as a bee on a nectar-gathering expedition.

Clue 5 Contrast

A contrast, or a *negative* comparison, tells what something is *not:* some contrast words—**not, although, though, never, instead, but, either-or.**

Paul felt he was a **nonentity,** not a person of real importance.

Clue 6 Sequence

Words in sequence show an increase in intensity; if you know one of the words, you can figure out the rest.

At the beginning Curren worried about Becker's serves, but they became even harder, more accurate, and **formidable** as the match went on.

Clue 7 Function Words

Often the meaning of a sentence depends on one function word. (See page 34 for a sampling of function words.)

When the stranger struck the first awful blow, Tom **retaliated** with all his might.

40   ENGLISH FOR THE COLLEGE BOARDS

Section II: Word Clues

PART 1

Word Clue: Connotation and Denotation

"I'd like you to meet my mommy."

"I'd like you to meet my mother."

"Mommy" and "mother" mean the same person, but the words seem quite different. An adult talks freely about his or her "mother" but rarely uses the word "mommy" outside the home. "Mommy" seems to belong to an earlier period of life. It is a word used by younger children or by adults in the company of small children. It has an altogether different tone from "mother."

Words have many meanings, but all these meanings can usually be divided into two broad types: (1) dictionary meanings and (2) suggested meanings. The first kind of meaning is called *denotation*; the second is called *connotation*. The denotations (dictionary meaning) of "mommy" and "mother" are pretty much the same. The connotations (suggested meanings), however, are quite different. "Mother" is more formal, more general, more applicable to many situations, even to other living creatures. "Mommy" has the flavor of childhood and expresses a certain tone and meaning.

The world of childhood is filled with words that have very special connotations, words like *choo-choo*, *ducky*, and *kitty*. Childhood words make especially good illustrations of connotation because they are so dramatically different from more adult words like *train*, *duck*, and *cat*. Sometimes words are rich in connotations for one individual and not another. *Snake* has a very negative connotation for the average camper and a very positive connotation for a naturalist.

No two words are exactly alike. As we shall see later, no two words—even close synonyms—are exactly the same, but many pairs of words are fairly close in meaning. Their denotations are similar, but their connotations may be farther apart. "Vision" and "sight" have similar denotations and are listed as synonyms. But they may have widely different connotations.

"That movie star is a vision."

"That movie star is a sight."

If you have a feeling for connotation as well as denotation, you'll do better in all portions of the verbal part of the SAT.

Dan and Merle are friendly (adversaries, antagonists, foes, rivals) for the affections of the new student in class.

All four words suggest that Dan and Merle are competing. The trick is to select the word with the most appropriate *tone*. The sentence says the competition is friendly. The strongly negative connotation of *adversaries*, *antagonists*, and *foes* is too powerful for friendship. *Rival* is more neutral. *Friendly rivalry* is more likely than *friendly antagonism*.

The spectators were gripped by sudden (consternation, dismay, dread, panic) and stampeded when the cry of "Fire!" was raised.

All four words suggest both fear and upset. The choice becomes a matter of connotation. *Consternation*, *dismay*, and *dread* are less overpowering than *panic*. *Dismay* and *dread* suggest long-term worry or concern. *Consternation* suggests fear that leads to inactivity. *Panic*, on the other hand, suggests wild, uncontrolled action.

As a word is used, and as a connotation becomes more widespread, the connotation may become part of the dictionary definition. The word *appease* was once a fairly neutral word. It meant simply "to quiet, to satisfy." In the expression "to appease one's appetite," the word is still neutral. But just before and during World War II, the word *appeasement* came to mean "giving in to the demands of a hostile power." It became a very negative word, and the growing negative connotation eventually became included in the dictionary definition.

Trial Test

Take the following trial test to make sure you understand this type of word clue. Write the letter for the word that best completes the meaning in each sentence.

EXAMPLE

The new nations of Africa were --- of their rights and their hard-won independence.

(A) suspicious   (D) unconcerned
(B) jealous   (E) weary
(C) fearful   **B**

Since *jealous* suggests a desire to hold onto what one has, (*B*) is the correct answer.

1. The ex-champion's muscles became --- from lack of exercise.
   (A) delicate   (D) limp
   (B) flabby   (E) loose
   (C) flimsy   1 ___

2. The photographer specialized in --- camera shots.
   (A) frank   (D) plain
   (B) open   (E) blunt
   (C) candid   2 ___

3. The characters in this novel are --- and bear no intentional resemblance to actual people.
   (A) fabulous   (D) imagined
   (B) mythical   (E) fictitious
   (C) legendary   3 ___

4. A mild --- blew in out of the west.
   (A) breeze   (D) tornado
   (B) blast   (E) gale
   (C) tempest   4 ___

5. Medieval monks spent a great deal of time --- ancient manuscripts.
   (A) imitating   (D) copying
   (B) mocking   (E) matching
   (C) aping   5 ___

6. When the four racing cars crashed, the spectators were stricken by sudden --- and ran in all directions.
   (A) dismay   (D) dread
   (B) panic   (E) anxiety
   (C) consternation   6 ___

7. The owner was unreasonable because he expected nothing short of --- in his employees.
   (A) merit   (D) quality
   (B) excellence   (E) perfection
   (C) virtue   7 ___

8. Although she had been away for years, when Sheila approached her house, everything suddenly seemed to become --- .
   (A) confidential   (D) exciting
   (B) intimate   (E) commonplace
   (C) familiar   8 ___

9. After a week in the desert without food and very little water, the returning hiker looked --- .

(A) haggard   (D) weary
(B) wan   (E) thin
(C) weak

9 ___

10. Three blocks of houses were burned in one great --- .

(A) blaze   (D) burning
(B) fire   (E) conflagration
(C) combustion

10 ___

Answers to Trial Test

1. (*B*) *Flabby* is a word applied to weak muscles. The alternatives are unsuitable. *Delicate* may be applied to an aroma. *Flimsy* may be applied to the construction of a house. *Limp* may be applied to the way hair hangs. *Loose* is a general word with many applications. None of these words can appropriately be applied to muscles.

2. (*C*) The five alternatives are rough synonyms and may generally be applied to a word like "speaking." When camera shots are mentioned, however, the correct word is *candid*.

3. (*E*) All the alternatives have something to do with "make-believe," but the term used for characters in a novel is *fictitious*.

4. (*A*) All the alternatives can be said of winds, but the word "mild" limits the possibilities. Only a *breeze* is mild.

5. (*D*) All the alternatives have to do with *copying*, but they all have different applications. *Copying* is a general word that covers many situations. *Mocking* and *aping* are unflattering words, unsuitable here. *Imitating* and *matching* do not describe the writing process. The only possibility is *copying*.

6. (*B*) The word "stricken" tells us that the spectators acted from terror. All the alternatives but one are inadequate to express their actions. The correct answer is *panic*.

7. (*E*) The word "unreasonable" suggests that the owner expected *perfection*, which is not a reasonable expectation. The correct answer is *perfection*.

8. (*C*) The alternatives are rough synonyms, but only *familiar* suggests the appearance of a place we might return to. The correct answer is *familiar*.

9. (*A*) All the alternatives suggest a weakened hiker. The extent of his deprivation—a week without food and with very little water—calls for the strongest word among the alternatives. The correct answer is *haggard*.

10. (*E*) When three blocks of houses burn, ordinary words for fire are inadequate. The correct answer is *conflagration*.

Examine two actual test questions.

Problem

It would be --- for any serious candidate to
--- such an influential constituency.

(A) profitable . .
    snub

(B) illogical . .
    appease

(C) foolish . .
    offend

(D) selfish . .
    overrate

(E) immaterial . .
    recognize

Strategy

If you have studied Context Clues (Section I), you already have many approaches to try in answering the question. The sentence as a whole eliminates alternatives (A), (D), and (E). They don't make sense. Only choices (B) and (C) seem possible. They provide similar words as first choices: *illogical* and *foolish*. The second choices, *appease* and *offend*, will help you to choose the right answer, (C). But suppose you don't know the second words. You can still work with *illogical* and *foolish*. Both obviously mean something like "unwise," but *illogical* suggests reasoning. *Foolish* does not. The sentence deals with actions, not with reasons. Therefore *foolish* seems a better choice. Substitute the suggested answers to see how they fit.

It would be **foolish** for any serious candidate to **offend** such an influential constituency.

They fit perfectly. In sentences of this type, the SAT question will often give similar words as alternatives to be chosen. In this test question, *snub* and *offend*, as well as *illogical* and *foolish*, are similar. Our strategy has two steps: (1) first, use context clues for unfamiliar words; (2) then, if this plan doesn't help, examine the connotations of similar words.

Problem

He had a delightfully indulgent way of showing his --- for his friends; these actions in themselves --- a kind heart.

(A) respect . .
    contradicted

(B) concern . .
    deprecated

(C) disdain . .
    established

(D) intolerance . .
    denoted

(E) fondness . .
    betokened

Strategy

You can immediately discard the negative alternatives *disdain* and *intolerance*, for the sentence as a whole has positive expressions like "delightfully indulgent," "friends," and "kind heart." *Concern* is a possibility, but *deprecated* is negative. *Respect* and *fondness* are both positive words and somewhat related. Pairs like this occur to make the question more challenging. Thus at first glance, either (*A*) or (*E*) seems to be a good possibility. If you know the second words, *contradicted* and *betokened*, you're home free, of course. *Contradicted* is a negative word, out of keeping with the positive words already mentioned. But if you know neither word, you can still make an educated guess by weighing the connotations of *respect* and *fondness*.

Both *respect* and *fondness* suggest positive attitudes. *Respect* is more a matter of the intellect. *Fondness* is more a matter of the emotions. Which tone is more suitable here? The key words "kind heart" tip the scales toward the emotions. It's a kind heart that develops *fondness*. So *fondness* is the better word. Incidentally, words like *betokened* can also be guessed at by looking at the smaller word within the larger word (pages 74–76).

Time Out for Review

Write the letter for the word that makes best sense in each sentence.

1. The moisturizing cream is supposed to make the complexion --- .
   (A) limp   (D) mushy
   (B) wet   (E) slippery
   (C) soft
                          1 ___

2. Many mobile homes are surprisingly --- .
   (A) palatial   (D) cavernous
   (B) roomy   (E) enormous
   (C) immense
                          2 ___

3. Garment sizes for the gowns were petite, small, medium, and --- .
   (A) jumbo   (D) large
   (B) fat   (E) bloated
   (C) overweight
                          3 ___

4. Some wrinkle-free fabrics are made of --- fibers.
   (A) fake   (D) synthetic
   (B) phony   (E) counterfeit
   (C) unreal
                          4 ___

5. The important executive --- into the room.
   (A) strode   (D) fell
   (B) trudged   (E) stumbled
   (C) wandered
                          5 ___

6. Millions of viewers --- the championship game.
   (A) ogled   (D) noticed
   (B) glanced at   (E) watched
   (C) stared at
                          6 ___

7. The rude audience's idle --- was annoying.
   (A) discourse   (D) debate
   (B) chatter   (E) speech
   (C) discussion
                          7 ___

8. The constant urban problem is --- streets and parkways.
   (A) infested   (D) congealed
   (B) overflowing   (E) stuffed
   (C) congested
                          8 ___

9. Buying defective merchandise hurriedly is a bit --- .
   (A) rash   (D) slothful
   (B) foolish   (E) tiresome
   (C) insane
                          9 ___

10. Homeowners must --- their property from theft.

    (A) barricade   (D) protect

    (B) militarize   (E) isolate

    (C) arm

                               10 ___

SUMMARY PART 1

Word Clue: Connotation and Denotation

No two words are exactly alike. Words have many meanings, but all meanings can usually be divided into two types: dictionary meanings called *denotation* and suggested meanings called *connotation*.

House and *home* are sometimes used interchangeably, but *home* has far richer connotations than *house*. "There's no place like a house" is not quite the same as "There's no place like home."

Recognizing connotation is especially helpful in answering reading comprehension questions on the SAT.

PART 2

Word Clue: Figurative Language

> March comes in like a *lion* and goes out like a *lamb*.
> When Ellen heard the news, her eyes *danced* and her smile *sparkled*.

In the sample sentences, March does not really resemble a lamb or a lion. Ellen's eyes don't actually dance, nor does her smile sparkle. These examples of "it is what it isn't" are good illustrations of *figurative language*, or *figures of speech*.

SIMILE

The March sentence provides an example of **simile** (SIM uh lee), the comparison of unlike things by using *like* or *as*. Some similes like *white as snow* and *sweet as sugar* have long since worn out their usefulness, and are avoided by careful speakers and writers. However, other phrases startle us by their freshness and appropriateness: *as lonesome as a bell buoy at sea.*

METAPHOR

In the Ellen sentence, "danced" and "sparkled" are examples of **metaphor** (MET uh for), comparisons without *like* or *as*. Metaphor is the poetry of everyday life. We can speak scarcely a sentence without using metaphor, either obvious or concealed. Action metaphors are everywhere, as we *run up* a bill, *go down* in math, *skirt* a topic, *win* approval, *hold down* a job, *catch* a cold, *kill* time, *flock* to a new idea, *find* a solution, or *go* over an answer. We may call a person a *rock*, a *tower of strength*, or a *chameleon*. We talk of an *arm* of the sea, the *eye* of a hurricane, the *teeth* of a gale, a *shoulder* of a mountain, or an *elbow* of land. Flowers are often gems of metaphor: *lady's slipper, baby's breath, buttercup, larkspur, Queen Anne's lace, snow-on-the-mountain, jewelweed.* The English language is incredibly rich in metaphor. Metaphors often appear in sentence completion and reading comprehension questions.

Though simile and metaphor are most familiar, there are other kinds of figurative language.

PERSONIFICATION

Personification (per SAHN uh fi KAY shun) gives some human traits to things not human. *Duty* calls. *Truth* cries out. *War* stalks the land. *Joy* flees the house. *Happiness* grows. *Justice* is sometimes blind. *Democracy* encourages citizen participation in government. *Violins* cry, and *trombones* wail. Personification is usually easy to identify.

METONYMY

Metonymy (met ON uh me) substitutes one word for another closely associated with it. If we say, "The kettle is boiling," we're using metonymy. The kettle itself isn't boiling; it's the water inside. "Kettle" is used to represent water. Other examples of metonymy follow.

The *pen* is mightier than the *sword*.
> (pen = writing; sword = force and violence)

I like the new *dish* you cooked.
> (dish = food in the dish)

No man can live by *bread* alone.
> (bread = food and the physical needs for survival)

SYNECDOCHE

Synecdoche (sin ECK duh kee) also relies on association. Synecdoche substitutes a part for the whole or the whole for a part. If we talk about hired *hands*, we really mean *laborers*. If we take a *head* count, we are really counting *people*. If we say, "North Carolina defeats Kentucky," we are really saying, "The basketball team of North Carolina defeats the basketball team of Kentucky."

HYPERBOLE

Hyperbole (high PURR buh lee) is exaggeration for effect. When someone says, "I ran a thousand miles before breakfast," *thousand miles* is certainly exaggerated! Occasional hyperbole is effective, but some speakers overuse this device. "I was absolutely *famished*. I drank *gallons* of water and gulped down a *ton* of hamburgers." Like all strong statements, hyperbole is most effective in small doses.

UNDERSTATEMENT

Understatement, the opposite of hyperbole, may also be used for emphasis.

> This dessert *isn't bad* at all! "It's excellent."
> After staying awake for 36 hours, I was a *little tired*. "I was exhausted."

IRONY

Irony is intentionally using words to say one thing and imply something quite the opposite. Suppose you take a clock apart and can't get it back together again. You might then say, "I guess I'm just a *skilled mechanic*," and mean the opposite. *Skilled mechanic* is an example of irony. Satire and sarcasm belong to the irony family.

Review of Figurative Language

A single expression may combine two or more figures of speech. Personification is closely related to metaphor. "Truth may whisper and falsehood shout." *Truth* and *falsehood* are personified. *Whisper* and *shout* are metaphors. No person or thing is actually whispering or shouting. "Buddy laughed till he burst" is certainly hyperbole. *Burst* is also a metaphor.

If you become sensitive to figurative language, you will be better able to handle the vocabulary and reading questions on the SAT. You'll also enrich all your reading and listening.

Notice how the same action may be reported differently. A clumsy young man enters a room, trips over a rug, breaks a priceless lamp, and pours coffee over an expensive sofa. He is unhurt, however. What are some reactions an observer might make?

> You're *like a bull in a china shop*! (Simile)
> You're a clumsy *clown*! (Metaphor)
> *Destruction* enters our quiet room! (Personification)
> Oh, mighty *toe*! (Synecdoche)
> You've just ruined *everything* in this room! (Hyperbole)
> You had a *bit of a fall*, didn't you? (Understatement)
> My, but you're an *agile* person! (Irony)

Trial Test

Write the letter for the name of the figurative language in boldface in each of the following sentences.

(A) Simile	(E) Hyperbole
(B) Metaphor	(F) Understatement
(C) Personification	(G) Irony
(D) Synecdoche	(H) Metonymy

EXAMPLE

When I broke the expensive butter dish, I **died** of embarrassment.

E

Died is an exaggeration. This is an example of hyperbole (*E*).

1. Jean stepped back from the rattlesnake in the path **like a mouse jumping away from a cat.**　　　1 ___

2. The **eyes** of the potato are really buds.　　　2 ___

3. Isn't all this rainy weather, with its hordes of mosquitoes, a **lot of fun**!　　　3 ___

4. Mr. Acton **hit the roof** when he saw the dent in his new car.　　　4 ___

5. We call our dog "**the nose**" because he can smell food a mile away.　　　5 ___

6. **Gloom** makes few friends.　　　6 ___

7. In reading the passage, I **stumbled** over the first word.　　　7 ___

8. It was as cold as the **north side of a January gravestone by starlight**.　　　8 ___

9. My six weeks in the hospital caused me a **bit of inconvenience**.　　　9 ___

10. **Love** conquers all.　　　10 ___

Answers to Trial Test

1. (*A*) Jean's quick action is compared with the action of a terrified mouse. Since the comparison uses **like** this is a simile.

2. (*B*) The buds of the potato are compared with "eyes," but no comparison word is used. Metaphor.

3. (*G*) Obviously rainy weather and mosquitoes are not fun. Irony.

4. (*E*) Mr. Acton may have been angry, but he didn't hit the roof. This exaggeration is hyperbole.

5. (*D*) "Nose" is being used for the entire dog. Synecdoche.

6. (C) "Gloom" is here given human qualities. Personification.

7. (B) The error in reading is compared with actual stumbling in walking. Metaphor.

8. (A) This is an extended comparison with **as**. Simile.

9. (F) Six weeks of hospital stay is much more than an inconvenience. Understatement.

10. (C) "Love" is given human traits. Personification.

Examine two other actual test questions.

Problem

He was suddenly thrown into a fit of despair,
his faith in himself infirm, his self-confidence
---.

(A) shattered   (D) inflated
(B) soaring   (E) delayed
(C) unassailable

Strategy

As it happens, all the alternatives provided are examples of figurative language. They are all metaphors. *Shattered* suggests breakage. *Soaring* suggests flight. *Unassailable* suggests conflict. *Inflated* suggests increase. *Delayed* suggests obstruction. Which implied comparison is most suitable here?

Two clues help: "fit of despair" and "infirm faith." Someone who is in despair and of infirm faith has lost his self-confidence. Which figurative meaning suggests the loss? *Shattered* fits. Self-confidence might well crumble and be lost. Quickly check the others to be sure.

Soaring and *unassailable* do not fit at all. They are positive words and suggest the wrong picture. *Inflated* also suggests an improvement in self-confidence, the opposite of the meaning we need. *Delayed* is a milder word than *shattered*. It suggests that self-confidence is slightly affected, but despair suggests something more drastic. (A) *Shattered*, the correct answer, uses a physical picture to make the point more strongly.

Problem

Ballet is known to be ---; once you go, you
are likely to find yourself going again and
again, loving the performances more each
time.

(A) addictive   (D) anticlimactic
(B) erratic   (E) interminable
(C) expendable

Strategy

Once again, figurative language is the key to the correct answer. *Addictive* is a word used originally for physical bondage to a habit. Drug addiction, for example, suggests a powerful need involving slavery to narcotics. But addiction, through metaphor, has acquired much wider uses. People say they're addicted to jogging, to square dancing, to tennis, or a host of other activities. Though addiction to jogging is quite different from addiction to drugs, there are enough points of similarity to make the comparison effective, especially the compulsive need to participate almost daily.

The sentence provides several clues, as is so often the case. "Going again and again" emphasizes the repetition. "Loving the performances" suggests the joy. Alternatives (*B*) to (*E*) are too negative or have the wrong tone for the sentence. Only (*A*), with its appropriate figurative meaning, is suitable as an answer.

Time Out For Review

Write the letter for the name of the figurative language in boldface in each sentence.

(A) Simile	(E) Hyperbole
(B) Metaphor	(F) Understatement
(C) Personification	(G) Irony
(D) Synecdoche	(H) Metonymy

1. The flight across the ocean was **as smooth as silk**. 1 ___

2. The old **house told** us of happier days. 2 ___

3. The humid, 100-degree day was **not especially refreshing**. 3 ___

4. The command was given: "**All hands on deck.**" 4 ___

5. Her delicate **laughter rippled** through the air. 5 ___

6. They talked and talked, while **ten thousand people were waiting** to use the phone. 6 ___

7. The entire **theater burst into laughter**. 7 ___

8. When she stumbled over the doorsill and fell flat, she earned the title **Miss Graceful**. 8 ___

9. Suddenly the child was **as quiet as a mouse**. 9 ___

10. Late as usual, Dexter had **an alibi that was a mile long**. 10 ___

SUMMARY PART 2

Word Clue: Figurative Language

SIMILE: comparison with **like** or **as**
Gray-haired Saturn, **quiet as a stone**. (John Keats)

METAPHOR: implied comparison
I felt a **cleavage** in my mind. (Emily Dickinson)

PERSONIFICATION: representing an object or idea as a person
Love laughs at locksmiths. (George Colman)

METONYMY: use of a word for another closely associated word
This hairy meteor did announce
The fall of **sceptres** and of **crowns**. (Samuel Butler)

SYNECDOCHE: use of the part for the whole, or the reverse
We dispatch you for bearers of this greeting to old **Norway**.
(William Shakespeare)

HYPERBOLE: exaggeration for effect
At every word a reputation **dies**. (Alexander Pope)

UNDERSTATEMENT: emphasis by saying less than is meant
The report of my death was **an exaggeration**. (Mark Twain)

IRONY: saying one thing and implying the opposite
Stick close to your desks and never go to sea,
And you all may be **Rulers of the Queen's Navee**. (W. S. Gilbert)

Mastering the types of figurative language will help you to answer many of the vocabulary test items on the SAT.

PART 3
Word Clue: Synonym Discrimination

Are you happy at this moment? How would you describe your happiness? Are you *cheerful, contented, elated, exuberant, joyful, jubilant, pleased, satisfied*? The English language supplies synonyms by the dozens. We have so many words with similar meanings because English has roots in many languages. Greek, Latin, Celtic, Anglo-Saxon, German, French, Italian—the roll call sounds like a list of the world's languages, dead and living.

Two main streams, the native Anglo-Saxon and Norman, came together when the Normans under William the Conqueror overran England. But before and since, English has borrowed from Latin, Greek, and other sources, to provide enrichment unparalleled in the world's languages. New coinages and borrowings occur today, enriching the treasure of English.

Notice how many degrees of happiness are suggested in the opening group of synonyms. *Happy* is a general word including many degrees of feeling. Some of the other words are more specific. *Elated, exuberant*, and *jubilant* suggest greater joy than *happy*. *Contented, pleased*, and *satisfied* suggest a moderate degree of happiness. *Cheerful* puts more emphasis on the obvious display of happiness. A person might be *happy* and not show anything. But a *cheerful* person makes an impression.

Although synonyms have generally similar meanings, no two words are interchangeable in all situations. Denotations and connotations vary enough to make every word slightly different from any other word. Synonyms may be as close as *pardon* and *excuse*, ... , and still be different. We may say, "Pardon me" or "Excuse me" and the words seem interchangeable. But a prison inmate may be *pardoned*, not *excused*.

Look at another group of synonyms. *Gleam, glitter, glow, shimmer*, and *sparkle* all refer to light, but each word has a specific application of its own. A beacon may *gleam* in the wilderness but not *glitter* or *shimmer*. Certain metals may *glitter* with reflected light but not *gleam*. Embers may *glow* after a fire has died down but not *sparkle*. Beautiful eyes may *sparkle* but not *glow*. Water may *shimmer* in moonlight but not *gleam*. And so it goes for all groups of synonyms. Subtle differences determine suitability for a given context.

> The lawyer brought on a surprise witness in an attempt to aid the almost hopeless cause of his (client, customer, patient, patron).

All four words apply to a person who pays others for a service, but we use the word *client* with "lawyer." A doctor has a *patient*. A store has a *customer*. A theater has a *patron*.

> The landlord went to court to get an order to (dismiss, eliminate, evict, expel) the tenant from the apartment.

All four words have something to do with getting rid of something or someone. The word used for the removal of a tenant from occupancy is **evict**.

Trial Test

Write the letter for the word that is most appropriate in each sentence.

EXAMPLE

The thirsty travelers thought they saw a pond of water in the shimmering sand, but the pond proved to be a ---.

(A) daydream   (D) mirage
(B) mistake   (E) fantasy
(C) vision   **D**

All alternatives suggest that the travelers were deceived, but the specific word for a trick-of-the-eye in the desert is *mirage* (D).

1. Young Mozart --- concertos, sonatas, and symphonies before he was 13.
   (A) constructed   (D) prepared
   (B) composed   (E) produced
   (C) created   1 ___

2. When planning her landscaping, Anne decided upon a (an) --- bed along the driveway.
   (A) eternal   (D) perennial
   (B) everlasting   (E) fadeless
   (C) perpetual   2 ___

3. Citizens who fail to cooperate with law agencies --- justice.
   (A) counteract   (D) curb
   (B) obstruct   (E) inhibit
   (C) repress   3 ___

4. Very little food is needed to --- Owen's appetite.
   (A) glut   (D) satisfy
   (B) cloy   (E) gorge
   (C) cram   4 ___

5. The boss sent around a brief --- reminding employees of the changed office hours.
   (A) catalog   (D) inscription
   (B) enumeration   (E) register
   (C) memorandum   5 ___

6. Yvonne's --- athletic ability almost guarantees her success as a tennis player.
   (A) native   (D) ingrained
   (B) inbred   (E) indispensable
   (C) internal   6 ___

7. Upon arising, Norm follows a rigid --- each morning.
   (A) habit   (D) fashion
   (B) routine   (E) practice
   (C) custom   7 ___

8. The two roads --- in the outskirts of Springfield.
   (A) mingled   (D) merged
   (B) mixed   (E) fused
   (C) intertwined   8 ___

9. The --- edition of Shakespeare's plays exactly reproduces the look of the First Folio.
   (A) facsimile   (D) copy
   (B) duplicate   (E) imitation
   (C) sample   9 ___

10. Sandra's --- mannerisms are charming, not unpleasant.
    (A) impudent   (D) haughty
    (B) defiant   (E) overbearing
    (C) pert   10 ___

Answers to Trial Test

1. (*B*) *Constructed* is usually used for structures. *Created* is a general word applied to a wide variety of abstractions like ideas and fusses. *Prepared* is a general word for anything from arguments to meals. *Produced* is another general word, often applied to words like masterpieces or films. The word especially applied to music is *composed*.

2. *(D)* All the words suggest something long lasting, but the word reserved for flowers that last more than a season is *perennial*.

3. *(B)* All the words suggest opposition, but the word associated with justice is *obstruct*.

4. *(D)* *Glut*, *cloy*, *cram*, and *gorge* suggest excess. Since the words "very little" are used, the correct answer is a milder word, *satisfy*.

5. *(C)* *Catalog* is too comprehensive for something brief. *Enumeration, inscription*, and *register* are too grand. The correct answer is *memorandum*.

6. *(A)* All words suggest inner qualities, but the word for athletic ability is *native*.

7. *(B)* All alternatives deal with frequent activities, but the word for a special, repeated activity is *routine*.

8. *(D)* All alternatives suggest a coming together, but the word reserved for roads that come together at one point is *merged*.

9. *(A)* All alternatives deal with duplication. When books are exactly reproduced, the correct word is *facsimile*.

10. *(C)* All words suggest cockiness and self-assurance. The key word "charming" tells us we need a word with pleasant connotations. The only word that qualifies is *pert*.

Look at other examples of synonym discrimination.

Problem

A truly --- historian of science, Meyer neither
--- the abilities of the scientists she presents
nor condescends to them.

    (A) unbiased . . scrutinizes
    (B) objective . . inflates
    (C) impressionable . . patronizes
    (D) reverent . . admires
    (E) analytic . . evaluates

Strategy

Answer *(E)* is incorrect. If the historian is *analytic*, she will not fail to *evaluate*. Answer *(D)* is incorrect. If the historian is *reverent*, she will not fail to *admire*. Answer *(C)* is incorrect. If the historian is *impressionable*, the answer *patronizes* does not fit. It has nothing to do with being impressionable or not being impressionable.

Answers *(A)* and *(B)* have words somewhat similar in meaning: *unbiased* and *objective*. When this situation occurs, look closely at the second alternative: *scrutinizes* or *inflates*. This time, the two function words, *neither* and *nor* suggest a comparison. We already know that the historian doesn't condescend to the scientists. If she doesn't condescend, then she also doesn't inflate their abilities.

Substitute the correct alternatives and look at the sentence again.

A truly **objective** historian of science, Meyer neither **inflates** the abilities of the scientists she presents nor condescends to them.

You might be led astray by thinking *unbiased* fits reasonably well in the first blank. The historian *is* probably *unbiased*, but *objective* is better. It has just the right meaning to fit here: "impersonal" and "fair." The clincher is the second alternative, *inflates*. It's opposed to "condescends" and keyed to **objective.**

Problem

He angrily ––– Plato as more consistently –––
than any other philosopher on all questions involving physical science, politics, ethics, or education.

(A) approved . .   (D) quoted . .
     debatable   brilliant
(B) defended . .   (E) derided . .
     refuted   acceptable
(C) condemned . .
     wrong

Strategy

The answers have two sets of similar words: *condemned* and *derided*, *approved* and *defended*. You will have to make a further anlaysis to find the correct answer.

Some answers can be rejected because they contradict themselves.

Answer (*A*) is incorrect. If he *approved* Plato, Plato would not be consistently *debatable*.

Answer (*B*) is incorrect. If he *defended* Plato, Plato would not be consistently *refuted*.

Answer (*D*) is incorrect. He wouldn't be *quoting* Plato "angrily" if Plato were more *brilliant* than any other philosopher.

Answer (*E*) is incorrect. If he *derided* Plato "angrily," he would not consider Plato *acceptable*.

Answer (*C*) fits perfectly. He angrily *condemned* Plato because he considered Plato so *wrong*. Both parts fit. Note that both *derided* and *condemned* are similarly negative. *Condemned* wins out because of the second alternative, *wrong*.

Sometimes close pairs like *condemned* and *derided* can lead you astray. In situations like these, the answer is usually found elsewhere, especially in the second alternative.

Time Out for Review

A. Following each sentence are three word choices in parentheses. Write the words in the spaces where they make best sense in the sentence.

1. Good, _____ food, prepared under _____ conditions, is influential in keeping us _____. (healthy, sanitary, wholesome)

2. Charles renounced the _____ of French nobility he hated, and adopted the _____ of Darnay to conceal his real _____ of Evremonde. (name, pseudonym, title)

3. In an _____ Ford, like the knights of _____ times, the _____ suitor for the hand of the town widow rode forth. (antiquated, elderly, olden)

4. The _____ hadn't done any real _____ to the body tissues, though the _____ was considerable. (damage, pain, wound)

5. She was _____ though perhaps not _____. Her very motion was _____. (beautiful, graceful, pretty)

6. He _____ his goal in life when he _____ the 440-yard race. The coaches all agreed that he had _____ the victory. (attained, earned, won)

7. The circus people considered it a great _____ for the aerialists to attempt their daring _____ at every _____. (achievement, feat, performance)

8. A petty _____ led to a long and bitter _____ that brought _____ to the little town. (feud, quarrel, strife)

9. The _____ whistles and the _____ crowd made for a _____ celebration. (boisterous, loud, shrill)

10. His costume was so _____ and his manner of speaking so _____ that all of us considered him extremely _____. (comical, witty, grotesque)

B. Many of our commonest words often have a number of colorful and discriminating synonyms. From the list of words below select a word to fill each of the blanks in the following sentences.

distinguished	recognized
gazed	scanned
glowered	scrutinized
observed	stared
peered	surveyed

1. The visitors _____ at the famous painting for a long time in admiration.

2. Deep in thought he _____ unseeingly out of the window.

3. His eye _____ the magazine hurriedly.

4. The small boy _____ earnestly through the knothole in an effort to see the baseball game.

5. He _____ the changes in society without alarm.

6. At that distance his eye just _____ the climbers on the ridge.

7. From his viewpoint on top of Mt. Washington he _____ the entire countryside around.

8. The travelers _____ in the distance the familiar towers of home.

9. The art dealer _____ the painting for any traces of retouching.

10. The angry knight _____ at his opponent before the battle.

SUMMARY PART 3

Word Clue: Synonym Discrimination

Synonyms are words of similar meaning, but no two words are always interchangeable. When you meet synonyms that need to be discriminated, consider connotation (page 41). Try the words out in sentences of your own to see where a word fits or doesn't fit.

If you cannot see the difference between *inability* and *disability*, for example, try them out in a sentence. ''Pete may have had a physical disability, but this meant no inability to play golf.'' If you interchange the words, the sentence doesn't work.

Synonym discrimination is especially helpful in sentence completion, analogy, and reading comprehension questions on the SAT.

PART 4

Word Clue: Antonyms and Opposed Words

The temperature dropped from *sweltering* to *freezing* in 12 hours.
In her attitude toward tennis, Caroline blows *hot* and *cold*. When Terry *arrived*, Dot *left*.

Opposites occur frequently in writing and conversation. Many common expressions include pairs of opposites: *feast* or *famine*, *thick* and *thin*, *friend* or *foe*, *ups* and *downs*, *win* or *lose*. These expressions, called **antonyms,** figure prominently on the SAT. Antonyms are often useful words for defining ideas, concepts, qualities. They suggest what something is by saying what it is *not*! Antonyms are common features of English.

Phyllis is not *ungenerous*. "She's *generous*."
Although his subject matter is difficult, Peter's writing is never *obscure*. "It's *clear*."
Tod tends to *disparage* where he should try *praise*.

Part 3 concentrated on synonyms, words of similar meaning. Part 4 will concentrate on antonyms, words of opposite meaning. A word may have both a synonym and an antonym. *Pride*, for example, may have a synonym, *arrogance*, and an antonym, *humility*.

Since words have different meanings in different contexts, a single word may have many antonyms. Clear is such a word of many meanings. We may talk about a *clear* day, a *clear* conscience, or a *clear* style of writing. Obviously one antonym will not do for all of these. The antonym of the first might be *overcast* or *cloudy*. Of the second it might be *troubled*. Of the third it might be *confusing*.

Take the following trial test to check your understanding of antonyms and opposed words.

Trial Test

In each sentence write the letter for the proper antonym for the word in boldface. Remember that the sentence context provides the clue to the specific meaning of the boldfaced word.

EXAMPLE

The old mariner's face was **craggy**, full of character.

(A) rocky   (D) level
(B) sandy   (E) smooth
(C) whiskery   E

Craggy here suggests *rough*. The opposite is *smooth* (*E*).

1. Most students do not object to a strictly run class as long as the teacher is **fair**.
   (A) dark   (D) ugly
   (B) stormy   (E) clever
   (C) unjust
                                1 ___

2. The wax **melted** as the candle burned.
   (A) awakened   (D) solidified
   (B) froze   (E) appeared
   (C) increased
                                2 ___

3. When the number of **idle** workers exceeds ten percent of the work force, a recession threatens the economy.

   (A) employed   (D) acute
   (B) active   (E) flourishing
   (C) alert

   3 ___

4. The lions used in circus acts are quite **tame.**

   (A) docile   (D) uncultured
   (B) barbarous   (E) fierce
   (C) impetuous

   4 ___

5. The meaning of your fourth sentence is **obscure.**

   (A) absolute   (D) unshadowed
   (B) evident   (E) famous
   (C) bright

   5 ___

6. Great writers have always been concerned with the power of **evil** in the world.

   (A) truth   (D) honesty
   (B) duty   (E) friendliness
   (C) good

   6 ___

7. Fulton's steamboat was hailed as nothing short of **marvelous.**

   (A) depressing   (D) contemptible
   (B) miserable   (E) drab
   (C) commonplace

   7 ___

8. By a **happy** coincidence the letter arrived just as we were leaving.

   (A) unfortunate   (D) grave
   (B) dreary   (E) gloomy
   (C) sad

   8 ___

9. Mark always felt **gloomy** as he heard the bells ringing in the new year.

   (A) bright   (D) acute
   (B) sunny   (E) clever
   (C) cheerful

   9 ___

10. The experts agreed that Jefferson's signature on the document was **genuine.**

   (A) forged   (D) smudged
   (B) pretended   (E) concealed
   (C) unclear

   10 ___

Answers for Trial Test

1. (*C*) In one sense or other, all alternatives are antonyms of **fair.** A **fair** complexion is contrasted with a *dark* complexion. A **fair** day is contrasted with a *stormy* day. A **fair** decision is contrasted with an *unjust* decision. A **fair** beauty is contrasted with an *ugly* person. A **fair** job is contrasted with an *excellent* job. The only alternative that fits the context is *unjust.*

2. (*D*) Two alternatives seem possible: *froze* and *solidified. Froze* is the opposite of **melted** when we talk about cold temperatures. That contrast is not the situation here. The correct answer is *solidified.*

3. (*A*) Again, in one sense all alternatives are antonyms of **idle.** When we talk about workers, however, we use the words *employed* and *unemployed*, or *idle.* The correct answer is *employed.*

4. (*E*) **Docile** is a synonym, not an antonym. *Barbarous* might be applied to a person, not an animal. *Impetuous* is a character trait not associated with lions. *Uncultured* cannot be applied to animals. The correct answer is *fierce.*

5. (*B*) The opposite of an **obscure** meaning is an *evident* meaning.

6. (*C*) **Evil** may be opposed to many qualities, but the best, most direct opposite is the simple word *good.*

7. (*C*) The opposite of **marvelous** is *commonplace*.

8. (*A*) In the sense used, **happy** means "fortunate," not "*joyful*." A *happy* coincidence is a *fortunate* coincidence. The correct answer is *unfortunate*.

9. (*C*) The word **gloomy** is here used to indicate a state of mind. The best antonym is *cheerful*.

10. (*A*) When applied to a signature, the opposite of **genuine** is *forged*.

Additional Helps In Working With Antonyms

In the SAT, antonyms account for twenty-five of the vocabulary test items, the largest single group. They also appear in reading questions and in sentence-completion items. Note how the following sentence uses antonyms to make the meaning clear.

> The actions of the speaker served to nullify the effect of the suggeston, not support it.
> The *not* tells us **nullify** and **support** are opposite in meaning.

The first test items you'll meet on the SAT will be antonym questions of the following type.

Problem

INDIGENOUS:
- (A) cheerful
- (B) wealthy
- (C) tasty
- (D) clever
- (E) foreign

Strategy

What can you learn by analyzing the example above?

1. Notice that the capitalized word (called the "given" word) is more difficult than any of the alternatives. Though this does not always happen, in most instances the least familiar word is the given word or the word in capital letters. In general, though you might be uncertain of the word to be matched, you will probably be familiar with the alternatives.

2. Notice that most of the alternatives, though unrelated, *sound* as though they might be antonyms. Some words may be inserted to trap you. If you know *indigent* (which means "poor"), for example, you might be tempted to choose *wealthy* as the opposite of **indigenous.**

3. Notice that all the alternatives are the same part of speech as the test word. An antonym should always be the same part of speech as the original word. CAUTION: In questions of this type be sure you look for the ANTONYM of the given word. Under stress of test taking, it is all too easy to pick out SYNONYMS by mistake instead of antonyms.

Other Ways to Analyze the Problem

1. Try to think of an expression which includes the test word. If you have heard of *indigenous populations*, for example, you have a helpful clue. Even if you are not sure what **indigenous** means in the expression, you can still try out the alternatives to see if they fit. *Cheerful populations* doesn't make much sense. Populations aren't uniformly cheerful. An individual is cheerful. *Cheerful populations* would be quite inaccurate. *Wealthy* might be applied to a person, a corporation, or a nation, but it would probably not be applied to populations. *Tasty populations* would be absurd. *Clever*, like *cheerful*, is applied to individuals, not to vast masses of people. *Foreign* populations does make sense, however. Even though you are not absolutely certain of **indigenous,** *foreign* seems like a reasonable answer. As it happens, *indigenous* means "native." *Foreign* (E) is an acceptable antonym for indigenous.

Though the prefix *in* sometimes means *not*, here it means *in*, "born *in* a country." You can usually tell when *in* appears in a word as *not*, for some of the alternatives help tip the answer. See item 4, below.

2. Consider another clue. Sometimes etymology (pages 84–163) can help. **Indigenous** contains the important Latin root *GEN*, meaning "birth," "origin," "species." *Indigenous* populations are those born within a country. Sometimes even a slight clue from word origins will help.

3. Sometimes a small word contained within a larger one (page 74) provides a good clue. You may not know *resplendent*, for example, but you do know *splendor* and can guess that *resplendent* has something to do with *shining*, *brilliance*. An antonym of *resplendent* might be *dim*, *gloomy*, or *murky*.

4. Sometimes it helps to use the negative-positive analysis, like the ones in sentence-completion questions (page 7). Look at the following problem.

Problem

INEXORABLE:
- (A) ruthless
- (B) commonplace
- (C) changeable
- (D) unimportant
- (E) mistaken

Strategy

In, like *un* and *dis*, is commonly a negative prefix that reverses the meaning of the word it is attached to. *Indiscreet* is "not discreet." *Unsophisticated* is "not sophisticated." *Dissatisfaction* is a "lack of satisfaction." When you note these clues, look for an opposite. Eliminate the alternatives that seem to have negative parts, for these are more likely to be synonyms, not antonyms. Note that *ruthless*, *unimportant*, and *mistaken* all have negative parts: *less*, *un*, and *mis*. (The importance of these little elements suggests you ought to spend some time working with prefixes and roots on pages 85-137.) Since you are looking for the opposite of **inexorable,** a negative word, you can discard the three negative alternatives.

Is there anything to lead you to choose between *commonplace* and *changeable*? One strategy is to put in an antonym of your own for both words and then compare your antonyms with the test word. An antonym for *commonplace* might be *rare*. An antonym for *changeable* might be *unchangeable*. Which of these two words, *rare* or *unchangeable*, seems more likely to be a synonym of **inexorable**? Note that *inexorable* and *unchangeable* end in *able*. A reasonable guess would be *unchangeable*. Therefore **changeable** (*C*) is the correct antonym for inexorable.

5. Putting in antonyms of your own is a helpful device—*if* you have time to go back over your answers. Sometimes the test question will help you eliminate some possibilities by supplying an alternative with no easily suggested antonym. What, for example, is the antonym of *greet*, *relief*, or *diet* (as a noun)? There is no good antonym for any of these. Alternatives like these can be eliminated. Your own previous reading and life experiences will help with some of these words. If, however, there are no helps and no clues, do not spend time agonizing over the question. Go on to the next question. Perhaps as you work on a later test item, an answer to a previous question will come to you and you can go back and fill it in. Get on with the test. Few candidates know <u>all</u> the answers!

Examine another problem.

Problem

IMPLEMENT:
- (A) help
- (B) carry
- (C) reveal
- (D) hinder
- (E) construct

Strategy

You are probably familiar with the word **implement**, meaning "tool," but clearly a verb is called for here, not a noun. Even if the verb meaning of **implement** is unfamiliar to you, use the resources you have to make an educated guess. If the noun **implement** means "tool," then the verb **implement** is probably related. Tools are used to do various jobs. The verb **implement** probably has something to do with completing a job. *Help* and *construct* are more like synonyms than antonyms, so they can be rejected. *Carry* and *reveal* don't seem to have anything to do with the meaning. *Hinder*, though, seems like a good choice. It would be in opposition to doing a good job. (*D*) is the correct answer.

Study another example.

Problem

MINIMIZE:
- (A) exaggerate
- (B) realize
- (C) belittle
- (D) scrape
- (E) chill

Strategy

If the word **minimize** is new to you, look at its elements. *Mini* appears in many words: *diminish*, *minimum wage*, *minimal*, and *mini-market*. All these words have one idea in common: *small*. Maybe you are familiar with the pair *minimum* and *maximum*. Look to see if *maximize* appears as a choice. It would be the ideal antonym. It does not, so you have to go further. If *mini* has something to do with *small*, its antonym should have something to do with *large*.

Does any alternative contain the idea of *large*? Yes, *exaggerate* means "to make something larger" than it really is. Some people *minimize* their achievements; others *exaggerate* them. **Exaggerate** (*A*) is an antonym of **minimize.**

If you have a good, sound answer and time is pressing, go on to the next question. If you have time, check the other alternatives quickly. *Realize* and *scrape* do not have antonyms. Reject these. The antonym of *chill* is *heat*—no relation to *minimize*. *Belittle*, or *make little*, is obviously a synonym, not an antonym. Your first impression was correct. The antonym is **exaggerate.**

Antonyms in Sentence-Completion Problems

Now examine some sentence-completion questions to see how understanding antonyms may help you find the correct answer.

1. Maryellen can be sophisticated in some situations and --- in others.

   (A) bright
   (B) angry
   (C) well-bred
   (D) immature
   (E) experienced

   1 ___

The linking of "in some situations" and "in others" suggests that contrasting ideas are being presented. What is needed here is an antonym for *sophisticated*. *Bright* and *experienced* are more like synonyms than antonyms. *Angry* and *well-bred* are not related. **Immature** (*D*) is an antonym. It fits perfectly into the sentence.

2. Whether Sarah is being subtle or ---, she always captures her audience and holds the members in her spell.

   (A) bitter
   (B) obvious
   (C) carefree
   (D) sly
   (E) interesting

   2 ___

Whether and *or* tell us we need contrasting words. The best antonym for *subtle* is **obvious** (*B*). *Sly* is almost a synonym. The other words are unrelated.

3. Unfortunately, the new members in the community are apathetic, not ---, about the gradual decline of our once-lovely neighborhood.

   (A) silly
   (B) concerned
   (C) uninterested
   (D) neighborly
   (E) tired

   3 ___

Not tells us an antonym for *apathetic* is needed. The sentence suggests that the new members should be doing something about the decline but are not. *Apathetic* means something like "indifferent." Its opposite is **concerned** (*B*). *Uninterested* and *tired* are almost synonyms, not antonyms. *Neighborly* is related but it is not opposed to *apathetic*. People *apathetic* about the community can still be friendly *neighbors. Silly* doesn't fit at all.

Function Words

Function words like **although, but,** and **however,** (page 34) also point toward antonyms. Try these examples.

1. Although Todd looked haggard after the ac-
   cident, Paula still looked ---.
   (A) pale   (D) distressed
   (B) relaxed   (E) tired
   (C) overwrought
                                         1 ___

"Although" tells us a contrasting word like **relaxed** is needed in the blank.

2. Sherry is always jovial, but Don is often
   ---.
   (A) happy   (D) arrogant
   (B) jubilant   (E) joyful
   (C) gloomy
                                         2 ___

"But" tells us a contrasting word like **gloomy** (*C*) is needed in the blank.

3. One twin is quite sedate; his brother, how-
   ever, is more ---.
   (A) dignified   (D) jaunty
   (B) solemn   (E) sophisticated
   (C) secure
                                         3 ___

"However" tells us a contrasting word like **jaunty** (*D*) is needed in the blank.

You are now ready to attempt some test-type questions dealing with antonyms. Use the clues you have learned. Good luck!

Time Out for Review

A. Write the letter for the antonym of each capitalized word.

1. PARASITE:
   (A) host   (D) motor
   (B) friend   (E) linguist
   (C) sponge
                                         1 ___

2. FORMIDABLE:
   (A) prudish   (D) terrible
   (B) feeble   (E) contemptible
   (C) active
                                         2 ___

3. CIRCUMLOCUTION:
   (A) transition   (D) brevity
   (B) abandon   (E) multiple
   (C) provincialism
                                    3 ___

4. BOLD:
   (A) impudent   (D) rude
   (B) modest   (E) vain
   (C) erroneous
                                    4 ___

5. FELONIOUS:
   (A) lawful   (D) dutiful
   (B) fake   (E) dreary
   (C) dynamic
                                    5 ___

6. CANDOR:
   (A) dullness   (D) levity
   (B) enlightenment   (E) inactivity
   (C) deceit
                                    6 ___

7. BUOYANT:
   (A) nautical   (D) unimpressed
   (B) dry   (E) melancholy
   (C) soapy
                                    7 ___

8. HARMONY:
   (A) melody   (D) rhythm
   (B) dissension   (E) sonata
   (C) tone-deafness
                                    8 ___

9. ALTERATION:
   (A) destruction   (D) revolution
   (B) variability   (E) peace
   (C) fixity
                                    9 ___

10. INSCRUTABLE:
   (A) clear   (D) manageable
   (B) witty   (E) portable
   (C) repetitive
                                    10 ___

B. In each group of three words in column B, one word is *not* opposed in meaning to the word in column A. Write the one word and check whether it is a synonym or unrelated. Use the dictionary if you need help.

EXAMPLE

| stout | lean, slender, portly |
| *portly* | Synonym ✓   Unrelated ___ |

| loyal | false, clumsy, unfaithful |
| *clumsy* | Synonym ___   Unrelated ✓ |

In the first group, **portly** is not an antonym of **stout,** but a synonym.

In the second group, **clumsy** is not an antonym of **loyal;** it is unrelated.

A	B
1. persist	falter, flinch, persevere
_____	Synonym ___ Unrelated ___
2. establish	eradicate, evade, extirpate
_____	Synonym ___ Unrelated ___
3. sadden	cheer, enliven, qualify
_____	Synonym ___ Unrelated ___
4. scarcity	abundance, deficiency, plenty
_____	Synonym ___ Unrelated ___
5. diminish	abbreviate, enlarge, increase
_____	Synonym ___ Unrelated ___
6. remain	embarrass, emigrate, migrate
_____	Synonym ___ Unrelated ___
7. crude	polished, refined, uncouth
_____	Synonym ___ Unrelated ___
8. boldness	efficiency, shyness, timidity
_____	Synonym ___ Unrelated ___
9. deny	acknowledge, admit, advise
_____	Synonym ___ Unrelated ___
10. discord	accord, agreement, disagreement
_____	Synonym ___ Unrelated ___

C. For each of the words numbered 1–20 select from the group of words that follows, one synonym and one antonym.

EXAMPLE

	Synonym	Antonym
discourteous	rude	polite

abandon	deathless	interrogate	respect
anguish	decrease	limited	restrain
answer	divide	loquacious	seldom
appetizing	doubt	majestic	shame
arouse	ease	mettlesome	silent
avoidable	easygoing	mortal	spiritless
broad	enlarge	often	tasteless
combine	flat	peevish	uneven
costly	ignoble	recover	worthless
credulity	inescapable	resist	yield

	Synonym	Antonym
1. belief	_____	_____
2. distress	_____	_____
3. frequently	_____	_____
4. honor	_____	_____
5. immortal	_____	_____
6. incite	_____	_____
7. increase (verb)	_____	_____
8. inevitable	_____	_____
9. irritable	_____	_____
10. level (adjective)	_____	_____
11. narrow	_____	_____
12. noble	_____	_____
13. precious	_____	_____
14. question (verb)	_____	_____
15. reclaim	_____	_____
16. separate (verb)	_____	_____
17. spirited	_____	_____
18. submit	_____	_____
19. talkative	_____	_____
20. tasty	_____	_____

SUMMARY PART 4

Word Clue: Antonyms

1. Antonyms occur in a great many common expressions.
   ins and *outs; friend* or *foe; live* or *die*
2. A word used in many senses may have many different antonyms.
   bright (light) – *dark; bright* (person) – *unintelligent; bright* (remark) – *dull;*
   bright (appearance) – *unattractive*
3. Some words do not have good antonyms.
   nouns like *tree*, *harbor*, *airplane*
   verbs like *fall*, *sing*, *look*
4. In the sentence-completion questions on the SAT, a word like *not* or *but* tells you an antonym may be coming.

   Antonyms account for twenty-five of the vocabulary test items on the SAT.

PART 5
Word Clue: Associated Words

When your life experience expands, so does your vocabulary. If you become interested in watching football, you soon learn what these words mean: *clipping, cornerback, pass interference, blitz, bomb,* and *touchback.* You know where the *end zone* is and what the *hash marks* are used for. You discover that a *goal line stand* is not a wooden structure, a *nose guard* is not part of a helmet, and a *quarterback sack* is not a kind of bag. Once you become interested in any new subject, you soon learn a great many new words.

Reading a book about the sea introduces you to words like *tiller, forecastle, boom, tack, jib, port,* and *starboard.* If you join a theater group, you learn what *upstage, downstage,* and *stage left* mean. If you collect coins, you meet *numismatist, mint, obverse,* and *uncirculated.* Carpentry brings you into contact with *awl, veneer, gimlet,* and *keyhole saw.*

The more activities you engage in, the larger your vocabulary. The more you read, the more you increase your word resources.

Association sometimes helps in answering questions on the SAT, as in the following antonym question taken from the test.

Problem

BLAND:
- (A) airy
- (B) golden
- (C) spicy
- (D) quick
- (E) distant

Strategy

You may not know the exact meaning of **bland,** but you may have associations with the word. You may have heard food referred to as *bland, hot, bitter, sour, delicious, aromatic, tangy, delicate, tasteless, sweet, pleasant, peppery, juicy, vinegary,* or *pungent.*

All these words are associated in some way with food. All have specific meanings. *Vinegary* is opposed to *sweet,* for example. If you come across *bland* on a test of this kind, you have some knowledge to use even if you're not sure of the exact meaning.

Since the question above calls for an antonym, the word to be selected should probably deal with food. Does any word deal with food? Yes, *spicy* is a good candidate. *Spicy* is actually an antonym for **bland.** Even if you did not know specifically what *bland* means, you could still answer this question. Use associations when other means fail.

Occasionally we may use *bland* in a figurative (page 47) sense. When applied to food, *bland* means *mild*, not *irritating*. When applied figuratively to a person or a personality, *bland* still means *gentleness*, *mildness*, even *dullness*. Even when words are used figuratively, they ordinarily keep their core of meaning.

Trial Test

Write the letter for the word in each of the following groups that is *not* ordinarily associated with the others.

EXAMPLE

(A) cracked   (D) mended
(B) broken   (E) split
(C) chipped   __D__

All alternatives suggest a breaking, but (*D*) emphasizes repair and is not as closely associated with the others.

1. (A) song   (D) hymn
   (B) rhapsody   (E) chant
   (C) struggle   1 ___

2. (A) dwell   (D) support
   (B) lodge   (E) occupy
   (C) reside   2 ___

3. (A) dye   (D) paint
   (B) stain   (E) sketch
   (C) tint   3 ___

4. (A) aid   (D) comply
   (B) heed   (E) obey
   (C) mind   4 ___

5. (A) medley   (D) ballad
   (B) mixture   (E) blend
   (C) hodgepodge   5 ___

6. (A) impetuous   (D) bold
   (B) brash   (E) impulsive
   (C) nervous   6 ___

7. (A) root   (D) bark
   (B) leaf   (E) violet
   (C) stem   7 ___

8. (A) differ   (D) dissent
   (B) argue   (E) debate
   (C) agree   8 ___

9. (A) majesty   (D) greatness
   (B) queen   (E) splendor
   (C) grandeur   9 ___

10. (A) flinch   (D) recoil
    (B) cringe   (E) shrink
    (C) scratch   10 ___

Answers to Trial Test

1. (*C*) *Song*, *rhapsody*, *hymn*, and *chant* are all musical forms. The word not associated with the others is **struggle**.

2. (*D*) *Dwell*, *lodge*, *reside*, and *occupy* have to do with living in a place. The word out of place is **support**.

3. (*E*) *Dye*, *stain*, *tint* and *paint* all have to do with applying color to something. Though *sketch* might involve applying color, the basic meaning does not include that process. The correct answer is **sketch**.

4. (*A*) All the alternatives but **aid** have the idea of listening to someone.

5. (*D*) All the alternatives but **ballad** have the idea of a mixture.

6. (*C*) All the alternatives but *nervous* suggest boldness. **Nervous** is actually opposed in meaning.

7. (E) All the words but **violet** refer to parts of a tree.

8. (C) All the alternatives but **agree** suggest differences. **Agree** is the opposite, not associated with the others.

9. (B) *Majesty*, *grandeur*, *greatness*, and *splendor* are words suggesting magnificence. **Queen** and *majesty* may be associated, but this association does not account for the other three.

10. (C) All the alternatives but **scratch** have to do with drawing back.

Examine an actual SAT antonym question to see how association can help.

Problem

AMATEUR:

    (A) spectator   (D) outsider
    (B) professional   (E) entrepreneur
    (C) genius

Strategy

When you see the word **amateur**, many associations come into your mind. Actors, golfers, cabinetmakers, craftworkers, quilters, and weavers may all be called *amateurs*. What distinguishes everyone in this group from other groups? Probably a love for the activity and no monetary payment for the work. You may also realize that the root *ama* has something to do with love.

What is a possible antonym for *amateur*? The word professional emphasizes activity for money. College tennis players play solely for the love of the sport. Professional tennis players are paid. *Professional* (B) is the closest antonym.

Examine another actual SAT antonym question to see how association can help.

Problem

PARODY:

    (A) singularity   (D) reverent imitation
    (B) abstinence   (E) unforgivable
    (C) monotony   insult

Strategy

Somewhere in your reading you have probably come across the word **parody**. If you search your memory, you will probably recall that this is some kind of literary work. You may remember that Lewis Carroll wrote parodies. James Thurber and S. J. Perelman also wrote parodies. As you let your mind work, other literary terms like *satire* and *caricature* may pop up. If you have the time, let the associations come forth freely.

If you are satisfied that *parody* has something to do with a kind of literary work, look at the alternatives. *Singularity* and *monotony* may describe a literary work, but your associations suggest a category, not a quality. *Abstinence* seems unrelated to a literary work altogether. You now have left (*D*) and (*E*). If you have somehow associated *parody* with *satire*, you know that an antonym of *parody* must have a positive meaning. (*E*) is negative. Therefore (*D*) seems the best choice. A **parody** is a literary work that pokes fun by imitating other works. The word *imitation* is there in (*D*), but *reverent* suggests that (*D*) is the antonym.

Time Out for Review

Write the letter for the word in each of the groups that is *not* ordinarily associated with the others.

1. (A) plain   (D) wealthy
   (B) ordinary   (E) common
   (C) simple
   1 ___

2. (A) house   (D) cabin
   (B) apartment (E) tent
   (C) car
   2 ___

3. (A) probable   (D) presumable
   (B) likely   (E) amusing
   (C) hopeful
   3 ___

4. (A) song   (D) anthem
   (B) ballad   (E) story
   (C) hymn
   4 ___

5. (A) cabinet   (D) cupboard
   (B) chair   (E) pantry
   (C) closet
   5 ___

6. (A) mystery   (D) solution
   (B) puzzle   (E) riddle
   (C) problem
   6 ___

7. (A) party   (D) banquet
   (B) feast   (E) championship
   (C) picnic
   7 ___

8. (A) beautiful (D) pretty
   (B) gorgeous   (E) friendly
   (C) handsome
   8 ___

9. (A) theater   (D) arena
   (B) stadium   (E) skyscraper
   (C) auditorium
   9 ___

10. (A) dollar   (D) lira
    (B) franc   (E) finance
    (C) peso
    10 ___

In questions of this sort, the best weapon is definite knowledge of the word. But, surprisingly, free association can be very helpful in working out antonyms.

The truth is that you know more than you think you know! Deep in the recesses of your mind is a treasure house of associations and information. Invite this hidden information to the surface, but remember—don't spend too much time on any one question.

SUMMARY PART 5

Word Clue: Associated Words

1. In general, you learn a cluster of words in a group, not just one word in isolation.
2. If you can associate a group of words on a test question, you can often answer the question correctly even if you are not sure of the *specific* meaning of a word. For example, if you know only that a *parody* is some kind of literary work, you can disregard all word choices that have nothing to do with literature.
3. Rely on free association to recall related words. A group of words somehow associated with a test word will often provide the clues you need. The SAT takes words from every area of life; so, the more words you know, the better you will be able to make word associations.

PART 6

Word Clue: Words Within Words

Which is probably a harder word, *foible* or *incomprehensibility*? Your first impulse might be to point to the longer word, but if you think about it a moment, you realize that *foible* is actually harder, even though it is much shorter. The length of a word may not be related to difficulty.

Look at two typical antonym questions.

Problem

1. INCOMPREHENSIBILITY:
   (A) favor
   (B) clarity
   (C) muddiness
   (D) steadiness
   (E) faith

2. FOIBLE:
   (A) weakness
   (B) gemstone
   (C) strength
   (D) mystical note
   (E) trial

Strategy

At first glance, question 1 seems much harder. **Incomprehensibility** is a forbidding word, overpowering in length and appearance. Yet it is easier than **foible**. Hidden inside the long word **incomprehensibility** is a common word, *comprehend*. You almost certainly know that *comprehend* means "understand." You therefore have the key to the whole question. The prefix *in* generally means *not*. This probably makes the concept negative: *not understand*. *Ible* suggests *able*. *Comprehensible* means "understandable;" therefore, *incomprehensibility* suggests the "quality of not being understandable." The antonym of **incomprehensibility** then is **clarity** (*B*). Note that *muddiness* is a related word, not an opposite. The others are not related in any sense.

The short word **foible** is a lot harder. There is no easy small word within the larger word. Don't spend too much time on a question like this, but don't pass it by completely. Though you may not *know* the word, you should still *guess*. The penalty for a wrong answer is only one-fourth point. So, even if you guess wrong three-fourths of the time, you still come out ahead. Don't guess wildly, but do guess intelligently if you have an idea of the word's meaning.

Is there any slight clue to help you arrive at the correct answer? Well, *foible* does sound like *feeble*. Actually, the two words are historically related. The opposite of *foible-feeble* is *strength* (*C*). The association with *feeble* works for **foible**. If you have no other clue, a guess of this sort is better than nothing.

Trial Test

Write the number for each word in column A next to its antonym in column B.

A	B
1. disorganization	____ hope
2. inconclusive	____ clearness
3. disillusionment	____ efficiency
4. unpalatable	____ certain
5. miscalculation	____ normality
6. incoherence	____ tasty
7. improvident	____ understanding
8. commensurate	____ unequal
9. eccentricity	____ criticism
10. endearment	____ thrifty

Look at another SAT-type antonym question.

Answers to Trial Test

3	hope
6	clearness
1	efficiency
2	certain
9	normality
4	tasty
5	understanding
8	unequal
10	criticism
7	thrifty

Problem

NONCOMMITTAL:

(A) neutral (D) chief
(B) extensive (E) partial
(C) vital

Strategy

Inside the larger word **noncommittal** is the common word *commit*. We may *commit* ourselves to an action, a philosophy, or an idea. If we are *noncommittal*, we refuse to promise, pledge, or participate. Which word is the opposite of such inaction or neutrality? The closest word is *partial* (*E*). *Neutral* (*A*) is a synonym of *noncommittal*. The others are unrelated.

In later sections you will deal with etymology. This is the study of word origins: prefixes, roots, and suffixes. A study of etymology will give you a powerful weapon for analyzing a word and studying its parts. But don't overlook the strategy outlined in this section. It sometimes works when etymology fails. The root of the word *unpalatable*, for example, is not a common one. It does not appear in lists of common roots. Yet you do know the word *palate*, meaning *the roof of the mouth*. You also know that palate has something to do with *taste*, as in the expression *tickle the palate*. You can guess that *unpalatable* is not *tasty*. Look for the smaller word within the larger.

Time Out for Review

Write the number for each word in column A next to its antonym in column B.

A	B
1. infantile	____ buyer
2. malevolent	____ important
3. indolent	____ mature
4. impoverished	____ energetic
5. cooperation	____ assets
6. vendor	____ believable
7. liabilities	____ pliable
8. obstinate	____ kindly
9. inconsequential	____ wealthy
10. incredible	____ conflict

SUMMARY PART 6

Word Clue: Words Within Words

1. Long words are sometimes easier to define than short ones.
2. Many long words contain within them familiar elements that provide a key to the meaning.
3. Sometimes you may guess at a completely unfamiliar long word by finding the short word within it. For example, within *noncommittal* is the known word *commit*. This word clue will help you to analyze long words that appear on the SAT.

PART 7

Word Clue: Allusions

An **allusion** is a reference to a literary or historical person, place, or event.

> In lifting the fallen tree trunk from the injured boy, the police officer showed *herculean* strength.
> Karate is one of the best-known of the Japanese *martial* arts.

If you are unfamiliar with *herculean*, you notice that the sentence suggests that it means "powerful." The lifting achievement is obviously out of the ordinary. *Herculean* comes from *Hercules*, the Greek hero noted for his feats of strength. The concealed allusion, or reference to Hercules, in the word enriches understanding and adds drama to the sentence.

If you know what "karate" means, you can guess that *martial* has to do with discipline, fighting, and war. If you are not sure, however, you have an allusion concealed within *martial*: the word *Mars*. *Mars* is the name of the fourth planet of the solar system and also of the god of war. Knowing the origin of *martial* enriches the meaning and makes it easier to remember.

Types of Allusions

CONCEALED ALLUSIONS: *Spartan* attitude, *stentorian* voice, *pasteurized* milk, *cashmere* sweater, *iridescent* colors, *mercurial* disposition—all have allusions concealed within them.

Spartans were noted for discipline, courage, moderation, and thrift. A *Spartan* attitude is characterized by discipline and bravery.

Stentor was a Greek herald during the Trojan War. His voice was as loud as that of fifty men all shouting together. *Stentorian* then means "very loud."

Louis Pasteur, a French scientist, pioneered in the study of microbes and the harm they could do. *Pasteurizing* is a method of killing harmful microbes by heat. (It doesn't have anything to do with a "pasture.")

Cashmere comes from Kashmir, a district of India noted for the fine wool made from Kashmir goats.

Iris was the goddess of the rainbow. *Iridescent* colors are brilliant, shifting like the colors of the rainbow.

Mercury, messenger of the gods and god of speed and travel, moved about rapidly. *Mercurial* suggests changeability, fickleness.

WORDS FROM NAMES: Some words have come from names without change; for example, *boycott*, *derrick*, *diesel*, *macadam*, *ohm*, *volt*, *watt*, and *maverick*.

Boycott arises from Captain Charles Boycott, an English agent in Ireland. The Irish peasants, under Charles Parnell's leadership, refused to work for Boycott or do any business with him. Thus the word *boycott* came to mean a refusal to buy, sell, or have anything to do with a person, a company, or a product. Ironically, Boycott was the victim of the strategy, not its organizer!

Derrick is named for Thomas Derrick, a London hangman. A derrick, an apparatus for lifting heavy objects, looked like a gallows to the first persons using the name.

A *diesel* motor or vehicle is named for the German engineer who invented this kind of engine, Rudolph Diesel.

Macadam is named for John Loudon McAdam. Even as a child, McAdam constructed miniature road systems in his backyard. He pioneered the type of pavement that even today is common around the world.

Ohm, *volt*, and *watt* are all named for pioneers in the field of electricity and mechanics: Georg Simon Ohm, Alessandro Volta, and James Watt.

Maverick was named for Samuel August Maverick, a fiery Texas rancher who did not brand his cattle. *Maverick* has the primary meaning of "an unbranded calf" and the secondary meaning of a "fiery independent person." *Maverick* cattle do not stay with their group. *Mavericks* in politics can't be tied down to a rigid doctrine or party line.

Now see how you can use allusions to figure out definitions in trial test items.

Trial Test

Select the alternative that best defines the word in capital letters. The explanation of the allusion appears in parentheses.

EXAMPLE

BLARNEY:

(A) clever flattery   (D) down-to-earth
(B) skin disease   reporting
(C) plea for funds   (E) repetition

A

(Blarney Castle in Ireland has a famous stone. The person who kisses it is supposed to gain great skill in giving compliments and charming people.) Great skill in giving compliments is allied to clever flattery. The answer is (*A*).

1. BEDLAM:

(A) noise and   (D) joy and
    confusion   contentment
(B) calm and   (E) time and tide
    serenity
(C) thoughtfulness
    and reflection

1 ___

(Bedlam was the name of a London hospital for the insane. The full name of the hospital was once *St. Mary of Bethlehem*.)

2. MARTINET:

(A) small bird   (D) long poem
(B) musical   (E) piece of
    instrument   furniture
(C) strict
    disciplinarian

2 ___

(Jean Martinet was a French general during the reign of Louis XIV. Martinet built the first modern army in Europe.)

3. MACHIAVELLIAN:

(A) forthright   (D) sound
(B) reliable   (E) crafty
(C) vital

3 ___

(Niccolo Machiavelli was an Italian writer who believed a ruler should use any means, honorable or deceitful, to maintain a strong government.)

4. QUIXOTIC:

(A) brave   (D) contemptible
(B) fearful   (E) impractical
(C) slow

4 ___

(Don Quixote, hero of Cervantes' novel, was a foolish dreamer, who resolved to remake the world by impossible knightly feats.)

5. ACHILLES' HEEL:

(A) funny bone
(B) source of weakness
(C) article of clothing
(D) unpleasant person
(E) ailment

5 ___

(In Greek mythology, the mother of the hero Achilles dipped him, while a baby, into the River Styx to render him safe from injury. She held him by his heel, which was thus not protected.)

6. BERSERK:

(A) speaking thoughtfully
(B) sleeping restlessly
(C) running evenly
(D) planning craftily
(E) raging violently

6 ___

(Berserkers were wild warriors, who in battle howled, growled, bit their shields, and foamed at the mouth.)

7. HOBSON'S CHOICE:

(A) dilemma
(B) no alternative
(C) cream of the crop
(D) strong preference
(E) argument

7 ___

(Thomas Hobson, stablekeeper, let out his horses in strict rotation, not by rider's choice.)

8. MEANDER:

(A) talk rapidly
(B) shout loudly
(C) wander aimlessly
(D) walk steadily
(E) run competitively

8 ___

(The Meander was a river in Asia Minor noted for its twists and turns.)

9. MESMERISM:

(A) philosophical disagreement
(B) hypnotic fascination
(C) dull repetition
(D) commonplace wisdom
(E) unchecked evil

9 ___

(Franz Anton Mesmer was an Austrian physician who believed that his hands had miraculous healing powers, "animal magnetism.")

10. PROTEAN:

(A) violently cruel
(B) very nutritious
(C) carefully selected
(D) extremely changeable
(E) attractive and appealing

10 ___

(Proteus was a sea god, who was able to change his shape at will.)

Answers to Trial Test

1. (*A*) There would be *noise and confusion* in such a hospital.

2. (*C*) A general would be associated with military *discipline*.

3. (*E*) If Machiavelli believed in possible deceit, *crafty* is the best answer.

4. (*E*) "Impossible feats" suggests Don Quixote was *impractical*.

5. (*B*) The unprotected heel was a *source of weakness*.

6. (*E*) Berserkers *raged violently*.

7. (*B*) "Strict rotation" eliminates the possibility of choice.

8. (*C*) The twisting, turning river suggests *wandering aimlessly*.

9. (*B*) Mesmer's powers suggest *hypnotic fascination*.

10. (*D*) Proteus's ability to change his shape suggests that **protean** means *extremely changeable*.

Now look at two **antonym** questions which can be answered by knowing the allusions.

Problem

PARADISIACAL:

    (A) blissful   (D) inappropriate

    (B) concerned   (E) unhappy

    (C) vital

Strategy

Although **paradisiacal** looks like a strange and forbidding word, it clearly contains a familiar noun, *paradise*. Paradise, the Garden of Eden, is a place of happiness and delight. Look at the alternatives. You can discard *blissful* (A) at once, for it is a synonym, not an antonym. Choices (B), (C), and (D) have nothing to do with the root idea of happiness. *Unhappy* (E) is the answer.

Problem

QUIXOTIC:

    (A) romantic   (D) down-to-earth

    (B) slothful   (E) careless

    (C) idealistic

Strategy

Most readers are familiar with the story of Don Quixote and his servant, Sancho Panza. Most will also recall Don Quixote's famous attack on the windmills, calling them *evil giants*. Don Quixote's major qualities are idealism, romanticism, courage, willingness to fight against all odds, and impracticality. Since an antonym is needed in this question, you can discard (A) and (C), since these words are synonyms of **quixotic**. *Slothful* and *careless* are not relevant. *Down-to-earth* suggests a quality lacking in Don Quixote. (D) is the answer.

SUMMARY PART 7

Word Clue: Allusions

1. Some words are taken with little change from names of actual people: *cardigan, mackintosh, raglan, silhouette, zeppelin*.
2. Others use names of actual people, but with some change in form: *dunce, galvanize, nicotine, philippic, saxophone, teddy bear*.
3. Still others use words based on characters in legends and myths: *aurora, cereal, janitor, jovial, saturnine, titanic, vulcanize*.
4. Some words are taken from place names: *china, currant, italic type, morocco leather, peach, sardonic, spruce*.
5. Many words have interesting stories to tell: *blarney, Cassandra, donnybrook, Frankenstein, hector, Job's comforter, Pandora's box, pooh-bah, utopian*.

You may wish to refer to the following books to help you with allusions:
Robert Hendrickson, *Human Words*
Nancy Caldwell Sorel, *Word People*
Willard Espy, *O Thou Improper, Thou Uncommon Noun*

Review Test
Word Clues

The sentences below provide clues to meanings. Write the letter of the word that makes best sense in each sentence.

1. It is natural and --- for a cat to keep itself clean.
   - (A) internal
   - (B) external
   - (C) instinctive
   - (D) learned
   - (E) accepted

   1 ___

2. The hand-rubbed finish on the custom-built furniture was as --- as silk.
   - (A) slippery
   - (B) slick
   - (C) shiny
   - (D) smooth
   - (E) soft

   2 ___

3. The winner's eyes were --- with excitement.
   - (A) reflecting
   - (B) sparkling
   - (C) fiery
   - (D) charged
   - (E) transparent

   3 ___

4. The government's --- in enforcing the new law encourages lawlessness.
   - (A) promptness
   - (B) cruelty
   - (C) kindness
   - (D) prudence
   - (E) carelessness

   4 ___

5. The religious service ended with a --- of praise and joy.
   - (A) tune
   - (B) melody
   - (C) book
   - (D) ballad
   - (E) hymn

   5 ___

6. The --- of the sandy soil caused the beachside buildings to be unsafe.
   - (A) beauty
   - (B) instability
   - (C) height
   - (D) age
   - (E) length

   6 ___

7. Because of his --- disposition, you can never predict what he will do.
   - (A) sound
   - (B) Spartan
   - (C) stentorian
   - (D) mercurial
   - (E) herculean

   7 ___

8. Use Renewo shampoo to give your hair its natural ---.
   - (A) shininess
   - (B) lustre
   - (C) reflection
   - (D) color
   - (E) strength

   8 ___

9. The clever politician was as --- as an eel.
   - (A) quick
   - (B) sharp
   - (C) shiny
   - (D) slippery
   - (E) smart

   9 ___

10. The reason for the special traffic lights and turning lanes is to --- traffic flow, not impede it.
    - (A) facilitate
    - (B) decrease
    - (C) hinder
    - (D) delay
    - (E) hamper

    10 ___

Summary
Section II: Word Clues

Review these word clues from time to time. If you understand how word clues help you learn new words, you will do better on the vocabulary and reading sections of the SAT.

Clue 1 Connotation and Denotation
Connotation is the tone and meaning acquired by use.
Denotation is the dictionary definition.
Model   Although we often use the terms porpoise and dolphin *interchangeably*, careful marine biologists observe the *distinctions between* the two.

Clue 2 Figurative Language
Simile: comparing by using *like* and *as*
Model   The clean sheets looked *as white as snow*.
Metaphor: implying a comparison of two different things without using like or as
Model   The lazy person could not *hold down a job*.
Personification: representing an object as a person
Model   The *truth cries* out for justice.
Metonymy: using a word for another closely associated word
Model   She prepared a new *dish* for dinner.
Synecdoche: using the part for the whole, or the reverse
Model   The show featured fifty *dancing feet*.
Hyperbole: exaggerating for effect
Model   I was *scared to death*.
Understatement: emphasizing by saying less than is meant
Model   After the marathon I was a *little tired*.
Irony: saying one thing and implying the opposite
Model   I love this as much as *going to the dentist*.

Clue 3 Synonyms: discriminating between words of similar meaning
Model   The unpleasant boss was *haughty* and *overbearing*.

Clue 4 Antonyms: discriminating between words of opposite, or nearly opposite, meaning
Model   Is the stranger a *friend* or *foe*?

Clue 5 Associated Words: thinking of related words you already know
Model   For my term paper I read ballads, sonnets, and many haiku.

Clue 6 Words Within Words: looking for the familiar smaller words in larger words
Model   She tried hard, but her efforts were *ineffectual* (effect).

Clue 7 Allusions: using a reference to a literary or historical person, place, or events.
Her *mercurial* (Mercury) personality made her unfit for the management position.

Section III: Clues from Etymology

PART 1

Latin Prefixes

Would you like the key to thousands of words? According to Dr. James I. Brown of the University of Minnesota, the following 14 words will help you master 100,000 words.

aspect	intermittent	oversufficient
detain	mistranscribe	precept
epilogue	monograph	reproduction
indisposed	nonextended	uncomplicated
insist	offer	

Epilogue and *monograph* are of Greek origin and will be treated in Part 4. All the others contain basic Latin prefixes and roots, which will be treated here in Parts 1–3. Several of the prefixes are Anglo-Saxon.

How is it possible for so few words to provide clues to the meanings of so many other words? English, like many other languages, builds words by putting elements together. We call these elements *prefixes*, *roots*, and *suffixes*. Here are some examples.

PREFIX: beginning word part

dislike   **re**port   **de**part

ROOT: main word part

dis**like**   re**port**   de**part**

SUFFIX: ending word part

dislik**ing**   report**er**   depart**ure**

Some words, like *aspect* and *insist*, contain prefixes and roots. Other words, like *victor* and *nutrition*, contain roots and suffixes. Some words contain prefixes, roots, and suffixes; for example, *reproduction* and *uncomplicated*. Some words contain only roots; such as, *course* and *pose*.

Where Our Words Come From

In the richness of its resources, English is different from most languages. There are four major streams in English: Greek, Latin, French (ultimately derived from Latin), and Anglo-Saxon. All four provide thousands of words for us to choose from. Synonyms abound in many possibilities. See how some synonyms of *mark*, all from a different source, enrich our language.

mark—from Anglo-Saxon. *Mark* is a general word suggesting a token, impression, feature.

signature—from Latin (modified). *Signature* is the special *mark*, usually handwritten, to identify a person.

imprimatur—from Latin (unchanged). *Imprimatur* is a *mark* of approval signifying that a book has been accepted for publication.

criterion—from Greek. *Criterion* suggests a *mark*, a test, a standard for judging.

vestige—from French (and ultimately Latin). *Vestige* suggests a small *mark*, a remnant of something that has disappeared.

graffiti—from Italian (and ultimately from Latin and Greek). *Graffiti* is a plural word designating *marks* that appear where they don't belong; for example, scribbling on public walls.

An average synonym dictionary suggests scores of other synonyms for *mark*; for example, *badge, blemish, blot, boundary, brand, characteristic, disfigurement*, and so on through the alphabet. These words have diverse origins. All contribute to the English treasure house and make distinctions finer and more subtle in English.

You have noticed that a number of words above, listed from other languages, ultimately come from Latin or Greek. *Vestige* and *graffiti*, for example, come through French and Italian, but their ultimate source is Latin. French, however, is a far richer source than Italian.

We have labeled French as one of the four great sources of English, even though it is basically derived from Latin. When William the Conqueror settled in England after the Battle of Hastings in 1066, he brought Norman (French) noblemen, ladies, customs, settlers, and language with him. We thus have pairs like *house* (Anglo-Saxon) and *mansion* (French) to enrich our language.

Many SAT questions, especially the antonym and analogy questions, rely on such words and word pairs for their answer choices.

Get the Dictionary Habit

To increase your vocabulary, get the dictionary habit. Look up words to find their derivations. Notice how the following excerpt from *Webster's New World Dictionary* tells the fascinating story of *volume*. Why should a word meaning *turn* be used to describe a flat book today? The meaning is there. *Volumes* were originally scrolls—rolled-up papers.

> **vol•ume** (väl′yoom, -yəm) *n.* [ME. < MFr. < L. *volumen*, a roll, scroll, hence a book written on a parchment < *volulus*, pp. of *volvere*, to roll: see WALK] 1. orig., a roll of parchment, a scroll, etc.   2. *a*) a collection of written, typewritten, or printed sheets bound together; book   *b*) any of the separate books making up a matched set or a complete work   3. a set of the issues of a periodical over a fixed period of time, usually a year   4. any of the individual phonograph records of a multirecord album, esp. of literary readings   5. the amount of space occupied in three dimensions; cubic contents or cubic magnitude   6.

a) a quantity, bulk, mass, or amount   *b*) a large quantity; bulk, amount, etc.   7. the quantity, strength, or loudness of sound   8. *Music* fullness of tone —*SYN.* see BULK[1] — speak volumes to be very expressive or meaningful *

Following a trail through the dictionary is like playing a video game—without the need for special equipment. The quest can be fascinating and the rewards great. If you get the dictionary habit now, you'll have a lifetime of fun and growth. If, for example, you find *scroll* associated with *volume*, look up *scroll*. You'll find that *scroll* is related to the English *roll*. The dictionary suggests that you look up *escrow*, another related word. *Escrow* introduces you to another expression: *in escrow*, a phrase you should know in adult life. And so it goes if you use your dictionary often.

Pause for a moment in your study of roots to analyze an SAT-type antonym question.

Problem

DECIDUOUS:

(A) careless
(B) evergreen
(C) hardy

(D) undecided
(E) narrow

Strategy

You may have heard the expression *deciduous tree*. A *deciduous* tree loses its leaves every year. That is, the leaves *fall down*. The root *cid* (from *cad*) means *fall*. The prefix *de* means *down*. The opposite of *deciduous* is *evergreen* (*B*). A tree may be both *deciduous* and *hardy*, so (*C*) can be rejected. *Careless* (*A*) and *narrow* (*E*) are unrelated. *Undecided* (*D*) is a clever trick to mislead the unwary. *Undecided* seems like a possible antonym for *deciduous* until you apply what you already know. If you know some prefixes and roots, you can figure out many meanings.

It has been estimated that 65% of the words in the dictionary come from Latin or Greek. Learning the basic Latin and Greek prefixes and roots is an excellent way to extend your vocabulary.

Latin Prefixes

In the following lists, the first column gives the prefix or root. The second column gives the basic meaning of the prefix or root. The third column gives a word or words showing the use of a prefix or root in a word. The fourth column explains how the prefix or root keeps some of its original meaning, even though the word may have come a long way from its introduction into English. This explanation often serves as a definition of the word, as well, though its major purpose is to show how a word acquires meanings.

ENGLISH FOR THE COLLEGE BOARDS

COMMON LATIN PREFIXES

Prefix	Meaning	Example	Explanation
a, ab	away, from	**a**vert	turn *away*
		abnormal	deviating *from* normal
ac, ad, a	to, toward	**ac**cess	coming *toward*
		advance	move *toward*
ambi	both	**ambi**dextrous	skilled with *both* hands
ante	before	**ante**cedent	coming *before*
circum	around	**circum**navigate	sail *around*
com, con	with	**com**pare	make equal *with*, regard as similar
contra	against	**contra**dict	say *against*
de	down, from, away	**de**pose	put *down*
dis, di	apart, from, not	**dis**enfranchise	*not* allow to vote
		digress	move *apart*
e, ex	out of	**ex**it	go *out*
		evict	cast *out*
extra	beyond, additional	**extra**ordinary	*beyond* the ordinary
in	into	**in**sert	put *into*
in	not	**in**imical	*not* friendly
inter	between,	**inter**vene	come between
intra, intro	among, within	**intra**mural	*within* a school
medi	middle	**medi**eval	pertaining to the *Middle* Ages
non	not	**non**productive	*not* productive
ob	against, toward	**ob**struct	build *against*, hinder
pen	almost	**pen**insula	*almost* an island
per	through, thoroughly	**per**nicious	*thoroughly* evil
		pervade	move *through*
post	after	**post**pone	put *after*
pre	before	**pre**arrange	arrange *before*
prim, prin	first	**prin**cipal	*first* teacher, leader
pro	forward, in place of	**pro**ceed	go *forward*
re	back, again	**re**mit	send *back*
		reread	read *again*
retro	back, backward	**retro**grade	*backward* motion
se	aside, apart	**se**cede	pull *apart*
sub	under	**sub**marine	*under* the sea
super, supr	above, beyond	**super**human	*beyond* the human
		supreme	*above* all others
trans	across	**trans**migrate	move *across*
ultra	beyond, extremely	**ultra**modern	*beyond* the modern
vice	in place of	**vice**-president	*in place of* the president

A few prefixes change the last letter to match the first letter of the root word. Thus **ad** becomes **af** (*affect*), **ag** (*aggression*), **al** (*alliteration*), **an** (*annex*), **ap** (*apply*), **ar** (*arrest*), and **at** (*attend*). **Sub** becomes **suc** (*succumb*), **suf** (*suffer*), **sug** (*suggest*), and **sup** (*supplant*). **In** becomes **il** (*illegal*), **im** (*imperfect*), and **ir** (*irregular*). If you know the prefix in its unchanged form, look for the double letter to find the modified prefix.

A word of caution about roots, prefixes, and word meanings: words change in use. Word meanings sometimes depart from the original strict meanings. *Extravagant*, for example, according to its root and prefix means "wandering beyond." The word has, however, acquired a wider, more figurative sense. *Extravagant* purchases, for example, "wander beyond" the normal and wise. *Extravagant* yarns "wander beyond" the reasonable. Once you know the roots, you will find these extended meanings especially interesting.

Trial Test

Take the following trial test for practice in using Latin prefixes. Fill in the blank in each sentence by writing a Latin prefix from the list above. The word in italics is a clue to the needed prefix. The number in parentheses tells the number of letters needed to complete each word.

EXAMPLE

As I went *back* in imagination to my childhood home, the old cottage seemed huge in *retro* spect. (5)

The italicized word *back* tells you the prefix **retro** should be inserted. *Retrospect* means "looking backward."

1. Most of the words in the description are _____fluous, for they go far *beyond* what is needed to make an effective picture. (5)

2. I feel _____valent toward Jennifer, for I find her *both* charming and annoying at times. (4)

3. A (An) _____mortem is an examination made *after* death to determine the cause of death. (4)

4. Doug gave his _____ry opinion and spoke vehemently *against* the proposal. (6)

5. Because he could *not* function in the game, the fullback was put on the _____abled list. (3)

6. A (An) _____patriate is a person who goes *out* of his country to settle elsewhere. (2)

7. The artist gave a (an) _____spective show and enabled her fans to look *back* at her illustrious past. (5)

8. Marie Antoinette had a (an) _____cluded villa, *apart* from the bustle of the palace. (2)

9. A (An) _____errant social group is one that deviates *from* the normal. (2)

10. That _____diluvian idea of yours must have originated *before* the flood! (4)

Answers to Trial Test

1. super	4. contra	7. retro	10. ante
2. ambi	5. dis	8. se	
3. post	6. ex	9. ab	

Use your knowledge of Latin prefixes for this sentence-completion question.

Problem

Although the agreement was finally signed in
October, under the terms of the pact, payments
of lost wages would be --- to April, the time
the original contract --- .

(A) retroactive . . expired
(B) charged . . began
(C) referred . . expanded
(D) conducive . . germinated
(E) applied . . deteriorated

Strategy

The prefix **retro**, meaning "back," provides the key to this answer. *Retroactive* suggests going back into the past, usually to a period before another event. Here the contract was signed in October, but the pact pretended it had been signed in April, with full benefits beginning at that time. The only choice that makes sense is (*A*). Wages are paid as though the new agreement immediately followed the expiration of the old.

None of the alternatives makes good sense when preceding the words "to April."

LATIN PREFIXES DENOTING NUMBER

Prefix	Meaning	Example	Explanation
bi	two	**bi**ennial	every *two* years
cent	hundred	**cent**imeter	*hundredth* of a meter
dec	ten	**dec**imal	system of *tens*
duo, du	two	**du**et	performance by *two*
duodec	twelve	**duodec**imal	system of *twelves*
mill	thousand	**mill**enium	a *thousand* years
multi	many	**multi**tude	*many* persons
nona	nine	**nona**genarian	*ninety*-year-old
novem	nine	**novem**ber	*ninth* month (originally)
oct	eight	**oct**et	group of *eight*
omni	all	**omni**scient	*all*-knowing
quadr	four	**quadr**ilateral	*four*-sided
quinqu, quint	five	**quinqu**ennial	every *five* years
		quintuplets	multiple birth of *five*
semi	half	**semi**circle	*half* a circle
sept	seven	**Sept**ember	*seventh* month (originally)
sex	six	**sex**tet	group of *six*
tri	three	**tri**ple	*three* times
uni	one	**un**animous	of *one* mind

Trial Test

Fill in the blank in each sentence by writing a Latin number prefix from the list above. The word in italics is a clue to the needed prefix. The number in parentheses tells the number of letters needed.

EXAMPLE

The setting sun made a perfect *semi*circle, as only *half* was visible on the horizon. (4)

The italicized word *half* tells us the prefix *semi* should be inserted.

1. Some colleges have a(an) _____ mestral organization, dividing the school year into *three* parts. (3)

2. A(An) _____ave is the *eighth* full tone above a given tone, having twice as many vibrations a second. (3)

3. Brock's plans are _____farious, having *many* angles and procedures. (5)

4. In a(an) _____nary system, *two* suns revolve about each other. (2)

5. Our town is celebrating its _____centennial, having been in existence *half* a hundred years. (4)

6. A truly _____que specimen is *one* of a kind. (3)

7. Superman was not _____potent, for he could not overcome *all* obstacles. (4)

8. A(An) _____angle is a *three*-sided figure. (3)

9. In the _____igrade, or Celsius, thermometer, the difference between the boiling point and the freezing point is divided into *100* degrees. (4)

10. A(An) _____ipede may seem to have a *thousand* legs, but the actual number is between 100 and 200. (4)

Answers to Trial Test

1. tri	4. bi	7. omni	10. mill
2. oct	5. semi	8. tri	
3. multi	6. uni	9. cent	

Here is an antonym question like those on the SAT.

Problem

UNANIMOUS:

    (A) anonymous   (D) disagreeing
    (B) incredulous   (E) excitable
    (C) indigenous

Strategy

You may have heard of a unanimous vote—one in which all persons voted the same way. **Uni** (shortened to **un**) means "all" and *animus* means "mind:" of one mind. It helps to know that **un** means "one" rather than "not." If you know this meaning, you can look for an opposite meaning.

Anonymous (A) sounds like a related word, but it is not; it means "unnamed" or "of unknown name." Remember, you are looking for an opposite meaning. *Incredulous* (B), meaning "unbelieving," is unrelated. Choice (C), *indigenous*, means "native," and is not related. *Disagreeing* (D) looks like a good choice—a unanimous vote occurs when everyone is agreeing. *Disagreeing* is its opposite. Also, the final choice, *excitable*, is not a possibility. The antonym is (D), *disagreeing*.

Time Out for Review

Fill in the blank in each sentence by writing the Latin prefix that makes best sense. The word in italics is a clue. The number in parentheses tells the number of letters needed.

1. An idea that is said to correspond *with* another is _____gruent with that idea. (3)

2. The _____urban bus service ran *between* towns. (5)

3. _____historic events took place *before* the invention of writing. (3)

4. The bottle held only a(an) _____iliter, or one-*tenth* of a liter, of liquid. (3)

5. If you're going *to* Walt Disney World, buy your ticket of _____mission at the main gate. (2)

6. The Patriots stated once *again* what they believed in and _____affirmed their allegiance to the cause of freedom. (2)

7. A presidential election is always a(an) _____ennial event, occurring every *four* years. (5)

8. A layer of _____cutaneous fat, *under* the outer layer of skin, provides insulation against the cold. (3)

9. Tiny _____mitters, powered by solar batteries, send messages *across* millions of miles of space. (5)

10. Because the chairperson had been delayed, the _____-chairperson acted *in place of* the chairperson and opened the meeting. (4)

11. A good _____ator takes a *middle* position, favoring neither one side nor the other. (4)

12. A(An) _____opus is so named because it has *eight* arms. (3)

13. Walt's _____terminable speeches seem *not* to have a purpose nor an end. (2)

14. When a seller offers a used car, he is often shocked to learn how much normal _____preciation has brought *down* the price of the car. (2)

15. A group of *five* musicians is called a(an) _____et. (5)

16. By _____polation Helen went *beyond* present statistics and estimated the probable population of Grimesdale by the year 2000. (5)

17. A(An) _____spect person looks *around* carefully before taking action. (6)

18. A(An) _____el is a formal fight *between* *two* persons. (2)

19. Our _____genitors, those who came *before* us, have left for us a valuable heritage of art and wisdom. (3)

20. For my taste the Cortland apple is _____lative, far *above* other apples in flavor and texture. (4)

SUMMARY PART 1

Clues from Etymology: Latin Prefixes

1. Etymology, the study of word origins, is extremely helpful in figuring out the meaning of new and unknown words.

2. A great many English words begin with common Latin prefixes and number prefixes. If you know the prefix, you have a good chance of figuring out the whole word.

3. A few prefixes change the last letter to match the first letter of the root word:

sub — suc (succumb)	**sub** — sug (suggest)
sub — suf (suffer)	**sub** — sup (supplant)

PART 2

Latin Roots: Verbs

Now we come to the longest list in our study of word elements: Latin roots. Though the lists seem overwhelmingly long, do not lose heart. You already *know* most of these roots because you see them every day in familiar words. You already know, for example, that *victory* involves *conquering* a person, a group, an obstacle. You may not have put that meaning into so many words before, but your knowledge gives you an advantage in working with the root **vic-vict,** meaning "conquer." When you meet *invincible*, you know it means "unconquerable."

When you go over the list below, associate a word with each root, preferably a word you already know. Doing so will expand your vocabulary enormously and will help you meet many new words with confidence. Note how a knowledge of roots helps with a question like the following antonym example from the SAT.

Problem

CONFLUENCE:
- (A) disparagement
- (B) disturbance
- (C) diffidence
- (D) divination
- (E) divergence

Strategy

The root **flu** meaning "flow" should strike you at once. You can remember **flu** by thinking of other words like *fluid* and *fluent*, all having something to do with *flow*. The prefix **con** meaning "together" is also familiar. You can remember this by thinking of other words like *congress* and *confer*, all having something to do with *together*. You can guess that *confluence* is a "flowing together."

Are there any alternatives that suggest the opposite of *flowing together*? All the words here begin with **di,** a tricky device, for you know that **di** means "away from." Sometimes the prefix gives the answer away, but not here. You can discard *divination*, however, for this obviously is related to *divine*. Does any root suggest something like *flowing*? **Verg,** meaning turn or bend, is present in a word like *converge, turn together.* **Verg** seems like a good companion root to **flu.** Since the prefix **con** means "together" and the prefix **di** means "away from," we can guess that *divergence* (*E*) is the opposite of **confluence.**

Don't underestimate what you already know. In your lifetime you have met a great many words. These familiar words lead you to the meanings of new words even without the benefit of context.

What if you have forgotten that **flu** means "flow?" Just think of a lot of related words like *fluid* and *fluent* to extract the meaning from the root. The other words in your vocabulary can help you remember roots and even discover the meaning of completely new roots. Even if you don't know *impel*, with its root **pel,** other words like *propel*, *repel*, and *dispel* provide clues that **pel** means something like "drive."

Latin Roots

The lists of Latin roots here are by no means all the roots used in English words, but they include most of the important and helpful ones. Don't forget, even if you meet a word with a root not included in the lists below, you can often guess at the meaning of the word by thinking of other words with the same root.

To make the lists more manageable, the words have been arbitrarily divided into two large categories: those derived from Latin nouns and adjectives and those derived from Latin verbs. Some words are borderline. *Labor*, for example, comes from a Latin noun which is related to a Latin verb. The lists 1, 2, and 3 (pages 94, 96, and 98) are for convenience, so that you can work with a small number of roots at one time. A trial test follows each list.

ROOTS FROM LATIN VERBS – 1

Root	Meaning	Example	Explanation
ag, act	do, act, drive	**ag**ile	*act*ive
am, ami	love	**ami**able	good-natured (originally *lov*able)
arbit	judge	**arbit**rate	*judge* between
aud	hear	**aud**ible	able to be *heard*
cad, cas, cid	fall	**cad**ence	*fall* of the voice in speaking
		coin**cid**ence	a *falling* together of events
cern, cert	perceive, separate	dis**cern**	recognize as *separate*, see clearly
can, cant, chant	sing	**cant**or	*sing*er
cap, capt, cip, cept	take	**cap**ture	*take* by force
ced, cess, cede, ceed	go	pro**ceed**	*go* forward
		re**cede**	*go* back
cis, cid, caed	kill, cut	sui**cid**e	*kill*ing of oneself
		in**cis**ion	*cut*ting into
clam, claim	cry out, shout	ex**claim**	*cry* out
		pro**clam**ation	*cry*ing forth
clud, claus, clus	shut, close	se**clud**ed	*shut* away
cogn	know	re**cogn**ize	*know* by some detail
col, cult	till, inhabit	agri**cult**ure	*till*ing the fields
cred	believe	**cred**ible	*believ*able
cresc, crease	grow	in**crease**	*grow* in size
curr, curs	run	in**curs**ion	*run*ning in, invasion
da, dat, don	give	**don**ation	*gift*
dic, dict	say	**dic**tate	*say* aloud

doc	teach	**doc**trine	*teach*ing
dorm	sleep	**dorm**ant	*sleep*ing, inactive
duc, duct	lead	ab**duct**	*lead* away, kidnap
err	wander	**err**ant	*wander*ing
fac, fec, fic, fy	do, make	magni**fy**	*make* large
		factory	place where things are *made*
fer, lat	carry	re**fer**	*carry* back
		trans**late**	*carry* across
flect, flex	bend	**flex**ible	easily *bent*
flu, flux	flow	**flu**id	something that *flows*
		in**flux**	a *flow*ing in
frang, fract, frag, fring	break	**fract**ure	*break*
		fragment	*broken* piece
fug	flee	**fug**itive	one who *flees*
fund, fus	pour	in**fus**ion	*pour*ing in
gen	cause, bear, produce	con**gen**ital	*born* with
ger, gest	carry	belli**ger**ent	one who *carries* war to another

Trial Test

Fill in the blank in each sentence by writing a Latin root from the list above. The word in italics is the clue to the needed root. The number in parentheses tells the number of letters needed.

EXAMPLE

Mark was too cre̲d̲ulous, *believ*ing everything he heard. (4)

The italicized *believ* tells us the root **cred** should be inserted.

1. A(an) _____ent moon soon after sunset tells us the moon is waxing, or *grow*ing. (5)

2. To prevent someone from *know*ing you, you might travel in_____ito. (4)

3. To *say* in advance is to pre_____. (4)

4. Our play group has a bene_____tor who has *done* many good things for us. (3)

5. He was charged with an in _____ion because he had *broken* the law about parking in restricted areas. (5)

6. Marcia is _____ent in French: her speech *flows* so effortlessly. (3)

7. The _____ry *carried* us across New York Harbor and back. (3)

8. Wally was in_____ed to wear the clown costume and was even *led* to performing a humorous routine. (3)

9. The _____itories in the cabin could *sleep* a dozen people in a pinch. (4)

10. The sports fans at the airport *shouted* when the plane landed and _____ored for a brief speech by the triumphant coach. (4)

11. When we decided to sell the house, we arranged for a real estate _____ent to *act* for us. (2)

12. When we opened the crowded closet, a pro_____ion of odds and ends *poured* forth. (3)

13. The _____erator *produced* enough current for a small village. (3)

14. Brett *ran* his eye over the manuscript, but his _____ory glance provided no clue to the importance of the contents. (4)

15. If you *go* beyond our budgeted expenditures and ex_____ the amount allotted to costumes, you'll put us in the red before we start. (4)

16. The witch doctor pronounced the in_____ation in a *singsong* voice. (4)

17. Ralph Waldo Emerson preached the _____trine of self-reliance and so *taught* his contemporaries to believe in themselves. (3)

18. Several wealthy _____ors *gave* sufficient funds to build a new rectory. (3)

19. Re_____ees were *fleeing* the city under attack. (3)

20. The *killing* of a brother is called fratri_____e. (3)

Answers to Trial Test

1. cresc	6. flu	11. ag	16. cant
2. cogn	7. fer	12. fus	17. doc
3. dict	8. duc	13. gen	18. don
4. fac	9. dorm	14. curs	19. fug
5. fract	10. clam	15. ceed	20. cid

ROOTS FROM LATIN VERBS—2

Root	Meaning	Example	Explanation
grad, gress	walk	pro**gress**	a *walk* forward
hab, hib	hold	**hab**it	something that *holds* us
her, hes	stick	co**here**	*stick* together
		ad**hes**ive	something that *sticks* to something else
it	go	ex**it**	*go* out
jac, ject	throw	re**ject**	*throw* back
jud	judge	pre**jud**ice	a *judging* in advance
jung, junct, jug	join	**junct**ion	a *joining*
jur	swear	**jur**or	one *sworn* to give a just verdict
leg, lect	choose, gather, read	il**leg**ible	not *read*able
		col**lect**	*gather* together
loqu, locut,	speak, talk	**loqu**acious	*talk*ative
mand	entrust, command	**mand**ate	a land en*trust*ed to another country
merg, mers	dip, plunge	sub**merg**e	*dip* below water
mit, miss	send	trans**mit**	*send* across
mon, monit	warn	ad**mon**ition	mild *warn*ing
mov, mot	move	**mot**or	something that *moves*
mut	change	**mut**able	*change*able
nasc, nat	born	**nat**ive	one *born* in a country
neg	deny	**neg**ative	*deny* truth of
ora	speak, pray	**ora**tor	*speak*er
orn	decorate	ad**orn**	*decorate*
pat, pass	suffer	**pat**ient	one who *suffers*, who receives care
pel, puls	drive	re**pel**	*drive* back
		com**puls**ion	*driv*ing force
pet	seek	centri**pet**al	*seek*ing the center

plac	please	im**plac**able	unable to be *pleased*
plaud, plus, plod, plos	clap, strike	ap**plaud**	*clap*
plic, plex, ply	fold	com**plic**ated	involved (*folded* in on itself)
pon, pos	place, put	post**pon**e	*place* after
port	carry	im**port**	*carry* in
prehend, pre-hens, pris	seize	com**prehend**	*seize* (as an idea)
press	press, print	im**press**ion	something *pressed* or *printed* on
prob	prove	**prob**ation	a period of test, of *prov*ing someone can perform as expected
pugn	fight	**pugn**acious	ready to *fight*
quir, ques, quis	seek	in**quis**itive	*seek*ing information
rid, ris	laugh	**rid**iculous	*laugh*able

Trial Test

Fill in the blank in each sentence by writing a Latin root from the list above. The word in italics is the clue to the needed root. The number in parentheses tells the number of letters needed.

1. Cheryl *sent* the re_____tance to the power company. (3)

2. In grammar, a con_____ion *joins* two elements together. (5)

3. Who will be chosen to ad_____icate the lawsuit, *judging* whether the plaintiff's case will prevail? (3)

4. Pauline in_____ed a few witty remarks, *throwing* them in casually at intervals. (4)

5. Humans are planti_____e creatures, for they *walk* on the soles of their feet. (4)

6. *Place* this envelope in the de_____it box. (3)

7. A (An) _____tionnaire is designed to *seek* information. (4)

8. Geraldine uses a(an) _____manteau for *carry*ing documents and letters. (4)

9. The minister *read* the Bible verse from the _____ern. (4)

10. Some col_____ial expressions are suitable for *speak*ing but not for writing. (4)

11. The judge re_____ed the prisoner to a detention home, *entrust*ing him to a pair of sheriff's deputies. (4)

12. Sheila im_____ed the dusty jacket in warm soapy water, *dip*ping it again and again until the stains were removed. (4)

13. The governor *changed* his mind and com_____ed the condemned man's sentence to life imprisonment. (3)

14. The re_____ent industrial life of many New England cities proves that a re-*birth* of vigor is not impossible. (4)

15. A (An) _____ligent driver may *deny* others the right to life. (3)

16. The police officers ap_____ed the smuggler and *seized* his cargo. (7)

17. The hero of Cotter's novel is *driven* by unpredictable im_____es. (4)

18. Naturally, Isabelle enjoyed the *clap*ping of the audience and the _____its of the critics. (5)

19. A com_____ent person is *pleased* with himself and quite smug. (4)

20. The _____ition *seeks* to bring to the notice of the authorities the dangerous intersection of Fifth and Main Streets. (3)

Answers to Trial Test

1. mit	6. pos	11. mand	16. prehend
2. junct	7. ques	12. mers	17. puls
3. jud	8. port	13. mut	18. plaud
4. ject	9. lect	14. nasc	19. plac
5. grad	10. loqu	15. neg	20. pet

See if you can figure out a SAT-type antonym question, using your knowlege of Latin roots.

Problem

MANDATORY:

(A) unhandy   (D) required

(B) manipulation   (E) managed

(C) optional

Strategy

The root **mand**, meaning "command," is the key to the meaning of **mandatory**: required by a command or an order. Remember, you are looking for an opposite meaning.

Required (D) is a synonym; ignore it. *Manipulation* (B) and *managed* (E) come from another Latin word meaning "hand;" they have nothing to do with **mandatory**. Only two choices are left. *Unhandy* (A) is a trap for anyone who may think **mandatory** means "handy." *Optional* (C) is left, and it is the correct choice: **mandatory** and *optional* are antonyms.

ROOTS FROM LATIN VERBS–3

Root	Meaning	Example	Explanation
rog	ask	inter**rog**ate	*ask*
rump, rupt	break	**rupt**ure	*break*
sal, salt, sult	leap	**sal**ient	*leap*ing out
sci	know	con**sci**ous	able to *know*
scrib, script	write	in**scribe**	*write* in
		in**script**ion	*writ*ing in
seg, sect	cut	bi**sect**	*cut* in two
sed, sess	sit	**sess**ion	a *sit*ting
sens, sent	feel	**sens**ation	*feel*ing
sequ, secu	follow	**sequ**el	work that *follows* another
solv, solut	loosen	**solv**ent	something that *loosens*
spec, spect	see	**spect**acles	device for *see*ing
spir	breathe	re**spir**atory	pertaining to *breath*ing
sta, sist, stit	stand	**sta**ble	able to *stand*

string, strict	bind	**string**ent	*bind*ing
stru, struct	build	de**struct**ion	opposite of *build*ing
tang, tact	touch	**tang**ible	able to be *touch*ed
tent, tin, tain	hold	**ten**acious	*hold*ing on
tend, tens, tent	stretch	ex**tend**	*stretch* out
torqu, tort	twist	dis**tort**ed	*twist*ed
trah, tract	draw	at**tract**ion	something that *draws*
trib	share, pay	**trib**ute	something *paid*
trud, trus	thrust	in**trud**e	*thrust* in
turb	agitate	dis**turb**	*agitate*
vad, vas	go	in**vad**e	*go* in
ven, vent	come	con**ven**e	*come* together
verg	lean, turn	con**verg**e	*turn* together
vert, vers	turn	re**vers**e	*turn* back
vid, vis	see	**vis**ible	able to be *seen*
vinc, vict	conquer	con**vinc**e	*conquer* (in a discussion)
viv, vict	live	re**viv**e	bring back to *life*
voc, vok	call	**voc**ation	*call*ing
vol	wish, will	in**vol**untary	against the *will*
volv, volut	turn	re**volv**e	*turn* around

Trial Test

Fill in the blank in each sentence by writing a Latin root from the list above. The word in italics is the clue to the needed root. The number in parentheses tells the number of letters needed.

1. The entertainer was able to *twist* his body into the strangest con_____ions. (4)

2. The boa con_____or *binds* and crushes its foe. (6)

3. The Ford *stand*ing in the garage will remain _____tionary until you replace the battery. (3)

4. Tele_____ion enables us to *see* events happening far away. (3)

5. The strong armies of Genghis Khan were in_____ible, *conquer*ing every force in their path. (4)

6. Ancient Egyptian _____es *wrote* on stone, messages that still survive. (5)

7. _____entary people *sit* too much, avoiding exercise. (3)

8. Although English royalty could not *hold* onto real power, it has re_____ed the pomp and glitter of centuries ago. (4)

9. Fred dreaded dis_____ing the frog in biology class, but after the first *cut* he became fascinated by the complexity of his subject. (4)

10. The cor_____ administration *broke* every moral and legal guideline in running the city. (4)

11. _____ion *stretches* mind and body almost to the breaking point. (4)

12. The purpose of the in_____ion was to *see* if the regulations had been followed. (5)

13. Some of our actions have important con_____ences that *follow* us all our days. (4)

14. The con_____ions of the brain show twists, *turns*, and folds on the surface. (5)

15. The storm *agitated* the formerly calm lake and caused dangerous _____ulence for small boats. (4)

16. Bene_____ent actions arise from feelings of good*will* toward others. (3)

17. To re_____e a license is to *call* it back and cancel it. (3)

18. A di_____ent point of view *turns* from the average. (4)

19. To inter_____e in a dispute is to *come* between the two parties in an attempt to settle the argument. (3)

20. The plastic models are formed by ex_____ ion, that is, by *thrust*ing the plastic through small holes to provide the desired shape. (4)

Answers to Trial Test

1. tort	6. scrib	11. Tens	16. vol
2. strict	7. Sed	12. spect	17. vok
3. sta	8. tain	13. sequ	18. verg
4. vis	9. sect	14. volut	19. ven
5. vinc	10. rupt	15. turb	20. trus

Here is another SAT-type antonym question. Can you answer it? Use your knowledge of Latin roots.

Problem

TURBULENT:
- (A) turgid
- (B) serene
- (C) torpid
- (D) distorted
- (E) impertinent

Strategy

Turbulent contains the Latin root **turb**, meaning "agitate;" *turbulent* means "agitated," "stormy," "violent." Its antonym is *serene* (*B*). *Turgid* (*A*) and *torpid* (*C*) may seem related, but they are not. (You are looking for an opposite meaning, not a similar one.) *Distorted* (*D*) and *impertinent* (*E*), because of their negative prefixes, may seem like appropriate antonyms, but they are unrelated in meaning.

Time Out for Review

Fill in the blank in each sentence by writing a Latin root from the lists. The word in italics is the clue to the needed root. The number in parentheses tells the number of letters needed.

1. We need an impartial _____er to *judge* the merits of the case. (5)

2. The letter expressed the ap _____ation of the council and *proved* that government was responsible to public needs. (4)

3. Daryl fancies he is omni_____ent, *know*ing everything about everything. (3)

4. The re_____e *shut* himself away from all society. (4)

5. The slightest sound on stage can be *heard* all through the _____itorium. (3)

6. The critic de_____ed the novel's purpose and *laugh*ed at the intended motivation of the central character. (3)

7. Humane societies protest _____ isection, research operations performed on *living* animals. (3)

8. Huge skyscrapers are *built* by specialized con_____ion contractors. (6)

9. Gail is so _____ulous she'll *believe* anything. (4)

10. The _____cle at Delphi *spoke* words that could be taken in many ways. (3)

11. The _____or *drew* the plow through the moist soil. (5)

12. Before the jet aircraft had been perfected, airplanes were *driven* by one or more pro_____lers. (3)

13. The spy inter_____ed the message and *took* it to the enemy contact. (4)

14. The referee ad_____ished the boxer, *warn*ing him that another foul would cost him the match. (3)

15. Some families are _____ile, *touch*ing and hugging each other on greetings and farewells. (4)

16. The keynote *speak*er delivered a lengthy _____tion. (3)

17. A manu_____tured article was once, by word origin, *made* by hand. (3)

18. Many elements of Victorian houses were purely _____amental, added for *decoration*, not function. (3)

19. The ex_____it *held* many items of interest to the visitor. (3)

20. Are insects _____ient creatures that *feel* some kind of primitive emotions, like fear? (4)

SUMMARY PART 2

Clues from Etymology: Latin Roots—Verbs

1. Because English contains more words from Latin than from any other language, Latin roots, as well as prefixes, can help you figure out meanings—and SAT answers.
2. Just one root can lead to several words:

    port ("carry")—import, deport, report, portable

PART 3

Latin Roots: Nouns and Adjectives

Latin verbs have provided a solid list of roots to help you in attacking new words. Latin nouns and adjectives also supply information you can use to master new and unfamiliar words. Spend time on these lists as you prepare for the SAT.

ROOTS FROM LATIN NOUNS AND ADJECTIVES – 1

Root	Meaning	Example	Explanation
al, alter, altr	other	**al**ien	person from *another* land
		altruism	concern for *others*
anim	life, mind	**anim**ated	*lively*
		un**anim**ous	of one *mind*
ann, enn	year	**ann**ual	*yearly*
		mill**enn**ium	period of a thousand *years*
apt, ept	suitable, appropriate	**apt**itude	*suitabil*ity for a task
		in**ept**	not *suitable*, unfit
aqu	water	**aqu**eous	*watery*
arm	arm, weapon	**arm**ament	*weapon*ry
art	art, craft, skill	**art**isan	a person skilled in a *craft*
bell	beautiful	em**bell**ish	make *beautiful*
bene, bon	good	**bene**factor	one who does *good*
brev	short	ab**brev**iate	*short*en
cand	white, glowing	in**cand**escent	*glow*ing
capit	head	**capit**al	chief* (*head*) city
centr	center	ec**centr**ic	off *center*
civ, cit	city, citizen	**civ**ic	dealing with problems of the *city*
cor	heart	**cor**dial	sincere, from the *heart*
corp	body	**corp**oreal	*bod*ily
crux, cruc	cross	**cruc**iform	*cross*-shaped
culp	blame, fault	**culp**able	deserving *blame*
cur	care	pedi**cur**e	foot *care*
dent	tooth	**dent**al	pertaining to *teeth*
dia, di	day	**di**urnal	*daily*
digit	finger	**digit**al	pertaining to *finger*
dom	house	**dom**icile	*house*
domin	master	**domin**ate	rule as a *master*
dur	hard, lasting	**dur**able	*lasting*
ego	I, self	**ego**centric	centered on the *self*
equ	horse	**equ**ine	pertaining to the *horse*
equ	equal	in**equ**ality	condition of being *unequal*
ev	age, time	co**ev**al	of the same *age*

felic	happy	**felic**ity	*happi*ness
ferv	boil, bubble	**ferv**ent	*boil*ing, ardent
fid	faith	**fid**elity	*faith*fulness
fil	son	**fil**ial	pertaining to a *son*

*Here's another example of the incredible richness of English. *Chief*, meaning head, comes to us through the French, but the French word itself comes from the Latin *capit*. When English borrows the same word twice, the borrowings are called *doublets*. See pages 158–159.

Trial Test

Fill in the blank in each sentence by writing a Latin root from the list above. The word in italics is the clue to the needed root. The number in parentheses tells the number of letters needed.

EXAMPLE:

The <u>cur</u>ator of a museum is a person who takes *care* of the exhibits.
The italicized word *care* tells you to use the root **cur**. The *curator* takes care of the museum.

1. The presti_____ator was a superb magician, as he demonstrated trick after trick with nimble *fingers*. (5)

2. _____ity in writing suggests that the writer take the *short*est path to his goal, avoiding all unnecessary words. (4)

3. Objects without *life* are in_____ate. (4)

4. A name *other* than your own is a(an) _____ias. (2)

5. The important testimony of the key witness ex_____ated the defendant, removing any *blame* from his actions. (4)

6. A(An) _____uity is an amount of money paid every *year*. (3)

7. A substance _____eficial to the health is *good* for you. (3)

8. A(An) _____ifrice is a powder for cleaning *teeth*. (4)

9. A(An) _____tist uses the pronoun *I* almost exclusively. (3)

10. At the horse show riders demonstrated _____estrian skills. (3)

11. A con_____ant is a close friend, someone we put *faith* in. (3)

12. A(An) _____ilian is a *citizen* not in the armed forces. (3)

13. Dis_____d, or disagreement, is a metaphor suggesting that two *hearts* are not beating together. (3)

14. A(An) _____ulent, obese person has just too much *body*! (4)

15. A per _____a distribution is literally according to each *head*, that is, equally to each individual. (5)

16. _____ifugal force flees the *center*. (5)

17. A(An) _____ry is meant to be kept faithfully, every *day*. (3)

18. An ef_____escent liquid *bubbles* and *boils*. (4)

19. A(An) _____ivalent payment is *equal* in value. (3)

20. Scrooge was a(an) _____eering boss, seeking to show himself the *master* in every situation involving his employees. (5)

21. Perkins has a medi_____al attitude toward labor, a point of view lifted straight out of the Middle *Ages*. (2)

22. A(An) _____ arium is a *watery* wonderland, with fish as the principal inhabitants. (3)

23. The _____ ator of a museum is a person who takes *care* of the exhibits. (3)

24. The victors dis _____ ed the losers, taking away all *weapons* and tools of war. (3)

25. A *cross*-shaped object is _____ iform. (4)

Answers to Trial Test

1. digit	8. dent	14. corp	20. domin
2. Brev	9. ego	15. capit	21. ev
3. anim	10. equ	16. Centr	22. aqu
4. al	11. fid	17. dia	23. cur
5. oner	12. civ	18. ferv	24. arm
6. ann	13. cor	19. equ	25. cruc
7. ben			

Try out your knowledge of Latin roots on this antonym question.

Problem

ALTRUISTIC:

(A) altered
(B) unchanged
(C) depth
(D) peaceful
(E) selfish

Strategy

The Latin root **altr** means "other;" someone who is altruistic is concerned with the welfare of others. Its antonym is obvious: *selfish* (*E*). *Altered* (*A*) may appear to be related, but it is not. Remember, you are looking for an opposite meaning. *Unchanged* (*B*), and *depth* (*C*), and even *peaceful* (*D*), may seem to be possible antonyms *if* you are unfamiliar with the root **altr**.

ROOTS FROM LATIN NOUNS AND ADJECTIVES – 2

Root	Meaning	Example	Explanation
fin	end	**fin**ally	at the *end*
firm	strong	in**firm**	not *strong*
flor	flower	**flor**al	pertaining to *flowers*
foli	leaf	**foli**age	*leaves*
form	form, shape	de**form**ation	change in *form* (for the worse)
fort	strong	**fort**ify	make *strong*
fum	smoke	**fum**es	*smoke*

grat	free, thankful, pleased	**grat**itude	expression of *thanks*
grav	heavy	ag**grav**ate	make worse, *heavi*er
greg	flock	con**greg**ation	*flock*ing together
herb	grass	**herb**ivorous	*grass*-eating
ign	fire	**ign**ite	set on *fire*
labor	work	**labor**atory	place to *work* in
leg	law	**leg**al	pertaining to *law*
lev	light	al**lev**iate	*light*en
liber	free	**liber**ate	*free*
libr	book	**libr**ary	storehouse of *books*
liter	letter	al**liter**ation	beginning with same *letter*
loc	place	**loc**ation	*place*
lud, lus	play, game	pre**lud**e	before the *game*, introduction
		col**lus**ion	conspiracy (a *play*ing together)
magn	great	**magn**ify	make *great*
mal	evil	**mal**efactor	one who does *evil*
man	hand	**man**ual	by *hand*
mar	sea	sub**mar**ine	beneath the *sea*
mater, matr	mother	**matr**iarch	rule by *mother*
maxim	largest	**maxim**ize	make *largest*
ment	mind	**ment**al	pertaining to *mind*
min	less, little, small	**min**imum	*least* amount
miser	wretched	**miser**able	*wretched*
mor	custom	**mor**es	*customs*
mort	death	im**mort**al	*death*less
nav, naut	ship, sail	**nav**al	pertaining to *ships*

Trial Test

Fill in the blank in each sentence by writing a Latin root from the list above. The word in italics is the clue to the needed root. The number in parentheses tells the number of letters needed.

1. An unfortunate person not in his right *mind* is de_____ed. (4)

2. The famous Rodgers and Hammerstein col_____ated on many musicals, *work*ing together as an effective team. (5)

3. _____eous rock had its origins in *fire* in the earth's early history. (3)

4. _____islators make *laws*; judges test them. (3)

5. Serious debates can be *light*ened by a touch of _____ity. (3)

6. _____itime regulations have developed from the unwritten laws of the *sea*. (3)

7. _____animity is a *great*ness of spirit reflected in good and generous actions. (4)

8. A(An) _____icure is care of the *hands*; pedicure, of the feet. (3)

9. It is hard for a human mind to conceive of in_____ity, space without *end*. (3)

10. One's *strong* point is called his _____e. (4)

11. A dis_____ated bone is out of its proper *place*. (3)

12. To _____ign someone is to say *evil* things about him. (3)

13. The female stickleback doesn't have _____nal instincts; the male fish acts as *mother* and father. (5)

14. In the battle off Cape Trafalgar, Admiral Nelson received a(an) _____al wound, but he won victory even in *death*. (4)

15. The strict laws were _____alized, *free*ing the citizens from many unnecessary regulations. (5)

16. _____ity on the moon is so much less than on earth that we'd feel much less *heavy*. (4)

17. People who like to *flock* together are _____arious. (4)

18. Keep that _____icide away from the *grass* or you'll kill it. (4)

19. Vince _____imized his injury, making it seem *less* than it really was. (3)

20. To interpret the law too _____ally may emphasize the *letter* of the law at the expense of its spirit. (5)

21. On the _____ly rations allotted them, the serfs lived a *wretched* life. (5)

22. The exterminators used a deadly *smoke* in _____igating the house and ridding it of pests. (3)

23. Because his speech was excellent, the speaker was given a _____uity to express the *thanks* of the audience. (4)

24. The _____ist sold a beautiful bouquet of *flowers* for Mother's Day. (4)

25. Some chemicals de_____ate trees, stripping them of *leaves* and often killing the trees. (4)

Answers to Trial Test

1. ment	8. man	14. mort	20. liter
2. labor	9. fin	15. liber	21. miser
3. Ign	10. fort	16. Grav	22. fum
4. Leg	11. loc	17. greg	23. grat
5. lev	12. mal	18. herb	24. flor
6. Mar	13. mater	19. min	25. foli
7. Magn			

See how well you can do on this antonym question.

Problem

DEFOLIATED:
- (A) unfolded
- (B) preceded
- (C) leafy
- (D) unruffled
- (E) foolish

Strategy

Check your Latin roots and find **foli**, meaning "leaf;" so **defoliated** must mean *leafless*. The opposite jumps out: *leafy* (*C*). *Folded* (*A*) and *foolish* (*E*) are traps for those who do not know the **foli** meaning. *Preceded* (*B*) might be tempting if you thought **defoliated** meant "followed." *Unruffled* (*D*) is unrelated.

ROOTS FROM LATIN NOUNS AND ADJECTIVES – 3

Root	Meaning	Example	Explanation
noc, nox	night	**noc**turnal	pertaining to *night*
norm	rule, standard	ab**norm**al	away from the *standard*
nov	new	**nov**elty	*new*ness
numer	number	e**numer**ate	list by *number*
ocul	eye	bin**ocul**ars	fieldglasses for two *eyes*
oper	work	co**oper**ate	*work* together
optim	best	**optim**al	*best*
pac	peace	**pac**ify	make *peaceful*
par	equal	**par**ity	*equal*ity
pater, patr	father	**pater**nal	pertaining to *father*
ped	foot	**ped**estal	*foot* of a column
plus, plur	more	**plur**ality	*more* than any other candidate
popul	people	**popul**ation	*people* of a country
prim, prin	first	**prim**ary	*first*
reg, rig	rule, straight, right	**reg**ent	*rule*r for another
salut	health	**salut**ary	*health*y
sanct	holy	**sanct**uary	*holy* place
sign	sign	**sign**al	*sign* giving warning
sol	alone	**sol**itary	*alone*
somn	sleep	in**somn**ia	*sleep*lessness
son	sound	re**son**ance	reinforcement of a *sound*
temp	time	**temp**orary	for the *time* being
tenu	thin	at**tenu**ate	*thin* out
term, termin	end, limit	**term**inal	*end* of a bus or train line
terr	earth	**terr**estrial	pertaining to *earth*
test	witness	**test**ify	bear *witness*
umbr	shade	**umbr**ella	screen to provide *shade*
urb	city	**urb**an	pertaining to *city*
vac	empty	**vac**uum	*empty* space
ver	true	**ver**acious	*truth*ful
verb	word	**verb**al	in *word*s
via	way	**via**	by *way* of
voc, vok	call	con**vok**e	*call* together
vulg	common	**vulg**arity	*common*ness

Trial Test

Fill in the blank in each sentence with a Latin prefix from the list above. Use the word in italics as a clue. The number in parentheses tells the number of letters needed.

1. Patrick was filled with *new* ideas, but not all his in_____ations proved practical. (3)

2. The equi_____es are the two periods each year when days and *nights* are equally long. (3)

3. Cervantes was a con_____orary of Shakespeare, living at the same *time* though in a different country. (4)

4. Perry's feet are e_____ous, requiring shoes far beyond the *standard* sizes. (4)

5. The government de_____ated the cities, forcing the *people* to go out into the countryside and face death by starvation. (5)

6. The new _____ime *ruled* with heartless disregard of human rights. (3)

7. The _____a donna is the *first* lady of the opera. (4)

8. The driver's license was *call*ed back and re_____ed for a year. (3)

9. To dis_____age someone is to make him lower in rank, not *equal*. (3)

10. A grain sur_____ means we have *more* than we need for domestic consumption. (4)

11. *Foot*paths over bridges usually delight _____estrians, but many bridges provide only for motor traffic. (3)

12. Vera refused the chance to sing _____o, for she dreaded standing *alone* before a crowded auditorium. (3)

13. On a very clear night the stars seem in_____able, but the *number* of visible stars is tiny compared with the number of stars beyond the range of sight. (5)

14. _____ambulists may walk in their *sleep*, but they usually get back to bed safely. (4)

15. Some modern composers combine *sounds* in harsh and unusual ways, seeking creative dis_____ance rather than harmony. (3)

16. A(An) _____ist considers this the *best* of all possible worlds. (5)

17. A city in the Australian Outback is sub_____anean, below the surface of the *earth* with its scorching heat. (4)

18. During the eclipse of the moon, the moon passed first into the pen_____a, the area of partial *shadow* caused by the earth's position between the sun and moon. (4)

19. _____anity, supposedly a quality of sophisticated *city* dwellers, is no longer a local quality. (3)

20. The Webers _____ated the house, *empty*ing it of all their possessions. (3)

21. The star _____ated her contract with the studio, *end*ing all contacts with one stroke of the pen. (6)

22. Many *holy* places are _____ified by the unselfish deeds of men and women in the past. (5)

23. A mon_____ar is a telescope with a single *eye*piece. (4)

24. The officer _____ified the witness's account and found he had given a *true* report. (3)

25. There's too much _____iage in your composition. Cut out half those *words*. (4)

Answers to Trial Test

1. nov	8. vok	14. Somn	20. vac
2. nox	9. par	15. son	21. termin
3. temp	10. plus	16. optim	22. sanct
4. norm	11. ped	17. terr	23. ocul
5. popul	12. sol	18. umbr	24. ver
6. reg	13. numer	19. Urb	25. verb
7. prim			

Which Word Parts Are Most Important?

Return for a moment to the 14 key words on page 84 at the beginning of this section. Which Latin prefixes and roots does Dr. Brown consider most important?

LATIN PREFIXES

ad, a	to	**a**spect
con, com	together	un**com**plicated
de	from	**de**tain
dis	apart from	in**dis**posed
ex	out of	non**ex**tended
in	not	**in**disposed
in	into	**in**sist
inter	between	**inter**mittent
non	not	**non**extended
ob, of	against, towards	**of**fer
pre	before	**pre**cept
pro	forward	re**pro**duction
sub, suf	under	over**suf**ficient*
re	back, again	**re**production
trans	across	mis**trans**cribe

Oversufficient is a good example of how words change through the years. "How," you may ask, "is it possible for a prefix meaning 'over' and a prefix meaning 'under' (**sub**) to appear in the same word?" *Sufficient* originally derived from **sub** and **fac**. How has it reached its present meaning? If you have *sufficient* funds, you have built a foundation *under* your position ("do under"). Thus *sufficient* has come to mean "as much as is needed." *Oversufficient* provides *more* than is necessary. The Anglo-Saxon prefix **over** has retained its common meaning, but the Latin prefix **sub** has lost its literal meaning and become part of a total concept. A word like *oversufficient* that uses elements from two different sources is sometimes called a *hybrid word*.

LATIN ROOTS

cept	take	pre**cept**
duct	lead	repro**duct**ion
fer	carry	of**fer**
fic	do, make	oversuf**fic**ient
mit	send	inter**mit**tent
plic	fold	uncom**plic**ated
pos	place, put	indis**pos**ed
scrib	write	mistran**scrib**e
sist	stand	in**sist**
spec	see	a**spec**t
tain	hold	de**tain**
tend	stretch	nonex**tend**ed

The remaining elements will be treated in the next two chapters, but for completeness they are included here also.

ANGLO-SAXON PREFIXES

mis	bad, badly	**mis**transcribe
over	above, too much	**over**sufficient
un	not	**un**complicated

GREEK PREFIXES

epi	on, after	**epi**logue
mono	one	**mono**graph

GREEK ROOTS

graph	write	mono**graph**
log	word	epi**log**ue

Although some of the words have moved away from their original meanings, the core of meaning in each word is still apparent. *Aspect* obviously has something to do with *seeing*. *Detain* has something to do with *holding*. *Epilogue* has something to do with *words*. And so on through the remaining words. The elements of these words lead to thousands of others.

Now analyze a typical SAT-type antonym question to see how roots and prefixes can help.

Problem

DISPARITY:

   (A) inefficiency   (D) toleration
   (B) pleasure   (E) equality
   (C) vividness

Strategy

If you remember your roots and prefixes, the question is easy. **Dis** means "apart from," "not." **Par** means "equal." **Disparity** means "condition of not being equal." The answer, (*E*), pops up immediately.

What if you don't recall the root and prefix exactly? You can still work out the answer by thinking of other words containing the elements in this word. You know that *disagree* means "not agree." **Dis**, you thus recall, means "not." **Par** appears in the simple word *par* itself and means "normal," "equal," as in the expression *on a par with*.

The best strategy is to know the root and prefix. The second best strategy is to recall the root and prefix by thinking of other words containing the same elements.

How can a knowledge of prefixes and roots help with SAT completion questions? Study an actual sentence completion test question to find out.

Problem

What makes the modern period in art --- is that this time, in most categories, the older --- has not been replaced by something equally substantial, accessible and satisfying.

   (A) exacting . .   (D) unprecedented . .
       efficiency   reality
   (B) ideal . .   (E) worthless . .
       illusiveness   depravity
   (C) unique . .
       ignorance

Strategy

This is a difficult question, but if you have been building power for the SAT, you have several ways to attack it.

1. Some students prefer to try out all the alternatives as a first step to see which "sound right" or "possible." This tactic sometimes allows you to reject one or more alternatives immediately. Usually you'll need to go on to the next step.

2. In sentence-completion activities always look for context clues. You know that smaller key words like *not*, *thus*, *like*, and *though* are always important, but there are longer key words, too. In this question the word "replaced" obviously carries a lot of weight. If the "older . . . has not been replaced by something satisfying," then you may assume that there is something unusual on the art scene this time.

3. Are there any words that suggest that this situation is unusual? *Exacting* (*A*), *ideal* (*B*) and *worthless* (*D*) don't seem to fit. *Unique* is a possibility. What of *unprecedented*?

4. Our familiarity with prefixes and roots comes in handy here. We recognize **un** ("not"), **pre** ("before"), and **ced** ("go"). If something is *unprecedented*, nothing like it has gone before. *Unprecedented* is clearly a possibility.

5. Check the second half of the (*C*) and (*D*) pairs. The word paired with *unique* is *ignorance*. Ignorance would not be *substantial* or *satisfying*. *Ignorance* is clearly incorrect, so we can discard (*C*) as an answer. The word paired with *unprecedented* is *reality*. This fits. The correct answer is (*D*). This is how the completed sentence looks.

> What makes the modern period in art **unprecedented** is that this time, in most categories, the older **reality** has not been replaced by something equally substantial, accessible and satisfying.

This detailed analysis reviews some of the skills you have been acquiring. As you become more and more familiar with this type of question, however, you will speed up your work. You will find your own shortcuts and draw upon your own special strengths.

Time Out For Review

A. Use context and etymology to figure out the answers. Write the letter for the word or word pair that best completes the meaning.

1. Seeking to magnify their own glories at the expense of earlier rulers, later pharaohs --- from tombs and monuments the names of their illustrious ---.
   - (A) humiliated . . contemporaries
   - (B) deciphered . . progeny
   - (C) obliterated . . predecessors
   - (D) plagiarized . . scribes
   - (E) reconnoitered . . generals

   1 ___

2. According to many therapists, the true function of a (an) --- is to --- energies and revive the spirit.
   - (A) chore . . humble
   - (B) anecdote . . dramatize
   - (C) avocation . . regenerate
   - (D) diatribe . . shrivel
   - (E) confrontation . . dissipate

   2 ___

3. Despite his reputation for hard-heartedness, the sergeant showed --- to the injured recruit, binding his injury and speaking encouraging words to the young soldier.
   - (A) merit   (D) indignation
   - (B) compassion   (E) firmness
   - (C) casualness

   3 ___

4. Some economists feel that a(an) --- distribution of all wealth would find great --- in actual holdings less than a year later.
   - (A) average . . equalization
   - (B) scheduled . . disappointment
   - (C) circumspect . . felicity
   - (D) equitable . . discrepancies
   - (E) unanticipated . . diminution

   4 ___

5. The departing guest thanked her host ---; still the cautious host --- avoided extending a second invitation.
   - (A) reservedly . . somehow
   - (B) reflectively . . angrily
   - (C) engagingly . . unconsciously
   - (D) tactlessly . . righteously
   - (E) effusively . . pointedly

   5 ___

6. Although Timothy much preferred to --- during the summer months, his father insisted --- that Timothy get a job.
   - (A) work . . tentatively
   - (B) vegetate . . vehemently
   - (C) travel . . vaguely
   - (D) compete . . unintentionally
   - (E) read . . carelessly

   6 ___

7. The purpose of the roller coaster is to provide --- thrills, to stimulate a sense of extreme ---, yet frightening people safely.
   - (A) vicarious . . vertigo
   - (B) inhuman . . illness
   - (C) casual . . indifference
   - (D) humdrum . . enthusiasm
   - (E) unimaginative . . terror

   7 ___

8. The fox's raid on the chicken coop was like a --- --- into an unprotected harbor.
   - (A) lion's . . rush
   - (B) sailor's . . navigation
   - (C) pirate's . . foray
   - (D) rower's . . sally
   - (E) pilot's . . approach

   8 ___

9. June's bursts of energy are ---; she is actually an expert in ---.
   - (A) sporadic . . placidity
   - (B) overpowering . . relaxation
   - (C) unexpected . . karate
   - (D) infrequent . . motivation
   - (E) illuminating . . electronics

   9 ___

10. That error is fortunately not ---; it can be corrected if we retrace our steps and follow correct procedures.
   - (A) relevant
   - (B) irremediable
   - (C) hopeful
   - (D) advertised
   - (E) compromising

   10 ___

B. Build your own vocabulary. Put together words of your own by taking prefixes from column A and combining them with roots from the two B columns. Write your words on the lines below.

A (PREFIXES)	B (ROOTS)	
a, ab	act	pel
ad, ac, af, ag, al, am, at	cede	pone
ante	claim	port
com, cof, col, com, con	credit	pose

contra	cur	prehend
de	date	rupt
dis, di	dict	scribe
ex, e	duct	sect
extra	fect	sense
in	fer	solve
inter	flux	spect
non	form	strict
ob, o, oc	gress	sult
per	ject	tain
post	junct	tract
pre	late	vene
pro	mand	verge
sub, suc, suf, sup, sus	merge	vert
super	mit	vise
trans	mute	volve

_____   _____   _____
_____   _____   _____
_____   _____   _____
_____   _____   _____
_____   _____   _____
_____   _____   _____
_____   _____   _____

SUMMARY PART 3

Clues from Etymology: Latin Roots—Nouns and Adjectives

1. English contains more words from Latin than from any other language.
2. Words are often built block by block. If you know what each block (word part) originally meant, you can probably figure out today's meaning—the one used in SAT questions.
3. The best strategy is to know the root and prefix. The second best strategy is to think of other words having the same elements.

ENGLISH FOR THE COLLEGE BOARDS

PART 4

Greek Prefixes and Roots

Though words derived from Greek prefixes and roots often look difficult, their meanings are sometimes easier to guess than words from other sources. First, the commonly used Greek roots are fewer in number than those from Latin. Secondly, the building blocks are often easier to see. A word like Dr. Brown's *monograph* (page 84), for example, is delightfully simple, once you know the elements **mono** and **graph**. Both elements have so many word-cousins, from *monotone* to *monotheism*, from *telegraph* to *biography*. The prefix **mono** clearly means "one" in those *mono* words. The root **graph** clearly means "write" in those *graph* words. A monograph is an article written about one special subject.

Words from Greek and Latin differ from each other in another way, too. Words from Latin usually have *one* root and one or more prefixes, but Greek often combines *two* roots. *Biography*, for example, combines two roots: **bio** and **graph**. We'll have more to say about this kind of combination later.

Before you begin studying lists of Greek prefixes and roots, try an experiment. You probably know more about word origins than you think you do. Take the following two-part test and prove to yourself that you can often derive the meanings of prefixes and roots on your own.

Trial Test

A. In each of the following ten groups, one root is common to all four words. You already know at least three of the four words in every group. Think of the meanings of the words you know, and try to determine the meaning of the root. You will find the answer among the words following the root. Write the letter for the meaning of the word.

EXAMPLE

telegraph, autograph, biography, graphic
GRAPH:

(A) distance   (C) friendship
(B) writing   (D) pictures

B ____

Since the words all have to do with writing, the correct answer is (*B*).

The meaning of the root **graph** is *writing*.

1. phonograph, telephone, radiophone, euphony
PHON:

(A) light   (C) sound
(B) heat   (D) water

1 ____

2. automatic, autograph, automobile, autocrat
AUTO:

(A) ruler   (C) only
(B) self   (D) written

2 ____

3. monotone, monopoly, monarchy, monogram
MONO:

(A) busy   (C) two
(B) loud   (D) one

3 ____

4. democrat, aristocrat, autocrat, bureaucrat
   CRAT:

   (A) person   (C) wealth

   (B) rule   (D) nature

   4 ___

5. synonym, antonym, homonym, patronymic
   ONYM:

   (A) name   (C) father

   (B) opposite   (D) same

   5 ___

6. bicycle, cyclone, cycle, encyclopedia
   CYCL:

   (A) storm   (C) play

   (B) circle   (D) two

   6 ___

7. centimeter, meter, metric, perimeter
   METER:

   (A) coin   (C) 100

   (B) instrument   (D) measure

   7 ___

8. biology, biography, autobiography, amphibian
   BIO:

   (A) book   (C) science

   (B) life   (D) water

   8 ___

9. antislavery, antitoxin, antidote, antipathy
   ANTI:

   (A) related   (C) against

   (B) before   (D) afterward

   9 ___

10. microscope, microphotograph, microbe, microcosm
    MICRO:

    (A) small   (C) germ

    (B) picture   (D) telescope

    10 ___

Answers to Trial Test – A

1. C	4. B	7. D	9. C
2. B	5. A	8. B	10. A
3. D	6. B		

Did you derive root meanings by yourself? Try a second part of the test to show how you can teach yourself Greek prefixes and roots.

B. Each word in the following pairs has one root (boldfaced) in common with the other. From the group of words below select the word that you feel best expresses the root meaning. Look up each unfamiliar word in the dictionary.

EXAMPLE

tele**scope**, micro**scope**.

Scope, which is common to both, probably means "to look" or "to see," since a telescope is used to look at the stars, and a microscope is used to look at very small things.

book	nature
breath	power
city	sight
concealed	skin
false	star

1. **Bibl**e, **bibl**iography   _____

2. **cryp**tic, **cryp**togram   _____

3. **dyna**mite, **dyna**mic   _____

4. epi**derm**is, taxi**derm**ist   _____

5. **astro**nomy, **astro**logy   _____

6. **opt**ometrist, **opt**ician   _____

7. **pol**ice, **pol**itics   _____

8. **pneu**matic, **pneu**monia   _____

9. **pseudo**nym, **pseudo**pod   _____

10. **physi**cs, **physi**ology   _____

Answers to Trial Test – B

1. book	4. skin	7. city	9. false
2. concealed	5. star	8. breath	10. nature
3. power	6. sight		

If you have taken the previous two-part test, you have discovered how easily Greek prefixes and roots combine. **Geo** meaning "earth" combines readily with **logy** to mean "the study of the earth" (*geology*), with **metry** to mean "the measure of the earth" (*geometry*), and with **thermal** to mean "heat from the earth" (*geothermal*). **Therm** combines with **meter** to mean "measure of heat" (*thermometer*), with **iso** to mean "lines of equal heat" (*isotherms*) on a map, and with **dynam** (*thermodynamics*) to mean "the study dealing with the transfer of heat into *power*." These easily formed words are a blessing to scientists, who must constantly invent new terms to fit the new discoveries they are making. You will find the following list of prefixes from the Greek helpful in meeting new words.

GREEK PREFIXES

Prefix	Meaning	Example	Explanation
a, an	no, not	**a**typical	*not* typical
		anarchy	condition of *no* government
amphi	around, both	**amphi**bian	on *both* land and sea
ana	up, again, back	**ana**lysis	examination of details (a loosening *up*)
anti	against	**anti**septic	*against* infection
apo	away from, off	**apo**stle	messenger sent *from* one place to another
auto	self	**auto**matic	running by it*self*
cata	down	**cata**clysm	a washing *down*, a flood
dys	bad, badly	**dys**pepsia	*bad* digestion
dia	across, through	**dia**meter	a measure *across* a circle

ec, ex	out of	**ex**odus	a going *out*
en	in, into	**en**gender	bring *into* being, cause
endo	inside	**endo**morph	a crystal *inside* another
epi	upon	**epi**taph	inscription placed *upon* a tomb
eu	well, good, pleasant	**eu**logy	a speaking *well*, praise
hyper	above, beyond	**hyper**bole	speech *beyond* truth, exaggeration
hypo	under, below	**hypo**thermia	body heat *below* normal
iso	equal	**iso**therm	line to show *equal* heat
mega, megal	great	**mega**lomania	personality disorder of assumed *great*ness
meta	after, beyond, over	**meta**morphosis	change*over* into another form
micro	small	**micro**meter	tool for making *small* measurements
mis	hatred of	**mis**anthropic	*hating* mankind
neo	new	**neo**logism	*new* word
pan, panto	all	**pan**chromatic	sensitive to light of *all* colors
para	beside	**para**phrase	a speaking *beside*, a re-wording
peri	around	**peri**meter	measure *around*
poly	many	**poly**syllabic	having *many* syllables
pro	before	**pro**phet	one who predicts the future (speaks *before*hand)
pseudo	false	**pseudo**science	*false* science
sym, syn	together	**sym**phony	a sounding *together*
		synagogue	a place for bringing people *together*

We have already called your attention to the fact that words sometimes travel far from their origins. Words introduced into the language long ago often have figurative meanings, but usually the basic meaning is still there. Ordinarily the more recently a word has come into the language, the closer the word is to its basic elements. The recent word *astrophysics*, for example, deals with the nature **(physi)** of the stars **(astro).**

Even though they seem simple, Greek prefixes are a little more difficult than Greek roots, because the prefixes have more meanings than the roots. A prefix like **meta,** for example, has many meanings (''along with,'' ''after,'' ''between,'' ''among,'' ''beyond,'' ''over'').

The word *metaphysics* has an interesting history. *Physics*, with its root **physi,** means ''nature,'' ''natural.'' When Aristotle was gathering his thoughts about nature and life, he came to those dealing with things *beyond* science, things that cannot be explained by experiment. He called these ideas *metaphysics* because they came *after* or beyond the *Physics.*

Try out your skill on the following Trial Test.

Trial Test

Fill in the blank in each sentence by writing a Greek prefix from the list above. The word in italics is a clue to the needed prefix. The number in parentheses tells the number of letters needed.

EXAMPLE

When two organisms live *together* with mutual benefit, this unique arrangement is called _____biosis. (3)

The italicized word *together* tells you the prefix **sym** should be inserted.

1. Although at times Pierce pretended to be a *hater* of women, he was not really a(an) _____ogynist. (3)

2. By definition, the two legs of a(an) _____sceles triangle are *equal*. (3)

3. Bert used a(an) _____phone and *great*ly increased the range of his voice. (4)

4. A(An) _____lyst may speed up or slow *down* the rate of a chemical reaction. (4)

5. A(An) _____cracy is a government in which one person, by him*self*, holds absolute power. (4)

6. The critics of astrology call it a(an) _____science, *false*ly assuming the mantle of a true science. (6).

7. Bennett was a true _____glot, writing and speaking *many* languages fluently. (4)

8. The _____eroid barometer, unlike the mercury barometer, uses *no* liquid. (2)

9. A(An) _____biotic works *against* the growth of harmful bacteria. (4)

10. _____trophy is the growth of an organ far *beyond* its normal size. (5)

11. Most colleges and universities now use many _____professionals to work *beside* fully licensed teachers and help with many education projects. (4)

12. A(An) _____scope enables a viewer to look *around* a corner. (4)

13. Despite its *small* size, _____film can store pages of material in a single frame. (5)

14. The _____phytes, all *new* members of the church, came to the altar in a group. (3)

15. Old-time medicine men used to offer their concoctions as _____aceas, guaranteed to cure *all* ailments from headache to pneumonia. (3)

16. In _____grams words are mixed *up* and then put *back* into different forms. (3)

17. In the Greek _____theater the seats curled *around* the stage. (5)

18. Pruitt _____chronized his watch with Helen's, making sure his time agreed *with* hers. (3)

19. _____thermia is a dangerous condition in which the body temperature falls far *below* normal. (4)

20. It is human nature to use _____phemisms, expressions that make unpleasant subjects sound neutral or *pleasant*. (2)

Answers to Trial Test

1. mis	6. pseudo	11. para	16. ana
2. iso	7. poly	12. peri	17. amphi
3. mega	8. an	13. micro	18. syn
4. cata	9. anti	14. neo	19. Hypo
5. auto	10. Hyper	15. pan	20. eu

Now try out your knowledge of Greek prefixes in a SAT-type antonym question.

Problem

PSEUDONYM:

(A) Mark Twain   (D) Samuel Clemens
(B) nom de plume   (E) alias
(C) Saki

Strategy

You know that **pseudo** means "false;" you can probably guess that **nym** means "name." So a **pseudonym** is a false name, or a name assumed for some purpose.

Mark Twain (A) is a pseudonym. *Nom de plume* (B) is a French phrase meaning "pen name," a kind of pseudonym. *Saki* (C) is a pseudonym or pen name for the author, H. H. Munro. *Alias* (E) is a false name. The only remaining choice, *Samuel Clemens* (D) is the real name of Mark Twain, and thus is an antonym of **pseudonym** in this problem.

GREEK NUMBER PREFIXES

Prefix	Meaning	Example	Explanation
hemi	half	**hemi**sphere	*half* a sphere
mono	one	**mono**tone	*one* tone
proto	first	**proto**type	*first* kind
di	two	**di**lemma	*two* choices (both bad!)
tri	three	**tri**cycle	*three*-wheeler
tetra	four	**tetra**meter	having *four* poetic feet
penta	five	**penta**gon	*five*-sided figure
hexa	six	**hexa**gonal	having *six* sides
hepta	seven	**hepta**meter	having *seven* poetic feet
octa	eight	**octa**ve	*eighth* tone above a given tone
deca	ten	**deca**logue	the *Ten* Commandments
hect	hundred	**hect**ograph	machine for making a *hundred* (*many*) copies
kilo	thousand	**kilo**gram	a *thousand* grams

Greek number prefixes occur in a great many English words. The field of geometry, for example, relies heavily upon Greek prefixes (as in *triangle* or *pentagon*), but these little elements appear in other English words, as well, such as *protozoan* and *monologue*. If you know the number prefix, you can usually figure out the right SAT answer.

Note how efficiently English borrows from both Latin and Greek. The Latin prefix for *thousand*, **mille,** appears in *millimeter* (a *thousandth* of a meter). The Greek prefix for *thousand*, **kilo**, appears in *kilometer* (a *thousand* meters). Neither prefix is wasted. Scientists keep drawing upon Greek for new words to express new ideas. A **milli**second, for example, is a *thousandth* of a second. But suppose you want a word to express a billionth of a second? The Greek word for dwarf is **nano.** A billionth of a second is a **nano**second ("a very small second"!).

Trial Test

Fill in the blank in each sentence with a Greek number prefix from the list. The word in italics is a clue to the needed prefix. The number in parentheses tells the number of letters needed.

EXAMPLE

A small child needs the *three* wheels on a tricycle to provide balance. (3)

The italicized word three tells you that *tri* is the correct Greek number prefix.

1. A(An) _____meter, which is *1000* meters, is approximately five-eighths of a mile. (4)

2. In the _____thlon each contestant takes part in *five* events. (5)

3. Jim spoke in _____syllables, allowing himself only *one* syllable at a time. (4)

4. _____gonometry, literally the measure of *three* angles, deals with the relationships of triangles. (3)

5. A(An) _____hedron is a solid figure with *four* triangular faces. (5)

6. _____zoans, one-celled animals, may resemble the *first* form of life on earth. (5)

7. In linguistics, a(an) _____phthong, combines *two* vowel sounds into one continuous sound. (2)

8. To win the _____thlon, a contestant need not win all *ten* events; he must, however, have the highest average over all. (4)

9. The great epics of Greece and Rome were written in dactylic _____meter, with *six* beats to every line. (4)

10. The unusual old building has a(an) _____gonal shape, with *eight* equal sides. (4)

Answers to Trial Test

1. kilo	4. Tri	7. di	9. hex
2. penta	5. tetra	8. deca	10. octa
3. mono	6. Proto		

Try the following SAT-type antonym question.

Problem

MONOTONOUS:
- (A) boring
- (B) repetitive
- (C) polygamous
- (D) multilingual
- (E) exciting

If you know that **mono** means "one," **ton** means "tone," and **ous** is an adjective suffix, you can see that **monotonous** describes something that has one and only one tone or quality. For example, it might be someone's voice or a kind of job or work. The opposite would be something with many tones or qualities—that is, a varied, interesting voice or job or performance.

The only choice that comes close is *exciting* (*E*). *Boring* (*A*) and *repetitive* (*B*) are synonyms, not antonyms. Someone who is *polygamous* (*C*) has more than one husband or wife. Someone who is *multilingual* (*D*) speaks more than one language.

GREEK ROOTS – 1

Now we come to one of the most helpful word groups in the study of etymology—Greek roots. Many of these are different from Latin roots because they may appear anywhere in a word—at the beginning, middle, or end. **Lith,** meaning "stone," may appear at the beginning in *lithography* and at the end in *monolith*. In some ways, Greek roots are more fun to combine because they combine so freely and in so many ways. **Meter,** meaning "measure," appears first in *metronome* and last in *diameter*. It also appears in the middle in *symmetrical*.

All the Greek roots are important and worth studying, but if you wish to concentrate upon some basic ones, study the starred (*) items first. These will be especially helpful as you prepare for the SAT. These Greek roots are also divided into two lists for your convenience.

Root	Meaning	Example	Explanation
alg	pain	neur**alg**ia	nerve *pain*
anthrop, andro	man	**anthrop**ology	study of *man*kind
		android	robot like a *man*
arch	chief, rule	**arch**bishop	*chief* bishop
		mon**arch**y	*rule* of one person
bar	weight, pressure	**bar**ometer	measure of *pressure*
bibli	book	**bibli**ophile	one who loves *books*
chiro	hand	**chiro**podist	*hand* and foot specialist
chrom	color	**chrom**atic	highly *color*ed
*chron	time	ana**chron**istic	out of proper *time*
cosm	universe	micro**cosm**	*universe* in little
crat, crac	rule	demo**crac**y	*rule* by the people
crypt	hidden	**crypt**ic	having *hidden* meaning
*cycl	circle	**cycl**one	storm that whirls in a *circle*
*dem	people	**dem**agogue	a rabble-rousing leader of *people*
derm	skin	hypo**derm**ic	beneath the *skin*
dos, dot	give	anti**dot**e	something *given* to counteract a poison

dyn, dynam	energy, power	**dynam**ite	*power*ful explosive
erg, urg	work	metall**urg**y	metal *work*ing
gam	marriage	poly**gam**y	many *marriages*
*ge, geo	earth	**geo**physics	dealing with the physics of the *earth*
gen	birth, cause, kind, race	homo**gen**ize	make uniform, of the same *kind*
*gram, graph	writing	autobio**graph**y	*writing* about one's own life
		mono**graph**	*writing* about a particular subject
heli	sun	**heli**otrope	flower that turns toward the *sun*
hem	blood	**hem**orrhage	unchecked flow of *blood*
*hetero	different, other	**hetero**geneous	of a *different* kind
*homo	same	**homo**geneous	of the *same* kind
hydr	water	de**hydr**ation	loss of *water*
iatr	healing	psych**iatr**ist	one who *heals* the mind
lith	stone	mono**lith**	single large block of *stone*
*log	word, study	geo**log**y	study of the *earth*

Trial Test

Fill the blank in each sentence with a Greek root from the list. The word in italics is a clue to the needed root. The number in parentheses tells the number of letters needed.

EXAMPLE

A bi*gam*ist has two *marriages* in force at the same time. (3) The italicized word *marriage*, tells you the Greek root **gam** should be used. One who has two marriages in force at the same time is a *bigamist*.

1. _____olysis is a chemical reaction in which a compound reacts with the ions of *water*. (4)

2. Copernicus upset the _____centric theory of the earth, pointing out that the *earth* is not the center of the universe. (3)

3. _____atitis is an inflammation of the *skin*. (4)

4. Ronny has _____ophobia; he has a morbid fear of *work*! (3)

5. An olig_____y is the *rule* of a few people. (4)

6. On a weather map iso_____s are lines of equal *pressure*. (3)

7. Eva is a(an) _____o of *energy*. (5)

8. The presence of _____um on the *sun* was first discovered during a solar eclipse in 1868, and the name reflects its origin. (4)

9. A(An) _____orama is a series of connected pictures in a *circular* room, often showing a landscape. (4)

10. Have you listed in your _____ography all *books* referred to? (5)

11. A basic treatment in _____practic is manipulation of the spine by the trained *hands* of the doctor. (5)

12. The *pain* of being separated from his friends and family gave the college student an acute case of nost_____ia. (3)

13. _____oid apes are so called because of their *man*like appearance and mannerisms. (7)

14. Ted usually adopts _____dox positions, *different* from those of his peers. (6)

15. At first _____ography used flat *stones* to reproduce a design on paper; later metal plates were introduced. (4)

16. People send *written* messages over distances via the tele_____. (5)

17. A(An) _____nym has the *same* pronunciation as another word but different meaning. (4)

18. _____atic aberration in a lens causes a margin of *colors* to appear around the edges of the image. (5)

19. An epi_____ic is a disease afflicting vast numbers of *people*. (3)

20. Ger_____ics deals with the *healing* of old people's ailments. (4)

21. A(An) _____ic ailment keeps coming back *time* and time again. (5)

22. A pluto_____ seeks the power to *rule* because of his wealth. (4)

23. In a(an) _____ogram the meaning is *hidden*, concealed in code or cipher. (5)

24. A bi_____ist has two *marriages* still in force at the same time. (3)

25. _____oglobin is the red coloring in the *blood*. (3)

Answers to Trial Test

1. Hydr	8. heli	14. hetero	20. iatr
2. geo	9. cycl	15. lith	21. chron
3. Derm	10. bibli	16. graph	22. crat
4. erg	11. chiro	17. homo	23. crypt
5. arch	12. alg	18. Chrom	24. gam
6. bar	13. Anthrop	19. dem	25. Hem
7. dynam			

Use your knowledge of Greek roots on the following antonym question like those on the SAT.

Problem

DYNAMIC:
- (A) explosive
- (B) lazy
- (C) active
- (D) unpleasant
- (E) familial

Strategy

Knowing the Greek root **dynam**, meaning "energy" or "power," allows you to figure out the meaning of **dynamic**: "energetic" or "powerful." You can see that a dynamic person is not *lazy*, and there is your antonym.

Explosive (A) and *active* (C) are synonyms, not antonyms. *Familial* (E) may trap someone who has *dynasty*, not **dynamic**, in mind. *Unpleasant* (D) is unrelated.

Prefix	Meaning	Example	Explanation
*log	word, study	geo**log**y	*study* of the earth
*meter, metr	measure	baro**meter**	*measure* of air pressure
morph	form, shape	a**morph**ous	*form*less
neur	nerve	**neur**itis	inflammation of *nerves*
nom, nomy	law, order, custom	astro**nom**er	one who studies the *order* of the stars
onym, onoma	name	an**onym**ous	*name*less
ortho	straight	**ortho**dontia	teeth *straight*ening
path	suffering, feeling	a**path**y	lack of *feeling*
phan, phen	show, appear	**phen**omenon	something *apparent* to the senses
*phil	love	**phil**anthropist	*lover* of mankind
phor, pher	carry, bear	sema**phor**	apparatus for signaling, for *bear*ing messages
*phos, phot	light	**phot**ography	producing images by use of *light*
pod	foot	**pod**iatrist	*foot* doctor
poli	city	metro**poli**s	main *city*
psych	mind	**psych**ology	study of the *mind*
pyr	fire	**pyr**otechnics	*fire*works
scop	see	tele**scop**e	device for *see*ing at a distance
soph	wise	**soph**isticated	worldly-*wise*
tax, tac	arrangement	**tac**tics	*arrang*ing forces in battle
techn	art, skill	**techn**ique	method of using *skills*
*tele	from afar	**tele**metry	measuring *from afar*
the, theo	god	**the**ist	believer in *God*
therm	heat	**therm**ostat	device for regulating *heat*
thes, thet	place, put	anti**thes**is	a *placing* against, contrast of thought
tom	cut	a**tom**	substance that cannot be *cut* or split (now proved wrong)
top	place	**top**ography	description of a *place*
trop	turn	**trop**ism	tendency to *turn* in response to a stimulus
typ	model, impression	**typ**ical	like a *model*
zo	animal	**zo**ology	study of *animals*

More About Greek Roots

A root like **therm** is easy to find in English words. It always means "heat." Some roots, however, travel a little farther afield. Like Latin roots, they sometimes have figurative meanings. The extremely useful root **graph**, for example, appears in a great many words. You notice the meaning of *writing* instantly in a word like *graphology*, the study of handwriting. But notice the figurative meanings in *phonograph* and *photograph*. *Photography*, by derivation, is "light written down." *Phonograph* is "sound written down." Here the concept of *writing* is much broader than usual. There's a poetic image in "written sound."

Fortunately, the words with figurative meanings have been in the language a long time. You certainly know *phonograph* and *photograph* anyway. But if you meet a new word like *thermograph*, you can reasonably guess it's a device for recording heat, or temperature. Even though the meanings are sometimes figurative, the core of meaning is usually clear.

Trial Test

Fill in the blank in each sentence with a root from the Greek roots list above. The word in italics is a clue to the needed root. The number in parentheses tells the number of letters needed.

1. In a syn_____is is ideas are *put* together to form a whole. (4)

2. Maurya is a pan_____ist and believes that *God* is manifest in everything, everywhere. (3)

3. The _____diac was so named because it was considered the zone of the *animals*: the ram, the lion, the bull, and others. (2)

4. In a tonsillec_____y the surgeon removes the tonsils by deft *cut*ting. (3)

5. The _____on is the structural and functional unit of the *nervous* system. (4)

6. Meta_____ic rock has been changed in *form* by heat, pressure, or chemical action. (5)

7. An acr_____ is a *name* formed by using the first letters of a series of words; for example, NATO for *North Atlantic Treaty Organization*. (4)

8. _____pedics is a branch of surgery whose goal is the *straight*ening of deformed parts of the body, especially in children. (5)

9. According to legend, Dido prepared a(an) _____e for herself, planning to cast herself upon the *fire* as the ships of Aeneas disappeared in the distance. (3)

10. _____ology is a *love* of learning. (4)

11. _____istry is a misleading but clever argument that gives the impression of being *wise*. (4)

12. A kaleido_____e is a specially designed tube for *see*ing beautiful forms and shapes. (4)

13. _____onomy is the science of the *arrangement* of animals and plants in orders, families, genera, and other groupings. (3)

14. A gastro_____ is a mollusk that has one large *foot* associated with its stomach. (3)

15. _____pathy, communication at a *distance* without using the normal sensory channels, is an attractive, if unproven, possibility. (4)

16. That plant is photo_____ic, *turn*ing to any light source for energy. (4)

17. The arche_____e is the original *model* from which all others of the same kind are made. (3)

18. Through the dia_____ous curtain on the stage, two shadowy figures suddenly *appeared*. (4)

19. Em_____y is the ability to share another's *feelings* by putting oneself in the other's place. (4)

20. An am_____ *measures* the strength of an electric current in amperes. (5)

21. Students who read very *badly* may be suffering from _____lexia. (3)

22. Maureen loved to _____gnosticate events, suggesting their outline *before* they happened. (3)

23. A(An) _____phyte, lives upon another plant but does not deprive the host plant of food. (3)

24. Sharon is a(an) _____lectic designer, picking *out* what she likes from many different periods and still making a harmonious total design. (2)

25. At _____gee the moon is farthest *away* from the earth. (3)

Answers to Trial Test

1. thes	8. Ortho	14. pod	20. meter
2. the	9. pyr	15. Tele	21. dys
3. zo	10. phil	16. trop	22. pro
4. tom	11. Soph	17. typ	23. epi
5. neur	12. scop	18. phan	24. ec
6. morph	13. Tax	19. path	25. apo
7. onym			

On the SAT you will probably encounter words from Greek prefixes and roots, often in antonym questions. Look at an actual SAT antonym question.

Problem

NEOLOGISM:

(A) nameless article
(B) foreign object
(C) exaggerated movement
(D) impoverished condition
(E) obsolete expression

Strategy

If you remember that **neo** means "new" and **log** means "word," you have no worries. If a *neologism* is a "new word," then the opposite is (*E*) *an obsolete expression*. What do you do if you cannot remember exactly what **neo** or **log** means? Do what you did for Latin roots and prefixes. Just think quickly of words containing the same elements. For **neo** there's *neoclassic* ("new classic"), *Neolithic* ("new Stone Age"), and *neophyte* ("a beginner"–"a new plant"). Of course, **neo** is similar to the English word *new*. If you're fairly sure that **neo** means "new," you can look for a word that means its opposite. *Obsolete* immediately comes to mind and guides you to (*E*).

Suppose you remember only that **log** means "word." A glance down the list points to *expression* (*E*). If the antonym depends upon **neo** and *obsolete*, you know at this point that *expression* and word are possible pairings. The other alternatives just don't fit.

Use your knowledge of Greek prefixes and roots in the following review.

Time Out for Review

A. Find and write the letter for the antonym of each capitalized word.

1. ACHROMATIC:
   (A) inharmonious
   (B) colorful
   (C) shopworn
   (D) tactful
   (E) emotional

   1 ___

2. HYPERCRITICAL:
   (A) crazed
   (B) authentic
   (C) hysterical
   (D) scandalous
   (E) lenient

   2 ___

3. MICROSCOPIC:
   (A) technical
   (B) huge
   (C) dismal
   (D) deplorable
   (E) essential

   3 ___

4. ARCHETYPE:
   (A) imitation
   (B) metal plate
   (C) watercolor
   (D) drama
   (E) spectacle

   4 ___

5. ANTAGONISTIC:
   (A) inquisitive
   (B) quiet
   (C) cowardly
   (D) isolated
   (E) amicable

   5 ___

6. HOMOGENEOUS:
   (A) dissimilar
   (B) of different colors
   (C) disagreeable
   (D) uniform
   (E) unilateral

   6 ___

7. ATHEIST:
   (A) judge
   (B) believer
   (C) church
   (D) reporter
   (E) skeptic

   7 ___

8. PHILANTHROPIST:
   (A) benefactor
   (B) miser
   (C) assassin
   (D) trickster
   (E) coward

   8 ___

9. SYMPATHETIC:
   (A) unlikable
   (B) busy
   (C) hardhearted
   (D) irreverent
   (E) morbid

   9 ___

10. MEGALOPOLIS:
    (A) small town
    (B) police state
    (C) condominium
    (D) minor official
    (E) self-important politician

    10 ___

B. Build your own vocabulary. Put together words of your own by taking elements from column A and combining them with elements from column B. You may use any element more than once.

You can easily make ten words.

EXAMPLE

A	B
auto (self)	graph (write) = *autograph*

A	B
auto	algia
chiro	cracy
cosmo	graph(y)
demo	logy
geo	meter
micro	nomic
neur	phone
photo	podist
tele	politan
theo	scope

_____
_____
_____
_____
_____
_____
_____
_____
_____
_____
_____
_____
_____
_____
_____

SUMMARY PART 4

Clues from Etymology: Greek Prefixes and Roots

1. The Greek language is an important source of English words.
2. When scientists create new words for new concepts and substances, they borrow freely from Greek. You are not likely to meet some of these technical creations, like *microencapsulate* and *neuroendocrinology*, but you will meet a great many others like *psychedelic* and *Xerox*.
3. Though words change in use, even words with figurative meanings can be guessed at by figuring out their basic elements. *Hydraulic* is derived from **hydr**, the root for *water*. The word has been expanded to mean other liquids: *hydraulic* brakes use *oil*. But if you know **hydr**, you can guess at the meaning of related words like *hydraulic* and *hydrometer*.
4. Some coinages, like *polyunsaturates* and *megavitamins*, borrow from both Latin and Greek.

PART 5
Anglo-Saxon Prefixes and Roots

You will feel at home with this section. You use Anglo-Saxon prefixes and roots in everyday English words you already know. As we have already seen, William the Conqueror overran England in 1066. He brought his own French language with him, but French did not replace the native English, or Anglo-Saxon. Instead of fighting English, it joined with it.

The French nobility lorded it over the Anglo-Saxon peasantry. Some words from French show this master-servant relationship: *dame*, *peer*, *prince*, *treasurer*, *minister*, *mayor*, *baron* and *noble*. The French upper classes enjoyed the fruits of Anglo-Saxon labor. The Anglo-Saxon *calf* was *veal* (*veau*) to the French nobility. And so we have both words, one for the living animal and one for the meat of the animal. *Bull* and *beef*, *sheep* and *mutton*, *pig* and *pork* all show this relationship.

French enriched the language with new words from the law: *plaintiff*, *jury*, *attorney*, *indictment*, *felon*, *bail*, *decree*, and *prison*. French provided religious words like *sermon*, *sacrament*, *prayer*, *parson*, *friar*, and *chaplain*. French provided words for clothing: *apparel*, *gown*, *embroidery*, *cape*, *cloak*, *frock*. French provided words for medicine: *surgeon*, *remedy*, *ointment*, *jaundice*, *pulse*. These are topics and words that often come up in SAT questions, especially the sentence-completion type.

We use some of these French words every day. Others, like *hauberk*, *barbican*, and *portcullis*, are fairly specialized and rarely used. This borrowing from French is, of course, also a borrowing from Latin secondhand. The double borrowing has enriched our language with doublets (page 158).

Anglo-Saxon Is Alive And Well

Despite the power of the new French language, Anglo-Saxon stubbornly held its own. A word count of conversation today would show that we use Anglo-Saxon words most of the time. Here's a typical brief dialog of greeting.

"How are you, John? I haven't seen you in months. How's everything?"
"Great! Did you hear the news? Joan and I are getting married next week. We're planning to live here, in the city."

This is the language of our everyday life. The Anglo-Saxon words have never given up. In this dialog there are a few words of French origin: *news*, *married*, and *city*. All the rest are Anglo-Saxon.

Occasionally, as time went on, a French word replaced the Anglo-Saxon. The briefer *news*, for example, has replaced the lengthier Anglo-Saxon *tidings*. When both words have survived and are frequently used, they usually take on somewhat different meanings. *Marriage* (from French) usually refers to the *state* of being married. *Wedding* (from Anglo-Saxon) usually refers to the *ceremony*. In general, however, the nuts-and-bolts words of English—the pronouns, the being verbs, the basic words for things around us—are Anglo-Saxon.

The first words we learn as children are mostly Anglo-Saxon words; for example, *mother, father, sister, dog, cat, love, like, good, see, home, house,* etc. Consequently, because they are associated with things we knew as children, they tend to arouse emotional responses in us.

At the end of Charles Dickens' *A Tale of Two Cities,* Sidney Carton muses on his way to the guillotine. His last thoughts are dramatic and famous:

"It is a far, far better thing I do, than I have ever done; it is a far, far better rest I go to than I have ever known."

Under the stress of great emotion—of happiness, grief, or anger—we tend to use Anglo-Saxon words which remain the backbone of English.

Scandinavian Words

Before the Normans took over, Viking raiders invaded again and again. They brought many Scandinavian words into the mainstream of English; for example, *sky, skin, skill,* and *whisk.* The *sk* sound is typically Scandinavian and so we have both *shi*rt (Anglo-Saxon) and *skirt* (Scandinavian).

Trial Test

In the following sentences the boldfaced words are all of Scandinavian origin. In each sentence write the letter for the word that is closest in meaning to the boldfaced word.

1. Suddenly there was a **rift** in the clouds.
   (A) crack   (D) bright spot
   (B) trap   (E) drift
   (C) storm   1 ___

2. He found the **snare** where he'd left it.
   (A) tuba   (D) knife
   (B) trap   (E) bite of food
   (C) rope   2 ___

3. Imitation **down** is made from milkweed.
   (A) seed   (D) flour
   (B) feathers   (E) milky beverage
   (C) mats   3 ___

4. He was large in **girth**.
   (A) stature   (D) size of hand
   (B) heart   (E) head
   (C) circumference   4 ___

5. The Spartans were **rugged** people.
   (A) sea-going   (D) hardy
   (B) sickly   (E) unusual
   (C) curious   5 ___

6. The ruthless dictator's followers were recruited from the **dregs** of society.
   (A) worthless   (D) businessmen
       section   (E) farmers
   (B) wealthiest
       people
   (C) pillars   6 ___

7. The day was **muggy**.
   (A) hot and dry   (D) warm and
   (B) cold and dry   moist
   (C) cold and moist (E) warm and dry
                                      7 ___

8. Hasn't he an unusual **gait**?
   (A) way of walking (D) half-door
   (B) door   (E) reading ability
   (C) manner of
       speaking   8 ___

9. Ichabod despised the **swains** who sought the hand of Katrina Van Tassel.

(A) old men
(B) young suitors
(C) wealthy landowners
(D) members of the nobility
(E) rivals

9 ___

10. They **ransacked** the house.

(A) burnt
(B) sold
(C) plundered
(D) bought at a sale
(E) painted

10 ___

Answers to Trial Test

1. A	4. C	7. D	9. B
2. B	5. D	8. A	10. C
3. B	6. A		

The Scandinavian words were thoroughly absorbed into English at the time of the Norman Conquest. For our purposes no further distinctions need be made between Scandinavian and Anglo-Saxon.

ANGLO-SAXON PREFIXES

Prefix	Meaning	Example	Explanation
be	completely	**be**draggled	*completely* soiled
by	near	**by**stander	one who stands *near*
for	not	**for**bid	*not* allow
fore	before, front	**fore**going	going *before*
mis	bad, badly, wrong, wrongly	**mis**take	take *wrongly*
in	in	**in**come	money that comes *in*
off	off, from	**off**set	set *off*
out	beyond	**out**law	*beyond* the law
on	on	**on**looker	one who looks *on*
over	too much, over	**over**pay	pay *too much*
		oversee	watch *over*
un	not	**un**happy	*not* happy
under	below, against	**under**pay	pay *below* reasonable amount
up	up	**up**heaval	a heaving *up*
with	against	**with**stand	stand *against*

Some words from Anglo-Saxon, like words from other sources, have acquired figurative meanings in use. *Understand*, for example, by derivation means "stand under." Now it means "get the meaning of." We can only guess how the current meaning came into being. Fortunately, the word has been used in the current sense for so long a time, it is an easy word. Ordinarily, the more figurative the meaning, the longer the word has been in the language and the more likely you are to know and use it.

Some Anglo-Saxon words almost exactly translate words of French or Latin derivation. *Dejected*, for example, is exactly parallel to the Anglo-Saxon *downcast*. Both *dejected* and *downcast* have evolved figurative meanings. *Downcast* does not require physical action; we don't throw or cast anything down. The word, like *dejected*, has become purely figurative.

Trial Test

Fill in the blank in each sentence by writing an Anglo-Saxon prefix from the list above. The word in italics is a clue to the needed prefix. The number in parentheses tells the number of letters.

EXAMPLE

The director's choice was *wrong*. Denny is *mis*cast as the lead in the school play. (3)

The italicized word *wrong* tells us to insert the prefix **mis**.

1. When Yvonne is _____ mused, she is so *completely* plunged in thought, she doesn't see or hear anything. (2)

2. We've cooked the chicken *too much*; it's _____ done. (4)

3. That _____ landish costume goes *beyond* any reasonable one I've ever seen! (3)

4. Looking back is easy; looking at the years in *front* of us is hard. Hindsight is 20–20, but _____ sight is not so certain! (4)

5. It takes a wise person to _____ bear saying, "I told you so," for it is hard *not* to gloat. (3)

6. Young children are _____ inhibited, *not* yet restrained by adult standards of decorum. (2)

7. _____ beat personalities differ *from* normal people in their unusual reactions to ordinary events. (3)

8. Many Americans are still _____ nourished, with diets *below* minimum standards for good health. (5)

9. A thousand shoppers descended *on* the store, and the ensuing _____ rush was like a riot. (2)

10. When teacher salaries were _____ graded, the average salary went *up* 10%. (2)

Answers to Trial Test

1. be	4. fore	7. Off	9. on
2. over	5. for	8. under	10. up
3. out	6. un		

No Roots?

At this point you would expect a list of Anglo-Saxon roots, like the ones for Greek and Latin. Such a list would contain a paradox: it would be both too long—and too easy! You already know most Anglo-Saxon roots. They are the word elements you used as a child.

Here's proof. There are two kinds of English verbs: weak verbs and strong verbs. Weak verbs add *ed* for the past tense and the past participle. Examples of weak verbs are *talk, talked,* (have, has, had) *talked* and *help, helped,* (have, etc.) *helped.* Strong verbs change in other ways in the past tense and the past participle. Examples of strong verbs are *go, went,* (have, etc.) *gone* and *sing, sang,* (have, etc.) *sung.* Verbs from French and other languages tend to be weak verbs; for example, *nominate* and *sympathize.* The strong verbs are Anglo-Saxon.

Here's a list of strong verbs in English. *You already know them.* You may have trouble with forms of the tenses, but you know the meaning of every word in the list. There is no need to list the Anglo-Saxon roots.

arise	draw	grind	shine	sting
beat	drink	grow	sink	stride
behold	eat	hold	sit	strike
bind	fall	know	slay	swing
bite	fight	lie	slide	take
blow	find	ring	speak	tear
break	fly	rise	spin	throw
choose	freeze	run	spring	weave
cling	get	see	stand	win
come	give	shake	steal	write

Examine an actual SAT antonym question.

Problem

UNDERSTATE:
(A) placate
(B) insulate
(C) embroider
(D) dissemble
(E) rebound

Strategy

The familiar prefix **under** and common root **state** tell us we have a word of Anglo-Saxon origin here. The meaning of the word is fairly clear from the sum of its parts: "to say less than is meant" ("state under" the truth). Does any alternative suggest *saying more* than is strictly accurate? *Embroidering* suggests *decoration.* *Decoration* suggests *something extra.* Though this is a figurative meaning, the central core of meaning is there.

Sometimes the figurative meaning is a little trickier, as in this actual SAT antonym question.

Problem

UPSHOT:
- (A) initial step
- (B) quick descent
- (C) severe punishment
- (D) complete silence
- (E) total destruction

Strategy

The familiar prefix **up** and common root **shot** tell us we have a word of Anglo-Saxon origin here. The **upshot** was once the final shot in an archery match. Thus it came to mean "conclusion." The opposite of *conclusion* is *initial step (A)*. You may have heard the word **upshot** in expressions like this: "The upshot of all the disagreement was the call for a new election." Recalling a familiar expression such as this will often give you clues to selecting the correct antonym on the SAT.

Time Out for Review

Write the letter for the antonym of each capitalized word.

1. BEWITCHMENT:
   - (A) embarrassment
   - (B) disenchantment
   - (C) sorcery
   - (D) conversion
   - (E) betrayal

   1 ___

2. UPLIFT:
   - (A) redesign
   - (B) depart
   - (C) prevail
   - (D) discard
   - (E) debase

   2 ___

3. OVERINDULGE:
   - (A) scan
   - (B) press
   - (C) strike
   - (D) fast
   - (E) clamor

   3 ___

4. WITHDRAWAL:
   - (A) retreat
   - (B) deposit
   - (C) authorization
   - (D) attainment
   - (E) decrease

   4 ___

5. UNDERTAKE:
   - (A) give up
   - (B) pursue
   - (C) disgrace
   - (D) carry on
   - (E) disclose

   5 ___

6. MISGIVING:
   - (A) assurance
   - (B) theft
   - (C) reluctance
   - (D) gift
   - (E) greed

   6 ___

7. FORBEARANCE:
   - (A) impatience
   - (B) allowance
   - (C) leniency
   - (D) refusal
   - (E) breakdown

   7 ___

8. UNWARRANTED:
   - (A) not sold
   - (B) garbled
   - (C) suitable
   - (D) scrutinized
   - (E) pressured

   9 ___

9. OFFSPRING:
   - (A) cousin
   - (B) sibling
   - (C) aunt
   - (D) sire
   - (E) infant

   9 ___

10. OUTGROWTH:
    - (A) cause
    - (B) appendage
    - (C) drop in profits
    - (D) result
    - (E) rock ledge

    10 ___

Compound Words

The Anglo-Saxons loved to build compound words, just as modern German does. (They are related languages.) For our modern word *traveler*, they had *earth-walker*. The *king* was a *ring-giver*. A *successor* was an *after-comer*. A *lamp* was a *light-vessel*. The *sea* was the *whale-road*. *Geometry* was *earth-craft*. A *boat* was *sea-wood*. Many compounds were poetically beautiful, like *day-red* for *dawn*.

Many of the old compounds were dropped. Some, like *ring-finger*, are still with us. Some compounds have been combined to make a single word. *Walrus*, for example, was a *whale-horse*.

Modern English still creates new compound words. Words like *counterculture* and *cost-efficient* are fairly recent additions. A living language never stops changing.

Try your hand at creating compounds from Anglo-Saxon word elements.

Match words from column A and words from column B to form present-day compound words. Write the compound words on the lines below.

EXAMPLE

basket ball. *Basket* plus *ball* equals *basket-ball*.

A		**B**	
back	rail	ache	mill
dress	saw	band	road
eye	sea	beam	rocket
foot	sky	boat	sickness
gate	snow	book	sight
gold	sun	fish	step
hand	tooth	ground	storm
home	water	less	stroke
life	work	maker	way
moon	wrist	man	works

_____   _____

_____   _____

_____   _____

_____   _____

_____   _____

_____   _____

_____   _____

_____   _____

_____   _____

_____   _____

SUMMARY PART 5

Clues from Etymology: Anglo-Saxon Words

1. Words from Anglo-Saxon predominate in most writing and nearly all conversation.
2. Words for basic human actions and for commonplace objects tend to be of Anglo-Saxon origin. In times of great emotion people tend to call upon Anglo-Saxon words.
3. Words long in use often have figurative meanings, but the central meaning of the words tends to be recognizable.
4. Anglo-Saxon words are particularly useful in making compound words.

PART 6

Suffixes

Suffixes are crucial little word elements. They make the difference between *hopeful* and *hopeless*, *journalist* and *journalese*, *elective* and *election*, *thirteen* and *thirty*. They make verbs of adjectives: *short*, *shorten*. They make adverbs of adjectives: *sweet*, *sweetly*.

Suffixes provide clues to the part of speech. Typical noun suffixes include **dom**, **ness**, **ship**, **ion**, and **tude**. Typical adjective suffixes include **ish**, **less**, **y**, **esque**, and **ose**. Typical verb suffixes include **fy**, **ize**, and **ate**.

Although English derives suffixes from Latin, Greek, and Anglo-Saxon, suffixes were not treated in those sections of the book. A major reason is that English tends to make all kinds of combinations, using Latin roots with old Anglo-Saxon suffixes (*gratefully*) and Anglo-Saxon roots with old Latin suffixes (*breakable*). A word like *hypothetically* has a Greek prefix **hypo** and Greek root **thes**. The Latin suffix **al** combines with the Anglo-Saxon suffix **ly**, and we have a word from three different sources—Greek, Latin, and Anglo-Saxon. When English creates new words, all languages are fair game. There is little practical point in classifying suffixes as of Latin, Greek, or Anglo-Saxon origin.

Suffixes You Already Know

You can instantly recognize many suffixes, like **less** and **able**. You already know the meaning of most suffixes. You can guess, for example, that *happiness* is the "state of being happy" and that **ness** means "state of." You can often identify the meaning of unfamiliar words with suffixes by recalling other words you already know that have the same suffix.

Suppose you come upon the word *quiescent*. You recognize the word *quiet* but what of the suffix, **escent**? Think of other words with the same suffix: *adolescent* and *convalescent*. Both suggest a *state of becoming*: *becoming* an adult and *becoming* well. The suffix **escent** does mean "becoming." *Quiescent* suggests the process of *becoming* quiet. You would never call the ancient stillness of an Egyptian tomb *quiescent*. It is not *becoming* quiet. It has been quiet for a long time.

If you come upon the word *senescent*, you have something to build upon. You have already decided that the **escent** suffix means "becoming," but what of the root, **sene**. You think of words like *senior*, *seniority*, *senile*, and *senility*. These have to do with age. Even *senate* and *senator* originally suggested the older, more experienced, wiser heads in government. You may reasonably decide that *senescent* means "becoming older," "aging." Suffixes help to make fine distinctions.

Some suffixes are so rich and helpful they deserve your special attention. **Fy**, meaning "make," is such a suffix.

Review the meanings of these **fy** words.

amplify	magnify	satisfy
clarify	mortify	simplify
codify	ossify	solidify
deify	pacify	stultify
dignify	petrify	testify
horrify	rectify	unify
identify	revivify	verify
indemnify	sanctify	vilify

The concept of *making* is apparent in all these words, even though in some words the meaning is more figurative than literal. *Mortify*, for example, by derivation means "make dead." Isn't that rather strange? Not at all. Speakers of English are prone to exaggeration. Think of a typical exclamation: "I was so mortified I thought I'd die!"

Suffixes Suggest Meaning

Suffixes go beyond denotation. They may also be clues to connotation. The **ish** suffix, for example, is a popular one. Often it has a negative connotation. Think of *boyish, babyish, childish, mannish, foolish, boorish, kittenish, cleverish,* and *clownish*. Contrast the neutral *childlike* with the negative *childish*. The **ster** suffix also tends to have a negative connotation, as in words like *trickster, mobster, gangster, prankster, gamester, huckster,* and *rhymester*. An occasional **ster** may be an exception. *Punster* may have had a mildly negative tone at one time, but now it seems almost affectionate. *Youngster* is a fairly neutral word, but for some people it seems patronizing. Still, the **ster** suffix is a good clue to negative words.

Some suffixes suggest affection. The suffix **y**, for example, appears in words like *kitty, aunty, Johnny, Elly,* and *sissy* (for sister). Some suffixes suggest science and learning: **ics** in *economics, agronomics, hydroponics, harmonics, astrophysics,* and *electronics*.

Some suffixes have sudden bursts of popularity. **Ette**, meaning "small," has been widely used in recent years to suggest compactness and charm. Most people would shun a *small kitchen*, but they're proud of a *kitchenette*. Words like *luncheonette, launderette,* and *statuette* are perfectly acceptable. One small grocery store proudly called itself a *superette*! The **ama** suffix, originally from *orama* meaning "to see," started with *cyclorama*, then made its way to *launderama*.

A living language has vitality, vigor, and the capacity for change. Suffixes play a role in that change.

Become familiar with the following lists of suffixes. Knowing suffixes will help you on the SAT. The suffixes here are in two sections for convenience.

Suffix	Meaning	Example	Explanation
able, ible	able to	manage**able**	*able to* be managed
		collaps**ible**	*able to* be collapsed
ac, ic	related to	cardi**ac**	*related to* the heart
		dramat**ic**	*related to* drama
aceous, scious	having quality of	ver**acious**	*having quality of* truth, true
age	state, quality, act	shrink**age**	*state* of shrinking
al, ical	related to, like	nav**al**	*related to* ships
		crit**ical**	*related to* criticism
an, ian	related to, one who	ur**ban**	*related to* the city
		magic**ian**	*one who* words with magic
ana	information about	Americ**ana**	*information about* America
ance, ence	state, quality	resist**ance**	*state of* resisting
ancy, ency	act	despond**ency**	*state of* being downcast
ant, ent	one who, that which	particip**ant**	*one who* takes part
		tang**ent**	*that which* touches
ar	like, related to, one who	circul**ar**	*like* a circle
		li**ar**	*one who* lies
ary, arium	place where	gran**ary**	*place where* grain is stored
		sanit**arium**	*place where* people go to regain health
ard, art	one who (usually negative)	bragg**art**	*one who* boasts
ate	make, act, one who	dehydr**ate**	*make* waterless
		advoc**ate**	*one who* pleads another's cause
	having quality of	moder**ate**	*having quality of* reasonableness
cle	small	parti**cle**	*small* element
craft	skill, practice of	witch**craft**	*practice of* being a witch
dom	state, quality	wis**dom**	*state* of being wise
ee	one who	employ**ee**	*one who* is employed
eer	one who	auction**eer**	*one who* auctions
el, le	little, small	parc**el**	*small* bundle
en	make	hard**en**	*make* hard
en	having quality	wood**en**	*having quality* of wood
er, or	one who, that which	sail**or**	*one who* sails
		wash**er**	*that which* washes
ern	related to	east**ern**	*related to* east
ery, erie	place where	hatch**ery**	*place where* fish are hatched

		menag**erie**	*place where* animals are displayed
ery, ry	state of, quality, act of	drudg**ery**	*state of* hard, dull work
		bigot**ry**	*state of or act of* prejudice
escent	becoming	obsol**escent**	*becoming* obsolete
ese	like, related to	Chin**ese**	*related to* China
esque	in the manner of	Whitman**esque**	*in the manner of* Whitman
ess*	feminine	act**ress**	*female* actor*
et, ette	little, small	ringl**et**	*little* ring
fic, fy	making, make	honori**fic**	*making* or conferring honor
		simpl**ify**	*make* simple
fold	times	ten**fold**	ten *times*
ful	having quality of	care**ful**	*having quality of* care
hood	state of, quality of	child**hood**	*state of* being a child
		false**hood**	*quality of* falseness
ics	science, system	linguist**ics**	*science* of languages
ice	act of, time of	serv**ice**	*act of* serving
id	related to	flu**id**	*related to* a liquid

*This suffix has been under attack as being sexist. Opponents argue that *actor* refers to both sexes. Words like *steward* and *stewardess*, they say, should give way to *flight attendant*. The suffix is included here for completeness, but you may wish to think about your own use of it.

Trial Test

Each of the words in column A contains a suffix from the preceding list. Each suffix is in boldface. Write the number for each word from column A next to its meaning in column B. Clues in column B are in *italics*. Note how suffixes can help to sharpen meaning.

A	B
1. avi**ary**	____ *make* systematic, arrange
2. benefac**tor**	____ *small*est speck
3. bliss**ful**	____ *science* of production, distribution, and consumption of wealth
4. cod**ify**	____ *place where* birds are kept
5. incorrig**ible**	____ *having quality of* happiness
6. econom**ics**	____ manual *skill*
7. handi**craft**	____ *related to* light, clear
8. luc**id**	____ *one who* does good deeds
9. parti**cle**	____ *in the manner of* a statue
10. sculptur**esque**	____ *not able to* be reformed

Answers to Trial Test

A	B
1. aviary	place where birds are kept
2. benefactor	one who does good deeds
3. blissful	having quality of happiness
4. codify	make systematic, arrange
5. incorrigible	not able to be reformed
6. economics	science of production, distribution, and consumption of wealth
7. handicraft	manual skill
8. lucid	related to light, clear
9. particle	smallest speck
10. sculpturesque	in the manner of a statue

Suffixes often help in answering SAT antonym questions such as the one that follows.

Problem

NULLIFY:

(A) use wisely   (D) make effective

(B) take seriously   (E) cause annoyance

(C) perform easily

Strategy

Notice the **fy** suffix, one of the most helpful of all. Clearly **nullify** is "to make null." You have probably heard **null** used in the expression *null and void* meaning "not binding." **Nullify** means "make not binding." If you haven't heard *null and void*, you may have heard the word *annul*, meaning "cancel." Or perhaps you've heard the word *annulment* meaning the "dissolution of a marriage."

Null contains the idea of "not in effect." Look at the choices. Does one of them seem the opposite of **nullify**? Knowing the **fy** suffix is helpful. The meaning of **fy**, "make," is actually a part of alternative (*D*), *make effective*. This use suggests that **null** and *effective* are antonyms. They clearly are.

SUFFIXES – 2

Suffix	Meaning	Example	Explanation
ie, y	small	dogg**ie**	*small* dog
		kitt**y**	*small* kitten
ine	like, related to	fel**ine**	*like* a cat
ion	state, quality, act of	suspic**ion**	*act of* suspecting
ish	like, related to	boor**ish**	*like* a boor
isk	small	aster**isk**	*small* star
ism	state of, quality act	egot**ism**	*state of* being self-centered
ist	one who	dent**ist**	*one who* works with teeth
ite	one who	favor**ite**	*one who* is favored
itis	inflammation	neur**itis**	*inflammation* of nerves
ity	state, quality, act	nobil**ity**	*quality* of being noble
ize	make, act	tranquil**ize**	*make* quiet
ive	one who, that which	capt**ive**	*one who* has been taken
ive	having power	creat**ive**	*having power* to create
kin	little, small	man**ikin**	*little* man
less	without	home**less**	*without* a home
let	little	book**let**	*little* book
like	like	ape**like**	*like* an ape

ly	having quality of	friendly	*having quality of* a friend
ly	in the manner of (adverb suffix)	hurriedly	*in a* hurried *manner*
ment	state of, quality, act	excitement	*state of* being excited
mony	state of, quality, that which	matrimony	*state of* being married
or	one who, that which	donor	*one who* gives
ory, orium	place where	factory	*place where* things are made
		auditorium	*place where* one can hear
ory	like, having quality of	regulatory	*having quality of* controlling
ose	having quality of	bellicose	*having quality of* quarrelsomeness
osis	state, condition, action	hypnosis	*state* resembling sleep
	abnormal or diseased condition	tuberculosis	*diseased condition* of lungs
ous	having quality of	famous	*having quality of* fame
ship	state of, quality of	ownership	*state of* being an owner
some	having quality of, full of	worrisome	*having quality of* worry
ster	own who	prankster	*one who* plays pranks
th	state, quality, that which	truth	*state of* being true
tude	state, quality of, act of	multitude	*state of* being numerous
ty	state of, quality of, that which	safety	*state of* being safe
ure	state of, quality of, act, that which	rupture	*state of* being broken
ward, wards	in direction of	homeward	*in direction of* home
wise	in the manner of, in a certain direction	clockwise	*in the direction* a clock rotates
y	having quality of	hasty	*having quality of* haste
	somewhat, tending to, suggestive of	yellowy	*somewhat* yellow
		drowsy	*tending to* drowse
		willowy	*suggestive of* a willow, gracefully slender

Trial Test

Each of the words in column A contains a suffix from the preceding list. Each suffix is in boldface. Write the number for each word from column A next to its meaning in column B. Clues in column B are in *italics*. Note how suffixes can help to sharpen meaning.

A	B
1. altru**ism**	___ *having quality of* being annoying
2. curat**or**	___ *inflammation* of the stomach
3. cut**let**	___ *little* slice
4. equ**ine**	___ *one who* is in charge of a museum or a library
5. eulog**ize**	___ *make* a speech of praise
6. gastr**itis**	___ *in the manner of* a greedy person
7. glutton**ously**	___ *place where* people work and experiment
8. laborat**ory**	___ *like* a horse
9. psych**osis**	___ *diseased condition* of the mind
10. vexati**ous**	___ *quality of* unselfishness

Answers to Trial Test

A	B
__10__	*having quality of* being annoying
__6__	*inflammation* of the stomach
__3__	*little* slice
__2__	*one who* is in charge of a museum or library
__5__	*make* a speech of praise
__7__	*in the manner of* a greedy person
__8__	*place where* people work and experiment
__4__	*like* a horse
__9__	*diseased condition* of the mind
__1__	*quality of* unselfishness

Here is another SAT-type antonym question.

Problem

BOOKLET:

(A) volume   (D) pamphlet
(B) leaflet   (E) schedule
(C) newspaper

Strategy

The **let** suffix, meaning "little," tells you that a **booklet** is a small book. In looking for an antonym, first rule out any other little items. That gets rid of *leaflet* (B) and *pamphlet* (D). Go on to *newspaper* (C) and *schedule* (E), neither of which can be considered an opposite of **booklet**. A *volume* (A) is usually a large or major book—quite the opposite of a small, minor booklet.

Use your knowledge of prefixes, roots, and suffixes in the following review exercise.

Time Out For Review

Write the letter for the antonym of each capitalized word.

1. RECONCILIATION:

    (A) relief   (D) reparation
    (B) vengeance   (E) demonstration
    (C) disappointment

    1 ___

2. RECIPIENT:

    (A) dispatcher   (D) caller
    (B) official   (E) recluse
    (C) grandfather

    2 ___

3. ANTIPATHY:

    (A) apathy   (D) amusement
    (B) compassion   (E) affection
    (C) weeping

    3 ___

4. VIVACIOUS:

    (A) petty   (D) lifeless
    (B) invisible   (E) tranquil
    (C) inevitable

    4 ___

5. MEDIOCRE:

    (A) medieval   (D) condensed
    (B) moderate   (E) breezy
    (C) outstanding

    5 ___

6. TRANSIENT:

    (A) permanent   (D) unstable
    (B) traveled   (E) poisonous
    (C) trained

    6 ___

7. SOMNOLENT:

    (A) drowsy   (D) shrewd
    (B) obedient   (E) wide-awake
    (C) open-minded

    7 ___

8. DISPARITY:

    (A) remuneration   (D) equality
    (B) reparation   (E) unintelligibility
    (C) replacement

    8 ___

9. SUPERFICIAL:

    (A) unnecessary   (D) reserved
    (B) profound   (E) experimental
    (C) undignified

    9 ___

10. IMPERTURBABLE:

    (A) plaintive   (D) sober
    (B) diplomatic   (E) excitable
    (C) informal

    10 ___

SUMMARY PART 6

Clues from Etymology: Suffixes

1. Suffixes provide important clues to the part of speech, word meanings, and word history.
2. English uses suffixes without regard for word origins. Anglo-Saxon and Latin suffixes are often used together.
3. You can find the meaning of most suffixes: think of other words containing the suffixes. Then decide what meaning all the words have in common.
4. Suffixes sometimes suggest connotation as well as denotation.

Suffixes can help you with SAT questions, especially when you need to know the part of speech—as you do in antonym and analogy questions.

PART 7

Foreign Words in English

Think of a typical American **barbecue**. In addition to the meat, there might be baked **potato**, baked **yam**, sliced **tomato**, all served with **lemonade**, **ginger** ale, iced **tea**, or iced **coffee**. Of course the inevitable bottle of **ketchup** would be on hand for the feast. For dessert there might be **orange sherbet**. Some guests might prefer **chocolate** ice cream, made from **cocoa**. In season, **apricots** and **avocados** might be welcome additions. **Bananas** would almost certainly be available.

Notice how much we depend upon foreign borrowings. Every one of the bold-faced words originally came from lands all around the world.

barbecue—American Indian	orange—Persian
potato—American Indian	sherbet—Arabic
yam—African	chocolate—Mexican
tomato—Mexican	cocoa—Mexican
lemon—Persian	apricots—Arabic
ginger—Indian	avocados—Mexican
tea—Chinese	bananas—African
coffee—Arabic	syrup—Arabic
ketchup—Malayan-Chinese	sugar—Arabic

These are just a few of the food words borrowed from other languages. Sometimes the borrowings provide a clue to the special contribution of a particular language. From Hebrew, for example, we get words like **amen**, **cherub**, **hallelujah**, **Jehovah**, **jubilee**, **Pharisee**, **sabbath**, and **shibboleth**. These words suggest our indebtedness to the ancient Hebrews for many religious terms.

Trial Test

A. Below are listed groups of words from various other languages. Decide from what language each group of words came and match each group with the proper language from the list below. What do you think was a major contribution of each nation?

EXAMPLE

arcade, **balcony**, **colonnade**, **corridor**, **portico**

Language: Contribution:

<u>Italian</u>   <u>Architecture</u>

These are all of Italian origin. Since all have something to do with parts of buildings, we can safely assume that Italian contributions to architecture have been considerable.

African	French
American	German
American Indian	Italian
Arabic	Persian
Dutch	Spanish

1. hominy, maize, pecan, succotash, squash

Language: _____   Contribution: _____

2. beret, cambric, chapeau, cretonne

Language: _____   Contribution: _____

3. deck, dock, hoist, jib, skipper, sloop

Language: _____   Contribution: _____

4. bismuth, cobalt, Fahrenheit, gneiss, quartz, shale, zinc

Language: _____   Contribution: _____

5. alchemy, algebra, chemistry, cipher, zenith, zero

Language: Contribution:

_____   _____

6. adobe, bronco, canyon, corral, lariat

Language: Contribution:

_____   _____

7. jasmine, lemon, lilac, orange, peach, tulip

Language: Contribution:

_____   _____

8. andante, aria, opera, piano, soprano

Language: Contribution:

_____   _____

9. chimpanzee, gnu, gorilla, ibis, quagga

Language: Contribution:

_____   _____

10. carborundum, cellophane, kodak, listerine, thermos, victrola

Language: Contribution:

_____   _____

A. Answers to Trial Test

1. American Indian	plants for food
2. French	fashion
3. Dutch	seafaring skills
4. German	science, chemistry
5. Arabic	science, mathematics
6. Spanish	opening up of the West
7. Persian	fruits and flowers
8. Italian	music
9. African	strange and new animals
10. American	technology and invention

B. The words in column A have all been based upon the names of places in other lands. Look up the origin and the meaning of each word in column A. Then write each word's number next to its country of origin in column B.

A	B
1. astrachan	____ China
2. bayonet	____ England
3. calico	____ England and Scotland
4. cantaloupe	____ France
5. cheviot	____ Germany
6. coach	____ Hungary
7. damask	____ India
8. frankfurter	____ Italy
9. muslin	____ Mesopotamia
10. oolong	____ Mexico
11. peach	____ Morocco
12. polka	____ Persia
13. tabasco	____ Poland
14. tangerine	____ Russia
15. worsted	____ Syria

B. Answers to Trial Test

	A		B
1.	astrachan	10	China
2.	bayonet	15	England
3.	calico	5	England and Scotland
4.	cantaloupe	2	France
5.	cheviot	8	Germany
6.	coach	6	Hungary
7.	damask	3	India
8.	frankfurter	4	Italy
9.	muslin	9	Mesopotamia
10.	oolong	13	Mexico
11.	peach	14	Morocco
12.	polka	11	Persia
13.	tabasco	12	Poland
14.	tangerine	1	Russia
15.	worsted	7	Syria

Word History

Among the ancient Greeks, citizens of Laconia, or Sparta, had the reputation of speaking directly, wasting no words. This characteristic has given us the word **laconic**. **Laconic** means "brief," "to the point." Many qualities or products of various places have given us new words. The American favorite, **hamburger**, is named after the city of Hamburg. **Italic** type originated in Italy. **Copper** took its name from Cyprus, as did **spaniel** from Spain. **China**, **turkey**, **cologne**, and **morocco** (leather) are self-explanatory. English has many such words.

Words from sources other than Latin, Greek, or Anglo-Saxon appear occasionally in the word sections of the SAT and the reading sections. The best preparation for this selection is also the best preparation for extending your vocabulary in general. Become word curious. When you meet an interesting new word, look up the definition, of course, but also check its history.

Note the interesting history behind the word **bizarre**.

> **bi·zarre** (bi zär′) *adj.* [Fr. < It. *bizarro*; angry, fierce, strange < Sp. *bizarro*, bold, knightly < Basque *bizar*, a beard] **1.** odd in manner, appearance, etc.; grotesque; queer; eccentric **2.** marked by extreme contrasts and incongruities of color, design, or style **3.** unexpected and unbelievable; fantastic [a *bizarre* sequences of events]—*SYN.* see FANTASTIC—**bi·zarre′ly** *adv.*—**bi·zarre′ness** *n.* *

Bizarre originally came from Basque *bizar* meaning "beard." The Spaniards borrowed the word as *bizarro* to mean "bold, knightly." Knights, we may assume, were *bearded*. The Italians then borrowed the word with the same spelling to mean "angry, fierce." Knightly battles were not gentle struggles! Then English borrowed the same word as **bizarre** to mean "odd," "eccentric." Reading the history makes an impression. (Note that the similar-sounding word, *bazaar*, is completely unrelated. *Bazaar* comes from the Persian *bazar*, meaning market.)

Karate comes from two Japanese words: *kara* meaning "empty," "open" and *te* meaning "hand." **Karate** literally means "open hand." A demonstration of karate clearly shows how the word originated, as thrusts are made with hands open.

Look at two actual SAT antonym questions.

Problem

BIZARRE:

    (A) underhanded   (D) polite
    (B) commonplace   (E) competitive
    (C) sincere

Strategy

Since we have discovered that the English meaning of **bizarre** is "odd," "eccentric," we can safely assume the antonym needed is *commonplace*, (*B*).

Problem

FLAMBOYANT:

    (A) unfamiliar   (D) amusing
    (B) unappealing   (E) unkempt
    (C) plain

Strategy

Try to recall expressions using the word **flamboyant**: a **flamboyant** personality, a **flamboyant** scheme, **flamboyant** decorations. All these carry the central idea of ornamentation, decoration, display. A good guess at the meaning of **flamboyant** would be "ornate," "showy." Don't stop there. Though **flamboyant** comes to us from the French, it has a recognizable English cousin: *flame*. *Dramatic display* is a characteristic associated with *flame*. The two clues together suggest that the antonym is *plain*, (*C*).

Time Out for Review

A. After each of the following test words, the origin of the word is given, along with its original meaning. Read the clues and write the letter for the answer which most closely explains the test word.

EXAMPLE

KOWTOW (from the Chinese meaning "knock head"):

(A) find unexpectedly
(B) respect excessively
(C) support enthusiastically
(D) understand poorly
(E) reject suddenly

B

Since the original meaning suggests a person touching his head to the floor in submission, alternative (B), *respect excessively*, is the correct answer.

1. UKASE (from the Russian "to order"):
   (A) container for bottles
   (B) kind of instrument
   (C) voting irregularity
   (D) official decree
   (E) all-purpose cement

   1 ___

2. AMOK (from the Malay "fighting furiously"):
   (A) sympathetic
   (B) at a standstill
   (C) in a rage
   (D) wearily accepting
   (E) quietly responsible

   2 ___

3. CHECKMATE (from the Persian "The king is dead"):
   (A) delay intentionally
   (B) replace secretly
   (C) marry in haste
   (D) support financially
   (E) defeat completely

   3 ___

4. PUNDIT (from Indian "learned person"):
   (A) authority
   (B) mayor
   (C) enthusiast
   (D) police officer
   (E) humorist

   4 ___

5. RUCKSACK (from German "back" plus "sack"):
   (A) potato sack
   (B) handbag
   (C) pocketbook
   (D) hiker's pack
   (E) wallet

   5 ___

6. ARGOSY (from Italian "vessel from Ragusa"):
   (A) merchant ship
   (B) newly published book
   (C) fan magazine
   (D) financial wizard
   (E) tall tale

   6 ___

7. MANDARIN (from Indian "minister of state"):
   (A) skilled chef
   (B) member of elite group
   (C) fruit punch
   (D) stringed instrument
   (E) mythological monster

   7 ___

8. NADIR (from the Arabic "opposite the highest point"):
   (A) kind of telescope
   (B) sunspot
   (C) good fortune
   (D) tropical fruit
   (E) time of dejection

   8 ___

9. MOGUL (from Persian "Mongol conqueror"):
   (A) superb athlete
   (B) member of endangered species
   (C) powerful person
   (D) falsehood
   (E) bill of sale

   9 ___

10. GARBLE (from Arabic "sieve"):
    (A) close
    (B) mix up
    (C) win at chess
    (D) wander aimlessly
    (E) find fault

    10 ___

B. Words from foreign sources are everywhere in English. They are found in every field of activity, every subject, at every level of difficulty. How many words in the following test are familiar to you? For each item, write the letter for the answer that best defines the test word. If you don't know a word, look it up.

1. FAHRENHEIT and CELSIUS are words dealing with
   (A) severity of earthquakes
   (B) degrees of heat
   (C) electronic calculations
   (D) atmospheric pressure
   (E) relative humidity

   1 ____

2. A SHIBBOLETH is a
   (A) monster
   (B) password
   (C) proclamation
   (D) flower
   (E) game

   2 ____

3. A SERAPH is a(an)
   (A) kind of printing
   (B) old woman
   (C) medicine
   (D) angel
   (E) mounted soldier

   3 ____

4. A FEZ is a kind of
   (A) fish
   (B) mythical animal
   (C) cap
   (D) coat
   (E) worship

   4 ____

5. A TABOO is a
   (A) mark
   (B) prince
   (C) restriction
   (D) narrative
   (E) permit

   5 ____

6. FANFARE involves
   (A) display
   (B) the use of a fan
   (C) charging admission
   (D) baseball
   (E) jealousy

   6 ____

7. CURRY is a
   (A) carriage
   (B) harness
   (C) pack animal
   (D) seasoning
   (E) comb

   7 ____

8. TURQUOISE is a kind of
   (A) fowl
   (B) plant
   (C) color
   (D) powder
   (E) French dish

   8 ____

9. AZIMUTH is a term used in
   (A) painting
   (B) music
   (C) navigation
   (D) handicraft
   (E) the study of minerals

   9 ____

10. A MAZURKA is a kind of
    (A) broiled chicken
    (B) dance
    (C) vehicle
    (D) herb
    (E) building

    10 ____

11. A FREEBOOTER is a
    (A) football player
    (B) member of a soccer team
    (C) fighter for freedom
    (D) pirate
    (E) weaver

    11 ____

12. A JUGGERNAUT is something that
    (A) plays a tune
    (B) crushes
    (C) works automatically
    (D) takes care of gardens
    (E) can perform acrobatic stunts

    12 ____

13. WAINSCOT is a
    (A) ceremonial car
    (B) kind of celluloid
    (C) formal dinner
    (D) roofing material
    (E) woodwork

    13 ____

14. QUININE is a
    (A) tropical disease
    (B) medicine
    (C) kind of dance
    (D) paint ingredient
    (E) beef tea

    14 ____

15. A CATAMARAN is a(an)
    (A) tiger-like animal
    (B) insect
    (C) Malayan hut
    (D) kind of boat
    (E) cure for malaria

    15 ____

16. A BAZAAR is a
  (A) cloak
  (B) strange tale
  (C) protest
  (D) musical instrument
  (E) fair

  16 ___

17. The ZENITH is
  (A) on the horizon
  (B) below one's feet
  (C) at a 45 degree angle
  (D) above one's head
  (E) at the equator

  17 ___

18. A PARIAH is a(an)
  (A) staunch friend
  (B) outcast
  (C) religious fanatic
  (D) oriental singer
  (E) weak-willed person

  18 ___

19. An ALPACA is a(an)
  (A) ballad
  (B) artificial fabric
  (C) light jacket
  (D) animal
  (E) special kind of stew

  19 ___

20. A JAGUAR is a(an)
  (A) medicinal root
  (B) animal
  (C) bird
  (D) savage
  (E) knife

  20 ___

SUMMARY PART 7

Clues from Etymology: Foreign Words in English

1. English has borrowed extensively from almost every language and culture it has come in contact with.
2. Borrowing has enriched the language by providing words for new objects and new ideas.
3. Finding the stories in foreign loan words enriches the study of vocabulary and impresses new words on the memory.
4. The borrowing goes both ways. English words also appear in almost every language in the original or changed form.

Studying foreign words in English and word histories will help you to prepare for the SAT.

PART 8

The Growth of English

Think of expressions like *space shuttle*, *launch window*, *computer chip*, and *video game*. A few years ago these expressions did not exist because the things they name did not exist. We need new words and expressions to name new processes and substances. Unfortunately, as our problems increase, we need new expressions for these, too: *hazardous waste*, *endangered species*, and *acid rain*.

Sometimes, as in the examples above, new expressions merely combine older words to create wholly new concepts. Sometimes, however, we need a wholly new word. When inflation strained the resources of a stagnant economy, we coined the new word *stagflation*. Words like *microprocessing* and *transistorize* show that we still have the ability to create new words from old roots.

The best way to learn new words is to listen carefully and read widely. Current newspapers and magazines are filled with new words and expressions. Words and expressions like *quark*, *jet lag*, *personal computer*, *word processor*, *laser*, and *burnout* have become commonplace in modern communication.

Because words enter the language at so rapid a rate, it is impossible to prepare an up-to-date book on new words, or *neologisms*, as they are called. Dictionaries of new words are out of date before publication day. If there is a knowledge explosion, there is also a language explosion. New words will not play a key role in the SAT, but it is always a good idea to keep up to date.

When you work with roots, be aware of the tendency of language to change. The root of *common* suggests "shared by all." But the word has acquired a negative connotation of "inferiority," even "coarseness." Similarly, *vulgar* once meant "general," "popular," "belonging to the great mass of people." Now a certain snobbishness in language has sent the word downhill to mean "coarse," "crude," "boorish."

Uphill in Meaning

Words can go up the social scale, too. A *knight* was once a "servant." A *marshal* was a "groom," a "horse servant." A *constable* was the "chief groom." A *chamberlain*, now a high official, was once just a "servant." A *steward* was the "guardian of the sty." *Chivalry* was just another word for "cavalry." Even *fame* once meant only "something spoken about someone." Now it suggests "a good reputation."

Narrower in Meaning

While some words are going up or down the social scale, others are changing in different ways. Specialization has changed *meat* from "any solid food" to the "flesh of animals." A *ballad* was once just a "song." Now it's a rather special kind of song. *Corn* was once any "grain." Now in America it refers to the plant the Indians called "maize." *Ghost* once meant just "spirit." Now it is usually applied to an "apparition" said to haunt houses. In fact, *apparition* itself once meant just "appearance."

Broader in Meaning

English often extends word meanings. A *journey* was originally a "trip of one day's duration." Now it means a "trip of any length." *Front* once meant merely "forehead." *Paper* was a substance made from "papyrus." Now paper can be made from many substances. A *scene* was once just "part of a theater stage." We still use it in that sense, but think of all the broader uses of the term, as in *the modern scene*. *Hazard* was once a "game of dice." Now it means a "chance occurrence" and, by extension, a "risk," a "danger."

Figurative in Meaning

One of the most common changes in English is figurative use of a word. *Deliberate* literally means "put on the scales." *Dilapidate* means "throw stones." A *pedigree* literally means a "crane's foot." If you look at a pedigree, or family tree (another figurative expression), you can see that foot! Pages 47–52 have already considered the importance of figurative language. The sections on roots have urged you to look for figurative meanings in many common words.

However, language grows and changes in other ways, too. If you know about these changes, you will have a better background for handling some of the questions on the SAT.

Look at an SAT-type antonym question.

Problem

ENORMITY:

(A) size
(B) digression
(C) fallibility
(D) enmity
(E) virtue

Strategy

Enormity once meant "something out of the normal." Then it became associated with *evil*. The expression *the enormity of the crime* suggests the approved modern definition of the word. The needed antonym here is *virtue*, (*E*).

Downhill in Meaning

Enormity suggests one way in which words change—for the worse. Once it meant merely "something unusual." Now it suggests "unusual in evil." Similarly, *boor* once meant merely "farmer." *Knave* meant just "boy." *Homely* meant "simple," and *sullen* meant "alone." A *villain* was a "farm servant," and a *hussy* was just a "housewife." *Servile* meant "not free." Now it suggests "cringing," "unnecessarily submissive." A *busybody* was just a "busy person," and a *hypocrite* was just an "actor."

Trial Test

In each sentence, write the word in parentheses that most suitably completes the meaning of the sentence.

EXAMPLE

The ending of the musical *Carousel* is so (poignant, pungent), it often brings a tear to every eye in the audience.

In this sentence *poignant* means "emotionally touching," "evoking pity." *Pungent* would be too strong. *Pungent* may be piercing to the mind; *poignant* to the emotions. *Pungent* can apply to taste. *Poignant* cannot.

1. An (abbreviated, abridged) dictionary keeps the most important words and omits infrequently used words.

    1 _____

2. Jim's speech was interesting, but his ideas were too (tenuous, thin) for a practical program.

    2 _____

3. When Caroline brought out the ping pong balls, the kittens became unusally (fresh, frisky) in playing with them.

    3 _____

4. After a morning in the garden, Don's complexion became (florid, flowery) from the heat.

    4 _____

5. Because of a disagreement, the two families (separated, severed) all ties that had once joined them.

    5 _____

6. Though Billy Dawn in *Born Yesterday* at first seemed (naive, native), she gradually developed a shrewd awareness of Brock's dishonesty.

    6 _____

7. From an early age, Teddy showed an (aptitude, attitude) for things mechanical.

    7 _____

8. Once Patty becomes interested in a subject, she (jealously, zealously) learns all she can about it.

    8 _____

9. By three, Jennifer could already (compute, count) from 1 to 10.

    9 _____

10. Pollen granules are (born, borne) on the wind.

    10 _____

Answers to Trial Test

1. abridged	4. florid	7. aptitude	9. count
2. tenuous	5. severed	8. zealously	10. borne
3. frisky	6. naive		

Problem

The petty --- of some persons in charge of others is often traceable to a basic --- in their lives.
(A) cheerfulness . . melancholy
(B) talkativeness . . charm
(C) vigor . . misunderstanding
(D) provincialism . . awareness
(E) tyranny . . insecurity

Analyze the possibilities. (*A*) contains a contradiction. *Cheerfulness* cannot logically be traced to *melancholy*. Although it might be argued that such an answer is not impossible, you are not asked to choose just a possible answer. You must choose the best answer. If a clue word like *although* had been included, things might be different. Notice the difference the following wording makes.

Although some persons in charge of others display *cheerfulness*, they may be concealing a basic *melancholy* in their lives.

Talkativeness and *charm* are negatively related, if at all. We can reject (*B*). *Vigor* and *misunderstanding* are not related. Misunderstanding would not logically lead to vigor. Reject (*C*). (*D*) also contains a contradiction. People who are *open and aware* are not likely to be *provincial*.

A process of elimination leaves you with (*E*). Do these answers fit? Yes, tyranny can arise from a feeling of insecurity. Those who feel insecure may try to generate security by being oppressive to others. (*E*) is correct.

Tyranny is a word that has gone downhill. A *tyrant* was once just a "ruler" in ancient Greece. Then, since rulers often abuse their powers, the word *tyrant* came to mean an "unjust, oppressive ruler." For the purpose of this question it is not necessary to know that *tyranny* has gone downhill, as long as you know its present meaning. But knowing a little about the history of a word makes it much easier to remember. Now that you know something about the origin of *tyranny*, you are unlikely to forget it.

Doublets

One of the most fruitful sources of the growth of English is borrowing. As we have already noted, English may borrow the same word twice or even more. This multiple borrowing enriches our language, increases the number of synonyms, and makes for finer discriminations in speaking and writing.

Both **potion** and **poison** come from the Latin word meaning "drink." These doublets have acquired different meanings. A **poison** is a deadly **potion. Loyal** and **legal** both come from the Latin *lex* meaning "law." **Loyal**, which reached English through French, has acquired a different meaning from **legal**. Similarly, **frail** has acquired a meaning slightly different from its doublet **fragile**. An ill person may become **frail** but not **fragile**.

Doublets may come from different languages. Here's a sampling.

Anglo-Saxon and Latin	eatable, edible
Anglo-Saxon and French	bench, bank
Anglo-Saxon and Scandinavian	shriek, screech
Anglo-Saxon and Dutch	slide, sled
Latin and French	concept, conceit
French and Italian	study, studio
French and Spanish	army, armada
Greek and French	cathedral, chair

Doublets may come from the same language, though at different periods.

Earlier and Later French	castle, chateau
Earlier and Later Latin	camp, campus

Doublets may come from various changes within English itself.

Loss of a Syllable	despite, spite
Change of Vowel	cloths, clothes
Change of Consonant	stitch, stick
Word Shortening	van, caravan
Spelling Variation	flour, flower

Words borrowed three times are called *triplets*.

French, Italian, Spanish	place, piazza, plaza

Some words have been borrowed four times and now appear in four different forms, each with a different meaning: **stack, stake, steak, stock.** Some words have been borrowed five times and appear in five different forms: **discus, disk, dish, desk, dais.**

Why are doublets important in a vocabulary-building program? They provide associated words and synonyms. When you take a test you must be able to discriminate meanings.

Time Out for Review

In each of the following sentences, doublets appear in parentheses. Write the word which most suitably completes the meaning of the sentence.

1. Mr. Hatheway (dealed, doled) out his son's allowance as if he were mortgaging the family homestead for the money.

   1 _____

2. Despite his advanced age, George Bernard Shaw remained surprisingly (hale, whole) and vigorous.

   2 _____

3. You'll need a(an) (example, sample) of your wallpaper if you want to buy a matching bedspread.

   3 _____

4. Making sure all five kittens had a good home was a (human, humane) action.

   4 _____

5. As a storyteller Maud is without a (pair, peer) in our club.

   5 _____

6. What seems like (concept, conceit) in Rod is really shyness.

   6 _____

7. With her new hairdo, Fran looks like a (spirit, sprite) from elfdom.

   7 _____

8. When Henry Ford started, his friends were critical of the risky (adventure, venture) he was engaged in.

   8 _____

9. Until Cynthia becomes 18, her uncle remains her legal (guardian, warden).

   9 _____

10. The sign in the window said, "We buy old furniture; we sell (antics, antiques)."

    10 _____

SUMMARY PART 8

Clues from Etymology: The Growth of English

1. As a living language, English adds new words constantly.
2. Some words are needed for technological advances and setbacks. Others are needed for new customs, fashions, and life-styles.
3. Some new expressions merely combine old words in new ways, but some actually create new words.
4. Most new words are constructed by putting together the building blocks of prefixes, roots, and suffixes.
5. Not only are new words created; words change. Some words go downhill; some, up. Some words become narrower in meaning; some, broader. Figurative use of existing words extends the possibilities of English.
6. Some words are borrowed twice, three times, or even more. These multiple borrowings enrich English with new synonyms and new concepts.

If you know how the language grows and changes, you will have a better background for verbal SAT questions.

Review Test
Clues from Etymology

A. Write the letter for the antonym of each capitalized word.

1. IMMEASURABLE:
   - (A) unmanageable
   - (B) genial
   - (C) small
   - (D) accurate
   - (E) allowable

   1 ___

2. INCOMPATIBILITY:
   - (A) suitability
   - (B) incorrigibility
   - (C) incongruity
   - (D) competence
   - (E) deficiency

   2 ___

3. DISINCLINATION:
   - (A) straightforward-ness
   - (B) discipline
   - (C) descent
   - (D) dejection
   - (E) receptivity

   3 ___

4. SELF-SUFFICIENCY:
   - (A) selfishness
   - (B) dependence
   - (C) ardor
   - (D) earnestness
   - (E) self-indulgence

   4 ___

5. UNPALATABLE:
   - (A) tasty
   - (B) improvable
   - (C) uninviting
   - (D) enlightened
   - (E) fertile

   5 ___

6. AMBIGUOUS:
   - (A) double-dealing
   - (B) lucid
   - (C) single-minded
   - (D) chronic
   - (E) zestful

   6 ___

7. DEFAMATION:
   - (A) commendation
   - (B) compensation
   - (C) slander
   - (D) representation
   - (E) silence

   7 ___

8. INCONCLUSIVE:
   - (A) indeterminate
   - (B) inapplicable
   - (C) decisive
   - (D) unanswerable
   - (E) nondescript

   8 ___

9. ENERVATE:
   - (A) exalt
   - (B) complicate
   - (C) strengthen
   - (D) dominate
   - (E) complain

   9 ___

10. UNKEMPT:
    - (A) restrained
    - (B) neat
    - (C) inoffensive
    - (D) constant
    - (E) impressive

    10 ___

B. Write the letter for the pair of words that best completes the meaning of the sentence as a whole.

1. For a true --- , democracy encourages --- opinions as well as those that support the existing state of affairs.
   - (A) inference . . complementary
   - (B) mandate . . conforming
   - (C) elimination . . haphazard
   - (D) juxtaposition . . straightforward
   - (E) consensus . . heterodox

   1 ___

2. Nature films on television frequently inject a powerful plea for regulations limiting the --- of natural areas and the inevitable --- of wildlife.
   - (A) closure . . hunting
   - (B) opening . . improvement
   - (C) depiction . . expansion
   - (D) exploitation . . destruction
   - (E) mapping . . census

   2 ___

3. Settlers from the Northeast sometimes find it difficult to --- themselves to the low humidity and --- beauty of the American Southwest.
   - (A) transport . . luxurious
   - (B) invite . . unexpected
   - (C) adjust . . dank
   - (D) will . . contrary
   - (E) acclimate . . austere

   3 ___

4. Television's --- appetite for novelty --- material at an ever-increasing rate.

   (A) insatiable . . devours
   (B) devious . . expands
   (C) indiscriminate . . creates
   (D) well-known . . resolves
   (E) amiable . . displays

   4 ___

5. Thor Heyerdahl, on the *Ra* papyrus boat, discovered floating --- of oil in the mid-Atlantic, pointing to the continuing --- of the seas.

   (A) cans . . commerce
   (B) mounds . . beautification
   (C) globs . . pollution
   (D) glimpses . . mining
   (E) tankers . . revival

   5 ___

6. Alice Neel is an artist whose art and life are --- , one feeding the other to the mutual --- of both.

   (A) exceptional . . surprise
   (B) intertwined . . enrichment
   (C) old-fashioned . . depiction
   (D) separated . . benefit
   (E) contemporary . . appeal

   6 ___

7. A Washington group teaches children how to --- with handicapped children by working with puppets that show various kinds of physical --- .

   (A) converse . . activities
   (B) compete . . variations
   (C) walk . . characteristics
   (D) win . . aids
   (E) interact . . disability

   7 ___

8. As video games become more and more --- , the players become more --- in their search for new challenges.

   (A) sophisticated . . discriminating
   (B) garish . . alert
   (C) metallic . . vigorous
   (D) alike . . idiotic
   (E) timely . . defiant

   8 ___

9. Mike McElroy, eminent scientist and --- professor of chemistry at Harvard, has --- interests that carry him from the atmosphere of planets to the origins of life.

   (A) dapper . . planetary
   (B) prestigious . . wide-ranging
   (C) retiring . . enjoyable
   (D) emaciated . . biased
   (E) susceptible . . meager

   9 ___

10. Charles made a --- bid to mend the broken relationship, but Laura --- refused to open his letter.

   (A) hopeless . . cheerfully
   (B) tentative . . disdainfully
   (C) lighthearted . . resentfully
   (D) fanatical . . casually
   (E) pointless . . modestly

   10 ___

Summary
Section III: Clues from Etymology

Review these clues from etymology from time to time. If you understand how etymology helps you learn new words, you'll do better on the SAT vocabulary test.

Clue 1 Latin Prefixes

Many English words begin with common Latin prefixes and number prefixes. Study these examples.

advance, **ex**it, **prin**cipal, **dec**imal, **tri**ple

Clue 2 Latin Roots—Verbs

English has more words from Latin than from any other language. One root can appear in several words.

re**fer**, con**fer**ence, trans**fer**, in**fer**red

Clue 3 Latin Roots—Nouns and Adjectives

If you know the root and prefix, you can figure out the meaning. If not, think of other words with the same elements. Then make a good guess.

benefac**tor**, **bene**diction, **fac**tory

Clue 4 Greek Prefixes and Roots

As with Latin, you can figure out words with Greek origins if you know the prefixes and roots. If not, think of similar words and make a guess.

autocra**tic**, **auto**biography, demo**cratic**

Clue 5 Anglo-Saxon Prefixes and Roots

Anglo-Saxon words are the everyday words. You already know the prefixes and roots because you use them all the time.

Clue 6 Suffixes

Suffixes are the third building block (after prefixes and roots). They give important clues to a word's part of speech, its meaning, and its history.

ampl**ify**, manage**able**, moder**ate**

Clue 7 Foreign Words in English

English is a great borrower. Find the stories in borrowed words to learn and remember them.

coach, tangerine, muslin, polka

Clue 8 The Growth of English

English keeps making new words, usually by putting together prefixes, roots, and suffixes. Words keep changing in meaning—uphill and down, broader and narrower.

Section IV: Clues from Analogies

You have undoubtedly noticed the *log* root in *analogy*. *Log* originally meant "word," but like words in English, the Greek word *logos* took on other meanings. Because words are crucial to thought, *log* was associated with thinking, as in *logic*. Then, since thinking involves weighing choices, *log* took on the additional meaning of "ratio" and "proportion." In fact, *analogy* comes from a Greek compound meaning "proportion," "in proper ratio."

In its broadest sense, an *analogy* is a *comparison*. Argument by analogy infers that two objects which are alike in some ways are also alike in another way. Here's a typical argument by analogy in a family.

> Johnny (age 10). Why can't I go on that whitewater canoe trip with Chuck and his friends? You're letting him go.
>
> Mother. Chuck is 18. He's had experience on rough water. He's an excellent swimmer, and you're not yet an accomplished swimmer. It's an expensive trip, and he's saved the needed money on his summer job.

Johnny is arguing from *analogy*. Because his brother is going, he feels he should be allowed to go, too. After all, they're both sons and should be given the same treatment. His mother knows that *argument by analogy is good only if the points of similarity outweigh the points of difference and there is no crucial difference.* She instinctively points out four essential differences: (1) Chuck is much older. (2) Chuck has had experience on whitewater trips. (3) He's an excellent swimmer. (4) He's paying for the trip himself.

In its simplest form, an analogy is like a mathematical equation.

$$2 : 4 :: 4 : 8$$

The equation says, "Two is to four as four is to eight." Four is twice two. In the same way, eight is twice four.

The SAT verbal sections use words, not numbers, to express relationships. The trick is to uncover what the word relationship is. Put an SAT-type question into equation form.

$$\text{swimming} : \text{water} :: \text{flying} : \text{air}$$

This equation says, "*Swimming* is to *water* as *flying* is to *air*." The relationship is clear. Water is the medium for swimming just as air is the medium for flying.

HOW TO DO ANALOGIES

To become familiar with the *form* of the analogy or word relationship questions, take the following test. For this warm-up activity, the relationships are synonyms or antonyms. This test will provide practice for taking the real test.

Trial Test

Write the letter for the word pair that best completes the analogy.

EXAMPLE

REPROOF : APPLAUSE :: ____A____

(A) harmony : controversy
(B) ignorance : indifference
(C) prejudice : mischief
(D) support : foundation
(E) nourishment : nutrition

Since **applause** is an antonym of **reproof**, look for a pair of antonyms. The only pair of antonyms is (A). The others are synonyms or unrelated. If the test words had been synonyms, then you'd look for synonyms in the answers.

1. EXHAUST : FATIGUE :: _____

(A) utensil : implement
(B) plunge : swim
(C) exertion : slumber
(D) confederation : officer
(E) generosity : greed

2. FRANKNESS : TRICKERY :: _____

(A) radical : tasty
(B) bankruptcy : insolvency
(C) benefit : harm
(D) memory : recollection
(E) mercy : commentary

3. AFFIRM : DENY :: _____

(A) converse : declare
(B) follow : pursue
(C) check : inhibit
(D) endeavor : attempt
(E) prosper : fail

4. MISFORTUNE : TRIBULATION :: _____

(A) affliction : sanitation
(B) fluid : food
(C) repute : uncertainty
(D) suggestion : denunciation
(E) injustice : unfairness

Answers to Trial Test

1. (*A*) Since **exhaust** and **fatigue** are synonyms, we need synonyms in our answer. *Plunge* and *swim* are neither synonyms nor antonyms. *Exertion* and *slumber* are opposed in meaning. An *officer* may be part of a *confederation*, but the words are not synonymous. *Generosity* and *greed* are opposed in meaning. The correct pair of words is (*A*), *utensil : implement*.

2. (*C*) **Frankness** and **trickery** are antonyms. We need antonyms in our answer. *Radical* and *tasty* are not related. *Bankruptcy* and *insolvency* are close in meaning. *Memory* and *recollection* are synonyms. *Mercy* and *commentary* are unrelated. The correct pair of words is (*C*), *benefit : harm*.

3. (*E*) **Affirm** and **deny** are antonyms. *Converse* and *declare* are loosely related. *Follow* and *pursue* are synonyms. *Check* and *inhibit* are synonyms, as are *endeavor* and *attempt*. (*E*), *Prosper* and *fail* are the antonyms we need.

4. (*E*) **Misfortune** and **tribulation** are synonyms. *Affliction* and *sanitation* are opposed in meaning. Fluid may be a food, but *fluid* and *food* are not synonyms. *Repute* and *uncertainty* are not related. *Suggestion* and *denunciation* are not related closely enough. (*E*), *Injustice* and *unfairness* are the synonyms we need.

25 TYPES OF ANALOGIES

You may find up to 25 types of analogies in achievement tests. For convenience, we will take up these types in groups of five, beginning with antonyms.

PART 1

Analogy Types A–E

TYPE A.   WORD : OPPOSED WORD

Problem

STRAIGHTFORWARD : LIAR :: _____
- (A) brilliant : genius
- (B) dreary : onlooker
- (C) popular : outcast
- (D) generous : friend
- (E) sympathetic : artisan

Strategy

Though this type of question is related to the antonym, there is a major difference. The two test words are of different parts of speech, *opposed* in meaning but *not* antonyms. A true antonym of **straightforward** would be *deceitful*, *dishonest*, *false*, or *untruthful*. Examine the other alternatives.

The idea of *brilliance* is associated with *genius*, not opposed to it. Eliminate (*A*). The idea of *dreariness* does not seem to be related to *onlooker*. Eliminate (*B*). The idea of *generosity* is more likely to be associated with *friend* than opposed to it. Eliminate (*D*). The idea of *sympathy* does not seem to be associated with an *artisan* (a skilled worker). Eliminate (*E*).

Elimination leaves us with (*C*). If you are *popular*, you will not be an *outcast*. *Popular* and *outcast* are opposed in meaning in the same way as are **straightforward** and **liar**. (*C*) is the correct answer. You may find the answer immediately without eliminating the others, but the process of elimination just demonstrated is an extra check.

It helps to put the analogy in the form of a sentence. In the example just given, the sentence would look like this:

Statement: If you are **straightforward**, then you will not be a **liar**.

Now put the alternatives into the same form to see how they fit.

- (*A*) If you are *brilliant*, then you will not be a *genius*.
- (*B*) If you are *dreary*, then you will not be an *onlooker*.
- (*C*) If you are *popular*, then you will not be an *outcast*.
- (*D*) If you are *generous*, then you will not be a *friend*.
- (*E*) If you are *sympathetic*, then you will not be an *artisan*.

Again (*C*) proves to be correct. You also have to know the word meanings to get the right answer.

Sometimes it helps to turn the word pair around. For the question just given, we might have constructed this sentence: A **liar** is not **straightforward**.

Both statements say essentially the same thing. Feel free to put your statement into the form most helpful to you. Always be sure that you keep the *same word order* when you test your possibilities in the statement.

Look at a question from the SAT.

Problem

IMMEDIATELY : DELAY :: _____

    (A) voluntarily : motive

    (B) urgently : aid

    (C) continuously : effort

    (D) flawlessly : error

    (E) accidentally : injury

Strategy

Once again the ideas are opposed, but the words are not antonyms. **Immediately** is an adverb and **delay** is a noun. (We can assume **delay** is not a verb here because the alternatives seem to have nouns as second words.) The ideas being contrasted are *immediate* action and *delayed* action.

Let's put the analogy into the form of a sentence.

Statement: If we act **immediately**, we'll not be subject to **delay**. We can put the alternatives into the same form.

    (A) If we act *voluntarily*, we'll not be subject to *motive*.

    (B) If we act *urgently*, we'll not be subject to *aid*.

    (C) If we act *continuously*, we'll not be subject to *effort*.

    (D) If we act *flawlessly*, we'll not be subject to *error*.

    (E) If we act *accidentally*, we'll not be subject to *injury*.

Clearly the only alternative that makes sense is *(D)*.

Some SAT questions, like this one, do not contain any difficult words. The problem is just to work out the relationship between the two test words. Sometimes, however, several words in the test are more challenging. Then you should draw upon the skills you learned earlier in this book.

Suppose, for example, you meet a pair like this: EUPHONIOUS : DISSONANT. A knowledge of common prefixes and roots is the key here. From *eu* (well) and *phon* (sound) we have a word meaning "having a beautiful sound," "harmonious." From *dis* ("apart") and *son* ("sound") we have a word with an opposite meaning: "having a bad combination of sounds," "discordant." These words are obviously antonyms.

The type of idea-opposition in the test question above is a frequent device in SAT analogy questions. Occasionally, however, idea-*similarity* appears in test words. Examine an SAT question.

TYPE B.   WORD : RELATED WORD

Problem

STRUT : OSTENTATIOUS :: _____
     (A) vacillate : modest
     (B) cringe : servile
     (C) flinch : indolent
     (D) waiver : arrogant
     (E) sputter : fastidious

Strategy

This time the words are almost synonymous in meaning, not opposed. As in the previous examples, however, the words are of different parts of speech. **Strut** is a verb and **ostentatious** is an adjective. To **strut** is to "walk showily, in a self-important way." Peacocks **strut**. Cocky persons **strut**. Persons who wear too much jewelry are **ostentatious**. People who act in extravagant ways are **ostentatious**. Call upon your previous associations with these words to get a sense of their central meaning. Then put the words into sentence form.

Statement: Those who **strut** are **ostentatious**.

If you put all the alternatives into sentence form, only one makes sense.

Those who *cringe* are *servile*.

Alternatives (*A*), (*C*), and (*E*) have words apparently unrelated. Alternative (*D*) has opposed words. Those who waiver are *not* likely to be arrogant. Alternative (*B*) is the correct answer.

Occasionally one of the words will be used figuratively. Study the following problem.

Problem

ADORN : EXAGGERATE :: _____
     (A) empower : diminish
     (B) replenish : reaffirm
     (C) furbish : absorb
     (D) soak : saturate
     (E) crochet : create

Strategy

Adorn and **exaggerate** are related, but how? The relationships in (*A*)–(*E*) are varied, but there is a pair of synonyms: *soak : saturate*. Could **adorn** and **exaggerate** be synonyms? Think of a sentence like the following:

Tom Sawyer loved to **adorn** his stories with fancy and imagination.

The word **adorn**, which basically means "add decorations to," has a figurative meaning. If we tell stories and *add decorations*, we **exaggerate**. The correct answer is (*D*).

TYPE C. PART : WHOLE—OR WHOLE : PART

Problem

HUB : WHEEL :: _____
(A) diameter : circle
(B) apex : triangle
(C) eye : hurricane
(D) clasp : tie
(E) top : desk

Strategy

The relationship between **hub** and **wheel** is that of the part to the whole. The relationship is a little more specific, though. What part of the wheel is the hub? The center. If we put the relationship into sentence form, it would look like this:

Statement: The hub is the center of the **wheel**.

Note that all the alternatives show the part-to-the-whole relationship, but only (*C*) has the exact relationship.

The *eye* is the center of the *hurricane*.

A hasty choice would be (*A*), since *circle* and **wheel** are so closely related. But the diameter is not the center of the circle.

Some questions are solved merely by finding general relationships, like *part : whole*. If *eye : hurricane* did not appear on this question, you'd be able to take the general answer, *diameter : circle*. Often, however, you must find special relationships within the general relationships, as in this question. The hub is not just *part* of the wheel. It's the *center* of the wheel. The eye is not just *part* of the hurricane. It's the *center* of the hurricane.

Remember that all the terms in this question could have been inverted without changing the essential relationship.

WHEEL : HUB :: hurricane : eye

As we analyze other analogies questions, consider that the relationships might also be expressed in inverted form. It would not, however, be correct to choose the following relationship.

HUB : WHEEL :: hurricane : eye

It's all right to reverse both pairs, but *not just one*.

TYPE D. CAUSE: EFFECT

Problem

WINCE : PAIN :: _____

    (A) forget : confidence
    (B) tremble : fright
    (C) grovel : embarrassment
    (D) glower : anguish
    (E) growl : delight

Strategy

In this question from a past SAT, **wince** and **pain** are directly related by cause and effect. **Pain** is the cause and **wince** is the effect.

Statement: **Pain** causes a person to **wince**.

Now if we put the possible answers into statement form, only one makes sense.

Fright causes a person to *tremble*.

The question might have been harder. One of the possible answers for (*A*) might have been *laugh : joke*. This possible answer also shows a causal relationship. A *joke* causes a person to *laugh*. Answer (*B*) is still better, however, because *fright* and **pain** are both negative, while *joke* is positive.

TYPE E. CONTAINER : SOMETHING CONTAINED

Problem

VALUABLES : SAFE :: _____

    (A) jewelry : gemstone
    (B) water : droplet
    (C) dessert : dish
    (D) corn : granary
    (E) fish : ocean

Strategy

This is a popular type of question, appearing in many forms. Here the container is **safe** and the thing contained, **valuables**. Put the relationship into statement form.

Statement: **Valuables** are stored in a **safe**.

Although *dessert* is *served* on a *dish*, it is not *stored* in a dish. We can reject (*C*). Although *fish* live in the *ocean*, they are not stored in the ocean. Note that the relationship is one where the storing is done by people. People store valuables in a safe. The correct answer is clearly (*D*). *Corn* is stored in a *granary*.

Time Out for Review

Type A. Word : Opposed Word
Type B. Word : Related Word
Type C. Part : Whole
Type D. Cause : Effect
Type E. Container : Something Contained

The five analogy types appear in the following five questions, but in a different order. Try your skill. To get you started, a statement is provided for the first question.

Write the letter for the word pair that best completes the analogy.

1. GROUCHY : COMPLAINER :: _____
   (A) dry : desert
   (B) flaky : teacup
   (C) pitiless : celebrity
   (D) comical : tragedian
   (E) barren : poetry

   Statement: **A complainer** tends to be **grouchy**.

2. STEM : LEAF :: _____
   (A) dog : kennel
   (B) wall switch : lamp
   (C) landscaping : house
   (D) toe : foot
   (E) letter : stamp

3. DEFIANT : RESIGNATION :: _____
   (A) vigorous : health
   (B) humdrum : weakness
   (C) commonplace : situation
   (D) lovable : laughter
   (E) humble : arrogance

4. HANGAR : AIRPLANE :: _____
   (A) waterfall : water
   (B) clock : numerals
   (C) book : novel
   (D) route : directions
   (E) terminal : bus

5. OPERATION : SCAR :: _____
   (A) fire : ashes
   (B) substitution : replacement
   (C) repetition : novelty
   (D) explosion : blast
   (E) landslide : tunnel

SUMMARY PART 1

Clues from Analogies: Types A–E

Type A. Word : Opposed Word
STRAIGHTFORWARD : LIAR :: popular : outcast

Type B. Word : Related Word
STRUT : OSTENTATIOUS :: cringe : servile

Type C. Part : Whole—or Whole : Part
HUB : WHEEL :: eye : hurricane

Type D. Cause : Effect
WINCE : PAIN :: tremble : fright

Type E. Container : Something Contained
VALUABLES : SAFE :: corn : granary

PART 2

Analogy Types, F–J

TYPE F. TOOL: ACTIVITY OR OBJECT
Problem

RACKET : TENNIS :: _____

    (A) puck : hockey
    (B) rifle : duck
    (C) hammer : nail
    (D) ball : soccer
    (E) bat : baseball

Strategy

Obviously this is a tool or implement and the activity or object it is used for. Put this analogy into statement form.

Statement: A **racket** is used in the activity of **tennis**.

Put the various possibilities into statement form.

(*A*) A *puck* is used in the activity of *hockey*.
(*B*) A *rifle* is used in the activity of *duck*.
(*C*) A *hammer* is used in the activity of *nail*.
(*D*) A *ball* is used in the activity of *soccer*.
(*E*) A *bat* is used in the activity of *baseball*.

We can discard (*B*) and (*C*) immediately, but (*A*), (*D*), and (*E*) all seem possible. When such a situation occurs, you must refine the statement even more. What is the special relationship between **racket** and **tennis**? A **racket** is held in the hand. When we spot that special relationship, we discard (*A*) and (*D*). We decide that (*E*) is correct. A *bat*, like a **racket**, is held in the hand.

We can state the special relationship like this.

A **racket**, held in the hand, is used in the activity of **tennis**.

TYPE G. LESSER : GREATER DEGREE OF INTENSITY
Problem

RIPPLE : TIDAL WAVE :: _____

    (A) breeze : hurricane
    (B) blizzard : avalanche
    (C) valley : earthquake
    (D) puddle : downpour
    (E) rock : waterfall

Strategy

What is the relationship of **ripple** to **tidal wave**? Both are obviously waves of a kind. A ripple is a tiny wave. A tidal wave is an enormous wave. The two objects are similar, but they differ enormously in degree. Look at the statement.

Statement: A **ripple** is a very minor form of a **tidal wave**.

If we try the statement with all the possibilities, only one makes sense: (*A*) breeze : hurricane. A breeze is a very minor form of a hurricane.

Though the other possibilities all show relationships, the relationships are not the same. A *puddle* is small compared with a *downpour*, but a puddle is not a small *form* of a downpour. It's the *result*. A *blizzard* may cause an *avalanche*, but a blizzard is not a small form of an avalanche. A *valley* may be created by an *earthquake* or afflicted by an earthquake, but the two are not related in intensity. *Rock* and *waterfall* are associated in space but not in degree.

TYPE H.   SMALLER : LARGER

Problem

MILL : PENNY :: _____

       (A) silver : quarter
       (B) currency : nickel
       (C) dime : dollar
       (D) check : cash
       (E) wallet : money

Strategy

A **mill** is a "thousandth of a cent." (Remember the number prefix *mill*? See page 89.) Though it is not an actual coin, it is used in various tax computations. The relationship, expressed in statement form, is simple.

Statement: A **mill** is a smaller percentage of a **penny**.

Silver is not a smaller percentage of a *quarter*. Silver is actually no longer used in a quarter. *Currency* is not a smaller percentage of a *nickel*. A nickel is currency. A *check* is not a smaller percentage of *cash*. A check is an alternative to cash. A *wallet* is not a smaller percentage of *money*. A wallet holds money. The only possible answer is (*C*), *dime : dollar*. A *dime* is a smaller percentage of a *dollar*.

TYPE I.   GENERAL TERM : SPECIFIC TERM

Problem

TALK : WHISPER :: _____

    (A) discover : deteriorate
    (B) fly : tour
    (C) listen : disagree
    (D) walk : amble
    (E) jump : marvel

Strategy

Both **talk** and **whisper** refer to the same basic activity, but one is a general term and one is specific. Put the relationship into statement form.

Statement: **Whispering** is a special kind of **talking**.

The only possibility is (D), *walk : amble*. *Ambling* is a special kind of *walking*.

TYPE J.   ACTION : OBJECT ACTED UPON

Problem

WEAVE : CLOTH :: _____

    (A) destroy : barricade
    (B) write : narrative
    (C) call : messenger
    (D) droop : trees
    (E) reduce : statue

Strategy

The simplest relationship is verb-object.

Statement: Someone **weaves cloth**.

The best answer is (B), *write : narrative*. Someone *writes* a *narrative*.

Both (A) and (C) make sense in the statement, but there is an important difference between these and the example pair. **Weaving cloth** is positive, constructive, creative. So is *writing a narrative*. There is, however, nothing particularly constructive in *destroying a barricade* or *calling a messenger*. Sometimes you have to take your statement a step further when you see how the various possibilities fit into the statement framework. If you wanted to revise the statement, it might look something like this.

Statement: Someone **weaves cloth** and performs a constructive action.

Time Out for Review

Type F.   Tool : Activity or Object
Type G.   Lesser : Greater Degree of Intensity
Type H.   Smaller : Larger
Type I.   General Term : Specific Term
Type J.   Action : Object Acted Upon

The five analogy types appear in the following five questions. Try your skill.

1. LAUGH : GUFFAW :: _____

   (A) look : scrutinize
   (B) lead : follow
   (C) discover : invent
   (D) drive : putt
   (E) missive : arrow

2. PLANE : CARPENTRY :: _____

   (A) beetle : gardening
   (B) tree : forestry
   (C) reel : fishing
   (D) house : painting
   (E) tiger : cage

3. SING : ARIA :: _____

   (A) devour : pastry
   (B) recite : poem
   (C) win : encounter
   (D) approve : decision
   (E) allow : exception

4. BOOKLET : TOME :: _____

   (A) essay : biography
   (B) tree : shrub
   (C) lake : waterfall
   (D) friend : foe
   (E) kitten : cat

5. ANNOY : ENRAGE :: _____

   (A) annex : reject
   (B) erase : disapprove
   (C) disembark : enlist
   (D) emancipate : flatter
   (E) decorate : embellish

SUMMARY PART 2

Clues from Analogies: Types F–J

Type F.   Tool : Activity or Object
              RACKET : TENNIS :: bat : baseball

Type G.   Lesser : Greater Degree of Intensity
              RIPPLE : TIDAL WAVE :: breeze : hurricane

Type H.   Smaller : Larger
              MILL : PENNY :: dime : dollar

Type I.   General Term : Specific Term
              TALK : WHISPER :: walk : amble

Type J.   Action : Object Acted Upon
              WEAVE : CLOTH :: write : narrative

Remember, if you think of analogies as challenging games rather than difficult types of verbal questions, you will have an easier time preparing for this part of the SAT.

PART 3

Analogy Types K–O

In this group of analogy types, someone is related to an activity, a quality, an instrument, a purpose, or a place. Look at some of these specifically.

TYPE K. PERSONS: WHAT THEY DO OR ACT UPON

Problem

MAGICIAN : DELUDES :: _____

    (A) potentate : obeys
    (B) swimmer : relaxes
    (C) comedian : entertains
    (D) welder : rivets
    (E) acrobat : complains

Strategy

Here someone is doing something to someone. The statement is simple.

Statement: The **magician deludes** an audience.

The only alternative that fits is (*C*), *comedian : entertains*. The *comedian entertains* an audience.

Although the other possibilities show someone doing something, they lack the idea of an audience associated with *magician*. After you have decided upon the relationship and checked the other possible answers, you may have to make the relationship a little more specific.

The question above showed the relationship between the person, the **magician**, and the verb **deludes**. Sometimes a question will show the relationship between the person and an object.

LOGGER : TREES

The **logger** acts upon the **trees**. A correct pair would have to show a similar relationship—for example, *farmer : wheatfield*.

In questions of this type an *animal* might replace a *person*:

MOLE : LAWN

A mole certainly acts upon a lawn.

TYPE L.   PERSON : QUALITY OR CONDITION ASSOCIATED WITH

Problem

PILGRIM : PIETY :: _____

    (A) explorer : curiosity
    (B) miser : poverty
    (C) gambler : winner
    (D) knight : beauty
    (E) monk : loneliness

Strategy

The relationship here is one of an essential quality. **Piety** is the central core of a **pilgrim**. The statement might look like this.

Statement: The essential quality of a **pilgrim** is **piety**.

Now analyze the answers. The essential quality of an *explorer* is indeed *curiosity*. (*A*) seems to be the correct answer, but try the others. *Poverty* is not the essential quality of a *miser*, though under certain circumstances a miser might be poor. Being a *winner* is, unfortunately, not an essential quality of a *gambler*. Losing may outweigh winning. *Beauty* is not the essential quality of a *knight*. Some monks may be lonely, but *loneliness* is not the essential quality of a *monk*. A monk usually chooses the monastery because he is able to be alone much of the time. (*A*) is indeed correct.

Don't be misled by similar words in the choices. In this question you might associate **pilgrim** and *monk*, since both have religious motivations. The relationship between **pilgrim** and **piety** on the one hand and between *monk* and *loneliness* on the other are not similar. Always look for relationships, not merely associations or shared meanings of a word in each pair.

TYPE M.   PERSON : PERSON, SUBJECT, OR PLACE ASSOCIATED WITH

Problem

LABORATORY : TECHNICIAN :: _____

    (A) stream : trout
    (B) studio : sculptor
    (C) factory : ranger
    (D) discovery : scientist
    (E) play : musician

Strategy

The relationship is between a worker and the place he works in. The statement is simple.

Statement: A **technician** works in a **laboratory**.

Though a *trout* is indeed found in a *stream*, it does not work there. The correct answer is (*B*), *studio : sculptor*. A *sculptor* works in a *studio*.

Note that we have reversed the order of words in our statement. We might also have created this statement.

Statement: A **laboratory** is a place where a **technician** works.

The first statement is a little simpler. It doesn't matter whether or not we reverse the paired words. The important point is to test the possibilities in the same order.

A *studio* is a place where a *sculptor* works.

TYPE N.   PERSON : PURPOSE

Problem

ALCHEMIST : TRANSMUTATION :: _____
- (A) traitor : loyalty
- (B) proselytizer : conversion
- (C) scientist : equivocation
- (D) anarchist : tranquillity
- (E) astronomer : consternation

Strategy

Here the relationship is between a person and his major goal. An alchemist sought to transmute baser metals into gold. Here's the statement.

Statement: A major purpose of the **alchemist** was **transmutation**.

As we have already noted, some analogies present fairly easy words, with the major problem that of finding relationships. Other analogies, however, present more difficult words as here. In your own reading you probably have come across the word **alchemist**. If you have, you probably remember the two major goals of these forerunners of modern chemistry: finding the elixir (or lengthener) of life and transmuting (or changing) other metals into gold. If you cannot recall anything about alchemists, your best course is an educated guess, using whatever clues you can derive from the pairs of words provided. *Even if you don't know one or both of the original pair, you can deduce the answer just by studying the possible answers.*

You know immediately that *loyalty* does not go with *traitor*. This is a negative association. You also know that *tranquillity* is not likely to go with *anarchist*. This is another negative association. If there are two negative pairs, the answer probably is *not* a negative pair. (Otherwise there might be a conflict between the two.) *Consternation* does not go with *astronomer*. (*Constellation* would be possible, but not *consternation*.) We now have three negative pairs.

Look further at the problem. *Equivocation* by derivation means "speaking equally." Equivocation is using terms with two or more possible meanings, being confusing. Scientists try to avoid being confusing. Thus (*C*) contains another negative pair. Negative elements are contained in all but (*B*). Thus (*B*) would be a good guess. As it happens, those who proselytize do try to convert. Just as **alchemists** are interested in **transmutation**, so *proselytizers* are interested in *conversion*.

This detailed analysis shows that even seemingly hopeless situations sometimes yield to careful analysis. Don't spend an excessive amount of time on any one question, however. (Review recommended procedures on page 164.) But if you do have time, don't give up without calling upon all your resources.

TYPE O. PERSON OR ACTIVITY : IMPORTANT TOOL

Problem

GARDENER : HOE :: _____
- (A) welder : apron
- (B) halfback : helmet
- (C) astronomer : chart
- (D) woodsman : axe
- (E) weaver : saw

Strategy

The relationship between **hoe** and **gardener** is that between tool and worker. A glance at the other possibilities suggests we have to be more specific. We cannot just say, "A **gardener** uses a **hoe**." A *welder* uses an *apron*. A *halfback* uses a *helmet*. An *astronomer* uses a *chart*. We can, at any rate, immediately discard (*E*). A *weaver* does not use a *saw*. But how shall we discriminate among the others? A **gardener** applies the **hoe** to the materials he or she works with. In the same way a *woodsman* applies the *axe* to the material he works with. Garden soil and wood are materials handled by hoe and axe. We can discard the other possibilities and word the sentence like this.

Statement: The **gardener** uses an important hand tool, the **hoe**.

Since *helmet*, *apron*, and *chart* are not tools in the same sense, we can be sure (*D*), *woodsman : axe* is the correct answer.

Here's a variation of the relationship just analyzed.

GARDENING : HOE

With this question you must find a similar relationship—for example, *lumbering : axe*.

Time Out for Review

Type K. Persons : What They Do or Act Upon
Type L. Person : Quality or Condition Associated With
Type M. Person : Person, Subject, or Place Associated With
Type N. Person : Purpose
Type O. Person or Activity : Important Tool

The five analogy types appear in the following five questions. Try your skill.

1. ROGUE : GUILE :: _____

   (A) dentist : drill
   (B) doctor : surgeon
   (C) philanthropist : generosity
   (D) denizen : cruelty
   (E) recluse : joy

2. CONDUCTOR : BATON :: _____

   (A) violin : bow
   (B) magician : wand
   (C) soldier : spectacles
   (D) globetrotter : shoes
   (E) senator : representative

3. COMBATANT : VICTORY :: _____

   (A) programmer : computer
   (B) professor : travel
   (C) pyromaniac : surgery
   (D) penitent : forgiveness
   (E) photographer : silhouette

4. INTERN : HOSPITAL :: _____

   (A) farmer : factory
   (B) flight attendant : travel agency
   (C) teller : bank
   (D) navigator : classroom
   (E) author : theater

5. ANGLER : CASTS :: _____

   (A) golfer : drives
   (B) soprano : sings
   (C) entrepreneur : loses
   (D) economist : delays
   (E) contributor : peruses

SUMMARY PART 3

Clues from Analogies: Types K–O

Type K. Persons : What They Do or Act Upon
MAGICIAN : DELUDES :: comedian : entertains

Type L. Person : Quality or Condition Associated With
PILGRIM : PIETY :: explorer : curiosity

Type M. Person : Person, Subject, or Place Associated With
LABORATORY : TECHNICIAN :: studio : sculptor

Type N. Person : Purpose
ALCHE-
MIST : TRANSMUTATION :: proselytizer : conversion

Type O. Person or Activity : Important Tool
GARDENER : HOE :: woodsman : axe

PART 4

Analogy Types P–T

In this group, relationships are expressed between something and something else: an activity, a quality, an instrument, a purpose, a place, a result. Examine some of these relationships.

TYPE P. SOMETHING : ASSOCIATED QUALITY

The associated quality may be negative as well as positive. Note the following SAT question:

PROBLEM

CIRCUMLOCUTORY : SPEECH :: _____

     (A) humorous : joke
     (B) meandering : path
     (C) tactless : remark
     (D) successful : attack
     (E) logical : conclusion

Strategy

Circumlocutory is a quality associated with some speeches. Here the special relationship is the indirectness of the speech. All five choices show associated qualities, like a *humorous joke* or a *tactless remark*. Here the special quality is the wandering nature of the speech. Therefore (*B*), *meandering : path* is correct. Just as some speeches wander, so some paths meander. Note that the associated word **circumlocutory** has a negative connotation. The associations may not always be positive. Look at another example.

Problem

OBSOLESCENCE : DISUSED :: _____

     (A) diversity : varied
     (B) obstinacy : voided
     (C) disability : vigorous
     (D) investigation : thorough
     (E) distress : curious

Strategy

If **obsolescence** is an unfamiliar word, you can use the smaller word inside the word as a clue: *obsolete*. You may recall the suffix *escent* meaning *becoming*. **Obsolescence** is the "condition of becoming obsolete, out of date." The helpful prefix *dis*, meaning *not*, suggests that **disused** means "not being used."

We can summarize the relationship here in our usual statement.

Statement: In **obsolescence**, things are inevitably **disused**.

The first possibility, (*A*) immediately pops out as an answer.

In *diversity*, things are inevitably *varied*.

Look at the other possibilities. The only one that must give us pause is (*D*).

In *investigation*, things are inevitably *thorough*.

Being *disused* is an essential characteristic of *obsolescence*. Being *thorough* is not an essential characteristic of *investigation*. An investigation may be careless, sloppy, or superficial.

The correct answer, (*A*), *diversity : varied*, best shows the relationship.

TYPE Q.   SOMETHING : A FORM OR DEGREE OF

Problem

DISAGREEMENT : ALTERCATION :: ―――――
- (A) distress : upset
- (B) equality : compensation
- (C) scheme : conspiracy
- (D) correspondence : envy
- (E) construction : blueprint

Strategy

An **altercation** is a form of **disagreement**. More specifically, it shows a greater degree of **disagreement**. An altercation is a heated, angry disagreement. The sentence might look like this.

Statement: An **altercation** is a more intense form of **disagreement**.

A *conspiracy* is a more intense form of *scheme*.

If we try the various possibilities we find that (*C*) fits.

Distress is a more intense form of *upset*, but the words are reversed, so (*A*), *distress : upset*, is incorrect. Although *blueprint* and *construction* (*E*) are related, *blueprint* is a help in *construction*. It is not a more intense form of *construction*.

You may not know one of the words in the example pair. If there are no clues within the unfamiliar word, try to guess the meaning by examining the possible answers. There is little apparent relationship between the paired words in (B) and (D). In (E), *blueprint* is used to guide *construction*. It is unlikely that an altercation (even if you don't know it) is used to *guide* argument. Eliminating (B), (D), and (E) reduces the possibilities to two and increases your chances of guessing right.

If you look at (A) and (C), you notice that one member in each pair is a more intense form of the other. **Disagreement** is negative, and so are *distress* and *scheme*. Both are good possibilities. Which shall you choose? Is **disagreement** a more intense form of **altercation**, or is **altercation** a more intense form of **disagreement**? Since **disagreement** is a fairly mild word, **altercation** is probably a more intense form. Thus you could guess that (C) is the answer even if you're not exactly sure what **altercation** means.

If you have time, you'll find many unexpected clues in the way the analogies are arranged and paired.

TYPE R.   SOMETHING : SOMETHING AFFECTED BY OR ASSOCIATED WITH

Problem

PLOW : SOIL :: _____

    (A) message : decipher
    (B) grow : vegetables
    (C) wear : clothes
    (D) prune : fruit trees
    (E) reach : solution

Strategy

Here something is being affected by an object. The **soil** is **plowed**. We can reject (A) because the words are reversed. We may *decipher* a *message*. We don't *message* a *decipher*. All the other possibilities seem to fit—on first check. We can *grow vegetables, wear clothes, prune fruit trees,* and *reach a solution*. Is there some special characteristic of plowing soil? Plowing involves cutting into the soil. *Pruning* involves cutting into branches of trees. The special relationship calls for (D), *prune : fruit trees*.

Statement: We **plow soil** by cutting into it.

Look at another example.

Often the relationship is quite specialized.

Problem

PARCHMENT : PAPER :: _____

(A) dog : kennel
(B) friend : acquaintance
(C) quill : ballpoint pen
(D) table : dining room
(E) title page : book

Strategy

All five possibilities are associated in some way. The task is to find the right relationship. Parchment was used before paper and eventually gave way to paper for all but highly specialized uses. In the same way a quill gave way to a ballpoint pen. Thus, (C), quill : ballpoint pen, is correct.

TYPE S. SOMETHING : SOMETHING STUDIED

Problem

PSYCHOLOGY : PERSONALITY :: _____

(A) physiology : philosophy
(B) genetics : heredity
(C) botany : animals
(D) ecology : finance
(E) oceanography : shipbuilding

Strategy

The relationship is that between a science and the subject of study.

Statement: **Psychology** is the study of **personality**.

Substituting the possible answers we find that (B), *genetics : heredity*, fits perfectly.

Genetics is the study of *heredity*.

Botany (C) is the study of plants, not *animals*. *Physiology* (A) is not related to *philosophy*. *Ecology* (D) has little direct relationship with *finance*. Shipbuilders (E) may help oceanographers by providing transportation, but the relationship stops at that point.

TYPE T. SOMETHING : UNIT OF MEASUREMENT

Problem

DISTANCE : KILOMETERS :: _____

      (A) emotion : laughter
      (B) duration : years
      (C) achievement : salary
      (D) light : brilliance
      (E) surgery : scalpel

Strategy

Our statement is simple.

Statement: **Distance** is measured in units called **kilometers**.

The best possibility is (*B*), *duration : years*.

        Duration is measured in units called *years*.

Emotion (*A*) and *laughter* are associated, but laughter is not a unit of measurement. *Brilliance* (*D*) is a quality of *light*, but again it is not a unit of measurement. *Scalpel* (*E*) is an instrument used in *surgery*, but it doesn't measure. To some people, *salary* may be a measure of *achievement*, but in any case salary is not a unit of measurement. If *dollars* had been provided instead of *salary*, you'd still have chosen (*B*). *Years* is a universally accepted unit of elapsed time. Dollars is not a universally accepted unit of achievement.

Time Out for Review

Type P.   Something : Associated Quality
Type Q.   Something : Form or Degree of
Type R.   Something : Something Affected by
          or Associated With
Type S.   Something : Something Studied
Type T.   Something : Unit of Measurement

The five analogy types appear in the following five questions. Try your skill. Write the letter for the pair that best completes each analogy.

1. HAPPINESS : ECSTASY :: _____

    (A) havoc : alertness
    (B) envy : boredom
    (C) valor : trust
    (D) depression : enthusiasm
    (E) fear : terror

2. CARTOGRAPHY : MAPS :: _____

    (A) ballistics : projectiles
    (B) hydraulics : sailboats
    (C) anatomy : surgeons
    (D) astronomy : physics
    (E) mineralogy : coins

3. DOLDRUMS : SLUGGISH :: _____

    (A) jollity : boring
    (B) elation : confusing
    (C) courage : fearless
    (D) assurance : blessed
    (E) compulsion : voluntary

4. CAPACITY : PECK :: _____

    (A) bushel : quart
    (B) size : nibble
    (C) pound : kilogram
    (D) volume : liquid
    (E) area : acre

5. EDIT : MANUSCRIPT :: _____

    (A) find : excuses
    (B) swallow : medication
    (C) revise : plans
    (D) scan : billboards
    (E) win : contest

SUMMARY PART 4

Clues from Analogies: Types P–T

Type P.   Something : Associated Quality
        OBSOLESCENCE : DISUSED :: diversity : varied

Type Q.   Something : A Form or Degree of
        DISAGREEMENT : ALTERCATION :: scheme : conspiracy

Type R.   Something : Something Affected by or Associated With
        PLOW : SOIL :: prune : fruit trees

Type S.   Something : Something Studied
        PSYCHOLOGY : PERSONALITY :: genetics : heredity

Type T.   Something : Unit of Measurement
        DISTANCE : KILOMETERS :: duration : years

The twenty analogy types provide a solid basis for attacking the analogy questions on the SAT. The strategies have shown you how to proceed and how to make the best use of your abilities and background. Sometimes the relationships will be in slightly different form, but the skills developed in this chapter will enable you to meet them all with some confidence.

You may find additional examples, often variations of the 20 already presented.

Type U. RAM : EWE (gender—
         male : female)
Type V. ABDICATE : ABDICATION (part
         of speech—verb : noun)
Type W. SHEEP : LAMB (par-
         ent : offspring)
Type X. STITCH : TIME (elements of one
         proverb : elements of another
         proverb)
Type Y. PHOENIX : IMMORTALITY
         (symbol : thing symbolized)

Time Out for Review

The five analogy types just mentioned appear in the following five questions. Try your skill. Remember: after you have formed the statement for each test pair, be sure you try out the possibilities in the same order as in your statement.

Write the letter for the word pair that best completes each analogy.

1. PUMPKIN : HALLOWEEN :: _____
   (A) election : ballot box
   (B) roast beef : Wyoming
   (C) money : finance
   (D) turkey : Thanksgiving
   (E) puppy : child

2. LOOK : LEAP :: _____
   (A) smoke : fire
   (B) horse : cart
   (C) babes : toyland
   (D) try : succeed
   (E) invest : speculate

3. MARE : COLT :: _____
   (A) lion : panther
   (B) cow : calf
   (C) cub : bear
   (D) egg : chicken
   (E) larva : butterfly

4. WIZARD : WITCH :: _____
   (A) countess : count
   (B) elk : moose
   (C) pickerel : pike
   (D) nephew : niece
   (E) grandfather : grandson

5. ATONE : ATONEMENT :: _____
   (A) firm : firmament
   (B) believe : adore
   (C) repeat : repetition
   (D) reconciliation : agreement
   (E) invigorate : renewal

Review Test
Clues from Analogies

Write the letter for the word pair that best completes each analogy.

1. NEUTRON : ATOM :: _____
   (A) circus : performer
   (B) molecule : quark
   (C) drop : lake
   (D) puppy : wolfhound
   (E) earth : satellite

2. HERD : SHEEP :: _____
   (A) meadow : ox
   (B) eyrie : eagle
   (C) pack : wolf
   (D) covey : lion
   (E) school : hamsters

3. GARRULOUS : TALKATIVE :: _____
   (A) placid : tranquil
   (B) noisy : considerate
   (C) wealthy : generous
   (D) complete : detailed
   (E) ethical : social

4. COOL : FRIGID :: _____
   (A) hot : lukewarm
   (B) fierce : gentle
   (C) vital : significant
   (D) unpleasant : contemptible
   (E) cold : north

5. PHARMACIST : PRESCRIPTION :: ____
   (A) diagnosis : doctor
   (B) baker : pastry
   (C) accountant : tax
   (D) veterinarian : horse
   (E) steeplejack : race

6. KITH : KIN :: _____
   (A) cousin : opponent
   (B) time : tide
   (C) neighbor : acquaintance
   (D) friend : enemy
   (E) buyer : seller

7. SMELL : FRAGRANT :: _____
   (A) touch : earsplitting
   (B) sound : tuneful
   (C) sight : slow
   (D) taste : musical
   (E) thought : fearful

8. VASE : FLOWERS :: _____
   (A) urn : barrel
   (B) apiary : bees
   (C) jar : glass
   (D) bowl : stove
   (E) kettle : handle

9. STING : SWELLING :: _____
   (A) wasp : anger
   (B) poison ivy : rash
   (C) flood : storm
   (D) thunder : lightning
   (E) infection : cut

10. BALLERINA : BALLET :: _____
    (A) carpenter : wrench
    (B) stage director : play
    (C) soprano : cantata
    (D) prima donna : marathon
    (E) cameraman : film

Summary
Section IV: Clues from Analogies

1. An analogy is a comparison.
2. The analogies question on the SAT compares two sets of words.
3. The question, stated in the form of an incomplete equation, evaluates the relationship of two pairs of words.
4. The words in the second pair must show the same relationship to each other as the words in the first pair.
5. Relationships are many and varied. The best way to evaluate each relationship is to put it into statement form. Substitute possible answers to find the correct pair.

Analogies are important! 20 SAT questions are analogies.

VOCABULARY DIAGNOSTIC TESTS

Now you have an opportunity to practice the vocabulary skills and strategies you have been using. First take Part A of the test. Allow yourself 30 minutes. Check your answers and go over the analysis for each of the 25 items. Note your incorrect answers. The page numbers in the Answers and Analysis Section will tell you where to turn in this book for additional help and strategy review.

Next take Part B of the test. See how your score compares with Part A. Study the reference pages for those items that you did not answer correctly or were not sure of the answer.

Find your weaknesses well in advance of the SAT testing date so that you will have ample time to work on the types of test items that you find most difficult. Remember you are building your personal power to take the SAT with confidence.

Vocabulary Diagnostic Test A

PART 1

For each question in this section, choose the best answer and write the letter for your choice in the space provided.

Each question below consists of a word in capital letters, followed by five lettered words or phrases. Choose the word or phrase that is most nearly *opposite in meaning* to the word in capital letters. Since some of the questions require you to distinguish fine shades of meaning, consider all the choices before deciding which is best.

EXAMPLE

GOOD:

(A) sour   (D) hot
(B) bad   (E) ugly
(C) red

<u>B</u>

1. CLARIFY:
   (A) bake   (D) direct
   (B) conceal   (E) elucidate
   (C) reopen

   1 ____

2. EMBITTERED:
   (A) unsweetened   (D) joyous
   (B) caustic   (E) hapless
   (C) aroused

   2 ____

3. ABSURD:
   (A) farcical   (D) threadbare
   (B) unhappy   (E) meaningful
   (C) unrelated

   3 ____

4. ALTRUISTIC:
   (A) otherworldly   (D) gentle
   (B) selfish   (E) gloomy
   (C) changeable

   4 ____

5. IMPEDE:
   (A) control   (D) collapse
   (B) desert   (E) fight
   (C) abet

   5 ____

6. IMPERTURBABLE:
   (A) dull   (D) excitable
   (B) interested (E) repeatable
   (C) invisible

   6 ____

7. BURN-OUT:
   (A) renewal
   (B) contemplation
   (C) collapse
   (D) conflagration
   (E) extinction

7 ___

8. AMORPHOUS:
   (A) misshapen
   (B) medical
   (C) symmetrical
   (D) overpowering
   (E) powerful

8 ___

9. IMPAIRED:
   (A) duplicated
   (B) seized
   (C) separated
   (D) approached
   (E) restored

9 ___

10. EQUITABLE:
    (A) unjust
    (B) lively
    (C) apparent
    (D) eventful
    (E) habitable

10 ___

PART 2

Each sentence below has one or two blanks, each blank indicating that something has been omitted. Beneath the sentence are five lettered words or sets of words. Choose the word or set of words that *best* fits the meaning of the sentence as a whole.

EXAMPLE

Although its publicity has been ---, the film itself is intelligent, well-acted, handsomely produced, and altogether ---.
   (A) tasteless..respectable
   (B) extensive..moderate
   (C) sophisticated..amateur
   (D) risqué..crude
   (E) perfect..spectacular

A

11. Despite the director's --- after the disastrous dress rehearsal, the opening night performance was a total success, with many curtain calls at its conclusion.
    (A) excitement
    (B) smugness
    (C) apathy
    (D) vigor
    (E) foreboding

11 ___

12. Indiana Jones seemed to have a --- love of danger, inherited, no doubt, from some swashbuckling adventurer in Francis Drake's navy.
    (A) tiresome
    (B) negative
    (C) congenital
    (D) grisly
    (E) rational

12 ___

13. Although Mandy --- responsibility for the accident, the jury decided it was a clear case of . . . on her part.
    (A) denied . . attentiveness
    (B) disclaimed . . negligence
    (C) accepted . . boredom
    (D) assigned . . dexterity
    (E) misinterpreted . . clairvoyance

13 ___

14. Unlike De Kooning, who --- the perils of modern living, his artist ---, Gorky, Smith, and Pollock, died tragic deaths.
    (A) belittled . . henchmen
    (B) delineated . . characters
    (C) survived . . peers
    (D) accepted . . namesakes
    (E) attacked . . kinsmen

14 ___

15. Charles Wheatstone, --- genius, --- the development of the telegraph, antedating Samuel F. B. Morse's famous demonstration by seven years.
    (A) unsung . . pioneered
    (B) erratic . . copied
    (C) conceited . . described
    (D) willful . . observed
    (E) notorious . . impeded

15 ___

PART 3

Each question below consists of a related pair of words or phrases, followed by five lettered pairs of words or phrases. Select the lettered pair that *best* expresses a relationship similar to that expressed in the original pair.

EXAMPLE

YAWN : BOREDOM ::
- (A) dream : sleep
- (B) anger : madness
- (C) smile : amusement
- (D) face : expression
- (E) impatience : rebellion

C

16. CANDID : HYPOCRITE ::
- (A) insatiable : glutton
- (B) curious : expert
- (C) cheerful : scientist
- (D) angelic : fiend
- (E) component : executive

16 ___

17. AQUARIUM : GUPPY ::
- (A) terrarium : lion
- (B) letter : file
- (C) dog : kennel
- (D) automobile : street
- (E) safe : jewelry

17 ___

18. GOLF : PUTTER ::
- (A) mallet : croquet
- (B) javelin : track
- (C) knitting : needle
- (D) football : line judge
- (E) cooking : onion

18 ___

19. POUND : KILOGRAM ::
- (A) century : year
- (B) foot : yard
- (C) liter : quart
- (D) centimeter : gram
- (E) calorie : heat

19 ___

20. REFEREE : IMPARTIALITY ::
- (A) chef : strength
- (B) winner : regret
- (C) counselor : understanding
- (D) pessimist : certainty
- (E) archer : arrows

20 ___

21. INSECT : BEETLE ::
- (A) reptile : cobra
- (B) porpoise : mammal
- (C) mollusk : jellyfish
- (D) frog : lizard
- (E) falcon : condor

21 ___

22. CONFUSION : CHAOS ::
- (A) poise : serenity
- (B) happiness : indifference
- (C) discord : conversation
- (D) headache : noise
- (E) recklessness : leadership

22 ___

23. INFECTION : ILLNESS ::
- (A) destruction : explosion
- (B) eclipse : disaster
- (C) bark : howl
- (D) sentimentality : ingenuity
- (E) cloudburst : flooding

23 ___

24. FONDNESS : INFATUATION ::
- (A) rage : irritation
- (B) enjoyment : rapture
- (C) excitement : indifference
- (D) comical : original
- (E) backward : deceitful

24 ___

25. COMPETES : ATHLETE ::

(A) plants : meteorologist
(B) plows : potter
(C) repairs : aerialist
(D) kills : matador
(E) sews : manicurist

25 ____

Answers and Analysis
Vocabulary Diagnostic Test A

PART 1   Antonyms (1–10)

Pages 59–68, "Antonyms and Opposed Words," provide a general review of antonyms. In addition to the analyses below, you will find cross-references to pages where more specific help can be found.

1. CLARIFY:

   (A) bake   (D) direct
   (B) conceal   (E) elucidate
   (C) reopen

   (B) The Latin roots are helpful here. **Fy** (page 95) means "make." **Clar,** allied to the English word *clear,* means "clear." *Clarify* means "make clear." The opposite of "make clear" is *conceal* (B). You can also call upon the English words *clarity* (state of being clear) and declare (make clear) to help you with **clar.**

2. EMBITTERED:

   (A) unsweetened   (D) joyous
   (B) caustic   (E) hapless
   (C) aroused

   (D) Finding the small word within the larger word is a clue here. (74–76). *Bitter* suggests that the word means something like "make bitter." *Unsweetened* and *caustic* are more like synonyms than antonyms of bitter. *Aroused* and *hapless* do not seem to be associated with bitter. Joyous (D) seems the closest opposite of **embittered.** If you are puzzled by the **em** prefix, you might have recalled other words beginning with **em.** *Embellish* means "make beautiful" (see *bell* on page 102). Use all your resources in tracking down meanings. Keep your wits about you. Do not spend too much time on any one word, but don't give up too easily either. You know more than you think you know!

3. ABSURD:

   (A) farcical   (D) threadbare
   (B) unhappy   (E) meaningful
   (C) unrelated

   (E) Sometimes you'll come across a word whose parts are unfamiliar. The root **surd,** meaning "deaf" or "stupid," is uncommon. There are too few English words with the **surd** root to justify its inclusion in a list of roots. What then?

Reach into your memory for contexts (page 6) containing the word. You may have heard sentences like these: "That's *absurd*." "That's an *absurd* conclusion." "Don't be *absurd*." The common meaning of absurd in all of these sentences is "stupid, foolish." The opposite is *meaningful*. Even when the cause seems hopeless, you will often find the answer in your experience and memory.

4. ALTRUISTIC:

    (A) otherworldly   (D) gentle

    (B) selfish   (E) gloomy

    (C) changeable

    (*B*) Once again, Latin roots are helpful. The root **altr,** meaning "other," is a key ingredient here (page 102). People who think of others before themselves are altruistic. Selfish (*B*) is an antonym.

5. IMPEDE:

    (A) control   (D) collapse

    (B) desert   (E) repeatable

    (C) abet

    (*C*) Searching your memory for associated words is always sound strategy (69–73). The word *impediment*, meaning "obstacle, something in the way," is probably more common than the word **impede**. If you know impediment, you may assume that **impede** means "provide an obstacle, hinder." The correct choice, *abet*, meaning "assist," may not be a familiar word, but here a process of elimination helps. None of the other alternatives is an opposite of *hinder*. Therefore *abet* is the best choice. Eliminating obviously wrong answers often leads to the right one.
    Impede also contains the Latin root **ped**, meaning "foot," but the derivation is a little indirect here.

6. IMPERTURBABLE:

    (A) dull   (D) excitable

    (B) interested   (E) repeatable

    (C) invisible

    (*D*) Some words present several clues to meaning. *Imperturbable* is a long word with a shorter word inside. The word *perturbed*, meaning "troubled," shows that **imperturbable** has something to do with "being troubled." The suffix **able** (139) is part of the complete word. The prefix **im**, meaning "not" suggests that *imperturbable* means "not able to be troubled." *Excitable* (*D*) is the antonym.

7. BURN-OUT:

    (A) renewal   (D) conflagration

    (B) contemplation   (E) extinction

    (C) collapse

    (*A*) Figurative language (47–52) is the key here. If a flame burns out, it is extinguished. If a person feels "burned out," he or she is exhausted. Choices (*C*), (*D*), and (*E*) are somewhat synonymous. *Contemplation* (*B*) is unrelated. *Renewal* (*A*) is the opposite of exhaustion.

8. AMORPHOUS:

   (A) misshapen   (D) overpowering
   (B) medical   (E) powerful
   (C) symmetrical

   (*C*) A knowledge of Greek roots and prefixes is helpful here. The root **morph**, meaning "shape" (page 126), and the prefix, **a**, meaning "not" (117), suggest that **amorphous** means "without shape." Since *symmetrical* suggests a definite shape, (*C*) is the correct response.

9. IMPAIRED:

   (A) duplicated   (D) approached
   (B) seized   (E) restored
   (C) separated

   (*E*) Some words may not present immediate clues. **Impaired** comes from a less familiar Latin root meaning "worse." **Impaired** means "made worse." You may, however, have to try a different tack.
   Try free association. Try to think of other contexts in which you may have seen or heard the word. Think of the word in shorter or longer form, as *impairment*. You may have seen a television program "for the hearing impaired." You may have heard of "the impairment of faculties." If you cull several examples, the concept of affliction, weakening, or damage may come through. The antonym *restored* (*E*) will suggest itself.
   Don't be dismayed if certain words do not become clear immediately. You are not expected to get a perfect score. Do the best you can.

10. EQUITABLE:

    (A) unjust   (D) eventful
    (B) lively   (E) habitable
    (C) apparent

    (*A*) There are two good clues: the suffix **able** (page 139) and the root **equ**, meaning "equal" (page 103). That which is not equal or fair is *unjust*.

PART 2 Sentence Completion (11–15)

Pages 6–40, "Clues from Context," provide a basic approach to this section. In addition, specific help will be found in Division A, Section II, "Word Clues," and Section III, "Clues from Etymology." The answers below suggest more specific cross references.

11. Despite the director's --- after the disastrous dress rehearsal, the opening night performance was a total success, with many curtain calls at its conclusion.

   (A) excitement   (D) vigor
   (B) smugness   (E) foreboding
   (C) apathy

   (E) "Despite" warns us immediately that a contrast (pages 26–29, 34–38), lies ahead. Something is being contrasted with the total success of the opening performance. The director did not expect the success. Therefore, he must have been worried. *Foreboding* (E) is the best choice. Note that in this type of question, many answers fit. The director might have been *excited* after the disastrous dress rehearsal. He might have shown *vigor* to bolster his morale. Choices (A) and (D) are not, however, as good as (E). You are asked not merely to supply an answer that fits. You are asked to supply the answer that *best* fits the meaning of the sentence as a whole. In this sentence the likelihood is that the director was worried. If *foreboding* is unfamiliar, you might reach it by a process of elimination or by analyzing the parts. **Bode** in "bodes no good" suggests bad possibilities. **Fore** obviously means "beforehand." *Foreboding* is thus a feeling that things will not turn out well. There are often many approaches to the right answer.

12. Indiana Jones seemed to have a --- love of danger, inherited, no doubt, from some swashbuckling adventurer in Francis Drake's navy.

   (A) tiresome   (D) grisly
   (B) negative   (E) rational
   (C) congenital

   (C) The clue here is a pairing of ideas (13–16). The word "inherited" is paired with the missing word. If something is inherited, it is part of the personality : *congenital* (C). If *congenital* is a hard word for you, work through Latin prefixes and roots (84, 94) or through a process of elimination. The other choices just don't fit.

13. Although Mandy --- responsibility for the accident, the jury decided it was a clear case of --- on her part.

   (A) denied . . attentiveness
   (B) disclaimed . . negligence
   (C) accepted . . boredom
   (D) assigned . . dexterity
   (E) misinterpreted . . clairvoyance

(B) Though it might seem more difficult to supply two words instead of one, actually supplying two words is often easier. Note how having two words, one of which is clearly wrong, helps us choose the right one. Choice (A) doesn't make sense. *Attentiveness* would have prevented the accident. Choice (C) provides a possible answer in *accepted*, but *boredom* does not fit the context. The word "although" clearly suggests a contrast (26–29), eliminating *boredom*. If "although" had been "because," the choices might have worked. *Dexterity* in (D) eliminates that possibility.

The choices in (E) are farfetched and inappropriate. Choice (B) fits perfectly. The jury did not accept Mandy's disclaimer and decided she had been negligent.

14. Unlike De Kooning, who --- the perils of modern living, his artist ---, Gorky, Smith, and Pollock, died tragic deaths.

    (A) belittled . . henchmen
    (B) delineated . . characters
    (C) survived . . peers
    (D) accepted . . namesakes
    (E) attacked . . kinsmen

    (C) Comparison and contrast often provide clues (22–25). If Gorky, Smith, and Pollock died tragic deaths and De Kooning is unlike them, we may assume he *survived* (C).

15. Charles Wheatstone, --- genius, --- the development of the telegraph, ante-dating Samuel F. B. Morse's famous demonstration by seven years.

    (A) unsung . . pioneered
    (B) erratic . . copied
    (C) willful . . observed
    (D) notorious . . impeded

    (A) The sentence as a whole provides the necessary context clues (6–40). The fact that Wheatstone succeeded before Samuel F. B. Morse suggests that *pioneered* (A) is the answer. The other word in the pair, *unsung*, also fits perfectly. The answer might also be derived by elimination of the other, faulty choices.

PART 3 Analogies (16–25)

The analogies section, pages 164–189, (Division A), provides a complete and detailed attack on the analogies questions, with helpful hints for handling them. Again, specific cross references to pages in the text will enable you to identify the kind of analogy being tested.

16. CANDID : HYPOCRITE ::

    (A) insatiable : glutton
    (B) curious : expert
    (C) cheerful : scientist
    (D) angelic : fiend
    (E) competent : executive

    (D) The relationship tested here is that of a word and an opposed word (166). We must therefore find among the choices two words opposed to each other. The first word in the pair must be an adjective and the second a noun. An excellent device is putting the relationship in the form of a statement (166). The statement for this analogy would look like this.
The statement:

        A **hypocrite** is never **candid**.

The correct choice:

        (D) A *fiend* is never *angelic*.

17. AQUARIUM : GUPPY ::

    (A) terrarium : lion
    (B) letter : file
    (C) dog : kennel
    (D) automobile : street
    (E) safe : jewelry

    (E) The relationship is that of container and something contained (170).
The statement:

        A **guppy** is kept in an **aquarium**.

The correct choice:

        (E) *Jewelry* is kept in a *safe*.

What's wrong with (B) and (C)? Isn't a *letter* kept in a *file* and isn't a *dog* kept in a *kennel*? Careful! the categories have been reversed. The container comes first in the original pair.

18. GOLF : PUTTER ::

    (A) mallet : croquet
    (B) javelin : track
    (C) knitting : needle
    (D) football : line judge
    (E) cooking : onion

    (C) The relationship is that of tool or implement and activity (172).
The statement:

        A **putter** is used in **golf**.

The correct choice:

> (C) A *needle* is used in *knitting*.

Note that (A) and (B) have been reversed and are therefore not acceptable. A *line judge* is used in *football* (D) and an *onion* is used in *cooking* (E). Why aren't these acceptable? Neither a *line judge* nor an *onion* can qualify as a tool.

19. POUND : KILOGRAM ::

    (A) century : year
    (B) foot : yard
    (C) liter : quart
    (D) centimeter : gram
    (E) calorie : heat

    (B) The relationship is that of the smaller to larger (173).
       The statement:

> A **pound** is smaller than a **kilogram**.

    The correct choice:

> (B) A *foot* is smaller than a *yard*.

A *century* is larger than a *year*. Therefore (A) is incorrect. A *liter* is larger than a *quart*. Therefore (C) is incorrect. A *centimeter* measures length and a *gram* measures weight. They cannot be compared. Therefore (D) is incorrect. *Calorie* is a measure of *heat*; it isn't larger than heat. Therefore (E) is incorrect.

20. REFEREE : IMPARTIALITY ::

    (A) chef : strength
    (B) winner : regret
    (C) counselor : understanding
    (D) pessimist : certainty
    (E) archer : arrows

    (C) The relationship is that of a person to a quality associated with the person (18).
       The statement:

> An essential quality of the **referee** is **impartiality**.

    The correct choice:

> (C) An essential quality of the *counselor is understanding*.

A *chef* does not need *strength*. (A) is incorrect. A *winner* does not tend to *regret*. (B) is incorrect. Though a *pessimist* may be *certain* about the terrible state of the world, *certainty* is not a crucial quality. (D) is incorrect. Though an *archer* needs *arrows* as a referee needs impartiality, the arrows cannot be considered a quality. When two or more choices seem to fit, go further. Refine the statement.

21. INSECT : BEETLE ::

(A) reptile : cobra
(B) porpoise : mammal
(C) mollusk : jellyfish
(D) frog : lizard
(E) falcon : condor

(A) The relationship is that of general term to specific term (174).
The statement:

A **beetle** is a kind of **insect**.

The correct choice:

(A) A *cobra* is a kind of *reptile*.

Choices (C), (D), and (E) are incorrect because one of the choices is not a general classification which contains the other. A porpoise is a kind of mammal. Therefore why not (B) also? Note that the terms have been reversed.

22. CONFUSION : CHAOS ::

(A) poise : serenity
(B) happiness : indifference
(C) discord : conversation
(D) headache : noise
(E) recklessness : leadership

(A) The relationship is that of something and its associated quality (177).
The statement:

Confusion is characteristic of (or associated with) **chaos**.

The correct choice:

(A) *Poise* is associated with *serenity*.

Choices (B), (C), and (E) are inappropriate. A *headache* (D) may be brought on by *noise*, but it is not necessarily linked with *noise*. *Noise* may even be a happy sound.

23. INFECTION : ILLNESS ::

(A) destruction : explosion
(B) eclipse : disaster
(C) bark : howl
(D) sentimentality : ingenuity
(E) cloudburst : flooding

(E) The relationship is that of cause and effect (170).
The statement:

Infection may bring on **illness**.

The correct choice:

(E) A *cloudburst* may bring on *flooding*.

An *explosion* may bring on *destruction* (A), but note that the terms are reversed. There is no cause-and-effect relationship between an *eclipse* and *disaster* (*B*), though ancient peoples may have thought so. *Bark* and *howl* (*C*) are similar, not causally related. There is no relationship between *sentimentality* and *ingenuity* (*D*).

24. FONDNESS : INFATUATION

    (A) rage : irritation
    (B) enjoyment : rapture
    (C) excitement : indifference
    (D) comical : original
    (E) backward : deceitful

    (*B*) The relationship is that of a lesser and a greater degree of intensity (173). The statement:

    Fondness is less than **infatuation**.

    The correct choice:

    (*B*) *Enjoyment* is less intense than *rapture*.

    Irritation is less *intense* than rage (*A*), but the terms are reversed. *Excitement* and *indifference* (*C*) are antonyms. (*D*) and (*E*) have unrelated pairs.

25. COMPETES : ATHLETE

    (A) plants : meteorologist
    (B) plows : potter
    (C) repairs : aerialist
    (D) kills : matador
    (E) sews : manicurist

    (*D*) The relationship is that of a person to what he or she does (176). The statement:

    An **athlete competes**.

    The correct choice:

    (*D*) A *matador kills*.

    The function of the matador in the bull ring is to kill the bull. The other choices do not show basic functions. The *meteorologist* doesn't *plant*. The *potter* doesn't *plow*. And so for the others.

Now that you have taken Part A and have read the analysis of the correct answers, try your skill at Part B. Again, at the end of the test correct answers will be analyzed for you, with cross-references to the pages which cover the skills being tested.

Taking both parts of the test may provide help in revealing areas where you are particularly strong as well as areas where you need special attention.

Vocabulary Diagnostic Test B

PART 1

For each question in this section, choose the best answer and write the letter for your choice.

Each question below consists of a word in capital letters, followed by five lettered words or phrases. Choose the word or phrase that is most nearly *opposite* in meaning to the word in capital letters. Since some of the questions require you to distinguish fine shades of meaning, consider all the choices before deciding which is best.

EXAMPLE

GOOD:
- (A) sour
- (B) bad
- (C) red
- (D) hot
- (E) ugly

B

1. AMIABLE:
- (A) lovable
- (B) indecisive
- (C) truculent
- (D) commonplace
- (E) frivolous

1 ___

2. ESSENTIAL:
- (A) unimportant
- (B) hypocritical
- (C) abnormal
- (D) hackneyed
- (E) habitual

2 ___

3. IMPLICIT:
- (A) ill-placed
- (B) expressed
- (C) uncompre-hending
- (D) exquisite
- (E) illogical

3 ___

4. DIMINISH:
- (A) illuminate
- (B) complain
- (C) terminate
- (D) increase
- (E) demur

4 ___

5. IMPARTIAL:
- (A) rapidly moving
- (B) unexpected
- (C) whole
- (D) complicated
- (E) unjust

5 ___

6. WITHSTAND:
- (A) yield
- (B) be quiet
- (C) derive
- (D) clobber
- (E) take a position

6 ___

7. SUMPTUOUS:
- (A) secretive
- (B) additional
- (C) modest
- (D) luxurious
- (E) painful

7 ___

8. SUPERANNUATED:
- (A) extraneous
- (B) up-to-date
- (C) yearly
- (D) extremely old
- (E) repetitive

8 ___

9. FLORID:
- (A) unpleasant
- (B) flowery
- (C) false
- (D) prodigal
- (E) plain

9 ___

10. CHIDE:
- (A) censure
- (B) slur
- (C) control
- (D) approve
- (E) repress

10 ___

PART 2

Each sentence below has one or two blanks, each blank indicating that something has been omitted. Beneath the sentence are five lettered words or sets of words. Choose the word or set of words that best fits the meaning of the sentence as a whole.

EXAMPLE

Although its publicity has been ---, the film itself is intelligent, well-acted, handsomely produced, and altogether ---.

- (A) tasteless . . respectable
- (B) extensive . . moderate
- (C) sophisticated . . amateur
- (D) risqué . . crude
- (E) perfect . . spectacular

A

11. Jean Henri Fabre shifted the --- of science from dead laboratory specimens to ---, living creatures in the field.
- (A) emphasis . . stodgy
- (B) scrutiny . . vibrant
- (C) mediocrity . . nameless
- (D) nomenclature . . unobserved
- (E) carelessness . . active

11 ___

12. The exhibit of American flower painting shows an --- diversity from the --- realism of Severin Roesen to the abstract design of Georgia O'Keeffe.
- (A) expected . . shoddy
- (B) unpretentious . . breezy
- (C) unbroken . . critical
- (D) exalted . . unattractive
- (E) incredible . . literal

12 ___

13. Although the chance of discovering --- intelligence may be slim, the SETI program continues to --- sounds from outer space.
- (A) superior . . transfer
- (B) extraterrestrial . . monitor
- (C) UFO . . disregard
- (D) galactic . . broadcast
- (E) inhuman . . clarify

13 ___

14. In light of the almost --- possibilities available, simple coincidence is neither mysterious nor ---
- (A) incomprehensible . . ridiculous
- (B) demonstrable . . expected
- (C) inconsequential . . purposeful
- (D) limitless . . miraculous
- (E) invariable . . substantial

14 ___

15. Like a meteor on an August night, the rock star --- across stages throughout the land and then --- into oblivion.
- (A) blazed . . faded
- (B) ran . . dashed
- (C) flew . . collapsed
- (D) marched . . hobbled
- (E) promenaded . . fell

15 ___

PART 3

Each question below consists of a related pair of words or phrases, followed by five lettered pairs of words or phrases. Select the lettered pair that <u>best</u> expresses a relationship similar to that expressed in the original pair.

EXAMPLE

YAWN : BOREDOM ::
- (A) dream : sleep
- (B) anger : madness
- (C) smile : amusement
- (D) face : expression
- (E) impatience : rebellion

C

16. GARDENER : TROWEL ::
- (A) aviator : signal
- (B) skater : net
- (C) amateur : tennis
- (D) angler : rod
- (E) chef : dairy

16 ___

17. FILAMENT : BULB ::
- (A) stamen : flower
- (B) tree : bark
- (C) blanket : warmth
- (D) novel : character
- (E) message : telephone

17 ___

18. MILLIGRAM : WEIGHT ::
- (A) capacity : liter
- (B) acre : area
- (C) heat : calorie
- (D) ecstasy : happiness
- (E) meter : foot

18 ___

19. ASTRONAUT : SHUTTLE ::
- (A) garage : mechanic
- (B) museum : botanist
- (C) cook : galley
- (D) canary : kennel
- (E) senator : White House

19 ___

20. CHISEL : MARBLE ::
- (A) burn : field
- (B) grow : asparagus
- (C) read : article
- (D) buy : newspaper
- (E) mold : clay

20 ___

21. EULOGIZE : COMPLIMENTARY ::
- (A) circumvent : weepy
- (B) reconcile : impatient
- (C) garnish : devious
- (D) gawk : noisy
- (E) economize : prudent

21 ___

22. GUIDES : MENTOR ::
- (A) memorizes : felon
- (B) repeats : prophet
- (C) opines : ascetic
- (D) deceives : impostor
- (E) triumphs : recipient

22 ___

23. CORRAL : MUSTANG ::
- (A) train : tiger
- (B) cage : antelope
- (C) paint : camel
- (D) spring : trap
- (E) herd : sheep

23 ___

24. RAINBOW : HOPE ::
- (A) patriotism : flag
- (B) sustenance : food
- (C) skeleton : Halloween
- (D) graduation : diploma
- (E) crown : wealth

24 ___

25. GENETICS : HEREDITY ::
- (A) seismology : earthquakes
- (B) aerodynamics : air pollution
- (C) volcanoes : vulcanology
- (D) meteorology : asteroids
- (E) metaphysics : subatomic particles

25 ___

Answers and Analysis
Vocabulary Diagnostic Test B

PART 1   Antonyms (1–10)

Pages 59–68, ''Antonyms and Opposed Words,'' provide a general review of antonyms. In addition to the analyses below, you will find cross references to pages where you can find more specific help.

Here, as in all word-test items, the best situation is to recognize at once the word being tested and know its meaning. But you will also meet test words that are not immediately familiar. Then you will need to draw upon all your resources, using the skills developed in this book. By understanding testing techniques and by applying your skill, you will be able to answer many test questions that seem difficult at first.

1. AMIABLE:

   (A) lovable   (D) commonplace
   (B) indecisive   (E) frivolous
   (C) truculent

   (*C*) The Latin root and prefix (pages 94, 109) tell us **amiable** means ''lovable.'' Beware! *Lovable*, a synonym, is provided as a choice. Sometimes a synonym will trap you unaware. Remember that an antonym is called for. *Truculent*, meaning ''cruel, savage,'' is the correct answer. Even if you are not completely sure about *truculent*, you can find the answer by eliminating the three obviously wrong numbers.

2. ESSENTIAL:

   (A) unimportant   (D) hackneyed
   (B) hypocritical   (E) habitual
   (C) abnormal

   (*A*) **Essential,** meaning ''extremely important,'' is not a difficult word. Think of associated words and contexts (69–73). You have undoubtedly heard the word in expressions like these: ''an essential ingredient,'' and ''minimum essentials.'' The correct answer is *unimportant* (*A*).

3. IMPLICIT:

   (A) illuminate   (D) exquisite
   (B) expressed   (E) illogical
   (C) uncomprehending

   (*B*) The word *imply* is concealed within the word **implicit** (94). Something that is implied, rather than expressed, is *implicit*. The opposite is *expressed* (*B*). Possibly helpful here also is the knowledge that the root **plic** means ''fold.'' Something implicit is ''folded in,'' not obvious.

4. DIMINISH:

   (A) illuminate   (D) increase
   (B) complain   (E) demur
   (C) terminate

(D) The root **min,** meaning "less, little" (105) helps. **Diminish** means "make less, become less." The antonym is *increase* (D).

5. IMPARTIAL:

    (A) rapidly moving   (D) complicated
    (B) unexpected   (E) unjust
    (C) whole

    (E) The prefix **im** meaning "not" (87) tells us **impartial** means "not partial." An impartial judge is *fair, just.* The antonym is *unjust* (E).

6. WITHSTAND:

    (A) yield   (D) clobber
    (B) be quiet   (E) take a position
    (C) derive

    (A) **Withstand** contains two Anglo-Saxon elements. "With" means "against" (132) and so withstand means "stand against, refuse to yield." The antonym is *yield* (A).

7. SUMPTUOUS:

    (A) secretive   (D) luxurious
    (B) additional   (E) painful
    (C) modest

    (C) **Sumptuous** is a hard word, but you can attack its elements. *Consume* and *consumption* are related. The root sum, sumpt suggests "using, taking, spending." If sumptuous involves spending, its opposite would suggest moderation, thrift. The closest word is *modest* (C). Perhaps you have heard the expression "a sumptuous banquet." This association (69–73) may give you another approach to the word, since a sumptuous banquet is extravagant.

        When all else fails, try to find in your memory the key word in a phrase or expression you have heard. This memory context may give you the needed clue. Don't spend too much time on any one word, however. You are not expected to get all the answers. Yet, you can do a great deal with what you already know!

8. SUPERANNUATED:

    (A) extraneous   (D) extremely
    (B) up-to-date   (E) repetitive
    (C) yearly

    (B) The prefix **super** (87), meaning "above, beyond", and the root **ann,** meaning "year" (102), provide clues. Something **superannuated** has lasted past the point of effectiveness. The antonym is *up-to-date* (B).

9. FLORID:

    (A) unpleasant   (D) prodigal
    (B) flowery   (E) plain
    (C) false

    (E) The root **flor,** meaning "flower" (104), provides the clue. If something is **florid,** it is not *plain* (E).

10. CHIDE:

    (A) censure   (D) approve

    (B) slur   (E) repress

    (C) control

    (*D*) Sometimes short, seemingly easy, words are difficult. Without easily recognized roots or sentence parts to help, such words present a real challenge. Then fall back on experience. Try to think of sentences or experiences during which you heard the word (69–73). Did a mother **chide** her children? Did a coach **chide** his players for lack of concentration? Such contexts suggest the meaning "scold."

        Sometimes the choices will give you a clue to the meaning of the test word. Note that there are two words here—*censure* and *slur*—that have the idea of disapproval. Both cannot be right. *Approve* (*D*) is the answer.

PART 2 Sentence Completion (11–15)

    Pages 6–40, "Clues from Context," provide a basic approach to this section. In addition, specific help will be found in the Vocabulary Division, Section II, "Clues in Words," and Section III, "Clues from Etymology." The answers below suggest more specific cross-references.

11. Jean Henri Fabre shifted the --- of science from dead laboratory specimens to ---, living creatures in the field.

    (A) emphasis . . stodgy   (D) nomenclature . . unobserved

    (B) scrutiny . . vibrant   (E) carelessness . . active

    (C) mediocrity . . nameless

    (*B*) The pairing of "dead laboratory specimens" with "living creatures in the field" tells us contrast (pages 26–29) is a major clue. We can pinpoint the meaning by filling the first blank or the second. Since "dead" is being contrasted with "living," find a word that appropriately describes living creatures. We can immediately eliminate (*A*) since *stodgy* is completely inappropriate. *Vibrant* and *active* seem the best possibilities. The other word along with *vibrant* is *scrutiny*. This word fits perfectly, but to be sure see whether the word with *active* fits: *carelessness*. This doesn't fit. The only pair that fits perfectly is *scrutiny* and *vibrant* (*B*). Frequently one word in the pair will fit but not the other, as in (*E*).

12. The exhibit of American flower painting shows an --- diversity from the --- realism of Severin Roesen to the abstract design of Georgia O'Keeffe.

    (A) expected . . shoddy   (D) exalted . . unattractive

    (B) unpretentious . . breezy   (E) incredible . . literal

    (C) unbroken . . critical

    (*E*) The sequence of ideas (30–33) and the function words **from** and **to** (34–38) provide the clues here. In addition, there is a contrast (26–29) of "realism" and "abstract design." Trying the possibilities suggests that (*E*) is the correct answer. *Literal* provides a sound contrast with *abstract*. With such contrast, the diversity may well be *incredible*.

13. Although the chance of discovering --- intelligence may be slim, the SETI program continues to --- sounds from outer space.

   (A) superior . . transfer
   (B) extraterrestrial . . monitor
   (C) UFO . . disregard
   (D) galactic . . broadcast
   (E) inhuman . . clarify

   (*B*) **Although** tells us a contrast (26–29) is a clue. In addition, the blank before "intelligence" is paired with "outer space." This is intelligence from outer space. A word linked with "outer space" is *extraterrestrial* (*B*). The prefix **extra,** meaning "beyond" (87) and the root **terr,** meaning "earth" (107), tell us *extraterrestrial* means "beyond the earth," another expression for "outer space." Though words like *superior* and *galactic* may seem to fit also, their paired words do not fit. Neither *transfer* nor *broadcast* makes sense in the context. This sentence demonstrates that there are often many ways to ferret out the answer.

14. In light of the almost --- possibilities available, simple coincidence is neither mysterious nor ---

   (A) incomprehensible . . ridiculous
   (B) demonstrable . . expected
   (C) inconsequential . . purposeful
   (D) limitless . . miraculous
   (E) invariable . . substantial

   (*D*) The sentence as a whole (6–12) provides the needed clues here, but there is another, the pairing of "mysterious" and the blank. The only suggested word that can be reasonably paired with "mysterious" is *miraculous* (*D*). Trying *limitless* in the first blank verifies our choice.

15. Like a meteor on an August night, the rock star --- across stages throughout the land and then --- into oblivion.

   (A) blazed . . faded
   (B) ran . . dashed
   (C) flew . . collapsed
   (D) marched . . hobbled
   (E) promenaded . . fell

   (*A*) What is the characteristic of a "meteor on an August night"? The trail is bright . . and brief. Here a comparison (22–25) provides the clues. The only word that fits the first blank is *blazed* (*A*). *Faded* fits neatly into the second blank. All the other possibilities have one or both inappropriate choices.

PART 3   Analogies (16–25)

The analogies section, pages 164–189, provides a complete and detailed attack on the analogies questions, with helpful hints for handling them. Again, specific cross-references to pages in the text will enable you to identify the kind of analogy being tested.

16. GARDENER : TROWEL ::

    (A) aviator : signal

    (B) skater : net

    (C) amateur : tennis

    (D) angler : rod

    (E) chef : dairy

    (*D*) The relationship tested is that of a person and an important tool (172). The statement:

> The **gardener** uses a **trowel.**

The correct choice:

> (*D*) The *angler* uses a *rod*.

The *aviator* may use a *signal* (A), but the *signal* is not a tool.

Though all the other pairs are related, the relationship is not the same as that of the test words.

17. FILAMENT : BULB ::

    (A) stamen : flower

    (B) tree : bark

    (C) blanket : warmth

    (D) novel : character

    (E) message : telephone

    (*A*) The relationship is that of part to the whole (168). The statement:

> The **filament** is part of the **bulb.**

The correct choice:

> (*A*) The *stamen* is part of the *flower*.

Check the other choices. *Bark* is part of the *tree* (B), but the words are reversed. *Warmth* is associated with a *blanket* (C), but *warmth* is not a physical part. Besides, the words are reversed. A *character* may appear in a *novel*, (D), but he or she is not a physical part of a novel. Again, the words are reversed. A *telephone* may carry a *message*, but the *message* is not a physical part of the *telephone* (E).

18. MILLIGRAM : WEIGHT ::

    (A) capacity : liter

    (B) acre : area

    (C) heat : calorie

    (D) ecstasy : happiness

    (E) meter : foot

    (*B*) The relationship is that of a unit of measurement and something to be measured (185). The statement:

> A **milligram** is a measure of **weight.**

The correct choice:

(B) An *acre* is a measure of *area*.

Choices (A) and (C) show correct relationships—but in reverse. *Ecstasy* and *happiness* are roughly synonymous (D), but neither is a unit of measurement. Both *meter* and *foot* (E) are units of measurement, but neither is something to be measured.

19. ASTRONAUT : SHUTTLE ::

(A) garage : mechanic
(B) museum : botanist
(C) cook : galley
(D) canary : kennel
(E) senator : White House

(C) The relationship is that of a person and the place associated with him or her (177).

The statement:

An astronaut **functions** in a (space) **shuttle.**

The correct choice:

(C) The *cook* functions in a *galley*.

Choices (A) and (B) would be possible, but they are presented in reverse. A *canary* does not function in a *kennel* (D). A *senator* does not function in the *White House* (E).

20. CHISEL : MARBLE ::

(A) burn : field
(B) grow : asparagus
(C) read : article
(D) buy : newspaper
(E) mold : clay

(E) The relationship is that of an action and the object acted upon (173).

The statement:

Someone can **chisel marble.**

The correct choice:

(E) Someone can *mold clay*.

Sometimes, as here, you have to carry the statement a bit farther. Every choice makes sense according to the simple statement:

Someone can *burn* a *field*.

Someone can *grow asparagus*.

Someone can *read* an *article*.

Someone can *buy* a *newspaper*.

What makes (*E*) better than the others? When an artist **chisels marble,** he or she is seeking an artistic creation. This goal is not true of the four incorrect choices, but it is true of (*E*). A person *molds clay* to create a work of art. After you have analyzed all the choices, if you like, you can rephrase your original statement to make it more specific.

Someone can **chisel marble** to create a work of art.

Then (*E*) becomes more obvious as the correct choice.

21. EULOGIZE : COMPLIMENTARY ::

(A) circumvent : weepy
(B) reconcile : impatient
(C) garnish : devious
(D) gawk : noisy
(E) economize : prudent

(*E*) The relationship is that of a word and a word similar in connotation, though not necessarily in part of speech (168).
The statement:

If someone **eulogizes,** he or she is **complimentary.**

The correct choice:

(*E*) If someone *economizes*, he or she is *prudent*.

Note that the first word in the pair is a verb and the second an adjective. Your correct choice should show the same parts of speech in the same order.

22. GUIDES : MENTOR ::

(A) memorizes : felon
(B) repeats : prophet
(C) opines : ascetic
(D) deceives : impostor
(E) triumphs : recipient

(*D*) The relationship is that of a person and his or her purpose (178).
The statement:

A **mentor guides.**

The correct choice:

(*D*) An *impostor deceives*.

The other choices do not show an essential relationship.

23. CORRAL : MUSTANG ::

(A) train : tiger
(B) cage : antelope
(C) paint : camel
(D) spring : trap
(E) herd : sheep

(*B*) The relationship again is that of an action and the object acted upon (174), but there is a difference between 20 above and this question. The purpose is not to create a work of art but to pen an animal.
The statement:

211

Someone can **corral** a **mustang.**

The correct choice:

(*B*) Someone can *cage* an *antelope.*

The other choices seem plausible at first, for someone can *train* a *tiger* (*A*) or *herd sheep* (*E*), but only (*B*) suggests the essential purpose: to put an animal into some kind of pen.

24. RAINBOW : HOPE ::

(A) flag : patriotism
(B) sustenance : food
(C) Halloween : skeleton
(D) graduation : diploma
(E) crown : wealth

(*A*) The relationship is that of the symbol and the thing symbolized (187). The statement:

The **rainbow** is a symbol of **hope.**

The correct choice:

(*A*) The *flag* is a symbol of *patriotism.*

The *diploma* is a symbol of *graduation* (*D*) and the *skeleton* is a symbol of *Halloween* (*C*), but the pairs are reversed. *Food* might, in some instances, be considered a symbol of *sustenance*, but the words are reversed (*B*). The *crown* (*E*) is really a symbol of *royalty* rather than *wealth.*

25. GENETICS : HEREDITY ::

(A) seismology : earthquakes
(B) aerodynamics : air pollution
(C) volcanoes : vulcanology
(D) meteorology : asteroids
(E) metaphysics : subatomic particles

(*A*) The relationship is that of a science and the subject of study (184). The statement:

Genetics is the study of **heredity.**

The correct choice:

(*A*) *Seismology* is the study of *earthquakes.*

Vulcanology is the study of *volcanoes* (*C*), but the words in the pair are reversed. *Meteorology* is the study of *weather*, not *asteroids* (*D*). *Aerodynamics* is not the study of *air pollution* (*B*). *Metaphysics* has nothing to do with *subatomic particles*, (*E*).

DIVISION B
Reading Comprehension

A Strategy for the Reading Tests

■ Now that you have mastered many of the skills of vocabulary building, you will find yourself ready for the reading tests. Begin to read each selection with calm confidence, for that is half the battle. If you consider each selection as a puzzle and as fun, you'll be more relaxed.

■ After you have read a selection, first look for the main idea. The test questions actually help you here, for they always provide five possibilities, one of which is the best. If you use the suggestions that follow in the text, you'll usually be able to spot the best answer.

■ Test questions usually fit into one of three broad categories: language, details, and inference. Even finding the title requires drawing inferences.

■ "Language in Action" builds directly on Part A and should be, for you, an extension of the work you've already been doing in this text.

■ "Finding Details" is fairly cut and dried. The answers are right there, in the passages themselves, and can be identified.

■ "Drawing Inferences" is a broad and challenging skill. It requires you to read between the lines as you draw inferences, predict what happens next, provide applications, and infer tones and attitudes. Though this kind of question is challenging, it can be more fun than merely picking out details. It leads to a disciplined approach that eliminates guesswork.

The chapters that follow will help you prepare for the SAT.

Section I: Drawing Generalizations and Finding the Main Idea

PART 1

Drawing Generalizations

One of the most important skills tested in the SAT is the ability to generalize. Questions of this type come in a variety of forms, but the essential task in each is to draw a conclusion from ideas or incidents presented in the passage. The most common type of generalization is finding the main idea or supplying a title—covered in subsequent pages. But sometimes you are asked to generalize from a segment of the passage. Here is a sample of such question forms.

1. The author apparently feels that . . .
2. With which statement would the author probably agree?
3. Which of the following terms would the author use to describe . . . ?
4. In the last sentence of the paragraph the word "it" refers to . . .

Trial Test

Read the passage. Choose the answer to the questions that follows it.

In Colin Wilson's science-fiction novel, *The Mind Parasites*, aliens have burrowed into human brains and are living there. To keep human beings from learning the truth,
5 the aliens keep us functioning at about 5% of our mental capacity. That we are all underachievers is not a new idea. William James once wrote, "There seems to be no doubt that we are each and all of us to some
10 extent victims of habit neurosis . . . We live subject to arrest by degrees of fatigue which we have come only from habit to obey. Most of us can learn to push the barrier further off, and to live in perfect comfort on much
15 higher levels of power." Wilson agrees. He is keenly interested in why we are *not* fully alive and alert all the time, why we cannot achieve all we are capable of achieving.

With which of the following statements would the author probably agree?

(A) Colin Wilson is unduly critical of William James.
(B) *The Mind Parasites*, though science-fiction, is a frightening glimpse of the future.
(C) The human mind ordinarily operates at a fraction of its capacity.
(D) Fatigue is a stimulus to achievement rather than a barrier.
(E) Wilson's point of view is a creative breakthrough, novel and ingenious.

———

Answer to Trial Test

(C) The human mind ordinarily operates at a fraction of its capacity. Examine each of the statements in turn. Since William James' quote supports the Wilson point of view, (A) is incorrect. There is no suggestion in the paragraph that *The Mind Parasites* is other than an ingenious bit of fantasy, with no relation to the future. Therefore, we can discard (B). That the human mind is idling most of the time is the point of view of the paragraph. Therefore, (C), is sound. Look at the other alternatives, just to be sure. Fatigue (D) inhibits achievement. It does not stimulate it. Wilson's point of view (E) was anticipated by James and others. The paragraph flatly says, "That we are all underachievers is not a new idea." The generalization stated in (C) is the only correct one.

Look at a typical SAT question and then analyze the possible answers.

Problem

If people are asked to name dangerous animals, they suggest tigers, rhinos, wolves, leopards, and bears. Yet a far more danger-
5 ous creature is the insignificant mosquito, carrier of discomfort, disease, and some-times death. Most people know about ma-laria-carrying mosquitoes, but few realize that some mosquitoes in the United States carry the dreaded encephalitis. This disease,
10 usually associated with the tropics, is found even in cold areas of the country, like LaCrosse, Wisconsin. It is transmitted by a nasty little fellow called the "tree-hole mos-quito." This woodland dweller tends to bite
15 in the late afternoon rather than the evening hours. But whenever it bites, the results can be painful, even deadly. It's just one repre-sentative of a dangerous family. Throughout the world the lowly mosquito is a vicious
20 enemy of human beings.

With which of the following statements would the author probably agree?

(A) Tigers are more dangerous than leop-ards, wolves, or bears.
(B) Most disease-bearing mosquitoes are found in Wisconsin.
(C) In classifying our natural enemies, we must realize that size is not proportional to the danger involved.
(D) Mosquito-control efforts are a waste of time, but public moneys are neverthe-less spent in the quest.
(E) Encephalitis is almost always fatal, but malaria has several cures.

Strategy

No judgment is made about the relative threat posed by leopards, wolves, or bears. (A) is incorrect. The passage admits that mosquitoes are found in Wisconsin but says nothing about comparative percentages of disease-bearing mosquitoes found in Wisconsin and elsewhere. (B) is incorrect. There is no mention of mosquito-control efforts and their relative effectiveness. (D) is incorrect. Encephalitis is called *dreaded* but not labeled "almost always fatal." Malaria is not mentioned. (E) is incorrect. That leaves (C). The major clue to this answer is the word *insignificant*. This tiny creature is called "far more dangerous" than the larger mammals. The conclusion to be drawn is clear: size is not proportional to danger in classifying dangerous beasts. (C) is correct.

Time Out for Review

Try your skill. The passage below is followed by questions based on its content. Use the preceding example to help you find the answers.

Arts and crafts fairs of recent years have displayed many unfamiliar skills, from the artistic arrangement of found objects and "junk" to the almost-forgotten handicrafts
5 of colonial America. One increasingly common newcomer is the Japanese bonsai, the miniature tree.

The bonsai combines the skill of artist and gardener, of sculptor and architect. Pot-
10 ted in a shallow dish, the young tree or shrub may be carefully shaped to resemble an ancient tree on a windswept mountain. For the creator of a bonsai garden, patience is the essential ingredient. The miniature trees are
15 trained, not tortured. Though in the wild, the effects of nature may weather and dwarf trees naturally, in a cultivated plant, the artist must duplicate the effects of nature.

Essential procedures include pruning, re-
20 potting, and wiring. Roots, trunk, branches, and foliage are all shaped in the process. Pruning is essential to keep the plant from outgrowing its root system. Repotting is necessary to trim the roots and to provide new
25 soil. Copper wiring is needed to shape the plant in desired forms.

Bonsai artists say their major purpose is to evoke the spirit of nature. Through "constant yet relaxed attention" they create a mi-
30 crocosm of serenity. If they are successful, they create a masterpiece that is a joy to behold. Their major goal is to achieve, through much direction and intelligent effort, a feeling of spontaneity, of natural beauty.
35 Bob Kataoka, bonsai master, says, "Viewing bonsai is restful, a brief contact with nature's calmness."

1. The author of the selection apparently feels that _____.
   (A) learning to create bonsai requires little experience
   (B) repotting the bonsai is an aesthetic rather than a practical necessity
   (C) bonsai have long been popular in American craft shows
   (D) bonsai trees are younger than they look
   (E) the best bonsai appear carefully planned

   1 ___

2. Which of the following terms would the author probably use to describe Bob Kataoka?
   (A) artisan   (D) nurseryman
   (B) landscaper   (E) forester
   (C) artist

   2 ___

3. "Microcosm" in line 29 refers to a _____.
   (A) painting   (D) replica
   (B) herb garden   (E) model
   (C) bonsai

   3 ___

SUMMARY PART 1

Drawing Generalizations and Finding the Main Idea: Drawing Generalizations

When drawing generalizations, first reread the passage carefully. Then get the feel of the passage as a whole.

Ordinarily the generalization grows out of that total evaluation. With that awareness of the total message, you can readily draw the generalization called for.

PART 2

Finding the Main Idea

A common device for testing the ability to generalize is asking the candidate to find the main idea. This kind of question focuses on the entire selection, not a section of it. If there are several ideas developed, you must weigh them all and determine the main *idea*. Here is a sample of question forms.

1. The major subject of the passage is . . .
2. The chief focus of the passage is on which of the following?
3. The main point of the passage is to . . .
4. The author apparently feels that . . .
5. Which of the following best describes the main idea of the passage?

Trial Test

Take the following trial test to evaluate your skill. Read the passage and choose the answer to the question that follows it. Write the letter for your answer.

One man's meat is another man's poison. Tadpoles thrive in situations that would be impossible for other species. Spring ponds that thrive for only a few months of the year
5 before drying up are ideal habitats for tadpoles. Even puddles formed by a heavy spring rain bring forth a batch of tadpoles struggling for survival. Most other species quickly perish in such circumstances, but not
10 the tadpoles.

Like busy Americans, the tadpoles are lovers of fast-food. Called "highly efficient, specialized feeding machines," tadpoles eat constantly in almost any aquatic habitat. In
15 some species newly swallowed food may account for 50% of their body weight. They eat and eat—and grow and grow. They thrive on uncertainty and instability. Their life cycles are tied to rapid changes in their en-
20 vironment.

Would tadpoles succeed in larger bodies of water that provide some stability? Oddly enough, the answer is *no*. The young creatures would probably succeed in their eating
25 goals, though they'd be competing with other species for the organic food on which they depend. The real problem would be hungry fish, which would soon gobble up the defenseless tadpoles. In fact, tadpoles and fish
30 rarely occur together. Thus, what seems like a happy, serene, nurturing environment is, for the tadpoles, a source of greatest danger.

When they grow in inhospitable conditions like the temporary pond or puddle, the
35 tadpoles have the opportunity to eat constantly in relative safety. These "safe" conditions are not guaranteed, however. If a pond or a puddle dries up too quickly, the tadpoles may starve to death or die from
40 desiccation.

The tadpoles are creatures of insecurity, taking advantage of short periods and apparently impossible living conditions. They are creatures of the seasons, appearing sud-
45 denly, feeding on the chance organic matter in a spring puddle, and then metamorphosing into frogs—if they are lucky.

Which of the following best describes the main idea of the passage?

(A) The life cycle of the tadpole resembles that of the fish.
(B) Tadpoles flourish in spring puddles.
(C) If a spring pond dries up, tadpoles perish.
(D) Tadpoles survive under conditions that seem unlikely and inhospitable.
(E) Tadpoles in large ponds or lakes have an excellent chance of survival.

Answer to Trial Test

(D) Tadpoles survive under conditions that seem unlikely and inhospitable. The life cycles of fish and tadpole are not compared. (A) is incorrect. (B) and (C) are correct statements, but they are details, not main ideas. They can be eliminated. (E) is incorrect. The passage specifically says that tadpoles could eat in ponds but could also be eaten. The paradoxical nature of tadpole survival is the theme of the passage. (D) is the correct answer.

Look at another SAT-type question and analyze the possible answers.

Problem

Hungarians are sometimes considered a sad and serious people, but the Hungarian sense of humor is delightful and unexpected. Hungarians say, "Disaster is a natural state
5 in Hungary. Every situation there is hopeless—but not serious."

The Hungarian playwright Ferenc Molnar was once asked, "What was the first sentence you learned in English?"
10 Molnar replied, "Separate checks, please."

Hungarians love their great twin city, Budapest. They say the Danube is the bluest there, the sunshine brighter and more per-
15 vasive than anywhere else in Hungary. "Even the midgets there are taller." Budapest has two million people and all of Hungary ten million. But all Hungarians insist they were born in Budapest.

20 The spice paprika is the national treasure. Someone asked, "Why do Arabs have oil and Hungarians paprika?"

The reply: "When God gave out the goodies, the Hungarians were pushier."

Which of the following best expresses the main idea of the passage?

(A) Hungarians are a sad and serious people.
(B) Ferenc Molnar is both witty and perceptive.
(C) To a true Hungarian, paprika is more valuable than oil.
(D) The Hungarian sense of humor is keen and enjoyable.
(E) Hungarians are unusually proud of their capital city, Budapest.

Strategy

Though all five answers have at least partial validity in one sense or another, only one expresses the *main* idea. The comment that Hungarians are sad and serious (A) is listed as a common idea, albeit a partial misconception. At best it is a detail and therefore unacceptable. Ferenc Molnar's wit (B) is suggested, but again the point is a small detail. The tongue-in-cheek comment about paprika and oil (C) is used to bolster the main point. It is not the main point. Hungarians are very proud of Budapest (E), but their pride is used as a humorous illustration of their sense of humor. All points reinforce the central point: Hungarians have a good sense of humor (D).

Time Out for Review

Try your skill. The passage below is followed by questions based on its contents. Use the preceding example to help you find the correct answers.

Dangerous drivers account for a disproportionately large number of traffic fatalities. Some drivers are multiple offenders. Keeping such drivers off the roads is a desirable
5 goal, but there are difficulties in enforcing such a plan. Up till now it has been possible for a driver with a suspended or revoked license in one state to get a license in another state. Some of these licensees had been in-
10 volved in several tragic accidents. The National Driver Register, which attempts to keep a nationwide, up-to-date file on drivers, has not, until recently, been especially prompt or effective in providing essential in-
15 formation to states requesting information. Now a bill passed by Congress provides more funds and puts more clout into the entire program. A California study has shown that license sanctions are the most effective
20 means of reducing accidents caused by problem drivers. This device is at least 30% more effective than jail terms, fines, driver-improvement classes, or alcohol-treatment centers. Proponents of the Register feel certain
25 that cooperation by the states and greater efficiency at the national level will reduce traffic deaths on tomorrow's highways.

1. Which of the following expresses the main idea of the passage?
   (A) Most dangerous drivers are multiple offenders.
   (B) The National Driver Register will help states to screen prospective applicants for a license.
   (C) Curbing the dangers posed by problem drivers is a problem disregarded by Congress.
   (D) Denying or limiting the issuance of drivers' licenses is a more effective means of driver control than jail terms or fines.
   (E) A loophole of past procedures is the ability of a problem driver to get a license in a state that does not know his or her record.

1 ___

2. With which statement would the author probably agree?
   (A) More active law enforcement is needed to protect the lives of innocent drivers.
   (B) The principle of the "second chance" should be a major consideration in handling the licenses of drivers who have had accidents.
   (C) Drivers who are at fault in serious accident cases should be jailed.
   (D) Though desirable, the National Driver Register presents a possible infringement on the rights of sovereign states.
   (E) Congress should play a purely advisory role in considering the problem driver.

2 ___

SUMMARY PART 2

Drawing Generalizations and Finding the Main Idea: Finding the Main Idea

There is a common expression, "You can't see the forest for the trees."
To find the main idea, you must see the forest *as well as* the trees. You must be able to see larger issues (the forest) concealed in smaller ones (the trees) and get to the heart of a reading passage.

PART 3

Providing a Title

A variation of stating the main idea is choosing the best title for the selection. Like the preceding type of question, this focuses on the entire selection. The major difference is that choices are not put into statement form but into headline form. Here is a common question requiring you to provide a good title:

Which of the following titles best summarizes the content of the passage?

Trial Test

Take the following trial test to evaluate your skill. Read the passage and choose the answer for the question that follows it.

Before 1883, local communities had their own time. Each town figured noon when the sun was at the zenith. Clocks in New York City, for example, were 10 minutes and 27
5 seconds ahead of those in Baltimore. Railroad schedules were a nightmare. Then, an unsung hero, William F. Allen, suggested that the country be divided into four time zones, eliminating those hundreds of differ-
10 ent local times. November 18, 1883, was called "The Day of Two Noons," for on that day Washington, D.C., gained four minutes as "local noon" was replaced by "standard noon." Some major cities resisted
15 change. Cincinnati held out for seven years, but gradually the entire country went on Eastern, Central, Mountain, or Pacific Time. This idea, so obviously good and so universally accepted today, was an idea whose time
20 had come, but the coming did not come easily.

Which of the following titles best summarizes the content of the passage?

(A) William F. Allen, A Man for All Seasons
(B) A History of the Calendar
(C) A Day to Remember in Washington
(D) The Introduction of Standard Time
(E) How Time Was Determined before 1883

Answer to Trial Test

William F. Allen (A) was indeed a man for all seasons, but the paragraph is about time. His contribution, while important, is not the whole story. (B) is irrelevant, off the topic. The paragraph deals with time, not with the calendar. (C) deals with a single sentence in the paragraph and is a detail. The same objection holds for (E). (D) tells what the paragraph is about. All sentences deal with this topic, beginning with a brief description of timekeeping before 1883. The central section deals with the transition from the old timekeeping methods to the new. The final section mentions the final victory of the four-zone agreement and comments on the importance of the change. Only (D) includes all three of these major sections.

Look at a typical SAT question and then analyze the possible answers.

Problem

Are you taking part in the Birkie this year?

This cryptic question would be no mystery to most active cross-country skiers. The Birkie, or *Birkebeiner* as it is correctly called, is North America's largest cross-country ski race. Held every February 25 in Cable, Wisconsin, it brings 10,000 skiers to a sleepy town of several hundred people. The race itself covers the 34 miles from Hayward, Wisconsin, to Cable. During the week before the race, Cable has ice-sculpture contests, skydivers, hot-air balloons, dancing, dozens of bands, ski clinics, a parade of nations and states, and good old Scandinavian smorgasbords. Incredible traffic jams develop. Housing facilities are stretched to the utmost. A thousand racers, for example, sleep in sleeping bags at the Hayward Middle School. The race must accommodate all these eager skiers. The starting area is a quarter-mile wide. Since top long-distance racers from around the world compete, the finishing time of the winning skier may be four hours ahead of the last skier. Yet all have a good time. Finishing the race is in itself a victory.

Which of the following titles best summarizes the content of the passage?

(A) America's Greatest Cross-Country Ski Race
(B) Fun in the Snow
(C) From Hayward to Cable, the Trip of a Lifetime
(D) The Comforts and Discomforts of Cross-Country Skiing
(E) The Race: A Victory Over Self

Strategy

There are several pitfalls in choosing titles.

1. Do not choose a title that is too broad. In this question (B) is much too broad. It says nothing about skiing. It could apply equally well to a great many other activities.
2. Do not choose a title that is too narrow. (C) focuses on an element of the selection, the start and finish.
3. Do not choose a title that sounds profound but is really off the topic. (E) sounds good, but there is nothing in the passage to suggest the philosophical implications in (E).
4. Do not choose a title just because it strikes a responsive chord in your memory. (D) looks like the kind of title you'd expect in a passage about skiing. If you did not read the paragraph carefully, you might choose (D).
5. Choose a title that fits, that is neither too broad nor too narrow, that is on the topic and generalizes about the entire passage. (A) is such a title. It encompasses the race and all the activities associated with the race. In any consideration about the race, the planners would have to take into account all the subsidiary activities, as well as the housing problems and traffic jams. (A) covers the entire passage effectively. The other alternatives do not.

Time Out for Review

Try your skill. The passage below is followed by questions based on its content. Use the preceding example to help you find the right answers.

The paradox of Gilbert and Sullivan continues to amaze music lovers. The two men, utterly different in temperament and personality, somehow managed to collaborate on
5 more than a dozen operettas of enduring charm. Both men were told they were wasting their talents on the inconsequential Gilbert and Sullivan operettas, but somehow they stayed together, through stormy years
10 and occasional unpleasant sessions, to create immortal songs like "Tell me, pretty maiden" from *Patience*, songs that were a fortuitous blend of lyric and melody.

William Schwenck Gilbert, who wrote
15 the lyrics and generally determined the plot and direction of the operettas, was a rather stern Victorian, intolerant of laziness, indifference, or lack of talent. His guiding hand in the actual production guaranteed the qual-
20 ity of the production and the integrity of the performances. His witty, often satirical, lyrics punctured Victorian pomposity and inefficiency and, it is said, even ruffled the feathers of Queen Victoria.

25 Arthur Sullivan, who composed the lovely music for Gilbert's words, was a contrast to Gilbert. Sullivan was a rather gentle person, aristocratic, fond of the good life, often melancholy. Awed by titles, he loved
30 to hobnob with the great. Seldom robustly healthy, he created some of the most beautiful music while racked with pain.

On many occasions, Sullivan said, "I don't want to do another operetta," but after
35 each refusal, Gilbert would tempt Sullivan with plots, snatches of dialog, production ideas. In the background, Richard D'Oyly Carte acted as impresario and referee, bringing the two men back together again and
40 again, despite the apparent refusal of Sullivan to go on. Somehow, despite altercations, disagreements, and misunderstandings the two men created 14 operettas, 11 of which are still frequently played.

1. Which of the following titles best summarizes the content of the passage?
   (A) Operettas of Victorian England
   (B) The Preeminence of Gilbert in the Gilbert and Sullivan Operettas
   (C) A Happy Collaboration
   (D) The Many Sides of Genius
   (E) Gilbert and Sullivan: A Study in Contrasts

   1 ___

2. With which statement would the author probably agree?
   (A) Richard D'Oyly Carte was an incompetent go-between, irritating both men.
   (B) Of the two men, Gilbert and Sullivan, Sullivan seemed more easygoing.
   (C) William Schwenck Gilbert was basically warm and forgiving.
   (D) *Patience* is probably the most popular of all Gilbert and Sullivan operettas.
   (E) If Gilbert and Sullivan had channeled their energies into other areas, their achievements would have been greater.

   2 ___

SUMMARY PART 3

Drawing Generalizations and Finding the Main Idea: Providing a Title

Choosing a title is very similar to finding the main idea. The major difference lies in the way the alternatives are phrased.

PART 4

Providing a Summary

This is another variation of finding the main idea, but the phrasing is somewhat different. Note the following sample question:

The passage as a whole is best described as . . .

Trial Test

Take the trial test to evaluate your skill. Read the passage and chose the answer for the question that follows it.

"Because it is there!" George Mallory's explanation of why he kept trying to scale Mt. Everest is not a satisfying answer to a nonclimber. But a true climber understands.
5 In an exciting report on his mountain adventures, *Savage Arena*, Joe Tasker attempts to add his explanation to Mallory's. Tasker endured terrible hardships on the Eigerwand in Switzerland, K2 in Kashmir, Dunagiri in In-
10 dia, and Everest in Nepal-Tibet. With fellow climbers he experienced hope and despair in a desperate ascent after an avalanche had covered their tents. In a climb on the West Face of K2 he lost Nich Estcourt, a beloved
15 comrade. Yet he always went back—at last

to his death in May 1982 not far from the summit of Everest itself, the ultimate challenge. In the book written shortly before his death, he confessed, "In some ways, going
20 to the mountains is incomprehensible to many people and inexplicable to those who go. The reasons are difficult to unearth and only with those who are similarly drawn is there no need to try to explain."

The passage as a whole principally deals with _____.

(A) the mystique of mountain climbing (or the mysterious appeal of mountain climbing)
(B) the heroism of Joe Tasker
(C) the highest peaks in Europe and Asia
(D) the dangers of rock climbing
(E) the waste of life in mountain climbing

Answer to Trial Test

(*A*) the mystique of mountain climbing (or the mysterious appeal of mountain climbing) The pitfalls in answering this question resemble the pitfalls discussed in choosing titles. (*B*) is too narrow. Of course, the heroism of Joe Tasker is an important element in the passage, but it does not deal with the passage as a whole. (*E*) is an inference based on a detail. It does not deal with the passage as a whole. In a sense, (*D*) is much too broad. It also fails to address itself to the major point of the passage. (*C*) is irrelevant to the point of the passage. Only (*A*) adequately sums up the point of the passage.

Look at a typical SAT question and then analyze the possible answers.

Problem

The migration of the monarch butterfly is one of nature's profoundest mysteries and most incredible stories. Each fall the monarchs set forth on the dangerous trip to their
5 winter homes—principally in California and Mexico. They come from diverse areas, fly different routes, and bivouac along the way, often with tens of thousands of their fellows. They are buffeted by winds, threatened by
10 long stretches of water, and soaked by downpours. Yet somehow or other they make their way to "butterfly trees" on the Monterey Peninsula, in the mountains near Mexico City, and in other less-well-known sites.
15 Each spring they mate and head north. Most of the original migrants die on the return journey. Their offspring somehow pick up the journey and fly to areas they have never seen before, only to repeat the process in the
20 fall. No other insects migrate so predictably, very much like birds. The monarch migration has been called "one of the world's great natural events, comparable to the immense mammal movements on Africa's Serengeti
25 Plain."

The passage as a whole is best described as a

——————.

(A) plea for protection of the monarch's nesting sites
(B) comparison of monarch migration with the migration of other insects
(C) description of a beautiful and mysterious natural phenomenon
(D) testament of courage
(E) scientific evaluation of an event known to everyone

Strategy

Which alternative should you choose? Note that this question asks you to find the main idea, but instead of expressing the idea in statement form, it provides a label (plea, comparison, etc.) with qualifying phrases. Remember that you are seeking the main idea. You are dealing with "the passage as a whole." (A) might well be a follow-up to the ideas expressed in the paragraph, but it is not the expressed *main* idea. (B) is too narrow. There is a brief comparison with the migration of other insects, but this is a detail. (D) is too broad. Then, too, whether to call the instinctive reaction of the monarch "courage" is debatable. It is certainly so in human terms but not necessarily in scientific terms. (E) could fit a myriad of other paragraphs. It's too broad. (C) is accurate. The paragraph is devoted to the migration (the mysterious phenomenon) and each sentence emphasizes its mystery.

Time Out for Review

The following selections test your ability to draw conclusions in a variety of formats.

1. How large a part will solar energy play in the future? When will the nonreplaceable petroleum begin to run out? How large a role will coal play in the energy program of the future? Is nuclear energy a feasible alternative? Can we depend upon mini-hydroelectric systems to produce electricity in small but economical chunks? Questions like these are bandied back and forth in television discussions, news reports, and newspaper articles. There is, however, another possibility, little considered but strategically important. We can create tiny habitats that conserve energy.

Experts estimate that energy-minded landscaping can cut home energy needs by 30%. Early societies knew the value of creative plantings to help people keep cool in summer and warm in winter. Much of today's architecture, however, overlooks creative possibilities for energy conservation, wasting precious resources through inefficient planning. Trees, shrubs, vines, and ground covers can be planted to protect against the summer's blazing sun. These plants are living air conditioners, evaporating water and cooling the air. Planting windbreaks can help keep out wintry blasts. Even small windbreaks around a foundation reduce heat loss by providing a wall of insulating air around the house. Winter and summer, living plants can work for us and save us energy dollars.

The passage as a whole is best described as a

_____ .

(A) warning against the depletion of coal resources
(B) comparison of today's architecture with that of another day
(C) suggestion for handling the cold of winter
(D) call for a partnership with nature in energy conservation
(E) criticism of nuclear energy as a solution to current energy problems

1 ____

2. Would you like to grow your own vegetables without cultivation, weeding, or soil preparation? Would you like to avoid problems of ground insects, moles, rabbits, or other animals? You may find hydroponic gardening your solution. This branch of gardening uses no soil. Vegetables grow in a nutrient solution in any place convenient to the gardener. Large tracts of land are not required, for plants grow rather close together in perfect harmony. Joe Corso of Altamonte Springs, Florida, hasn't bought a vegetable in 15 years. He grows several varieties of lettuce, tomatoes, cucumbers, green peppers, zucchini, broccoli, basil, scallions, and escarole. He insists a complete garden can be set up for $20–$35 as a one-time cost. The nutrients will cost $15–$20 a year for a complete garden. Soilless gardening has many possibilities. Principles of hydroponic gardening, for example, are used for desert gardens where sand contains little or no natural nutrients.

Which of the following titles best summarizes the content of the passage?

(A) Growing Vegetables the Easy Way: Without Soil
(B) A Florida Experiment That Paid Off
(C) Desert Gardens: Using the World's Barren Lands
(D) A New Product for Attacking World Hunger
(E) A Backyard Garden with a Different Approach

2 ____

3. Until relatively recently the exploitation of the vast Amazon Basin was minimal. Extensive clearing of forests and overfishing of rivers was unknown. The
5 primitive dwellers in the region harvested the resources conservatively and thus preserved, until recently, the tremendous natural wealth of the entire area. A restraining influence, not altogether lost on the little farmers and
10 hunters of today, was a belief in supernatural game wardens and forest demons. These creatures, the forest dwellers believed, punish those who abuse nature's generosity. Some of these spirits watch over game. Oth-
15 ers harass those who venture too far into the jungle. These deterrents averted the greedy, mindless destruction that has characterized man's treatment of nature in other parts of the world. Though the rise in population and
20 new economic pressures are now threatening the entire basin, there are still signs of primitive beliefs held by the rural population of Amazonia.

Which of the following expresses the main idea of the passage?

(A) A belief in supernatural game wardens and forest demons is a sign of ignorance.
(B) Too often man has exploited the natural resources around him.
(C) A tremendous population explosion has upset the balance of nature in Amazonia.
(D) Primitive dwellers are in reality more sophisticated than urban residents.
(E) A belief in spirits kept men from exploiting the Amazon basin.

3 ____

SUMMARY PART 4

Drawing Generalizations and Finding the Main Idea: Providing a Summary

The ability to summarize the essential point of a paragraph is closely related to the ability to choose the correct title and express the main idea. Be sure you are not sidetracked by details, or by generalizations broad enough to cover an article, not a reading passage.

Summary
Section I: Drawing Generalizations and Finding the Main Idea

The ability to generalize takes many forms: You may be asked to generalize about a portion of the reading passage: a paragraph or even an important sentence. Or you may have to find the central point of the paragraph in a variety of question formats. The ability to extract main ideas is a crucial skill in note-taking and in study.

The strategies for drawing generalizations and finding the main idea will help you prepare for the SAT.

PART 1 Drawing Generalizations

A. Read the question carefully so that you are sure of the generalization asked for.
B. Find and reread the portion of the passage that has the information for making the generalization.
C. Draw the generalization asked for. Base it on the portion you reread.

PART 2 Finding the Main Idea

A. Reread the entire passage.
B. Get a feel for the *whole passage*, not just a part of it.
C. If several ideas are developed, weigh them all. Then decide on the main idea.

PART 3 Providing a Title

Choosing a title is similar to finding the main idea.

A. Get a feel for the whole passage, not just a part of it.
B. Notice that the title choices are in headline form, not sentence form.
C. Choose the ''headline'' that best covers the whole ''story.''

PART 4 Providing a Summary

Choosing a summary is similar to finding the main idea and choosing a title.

A. Keep the whole passage in mind; reread it if you are unsure.
B. Don't be sidetracked by details; on the other hand, don't go beyond the limits of the passage.
C. Choose the statement that sums up the whole passage and that does not go beyond it.

Section II: Drawing Inferences

PART 1

Identifying Inferences

"Sue just sneezed. She must have a cold."

These two statements that sound alike are quite different. The first is a factual observation. The second is an inference. The first is based on a verifiable observation. The second is a judgment that may or may not accord with the facts. Sue may have an allergy. The room may be dusty.

There is nothing wrong with drawing inferences. We often run our lives on the basis of inference. We see people bundled up outside our window and prepare for a cold day. The danger arises when we take an inference for a fact. If we understand the difference between fact and inference, we manage our lives intelligently.

There are good, reasonable inferences; there are poor, irrational ones. When we hear the teakettle whistling, we reasonably infer the water is boiling. When a friend fails to appear for a meeting, we should not infer he or she is rejecting us. There may be dozens of good reasons for his or her failure to come.

Inference plays an important role in SAT reading questions. The following words and phrases are often used to test your ability to draw inferences.

1. assume
2. hint
3. imply
4. indicate
5. presume
6. presuppose
7. suggest
8. suppose
9. apparently believes
10. can be inferred
11. can best be described as
12. may be interpreted

Trial Test

For the following test question select the best inference.

The barometric pressure dropped rapidly. The wind, formerly at calm, suddenly began to whip up. The harbor flag, which had been flapping listlessly, stood out with
5   the force of the wind. Owners of boats in the marina dashed about, fastening boat covers securely and checking all mooring ropes. A few drops of rain splattered the pavement. The sun had already disappeared, and the
10 world was dark.

The part of the storm being described is
_____.

(A) the warning
(B) the beginning
(C) the height
(D) the end
(E) the aftermath

Answer to Trial Test

(B) The entire passage suggests the beginning of a storm, but there are more specific clues, too: the sudden whipping of the wind, the frantic activity of boat owners, the beginning of the rain. The full force of the storm has not yet struck, but its impact is beginning to be felt. We can infer from the clues that the worst is yet to come.

Now look at a typical question and analyze the possible answers.

Problem

There is one creature perfectly adapted and temperamentally suited to some of the most inhospitable areas of the world: the camel. In the ecology of the Sahara Desert,
5 the nomad and the camel live in a mutually satisfactory dependence on each other. The nomad provides the camel with water and food. The camel provides the nomad with milk, wool, transportation, and meat. Above
10 all, the camel provides work and gives meaning to the lives of the tribes that criss-cross the Sahara. The camel provides the only means by which human beings can con-structively utilize the desert. Camel herding,
15 combined with nomadism to take advantage of seasonal rains and recurrent scattered veg-etation, is the only feasible solution to sur-viving on the desert. The camel is at the heart of all efforts to live in harmony with
20 the desert.

1. The passage implies that _____ .
   (A) human beings should give up the challenge of living on the desert
   (B) no other creature can replace the camel
   (C) nomads unfairly exploit their camels
   (D) the Sahara Desert is less hospitable than any other desert
   (E) camels are less satisfactory than cattle in many ways

2. The essential point made about nomads is that they are _____ .
   (A) kindly toward their camels
   (B) essentially traders and merchants
   (C) experts on camel wool
   (D) wanderers
   (E) poets in harmony with life

Strategy

1. Nowhere does the writer suggest that human beings should give up the challenge of living on the desert. Instead, the author commends survival under difficult conditions. (A) is incorrect. The first sentence, on the other hand, does suggest that the camel is one of a kind. The rest of the paragraph supports that suggestion. (B) sounds right. There is no mention of unfair treatment of camels. Reject (C). There is no comparison of the Sahara with other deserts. Reject (D). Cattle are nowhere mentioned or implied. Reject (E).

2. There are two clues to (D) as the correct answer: crisscrossing the Sahara and movement to take advantage of rains and scattered vegetation. (A), (B), and (C) are nowhere suggested. (E) is much too grandiose, out of keeping with the straightforward, serious note of the passage. Note that this question is allied to "drawing generalizations," as outlined in Part 1 (pages 214–216). The *essential* point is a kind of generalization.

Time Out for Review

Try your skill. Use the preceding example to help you find the right answers.

Amateur photographers constantly seek more complete cameras, with faster and faster lenses. They want cameras that focus automatically, determine the correct expo-
5 sure, provide flash when needed—all to produce the perfect picture. Some photographers, however, think automation has taken some of the fun out of photography. For these photographers, a return to basics can
10 be fun.

There is nothing more basic than a pinhole camera. Pinhole photography depends on the passage of light through a small hole in an opaque screen. The pinhole acts like a
15 lens. The light falls on film to construct the image, as in a lens camera. Aristotle mentioned images from pinholes. Leonardo da Vinci explained the principle involved. Lord Rayleigh formally analyzed the process. The
20 pinhole camera has an ancient history, but it has some modern appeals.

The major advantage of the pinhole camera is simplicity. Pictures made with the pinhole camera do have a special quality. But
25 the fun is the challenge of deciding how large the pinhole is to be and how the picture is to be taken. The pinhole camera will never replace the lens camera, but for the amateur enthusiast, it can provide hours of challenge
30 and experimentation.

1. The passage implies that _____.
   (A) the pinhole camera may replace the lens camera in years to come
   (B) Leonardo took pictures with a pinhole camera
   (C) light passes through a pinhole in much the same way it passes through a lens
   (D) vast numbers of amateur photographers have temporarily given up lens photography for pinhole photography
   (E) pictures taken with the pinhole camera are superior to those taken with the lens camera

   1 ____

2. It may be inferred that _____.
   (A) a pinhole camera is a true camera
   (B) automation in cameras should be discarded
   (C) Aristotle used a lens camera
   (D) the size of the pinhole is not important in pinhole photography
   (E) images from a pinhole camera are not inverted

   2 ____

SUMMARY PART 1

Drawing Inferences: Identifying Inferences

An inference differs from a factual statement, but a good inference is an educated guess that is closely tied to the facts.

For an SAT answer, read between the lines and make your inference a reasonable one.

PART 2

Drawing Inferences: Supplying an Interpretation

"Joe said he won't play football this Sunday under any circumstances."

"What he really meant was that he wouldn't play unless he could start as quarterback."

Life is filled with situations in which one person interprets the words of another. Doing so requires drawing inferences. SAT questions sometimes ask for interpretations using wording like this.

Trial Test

Read the following and choose the answer for the question that follows it.

Most people are aware that ammonia, bleach, and household cleaners are poison, but few people realize that cosmetics, shampoos, shaving creams, and lipstick can be
5 deadly if swallowed by small children. The list of dangerous substances is surprisingly large, including hair spray, toothpaste, nail polish and nail polish remover, makeup, and deodorants. Of course, these substances are
10 used by adults only in small quantities and are not swallowed. Thus, many parents fail to realize that since small children put almost anything into their mouths, they may swallow dangerous amounts of what are usually
15 considered "perfectly safe" substances. Eternal vigilance is the price of safety as well as liberty.

Which of the following best expresses the meaning of the sentence, "Eternal vigilance is the price of safety as well as liberty"?

(A) Parents should probably keep hair spray out of the house.
(B) Young children should never be left unsupervised.
(C) Children should assume a share of responsibility for dangerous substances.
(D) Safety and liberty always go together.
(E) Parents need to be constantly aware of dangers in the home.

Answer to Trial Test

(*E*) The major thrust of the paragraph is the danger in many common household substances. The summarizing statement suggests that the dangers require constant vigilance on the part of parents. This is the idea contained in (*E*). The statement parallels a famous quotation: "Eternal vigilance is the price of liberty." Knowing the quotation adds interest to the question, but such knowledge is not necessary for the correct answer.

Now look at a typical question and analyze the possible answers.

Problem

"Prairie fire!" The words struck terror into the hearts of many settlers. Dry grass burns rapidly. Out of control, a prairie fire can be an awesome sight. Yet today con-
5 trolled fires are set to help the grasslands survive. Without occasional fire, undesirable intruders like red cedar begin to take over the land. Unwelcome smaller plants, like Kentucky bluegrass, soon replace native
10 grasses and change the character of prairie islands preserved as examples of the American natural heritage. Litter on the prairie floor also changes the ecology of an area and permits aggressive exotic plants to move in.
15 Fire removes litter and provides the opportunity for native grasslands to be preserved for generations to come. But the fires must be set only after extensive study and analysis of wind, wind speed, relative humidity, tem-
20 perature, and the physical factors of the vegetation to be burned.

1. Which of the following best expresses the meaning of the phrase "changes the ecology of an area and permits aggressive exotic plants to move in?"
   (A) upsets the natural balance in favor of non-native species
   (B) evaluates natural conditions and restrains newcomers
   (C) introduces nonproductive changes and starts fires
   (D) accelerates proper soil management by allowing diversification
   (E) expresses admiration for the forces of nature and survival of the fittest

   1 ___

2. A "controlled fire" is set _____.
   (A) when the native grasses need burning
   (B) after a summer storm
   (C) as soon as a red cedar appears on the grassland
   (D) when environmental factors are right
   (E) on a consistent and regular basis

   2 ___

Strategy

1. On first reading (A) seems to be the best answer, but let's check the others just to be sure. Litter changes the ecology but doesn't evaluate it. (B) is incorrect. Litter may permit nonproductive changes, but of itself it does not start fires. (C) is incorrect. (D) has the wrong meaning altogether. The selection speaks against diversification with exotic plants. (E) is also contrary to the idea of the passage. The passage is concerned with the survival of native plants, not necessarily with the survival of the fittest.

2. We may infer that a "controlled fire," by definition, is set when conditions can be controlled. (D) provides the right suggestion. The fire is not set when native grasses need burning (A), but when total conditions suggest the need for a fire. A summer storm (B) might provide one of the safety conditions for the fire, but it is not the determining factor. The removal of a single red cedar (C) does not require a fire. There is no indication anywhere that fires are set (E) on a regular basis. (D) is indeed the correct answer.

Time Out for Review

Try your skill. The passage below is followed by four questions based on its content. Use the preceding example to help you find the right answers.

Patan is the oldest of the "Three cities of the ancient Kathmandu Valley," whose origins are lost in the mists of history. Visitors to Nepal can take a taxi from the cap-
5 ital, Kathmandu, and find themselves transported to a mystical past, where shrines of Hindu and Buddhist deities rub elbows. On the facades of ancient temples are ornate carvings with religious and historical signif-
10 icance. Most of these temples have been built in a superb architectural style.

Durbar Square, in the center of the city, is a colorful blend of architectural inspirations and historical associations. Along the
15 cobble-lined streets are the houses of skilled craftsmen, whose arts, processes, and designs have been passed from father to son. Here three generations of a family sit side by side, creating art of exquisite beauty. The
20 imposing Krishna Mandir, temple of the Lord Krishna, dominates the picturesque square, which is always vibrant with life.

1. Which of the following best expresses the meaning of the phrase "a colorful blend of architectural inspirations and historical associations"?

    (A) a subtle attempt to sway the religious beliefs of observers
    (B) a center for folk art and the treasures of another day

    (C) a picturesque mixture of modern and historical arts and crafts
    (D) brilliantly conceived architecture with historical significance
    (E) a number of functional buildings created for long-forgotten deities

    1 ___

2. An excellent adjective to describe Patan is _____.

    (A) huge   (D) sparkling
    (B) financially   (E) grim
        sound
    (C) unvaried

    2 ___

3. Which word best summarizes the work of Nepalese craftsmen?

    (A) fatigue   (D) indifference
    (B) continuity   (E) rigidity
    (C) improvisation

    3 ___

4. Which of the following titles best summarizes the content of the passage?

    (A) Durbar Square: Heart of Patan
    (B) From Kathmandu to Patan: A Royal Road
    (C) Nepalese Temples: History in Stone
    (D) Patan: A Many-Splendored City
    (E) Architecture in Nepal

    4 ___

SUMMARY PART 2

Drawing Inferences: Supplying an Interpretation

An interpretation calls for drawing inferences about actions, statements, or events. Watch for interpretation questions on the SAT. You will be asked to supply another way of saying something. If you restate the phrase or sentence in your own words, you can then find the answer closest to your own.

PART 3

Drawing Inferences: Providing a Paraphrase

Sometimes you will be asked to provide an interpretation slightly longer than that called for in Part 2. Such an extended interpretation is a **paraphrase**. You might tend to consider such a lengthy interpretation a summary, as in Section I, Part 4. There is, however, a great difference between a summary and a paraphrase. A summary condenses, provides the gist of a selection in far fewer words. A paraphrase, on the other hand, gives the sense of a given segment in different words, but roughly in the same number of words. A good paraphrase calls for comprehension and the drawing of sound inferences. On the SAT you may meet a question with wording like the following.

Which of the following is the best interpretation of lines –––?

Trial Test

Choose the best answer for the question at the end of the selection.

The Information Explosion adds knowledge at an incredible rate. Some say that knowledge has been doubling every ten years. Others agree and add that the rate is
5 increasing. The new industries spawned by computers alone are increasing at a phenomenal rate. What is behind this breath-taking growth? What spurs people on to new inventions and broader applications of existing
10 technology? Ralph Hinton, an American anthropologist, had an unusual answer: "The human capacity for being bored, rather than man's social or natural needs, lies at the root of man's cultural advance."

Which is the best interpretation of the quotation by Ralph Hinton?

(A) A man's reach should always exceed his grasp.
(B) The Information Explosion is not necessarily a desirable thing.
(C) Man's restless spirit, not his needs, brings advances.
(D) Boredom takes time away from caring for people's needs.
(E) To be bored is to be creative; to be happy is to be lazy.

Answer to Trial Test

(C) The last sentence of the selection gives the central idea. The best paraphrase of the idea is (*C*): "Man's restless spirit, not his needs, brings advances." Note that both the original statement and the paraphrase say essentially the same thing.

Now look at a typical question and analyze the possible answers.

Problem

"I like my football players agile, mobile, and hostile." Coach Tom Burrows' successful philosophy was summed up in that favorite statement. Not an exponent of trick
5   plays, strange formations, and razzle dazzle, Burrows concentrated upon fundamentals: clean, hard tackling; crisp, sure blocking; thorough preparation; and a methodical, consistent game plan. He didn't depend upon
10 surprise. If his opponents knew his next play was a plunge off right tackle, Burrows didn't care. He depended upon complete cooperation of all his players, superb execution, split-second timing, and the will to win.
15 Burrows would have agreed with Austin O'Malley, who said, "In dealing with a foolish or stubborn adversary, remember your own mood constitutes half the force opposing you." Other coaches belittled Bur-
20 rows' coaching philosophy and mentally put him back in the dark ages, but they could not fault his incredible string of victories.

1. Which is the best interpretation of the quotation by Austin O'Malley?

   (A) In a close game your opponent may foolishly or stubbornly refuse to play your game.
   (B) In any sport emotion is as important an ingredient as thought and preparation.
   (C) Your opponent may defeat you by doubling his efforts while you halve yours.
   (D) In a hard game you may be your own worst enemy.
   (E) If your players do not play hard, emotions may help your opponents win.

   1 ___

2. The attitude of other coaches toward Burrows might be considered _____ .

   (A) condescending but respectful
   (B) baffled but cheerful
   (C) inconsistent and terrified
   (D) hostile and uncooperative
   (E) curious and imitative

   2 ___

3. Burrows probably did not rely on trick plays because _____ .

   (A) he preferred razzle dazzle
   (B) he thought they weren't necessary
   (C) other coaches liked them
   (D) they made his players careless
   (E) they needed too much planning

   3 ___

Strategy

1. The answer which best paraphrases the quotation is (D). The quotation says that "your own mood constitutes half the force opposing you." If that mood is negative, you help to defeat youself. (A) is off the topic. Nothing is said about the opponents' game. For the same reason (C) is incorrect. (B) is too broad. (E) seems plausible, but there is no suggestion about whether or not the players play hard.

2. The final sentence is the clue to this answer: (A). "Belittled" suggests condescension, but the victories suggest respect.

3. The selection says that Burrows concentrated on fundamentals instead of relying on trick plays. The answer is (B).

Time Out for Review

Try your skill. The passage below is followed by questions based on its content. Use the preceding example to help you find the right answers.

Grandpa was a monument to sanity in a crazy world. He never set the world on fire or put his name up in lights. He had a modest job at the post office all his working life and
5 retired to hobbies, crafts, and volunteer work. It was his personality that endeared him to all who knew him. It was his philosophy of life that enriched the lives of his friends and relatives. He embodied Reinhold
10 Niebuhr's prayer never to worry about what could not be changed and to concentrate only on what could be changed. He lived today and let those two impostors, yesterday and tomorrow, worry about themselves. He was
15 bright, sunny, jovial, optimistic, and a joy to be with. He often quoted a common quotation to sum up his own beliefs: "Inch by inch, life is a cinch. Yard by yard, life is hard."

1. Which is the best interpretation of the quotation in the selection?
   (A) Life can be measured in inches or in yards.
   (B) Life is tragic if we stop to think about it too much.
   (C) Life is easy or hard depending on your point of view.
   (D) To avoid worry and stress, take life a small step at a time.
   (E) If you don't plan for the future, you won't have one.

   1 ___

2. Yesterday and tomorrow are called "impostors" because _____ .
   (A) the future is uncertain and the past is gone
   (B) worry is always destructive
   (C) fortunetellers take advantage of gullible people
   (D) we truly live in thinking about the future
   (E) they contradict Reinhold Niebuhr's prayer

   2 ___

3. The best word to describe Grandpa is _____ .

   (A) skilled   (D) anxious
   (B) cautious   (E) ambitious
   (C) sensible

   3 ___

SUMMARY PART 3

Drawing Inferences: Providing a Paraphrase

A paraphrase is a restatement of a sentence or a selection, not a summary. A paraphrase presents the essential point in other words. It parallels the material; it doesn't condense it.

PART 4

Drawing Inferences: Making a Comparison

Inferences come in many forms. Sometimes on the SAT you will be asked to compare two ideas, persons, expressions, or arguments. Comparisons like these require you to draw several inferences. One SAT question used this phrasing.

In the second paragraph, the author's chief distinction is between which of the following?

Trial Test

Read the following. Then choose the answer to the question at the end.

Stamp collectors sometimes have to make a key decision: whether to concentrate on stamps that have been postally used or to collect only clean, pure, unused stamps,
5 often direct from the printing presses. Postally used stamps are not as pretty as mint stamps. Portions of their designs have been obliterated by cancellation marks. Mint stamps, on the other hand, are sparkling and
10 clear, with every design detail clearly visible. But used stamps have something extra: actual use in the mails. Often their cancellations provide information about date and place of use. They often demonstrate the ro-
15 mance of the mails. Collectors of only used stamps call stamps *mere labels* until they perform their function in the mails. Postally used stamps may conveniently be put into an album with stamp hinges, without any con-
20 cern about a loss in value. On the other hand,

mint stamps that have been hinged lose part of their value in the marketplace. They must thus be encased in transparent envelopes and pockets that show the stamps without stick-
25 ing hinges to them. Mounting mint stamps thus takes more time, energy, and money. There is something to be said for both decisions, and some collectors collect both kinds of stamps. But usually a collector has
30 a secret preference.

In this selection the author's chief distinction is between which of the following?

(A) used stamps and mint stamps
(B) the arguments for collecting two types of stamps
(C) good stamps and worthless stamps
(D) the market values of two different types of stamps
(E) the aesthetic value of a used stamp as contrasted with that of a mint stamp

Answer to Trial Test

(*B*) The selection is an extended comparison of the arguments for collecting two types of stamps: mint and used. Though all five choices suggest comparisons, only (*B*) states the essential comparison: the *arguments* for collecting the two types of stamps. (*A*) is incomplete. (*C*) and (*D*) are not touched upon. (*E*) is a detail only partially covered.

Now look at a typical question and analyze the possible answers.

Problem

Distinguishing between the speaker and his argument is difficult but essential. We tend to accept the statements of those we like and reject the statements of those we dislike.
5 Yet our friends may be speaking nonsense and our enemies, the truth. An obnoxious person may have something valuable to say. A major task is focusing attention on what is said and not on who is saying it. There
10 are four possible reactions. We may accept the speaker and accept his argument. We may reject the speaker and reject his argument. We may accept the speaker and reject his argument. We may reject the speaker and
15 accept his argument. The first two are easy. A person with a closed mind finds no prob-
lem here. The person with an open mind must, however, be able to have all four reactions. To focus on the argument and not
20 be swayed unduly by the personality of the speaker is true maturity.

In this selection the writer's chief distinction is between which of the following?

(A) personality and maturity
(B) speakers and their points of view
(C) acceptance and rejection
(D) inductive and deductive reasoning
(E) the open mind and the closed mind

Strategy

Personality (*A*) is mentioned as an influence on reaction to argument. It is not contrasted with maturity. Speakers (*B*) do have different points of view, but the major point deals with listeners' reactions to speakers' arguments. As an answer, *acceptance* and *rejection* (*C*) is much too broad for this paragraph. Inductive and deductive reasoning (*D*) are neither mentioned nor implied. The basic contrast is between the open mind, which accepts all four possibilities, and the closed mind, which accepts only the first two. (*E*) is correct.

Time Out for Review

Try your skill. The passage below is followed by four questions based on its content. Use the preceding example to help you find the right answers.

"The left hand is the dreamer; the right hand is the doer."

Scientists often discover wisdom in folk sayings. There has been much recent spec-
5 ulation about the hemispheres of the brain and their various functions. The right hemisphere of the brain controls the left side of the body. The left hemisphere controls the right side. But there is more to the division.
10 In most people language and language-related abilities are located in the left hemisphere. Because language is so closely related to thinking and reasoning, the left hemisphere is concerned with conscious
15 thought processes and problem solving. It was once considered the major hemisphere. But recent investigations have shown that the right hemisphere also plays an important role in the total functioning of the personality.
20 This hemisphere provides nonverbal skills and a different mode of thinking. Whereas the left hemisphere tends to be verbal and analytic, the right hemisphere tends to be nonverbal and global. The right hemisphere
25 is not inferior to the left. It processes information differently, often providing creative leaps and sudden insights not available to the left hemisphere. The left hand, controlled by the right hemisphere, is "the dreamer," but
30 the label should not suggest inferiority or incapacity. Both hemispheres play an equivalent, though different, role in the functioning of the personality.

1. In this selection the writer's chief distinction is between which of the following?
   - (A) the left hand and the right hand
   - (B) dreamers and doers
   - (C) the functions of two brain hemispheres
   - (D) nonverbal skills and analytic abilities
   - (E) applied science and folk wisdom

   1 ___

2. Of the following skills, which would probably belong to the right hemisphere?
   - (A) writing a summary
   - (B) creating music
   - (C) classifying objects
   - (D) translating an article
   - (E) criticizing a movie

   2 ___

3. The article suggests that _____.
   - (A) the left brain controls left-handedness
   - (B) the left brain is the major hemisphere
   - (C) a left-handed person is at a disadvantage in a right-handed world
   - (D) both hemispheres are important for a complete personality
   - (E) scientists have discredited the theory that there are two hemispheres

   3 ___

4. Which of the following titles best summarizes the content of the passage?
   - (A) Creativity and the Human Brain
   - (B) Poetry: A Left-Brain Function
   - (C) The Brain: A Two-Part Mechanism
   - (D) Personality Types
   - (E) Language and the Human Brain

   4 ___

SUMMARY PART 4

Drawing Inferences: Making a Comparison

When asked to evaluate comparisons, be sure to isolate the two important things being compared. Don't hit upon a minor comparison. Alternative *1A* above singles out a minor illustration though the question calls for the *chief distinction*.

Summary
Section II: Drawing Inferences

An inference is an educated guess. Though it is based on facts, it goes beyond facts. It reads between the lines and makes a judgment. Often many inferences can be drawn from a single statement or situation. Always choose the most reasonable one, the one most consistent with the facts.

Review the strategies for drawing inferences often as you prepare for the SAT.

PART 1. Identifying Inferences

A. Recognize an inference question. Look for such words as: *imply*, *assume*, *suggest*, *apparently believes*.
B. Look for the facts related to the inference question.
C. Base your inference (your "educated guess") on the facts.
D. Remember, a fact is an observation you can prove. An inference is a guess or a judgment. Don't confuse the two.

PART 2. Supplying an Interpretation

A. Recognize an interpretation question, asking you to say something in another way. Look for such wording as:
    Which best expresses the meaning of . . .
    An excellent adjective to describe _____ is . . .
B. Find the word or phrase in question.
C. Use your own word or phrase to say the same thing.
D. Choose the answer that corresponds most closely to what you have said in your own words.

PART 3 Providing a Paraphrase

A. A paraphrase question asks for a restatement (or "interpretation") of an entire sentence or paragraph or more.
B. Find the material to be paraphrased.
C. Put it in your own words; be sure you are saying the same thing. Restate; don't summarize.
D. Choose the answer that corresponds most closely to what you have said in your own words.

PART 4 Making a Comparison

A. A comparison question asks you to compare two ideas, persons, expressions, or arguments.
B. Look for comparison words such as *difference between* or *distinction between*.
C. Be sure you know what is being compared.
D. Focus on the *important* things being compared.

Section III: Finding Details

PART 1

Spotting Details in the Text

In reading tests, you must be able to find more than generalizations. You'll need to pick out details, specific items in the text. These test items occur in a variety of forms. Here's a skeleton sample.

1. The author refers to . . . as an example of . . .
2. The author bases the answer to the question . . . on . . .
3. According to the passage what happens to . . . ?
4. Sousa's work is "practical" in the sense that it is . . .
5. According to the passage, one of the cultural lessons taught by African art is that art should be . . .
6. The author mentions fluorescent lamps and transistors as examples of . . .
7. According to the passage a cohort study is one that . . .
8. The author cites . . . for their . . .
9. The author mentions which of the following as experiences common to . . . ?
10. According to the passage, a true work of art can be the product of all the following EXCEPT . . .

Again, despite the variety of formats, the essential task is straightforward. With these questions you must comb the selection for *specific* phrases and sentences being asked for.

Trial Test

For the following test questions write the letter for the best answer.

The long association of Joseph Duveen and Henry E. Huntington resulted in an art collection of unquestioned excellence. Like many other wealthy men of his time, Hunt-
5 ington distrusted his own judgment, relying instead upon the impeccable taste of an art dealer who had the knack of matching millionaire and painting. It was Joseph Duveen who bought for Huntington and his wife Ar-
10 abella the two famous paintings often paired in the eyes of the public: Gainsborough's *The Blue Boy* and Lawrence's *Pinkie*. Without prodding from Duveen, Huntington would never have bought Turner's *The*
15 *Grand Canal*. Over the protest of Arabella Huntington, Duveen persuaded Huntington to buy Reynolds' masterpiece, *Sarah Siddons as the Tragic Muse*. Arabella had at first objected to having a picture of an actress
20 in her home. Another Reynolds gem, *Georgiana, Duchess of Devonshire*, was added to the Huntington collection. One painting that Arabella Huntington bought, with Duveen's help, is the priceless painting, Rogier van
25 der Weyden's *The Virgin and Christ Child*. Visitors to the Huntington Gallery in San Marino, California, owe a debt to Henry E. Huntington, who accumulated the art now available to the public. But it was Joseph
30 Duveen who made it all possible.

242

1. The painting Arabella was reluctant to buy
was _____ .
   (A) *The Grand Canal*
   (B) *Georgiana, Duchess of Devonshire*
   (C) *Sarah Siddons as the Tragic Muse*
   (D) *The Blue Boy*
   (E) *The Virgin and Christ Child*

                                              1 ___

2. Two paintings often paired by the public
are _____ .
   (A) *The Grand Canal* and *Pinkie*
   (B) *Sarah Siddons as the Tragic Muse*
       and *Pinkie*
   (C) *The Virgin and Christ Child* and *The
       Blue Boy*
   (D) *Pinkie* and *The Blue Boy*
   (E) *Georgiana, Duchess of Devonshire*
       and *Sarah Siddons as the Tragic
       Muse*

                                              2 ___

Answers to Trial Test

1. (*C*) The selection specifically says, "Over the protest of Arabella Huntington, Duveen persuaded Huntington to buy Reynolds' masterpiece, *Sarah Siddons
as the Tragic Muse*."

2. (*D*) The selection talks about "the two famous paintings often paired in the
eyes of the public: Gainsborough's *The Blue Boy* and Lawrence's *Pinkie*."

Look at a typical SAT-type question and then analyze the possible answers.

Problem

In June, 1981, Jay Johnson started out
on an incredible journey—a self-propelled
trip around the United States. At no time did
Johnson rely on any motorized transporta-
5 tion, though he used a variety of methods.
He started in northern Maine and backpacked south along the Appalachian Trail to
Georgia. Still on foot, he reached Montgomery, Alabama. He picked up a 15-foot dory
10 in Montgomery and rowed down the wild
Alabama River to the Gulf of Mexico. Rowing 1200 miles along the Gulf coast, he
reached Brownsville, Texas. Then he chose
a bicycle for his 3000 mile trip through the
15 Southwest. He gave up the bicycle in southern California and backpacked north on the
Pacific Coast Trail all the way to British Columbia, arriving in late September, 1982. His
trip had lasted 16 months and covered nearly
20 10,000 miles. To help him along his unusual
journey, he estimated his needs in advance
and then used the Postal Service for delivery
of supplies to prearranged points. He plotted
his journey like a military campaign, with a
25 thorough evaluation of his abilities and
needs. This was a magical experience, but
there was no magic behind its success.

1. The bicycle portion of the journey took place
_____ .
   (A) in Montgomery, Alabama
   (B) at the very end
   (C) in British Columbia
   (D) before the arrival in Brownsville
   (E) in the Southwest

                                              1 ___

2. As used in the selection "self-propelled"
means _____ .
   (A) highly motivated
   (B) carrying a backpack
   (C) without motorized help
   (D) well planned
   (E) using the Postal Service

                                              2 ___

3. Jay Johnson used each of the following
methods EXCEPT _____ .
   (A) bicycle
   (B) dory
   (C) backpack
   (D) mule
   (E) rowing

                                              3 ___

Strategy

This is a fairly easy selection to get you started and help you see various strategies used in testing for details.

1. Often the answer is found in a single sentence: "Then he chose a bicycle for his 3000 mile trip through the Southwest." Go no further. (*E*) is correct.

2. All five answers relate to the passage, but only (*C*) is responsive to the question. Sentence 2, following immediately after Sentence 1, provides a ready definition of "self-propelled." (*C*) is correct.

3. This type of question is sometimes confusing because of *except*. Under stress and in haste, sometimes candidates fail to read carefully. They see *bicycle* and say, "He used a bicycle." But the *except*, of course, excludes *bicycle*, *backpack*, and *dory*. Note, too, that *rowing* and *dory* are essentially the same. There is no mention of using a mule. Therefore (*D*) is correct.

Time Out for Review

Try your skill. The passage below is followed by questions based on its content. Use the preceding example to help you find the right answers.

What happens when a climate change occurs swiftly? When living conditions change almost overnight, how do various species react to the sudden demands upon them? The
5 appearance of El Niño in 1982–83 helped scientists to study, in a short period, effects that normally take much longer to appear. El Niño—a stream of unusually warm western Pacific water—had a far-reaching impact
10 on all fish, bird, and mammalian life in an area from Chile to southern Alaska and west as far as the central Pacific.
  The unusually warm water upset the balance, starting a chain of events that did in-
15 calculable damage. The normally cold water off the coast of Peru is rich in nutrients. These nutrients support microscopic plants called *phytoplankton*, the base of the food chain. When the phytoplankton population
20 dropped to 5% of normal, anchovies, sardines, jack mackerel, and other fish began to disappear. Then the species depending upon fish had to look elsewhere. Cormorants and boobies headed north for food. Penguins
25 and seals headed south. Though adults tended to survive, the young birds and animals could not be fed and were abandoned. Even seal mothers, normally the most maternal of animals, abandoned their pups to
30 starvation. Whole colonies of nesting birds disappeared. Even ecosystems far from El Niño were affected by the climatic changes and disappearance of food in the normally bountiful Pacific. Yet, scientists say, there
35 have been drastic swings before, appearances of unpredictable El Niño in past history. Without additional pollution or overfishing by man, species will recover in time. There is one good result despite the difficul-
40 ties: scientists appreciate the natural laboratory provided by the unwelcome visitor.

1. To support marine life along the coast of Peru, which of the following is most important?
   (A) abundant sunshine
   (B) an occasional tropical storm
   (C) a large school of sardines
   (D) El Niño
   (E) cold water

   1 _____

2. One positive contribution of El Niño is _____ .

   (A) the natural laboratory it supplied
   (B) the improvement in bathing facilities along the coast of South America
   (C) the possibility of new tourist resorts in Alaska
   (D) an indication that the conditions will never be repeated
   (E) a great increase in phytoplankton

                                          2 ___

3. Apparently contradictory behavior was exhibited by _____ .

   (A) anchovies   (D) seals
   (B) phytoplankton   (E) jack mackerel
   (C) penguins   3 ___

4. The effects of El Niño can best be described as _____ .

   (A) far reaching
   (B) beneficent
   (C) largely unobserved
   (D) minimal
   (E) of little scientific interest

                                          4 ___

5. In terms of species survival, the abandonment of the young by seal mothers was _____ .

   (A) prudent
   (B) cruel
   (C) an indication of indifference
   (D) ill-advised
   (E) characteristic

                                          5 ___

6. The most serious damage done by El Niño was _____ .

   (A) hurricanes as far away as the Caribbean
   (B) an imbalance between mackerel and anchovies
   (C) a threat by the activities of man
   (D) a drought over the deserts of Chile
   (E) the death of young animals

                                          6 ___

7. Which of the following titles best summarizes the content of the passage?

   (A) Bird Life under Stress
   (B) El Niño—A Devastating Visitor
   (C) A Study in Climate
   (D) Weather in the Western Pacific
   (E) Fish Migration and Polluted Water

                                          7 ___

SUMMARY PART 1

Finding Details: Spotting Details in the Text

When checking for details in a reading passage, look for specific phrases and sentences to support your choice. If more than one answer applies to the passage, be sure you choose the answer that is responsive to the question.

PART 2

Finding Details in Combination

Sometimes the test question will call for a combination of possibilities. Your answer must include all details called for and no details not in the selection.

Trial Test

For the following test question select the best answer.

Oats, wheat, rye, and other grains are well known and often used in America. Barley, however, has been neglected. As Raymond Sokolov has observed, "In this country, today, few people cook barley at all. Most of us taste it rarely and almost exclusively in soup." Though known from Biblical days, barley is "the all-but-forgotten grain, orphan among staples." It deserves to be better known and more often used.

Barley is a superbly hardy grass, growing everywhere from Egypt to Norway and Tibet. It thrives in climates too cold for wheat. It is a versatile grain. Bread made from barley is dark and tasty. It keeps well and is still pleasantly edible when dry. Barley can be used for cakes, breads, pancakes. It is a subtle flavoring when used in combination with other grains. Why, then, has barley done so poorly in modern America?

Wheat is the culprit in the story of barley's retreat. Though less sturdy than barley, wheat can, with modern methods, be transported and preserved more easily than in the past. Wheat has more gluten, thus allowing bread from wheat to rise. Barley bread, by contrast, is flat. Barley cannot replace wheat, but it has a niche to fill.

How can we take advantage of this neglected grain? We can combine barley with wheat for a tasty, nutritious bread. We can, of course, use it in soup, where its delicate flavor is a plus. We can eat barley as a side dish with most main courses. We can bake it with mushrooms in a pie crust. We can, like the Koreans, serve it with rice. We can also brew a tea from roasted barley, as the Japanese do. However we use it, we ought to rescue this overlooked grain from its undeserved oblivion.

Which of the following statements may be accurately derived from the selection?

   I. Barley makes a bread superior to wheat bread.
  II. Barley has an adaptability unsuspected by most Americans.
 III. Barley is a member of the grass family.
 IV. Barley combines with other grains for tasty foods.
  V. Oats and wheat grow in Tibet.

    (A) I only
    (B) IV only
    (C) II, III, and IV
    (D) I, III, and V
    (E) I and IV

Answer to Trial Test

(*C*) Statements I and V are nowhere stated or implied. Any answer with either of these can be dismissed at once. We can thus eliminate (*A*), (*D*), and (*E*). (*B*) contains a correct statement, but since it says "IV only" it cannot be the desired answer.

Look at a typical question and then analyze the possible answers.

Problem

The Mayan Empire once stretched from the Yucatan to western Honduras. Its power and extent are constantly being restudied as new discoveries rescue important Mayan
5 sites from the jungle. Sites like Uxmal and Chichen-Itza in Yucatan, Tikal in Guatemala, and Copán in Honduras reveal the awesome achievements of the civilization that flourished many centuries ago. The lat-
10 ter two, discovered in the 1840s, "rank in archaeological importance with the pyramids of Egypt."

A more recent discovery is causing a complete reappraisal of the Mayan influence
15 and the duration of the Mayan Empire. It had previously been thought that the Mayan civilization did not mature before 300 A.D. Then in 1978 Bruce Dahlin uncovered bits of pottery dating from 400 B.C. There, in
20 the lost city called *El Mirador*, not far from Tikal, a civilization flourished centuries before the date usually assigned to its arrival.

The architecture at El Mirador reveals the sophistication of its artisans: master
25 builders, stonecutters, and sculptors. The various structures also suggest a high level of social organization. Here, too, are beautiful carvings with hieroglyphics as yet undeciphered. This graphic style of writing
30 provided much of the communication upon which a civilization ultimately rests.

The new discoveries suggest that the Mayan Empire lasted not 500 or so years but 1500 years or more. John Graham of Berke-
35 ley flatly states, "Mayan civilization represents the longest sustained civilization in the New World." Further explorations at El Mirador suggest that we have just scratched the surface of our knowledge about the
40 Maya.

Which of the following statements may be accurately derived from the selection?

    I. Writing is crucial to the success of a civilization.
    II. Mayan sites are predominantly in Yucatan.
  III. The duration of Mayan civilization is under reappraisal and revision.
  IV. The buildings at El Mirador are contemporary with the pyramids of Egypt.
   V. Hieroglyphics are associated with, and restricted to, Egypt.

    (A) III only
    (B) IV only
    (C) I and V
    (D) II and IV
    (E) I and III

Strategy

Statements II, IV, and V are false. Therefore any answer containing one of these statements is wrong; that is, (B), (C), and (D). Statement III is true, but (A) is wrong because it suggests that only III applies. The correct answer, (E), lists both correct statements: I and III.

Time Out for Review

Try your skill. The passage below is followed by questions based on its content. Use the preceding example to help you find the right answers.

American folklore is filled with tales of hoboes, wanderers who rode the rails and traveled the country as uninvited guests of the railroads. But there is another group of
5 rail-riders, whose presence is never felt by the train but whose journey is made possible by the Iron Horse: weeds! These courageous adventurers establish themselves on sites that look forbidding, even deadly, to living
10 things. The cinders along the railbed and the borders seem an impossible nursery for any living organism. Yet many plants survive in the hostile environment.

Seeds are carried by trains and dispersed
15 along the right of way. Queen Anne's lace, ragweed, and wild parsnip flourish where a railroad intersects with a road. Clovers, horseweed, and wood sorrels do well at railroad crossings in farm country. Some plants
20 seem to thrive especially well along the forbidding tracks. Dwarf snapdragon, for example, grows more abundantly along railroad tracks than anywhere else.

It's hard to think of a more inhospitable
25 environment than the land along the railroad tracks. The cinders contain little if any humus. The area is dry, sun-baked, and often sprayed with weed killers. Speeding trains lop off the heads of taller species. Even
30 smaller plants are subjected to the air stresses created by passing trains. Yet persistent plant life struggles and often perpetuates its kind, despite the odds against survival. The track area may not be a luxurious garden, but it
35 nurtures many train-borne weeds.

1. Which of the following statements may be accurately derived from the selection?
   I. A railbed is a better place to grow plants than a city garden.
   II. Different plants thrive in different conditions.
   III. The dwarf snapdragon thrives especially well along a railroad line.
   IV. Ragweed and Queen Anne's lace seem to grow well in similar environments.
   V. American folklore features the vitality and dispersion of native weeds.
   (A) II only
   (B) IV only
   (C) II, III, and IV
   (D) III and V
   (E) I, II, and III

   1 ___

2. The "courageous adventurers" referred to in line 8 are _____.
   (A) hoboes
   (B) trains
   (C) dwarf snapdragons
   (D) smaller plants
   (E) weeds

   2 ___

3. It is reasonable to infer that _____.
   (A) some weeds can store moisture for survival
   (B) the wood sorrel is more adaptable than the dwarf snapdragon
   (C) hoboes paid a small railroad fare
   (D) cinders have hidden pockets of soil
   (E) the wild parsnip is sturdier than the ragweed

   3 ___

4. Which two are compared in the selection?
   - (A) hoboes and weed killers
   - (B) luxurious garden and a railbed
   - (C) the Iron Horse and the tracks
   - (D) impossible nursery and hostile environment
   - (E) railroads and automobiles

4 ___

5. Which of the following titles best summarizes the content of the passage?
   - (A) Weeds and Their Ways
   - (B) Railroads: Preservers of American Wildlife
   - (C) Those Unlikely Railroad ''Gardens''
   - (D) Endangered Species: Railroad Weeds
   - (E) Weeds: the Railroads' Persistent Problem

5 ___

SUMMARY PART 2

Finding Details: Finding Details in Combination

When checking for a combination of details in a reading passage, be complete. Include only those details actually included—but don't leave any out.

Combining Skills

The reading skills tested are rarely pure examples of only one skill. Frequently two or more skills are needed to ferret out an answer.

An inference, for example, is frequently built upon a key detail in the selection, even though it is not, itself, a detail. You have to do two things: find the detail and make the inference. A title is frequently based on a conclusion that balances various inferences. You have to do three things: make the inferences, form a conclusion, and choose a title.

Some SAT questions require you to figure out details and then make judgments about the details. Note that the wording of the following SAT-type question does more than call for identification of details. It also calls for an inference based on details.

1. In which of the following lines is an appeal made to curiosity?

   (A) 1–5
   (B) 6–10
   (C) 11–15
   (D) 16–20
   (E) 21–25

   Here's a combination in which you are not expected to state the main idea but to identify the lines in the passage which contain the main idea.

   The same skills may be tested in different forms.

2. During which ten-year period was there the greatest unrest in the United States?
   (A) 1896–1905
   (B) 1905–1914
   (C) 1920–1929
   (D) 1945–1954
   (E) 1962–1970

3. The central thought of the passage is most clearly expressed in which of the following lines?
   (A) 1–5
   (B) 6–10
   (C) 11–15
   (D) 16–20
   (E) 21–25

Trial Test

Select the best answer for the following test question.

You can have your own drugstore right on your windowsill. The aloe vera plant, which is often grown as a pot plant, has some remarkable medicinal properties. The fresh
5 leaf juice of the plant contains the drug aloin, which has many soothing properties when it is used externally.

The roster of the skin problems helped by aloe is impressive. The juice has healing
10 properties for insect bites, minor burns, poison ivy, and athlete's foot. It can also relieve summer sunburn and dry skin.

For minor burns, victims may break off the largest leaf of the aloe plant and squeeze
15 it gently, like a tube of toothpaste or ointment. The sticky clear gel is applied directly to the burn.

Aloe is not a recent newcomer to medication. The ancient Greeks and Egyptians
20 knew of its medicinal properties. Cleopatra used aloe as part of her beauty treatments and medications.

The plant itself is inexpensive. It makes a beautiful pot plant. Because it is a succu-
25 lent, it requires little watering. It does, however, need good drainage and lots of sun. Some people may have a mild allergy to aloe vera, but for most people, the plant can be a multipurpose medicine shelf—and a com-
30 pact, decorative one besides.

In which of the following paragraphs is a possible drawback to the use of aloe mentioned?
  (A) 1
  (B) 2
  (C) 3
  (D) 4
  (E) 5

Answer to Trial Test

(*E*) The last paragraph specifically says, "Some people may have a mild allergy to aloe vera." The statement goes on to say that most people find aloe beneficial. Yet this one drawback tells us that (*E*) is the right answer. No other paragraph mentions a disadvantage.

Look at a typical question on the following page and analyze the possible answers.

Problem

Accidents will happen—but many needn't. Among the most common type of automobile accidents are rear-end collisions. In a ranking of types of automobile road accidents, these collisions rank second. Over $3\frac{1}{2}$ million drivers are involved each year in this particular road hazard. Yet much can be done to cut down the number of such accidents.

The best way to reduce rear-end collisions is to improve visibility. One experimental device was the installation of a third brake light on the back of cars. In an experimental study this minor addition resulted in a drop of 50% in the number of rear-end collisions. Placing the new light centrally on the trunk, just below the rear window, provides certain new advantages. It is not used as a directional signal, nor is it used to illuminate the back of the car at night. It stays dark until the driver brakes. This is a clear signal that the car is slowing or stopping. Because it is about at eye level of the driver in the car behind, it is easily visible.

Installation of such a light is inexpensive—generally under $30. Wires go directly into the car trunk and are connected to the existing brake lights. The average motorist can install the light himself, or an auto mechanic can complete the installation in minutes.

The second method for avoiding rear-end collisions is to drive a light-colored car. When visibility is poor, accidents often occur because a driver doesn't see the other vehicle until it's too late. According to safety tests, drivers can see light, bright cars from a distance of up to four times farther away than they can see cars in darker tones. A white car is the most visible of all.

1. The advantage of placing the third light just below the rear window is mentioned in which of the following lines?
   (A) 1–5
   (B) 6–8
   (C) 9–16
   (D) 27–30
   (E) 34–40

   1 ___

2. The central thought of the passage is most clearly expressed in which of the following lines?
   (A) 1–5
   (B) 9–15
   (C) 15–20
   (D) 25–30
   (E) 35–40

   2 ___

Strategy

1. The advantage of placing the light at eye-level height is mentioned in lines 10–13. Since answer (C) includes lines 10–13 (C) is the correct answer. The rest of the selection does not deal with that particular detail.

2. The central idea of the entire selection is stated in lines 10–11.

"The best way to reduce rear-end collisions is to improve visibility." The entire passage is devoted to the question of visibility, with the third light discussed at length and the color of the car discussed in the last paragraph. Since lines 10–11 are in 9–15, (B) is the correct answer.

Time Out for Review

Try your skill. The passage below is followed by questions based on its content. Use the preceding example to help you find the right answers.

"Why bother saving wild and endangered species? It is the fate of species to become extinct some day anyway. Why bother with snail darters and wild grains?
5 Let's spend more time on more important problems."

These arguments have a specious reasonableness, but they couldn't be more wrong. We have a selfish interest in wild species.
10 We need to protect them for our own survival.

As Norman Myers has pointed out, "We use hundreds of products each day that owe their existence to plants and animals. The
15 ways in which wild species support our daily welfare fall under three main headings: agriculture, medicine, and industry."

In agriculture, for example, we need a constant infusion of new genetic material
20 from wild plants. Plant geneticists have done more to improve crop yields than artificial additives like fertilizers and pesticides. Natural immunities to pests and extremes of climates are bred into native plants with the
25 help of wild stock. Blight-resistant genes from a wild Mexican plant helped preserve the threatened American corn crop. A wild wheat strain from Turkey is resistant to several diseases afflicting domestic grain. Its in-
30 troduction saved the farm industry millions of dollars worth of crops each year.

The same situation is true in medicine. Wild organisms continue to contribute remedies for many of our ills. A child suffering
35 from leukemia once had only a 20% chance of remission. With the help of rosy periwinkle, a tropical forest plant, the child now has an 80% chance. Other anticancer drugs may well be found in the vast jungles of the Am-
40 azon basin.

The seas provide other medicinal materials. A Caribbean sponge may be an important antiviral agent. Menhaden, a marine fish, provides an oil that may help in treating
45 atherosclerosis. Sea snakes can yield an anticoagulant. Extracts from the toxin of the octopus may be used as an anesthetic in modern surgery. Potential anticancer drugs may come from corals, sea anemones, mol-
50 lusks, sponges, sea squirts, and even clams.

Industry also depends upon wild species for many products. Seaweeds, for example, contribute to hundreds of products, including waxes, detergents, soaps, shampoos, paints,
55 lubricants, and dyes. Land plants like the jojoba play a large part in industrial production. The liquid wax from the jojoba is a brilliantly efficient lubricant. The expansion of the chemical industry suggests that we'll
60 need many more supplies of organic industrial chemicals. As yet untapped or undiscovered species can make major contributions to industry.

The wild species of the world are not
65 merely decorative at best or essentially useless at worst. They are a storehouse of genetic material and products that can help us improve our lives—even survive. An investment in the survival of wild species is an
70 investment in the survival of another species—our own.

1. Genetic experimentation with plants is discussed in which of the following lines?
   (A) 1–10
   (B) 11–17
   (C) 18–31
   (D) 32–50
   (E) 51–70

   1 ___

2. A wild species that contributes hundreds of products is _____.
   (A) jojoba
   (B) rosy periwinkle
   (C) seaweed
   (D) octopus
   (E) sea snake

   2 ___

3. The central thought of the passage is most clearly expressed in which of the following statements?

    (A) In agriculture, for example, we need a constant infusion of new genetic material from wild plants.
    (B) It is the fate of species to become extinct some day anyway.
    (C) The seas provide other medicinal materials.
    (D) As yet untapped or undiscovered species can make major contributions to industry.
    (E) An investment in the survival of wild species is an investment in the survival of another species—our own.

                                    3 ___

4. From the selection, it may be inferred that _____ .

    (A) wild plants are always superior to domestic plants
    (B) a cure for cancer will come from the blight-resistant Mexican wheat
    (C) domestic plants often have limited resistance to ills
    (D) we need not be concerned about the extinction of wild species
    (E) industry is blindly reluctant to accept the products derived from wild species

                                    4 ___

5. Which of the following pairs is correctly matched?

    (A) seaweed–anticancer
    (B) jojoba–anesthetic
    (C) sea snake–detergent
    (D) mollusk–leukemia
    (E) menhaden–atherosclerosis

                                    5 ___

6. To save wild species we must _____ .

    (A) preserve their natural habitats
    (B) cultivate them in our gardens
    (C) carefully monitor climate
    (D) stop using their genetic material
    (E) experiment with changing their genetic structure

                                    6 ___

SUMMARY PART 3

Finding Details: Combining Skills

Some questions test a combination of skills. First read the question carefully. Then, to double check your answer, carefully rule out the incorrect alternatives.

Summary
Section III: Finding Details

Although you cannot ordinarily point specifically to a sentence or section in the text to prove an inferred answer, you can usually find in the text itself the answer to a question turning upon a detail in the selection.

Review the strategies for finding details as you prepare for the SAT.

PART 1   Spotting Details in the Text

A. Look for specific phrases and sentences with the details you want.
B. When you find details for *more than one* answer, do the following:
   1. Reread the question to be sure you understand it.
   2. Choose the answer with the details that specifically answer the question.

PART 2   Finding Details in Combination

When a question calls for two or more details together:

A. Read the passage carefully.
B. Choose the answer with *only* the details that you have read.
C. Be sure you don't leave out any of the details.

PART 3   Combining Skills

When a question asks you to combine skills, usually making an inference or judgment based on details:

A. Find the details you need.
B. Use the details to make the inference or judgment called for.
C. Make any more choices as needed (such as choosing a title or a central idea) based on what you have found and decided.

Section IV: Understanding the Author's Role

PART 1

Evaluating the Author's Tone

When we speak, we indicate the tone of the message by our tone of voice. When we write, we indicate tone in other ways. SAT questions frequently ask candidates to describe the tone of a passage. The following are some typical adjectives and nouns to describe tone.

"TONE" ADJECTIVES

aggressive and dogmatic	indifferent
argumentative	inquisitive
conciliatory and apologetic	inspirational
honest and straightforward	instructional and explanatory
humble	ironic
objective	scholarly
reflective	sensational and melodramatic

"TONE" NOUNS

apprehension	hope	resignation
deference	indifference	reverence
despair	irrationality	sarcasm
disdain	mistrust	self-pity
enthusiasm	relief	urgency

To answer questions about tone, you must get the "feel" of the passage. You must "read between the lines" and determine what mood is suggested.

Trial Test

The morning dawned cold and gray. The freezing winter rain had stripped all but a few tenacious oak leaves from the trees outside the study window. The colors were
5 muted, with shades of gray and brown predominating in a Rembrandtesque landscape. The autumn distractions of brilliant color were gone, and the tree trunks stood stark and austere a few feet from the window. The
10 corrugations of the bark were clear and distinct. The tiny patches of moss and lichen here and there accentuated the grooves rather than diminished them. Through the tree silhouettes could be discerned the olive-green
15 needles of young Southern pine, struggling for survival in the oak forest. The ground was littered with brown oak leaves, whose otherwise monochromatic appearance was challenged by their curl and twist on the for-
20 est floor. Here and there, fallen gray twigs punctuated the rust mattress, adding a pleasant break in the superficial uniformity. This was a subtle scene, a scene demanding close observation to find the beauty of color and
25 form that was everywhere.

The tone of the passage can best be described as _____.

(A) self-satisfied   (D) argumentative
(B) conciliatory   (E) apprehensive
(C) reflective

____

Answer to Trial Test

(*C*) This is a quiet sketch of a natural scene, emphasizing the subtle elements frequently overlooked in a cursory glance. This invites the reader to stand still a moment and recreate in imagination the stillness of a winter morning. The tone is *reflective*.

Look at a typical question and then analyze the possible answers.

Problem

OLD IRONSIDES

Ay, tear her tattered ensign down!
  Long has it waved on high,
And many an eye has danced to see
  That banner in the sky;
5 Beneath it rung the battle shout,
  And burst the cannon's roar;—
The meteor of the ocean air
  Shall sweep the clouds no more.
Her deck, once red with heroes'
10   blood,
Where knelt the vanquished foe,
When winds were hurrying o'er the
    floods,
  And waves were white below,
15 No more shall feel the victor's tread,
  Or know the conquered knee;—
The harpies of the shore shall pluck
  The eagle of the sea!

Oh, better that her shattered hulk
20 Should sink beneath the wave;
Her thunders shook the mighty deep,
  And there should be her grave;
Nail to the mast her holy flag,
  Set every threadbare sail,
25 And give her to the god of storms,
  The lightning and the gale!

1. The tone of the poem as a whole can best be described as _____.
  (A) amiable   (D) indifferent
  (B) doubtful   (E) angry
  (C) acquiescent
                1 ___

2. Lines 3–4 convey a sense of _____.
  (A) humor   (D) delight
  (B) pride   (E) worry
  (C) uncertainty
                2 ___

3. Which of the following lines can best be described as *sarcastic*?
  (A) 1   (D) 19
  (B) 9   (E) 21
  (C) 13
                3 ___

4. The "harpies of the shore" (line 15) are treated with _____.
  (A) suspicion   (D) anticipation
  (B) contempt   (E) resignation
  (C) fear
                4 ___

Strategy

1. The poet resents the fact that the historic ship is going to be scrapped ("tear her tattered ensign down"). This attack is angry, as other lines confirm. The answer is (E), angry.

2. If an eye "dances" to see the banner in the sky, the emotion described is pride: (B).

3. From the rest of the passage, it is clear that the poet does not want the "tattered ensign" torn down. Quite the opposite. Since sarcasm seems to say one thing while clearly implying the other, the answer is (A), line 1. The other alternatives are straightforward and positive.

4. Contrasting the "harpies of the shore" with "the eagle of the sea" clearly suggests the poet's venomous attitude toward the harpies. Contempt, (B), is an accurate word to suggest the tone of the lines.

Time Out for Review

Try your skill. The passage below is followed by questions based on its content. Use the preceding example to help you find the right answers.

"Who Cares Who Killed Roger Ackroyd?" The title of Edmund Wilson's 1945 essay clearly indicates the writer's bias. Wilson called detective stories "wasteful of time
5 and degrading to the intellect." Since that time other critics have sneered, condescended, and scorned the whodunit, but its popularity has rarely faltered. The detective story and related types like the spy story, the
10 horror tale, and the Dashiell Hammett type of thriller are often lumped under the general heading *Mystery* and earn a special shelf in most libraries. The mystery shelf is one of the most popular in every library. The books
15 on these shelves have been worn with use. Novels by old favorite writers like John Dickson Carr vie with current favorites like those by Ruth Rendell. Why do mysteries, and especially detective stories, often outlast
20 their critics?

In an era when much modern fiction is plotless and loosely structured, the detective story, with its solid plot, tells a story that appeals to the child in everyone. The detec-
25 tive story begins somewhere and ends somewhere. In between, readers are treated to twists of plot, surprises in characterization, and challenging puzzles.

Detective stories and other mysteries,
30 though often maligned, have influenced other current fiction. Even "literary" fiction has been affected by the mystery and its close relatives. Paul Theroux's *Family Arsenal*, Robert Stone's *A Flag for Sunrise*, and Mar-
35 garet Atwood's *Bodily Harm* all use the conventions of the thriller.

Some writers have gone further. Michiko Kakutani has pointed out that some prestigious writers "have used the conventions of
40 the mystery to make philosophical points about the nature of storytelling itself." Joyce Carol Oates in *Mysteries of Winterthurn*, Alain Robbe-Grillet in *The Erasers*, and Jorge Luis Borges in *Death and the Compass*
45 have added a dimension to the possibilities inherent in the mystery form.

1. The tone of the selection as a whole can best be described as _____.
   (A) instructional and explanatory
   (B) inquisitive and investigatory
   (C) sensational and dogmatic
   (D) biased and poorly represented
   (E) careless and unconcerned

   1 ___

2. The tone of the title "Who Cares Who Killed Roger Ackroyd?" is intended to be _____.

   (A) sympathetic and curious
   (B) wittily negative
   (C) brutally callous
   (D) straightforwardly informative
   (E) earnest and prudent

   2 ___

3. As a category name, *mystery* can be best labeled _____.

   (A) inaccurate   (D) worthless
   (B) humorous   (E) noteworthy
   (C) broad

   3 ___

4. The major strength of the detective story is its _____.

   (A) philosophical content
   (B) sense of direction
   (C) imitation of the best writing of Joyce Carol Oates
   (D) conventional characterization
   (E) use of exotic settings

   4 ___

5. The sentence "Why do mysteries, and especially detective stories, often outlast their critics?" can be interpreted as _____.

   (A) an unanswerable question
   (B) a petty swipe at mysteries
   (C) a baffling comment of "literary" fiction
   (D) an apologetic defense of literary critics
   (E) a commendation of the detective story

   5 ___

6. The word "literary" in " 'literary' fiction" is in quotation marks because _____.

   (A) it is quoted from a novel by Paul Theroux
   (B) it exposes a critical snobbish attitude
   (C) here it means exactly the opposite of its usual meaning
   (D) it suggests that the novels mentioned are largely biographical
   (E) mystery writers lack true narrative gifts

   6 ___

7. We may reasonably infer that Roger Ackroyd is _____.

   (A) a mystery writer
   (B) a book reviewer
   (C) a real-life crime victim
   (D) a character in a famous mystery
   (E) an imaginary name invented by Robert Stone

   7 ___

8. It may be assumed that the writer of this selection considers Paul Theroux's *Family Arsenal* as _____.

   (A) a true detective story
   (B) a philosophical novel
   (C) "literary" fiction
   (D) a book to be grouped with *The Erasers*
   (E) a book for the mystery shelf

   8 ___

9. The main point of the passage is to _____.

   (A) give the mystery its rightful due in current fiction
   (B) explain why Dashiell Hammett's novels have had ups and downs
   (C) present Michiko Kakutani's point of view about spy stories
   (D) answer the critics of John Dickson Carr and Ruth Rendell
   (E) explore the origins of the whodunit

   9 ___

SUMMARY PART 1

Understanding the Author's Role: Evaluating the Author's Tone

The tone of a passage cannot be found in a detail of the selection. It can ''be found only in the overall impression created by the combination of descriptive and connotative words.'' (See connotation and denotation, pages 41–46.) Most SAT selections tend to have a fairly neutral tone, with emphasis upon the presentation of information. Others, like ''Old Ironsides,'' crackle with a special life of their own, a mood that colors the piece.

PART 2

Evaluating the Author's Attitude

Closely related to the tone of a reading passage is the attitude displayed or suggested. A typical SAT question requires you to discover the author's attitude toward someone or something. The following are examples of questions of this type.

1. Which of the following best expressed the author's attitude toward . . . ?
2. The attitude toward . . . is one of . . .
3. It can be inferred from the passage that the author's attitude toward the . . . is one of . . .
4. The author's attitude toward . . . is primarily one of . . .
5. The attitude toward . . . conveyed by the author's use of the words . . . is best described as one of . . .
6. The author's attitude toward the . . . mentioned in lines 1–20 is best described as . . .

Here is a brief cross-section of typical attitudes tested.

admiration	disdain
ambivalence	exasperation
anxiety	nostalgia
apathy	puzzlement
disbelief	skepticism

Sometimes the attitudes are more narrowly and specifically labeled.

delighted amazement	clear distaste
growing anger	apologetic embarrassment
reluctant approval	cold objectivity
mild condescension	admiring support
veiled disdain	detached sympathy

Other questions display a slightly different phraseology which requires a different type of answer.

The author's attitude toward . . . is that of a . . .

A correctly completed statement might look something like this:

> The author's attitude toward the absentee employees is that of a parent correcting a misbehaving child.

Note that all these questions are quite different from those for tone. Questions about tone are usually general. Questions about attitude are more specific. In these questions you must uncover the author's attitude *toward someone or something*. Though the phraseology varies from question to question, the essential requirement is the same.

There is no substitute for trying your hand at a typical question.

Trial Test

Take the following trial test to evaluate your skill.

Those who see professional football on television are missing half the fun and half the show: the fans. Though the television cameraman occasionally provides tantalizing
5 shots of oddball enthusiasts, the glimpses are not enough. Through the years there have been colorful characters on the field with picturesque names like "Crazylegs," "The Catawba Claw," "the Juice" and "the Fun
10 Bunch." But the real characters are in the stands.

The Pittsburgh Steelers once numbered among their stalwart fans "Franco's Italian Army" and "Gerela's Gorillas." The "Go-
15 rillas" came, appropriately enough, dressed in gorilla suits. "Cowboys," "Indians,"
"Pirates," and "Vikings" regularly appear in the stands to root their teams on. Entire sections join in the fun, wearing orange
20 sweaters and waving orange banners or singing "Hail to the Redskins." There's *active* fun in the stands, too. Stadium hijinks at halftime include passing around play footballs in the stands to the roaring approval of
25 the crowd. There is much to see and hear at a football game—and much of that is not on the field.

The author's attitude toward football fans is one of _____.

(A) righteous indignation
(B) concealed intolerance
(C) vigorous denunciation
(D) amused affection
(E) calculated indifference

Answer to Trial Test

(*D*) This is by no means a negative appraisal. Therefore, (*A*), (*B*), and (*C*) can be immediately rejected. It is positive, amused, interested in the behavior of the fans. It is not indifferent. Eliminate (*E*). It does write with amused affection of the unusual characters who cheer on their football teams.

Look at a typical question and then analyze the possible answers.

Problem

"The redwing blackbirds are back!" This cry in February or March reassures a winter-weary land that spring will come again. Migrating birds bring song, color, and joy into
5 our lives. Their migrations have been cheered, observed, and analyzed for many years, but the mysteries remain.

Most birds apparently migrate to follow the food chain. When insects start to become
10 abundant in northern meadows, migrating insect-eaters return. The appearance of flowers entices the hummingbirds. Food requirements of all species are relatively specialized and keyed to the environment.

15 There are many hazards, however, in migration. Storms may blow birds far off course over open water, an often fatal accident.
Flying at night, birds crash into towers and tall buildings. They may arrive at their usual
20 destination only to find a shopping center where their territories once were.

Birds make these incredible journeys each year, but the how and the why are often obscure. Why does the Arctic tern spend
25 eight months each year migrating from the Arctic to the Antarctic and back again? How can this tiny creature successfully navigate vast areas of open seas? Though migration has been studied since the time of Aristotle,
30 we are still in the dark. We can, however, make a contribution by protecting breeding habitats and protecting the way stations the long-distance travelers frequent on their hazardous trips.

1. The author's attitude toward migrating birds is one of _____.
   - (A) satisfied curiosity
   - (B) cautious skepticism
   - (C) mild irritation
   - (D) affectionate respect
   - (E) unfeeling analysis

1 ___

2. The author's attitude toward the flight of the Arctic tern can best be characterized by the word _____.
   - (A) wonder
   - (B) disbelief
   - (C) approval
   - (D) indifference
   - (E) anxiety

2 ___

Strategy

1. Eliminate some of the alternatives and see what is left. Curiosity about bird migration has not been satisfied; (A) is incorrect. *Skepticism* is not the word needed. Skepticism implies doubt about the truth or falsity of a statement or belief. Uncertainty does not generate skepticism; dogma does. (B) is incorrect. There is no hint of irritation; (C), *mild irritation*, is incorrect. The author is emotionally but positively involved. *Unfeeling* tells us (E) is wrong. That leaves (D), *affectionate respect*, clearly the attitude of the author.

2. The author takes no direct stand about the flight of the tern (C), but he is not indifferent (D). There is no question of disbelief (B). That leaves us with (A) and (E). The use of *incredible* and the sentences following tell us the correct answer is *wonder*, (A).

Time Out for Review

Try your skill. The passage below is followed by questions based on its content. Use the preceding example to help you find the right answers.

Though often taught as merely a pretty decoration in poetry, metaphor is in reality a basic element in language, transcending mere ornamentation. Simply defined as "an
5 implied comparison between unlike objects," metaphor is really a flash of insight, a leap of imagination, a poetic explosion. When the poet Alfred Noyes in "The Highwayman" calls the road "a ribbon of moon-
10 light," he is superficially comparing a road and a ribbon, but he is really going farther. He is investing the road with the emotional, imaginative qualities associated with moonlight. He is pouring into that solid, substan-
15 tial road all the ethereal qualities of moonlight.

Our entire language is metaphorical. Many of our commonest expressions are overlooked metaphors. Think, for a mo-
20 ment, of the actual images concealed in "run out of patience," "a cutting remark," "drop the subject," "fly into a rage," "pull strings," "turn down a suggestion," and "pick up the threads of a story."
25 Metaphor enlarges language. It takes commonplace building blocks and by combining them creates new and beautiful meanings. Shakespeare says, "Life's but a walking shadow, a poor player that struts and
30 frets his hour upon the stage and then is heard no more." The individual words are common, but the extended comparison—of life and an actor—is uncommon.

Metaphor is concealed in many common
35 words. By derivation, a *coherent* story "sticks together." A *subliminal* impulse lies "below the threshold" of consciousness. A *chrysanthemum* is "a flower of gold." *Planets* are "wanderers." Most words travel
40 far from their original, narrow, literal meanings. In the process they acquire metaphorical meanings.

Metaphor is everywhere—in sports telecasts, on the editorial pages, on the stage, in
45 our everyday speaking and writing. Even the word *metaphor* contains a hidden metaphor—from the Greek words to "carry beyond." Metaphor indeed *carries* meaning *beyond* the narrow and literal.

1. The author's attitude toward the subject of metaphor is one of _____.
   (A) amused boredom
   (B) scholarly debate
   (C) mandatory approbation
   (D) excessive enthusiasm
   (E) alert interest

   1 ___

2. The author's attitude toward Shakespeare is _____.
   (A) flattering
   (B) appreciative
   (C) curious
   (D) uncritical
   (E) contradictory

   2 ___

3. According to the selection a concealed metaphor is contained in the word _____.
   (A) comparison
   (B) literal
   (C) coherent
   (D) derivation
   (E) beautiful

   3 ___

4. The writer would probably classify the expression "leap of imagination" as a(an) _____.
   (A) ribbon of moonlight
   (B) metaphor
   (C) decoration
   (D) poem
   (E) extended comparison

   4 ___

5. The paragraph devoted exclusively to the physical imagery of the metaphor is _____.
   (A) 1   (D) 4
   (B) 2   (E) 5
   (C) 3

   5 ___

6. The main point of the passage is to _____.
   (A) extol the art of poetry
   (B) compare Noyes and Shakespeare as poets
   (C) encourage the more extensive use of metaphor
   (D) give metaphor its due as a crucial element in language
   (E) provide an implied comparison of metaphor and simile

   6 ___

7. Using clues from the selection, we might guess that the original meaning of *eliminate* was _____.
   (A) cast over the threshold
   (B) discard abruptly
   (C) wander from the truth
   (D) carry beyond
   (E) strut upon the stage

   7 ___

8. We may reasonably infer that "The Highwayman" is a(an) _____.
   (A) essay
   (B) article
   (C) historical memoir
   (D) novel
   (E) poem

   8 ___

9. The quotation from Shakespeare is called an "extended comparison" because _____.
   (A) it contains several images
   (B) it compares life and an actor
   (C) it is more literal than metaphorical
   (D) Shakespeare rarely created simple metaphors
   (E) it is a better image than that created by Noyes

   9 ___

10. Two words that are intentionally paired and opposed are _____.
    (A) road and moonlight
    (B) struts and frets
    (C) substantial and ethereal
    (D) chrysanthemun and planets
    (E) life and actor

    10 ___

SUMMARY PART 2

Understanding the Author's Role: Evaluating the Author's Attitude

Searching out the author's attitude requires rereading of the selection as a whole. If you read the selection quietly to yourself, you will begin to sense the author's feeling toward his material. Individual words may provide clues, but you must get a feeling for the selection in its entirety. Think of the author as speaking to you. What feeling is he trying to convey?

PART 3

Evaluating the Author's Purpose

As we have seen, in a reading passage the author's attitude and the tone of the selection are often linked closely together. A third ingredient, the author's purpose, also influences a reading selection. SAT questions frequently challenge you to decide just what the author is trying to achieve.

The following are examples of questions designed to uncover and probe the author's purpose:

1. Which of the following best describes the purpose of the passage?
2. The primary purpose of the passage appears to be to . . .
3. The author includes statistical information specifically to . . .
4. The author's primary purpose in this passage is to . . .
5. The author quotes . . . in order to . . .

Trial Test

Take this trial test to evaluate your skill.

"You smash and slapdash the idea while it's red hot with you. Get it down on paper." This advice by Bergen Evans should be en-graved in every writer's memory. Every au-
5 thor experiences writer's block at some time or other. Just looking at an empty paper waiting to be filled is enough to paralyze the will and freeze determination. But Evans's advice can help break down the barriers.
10 When you have a writing assignment of any kind, don't sit numbly waiting for the perfect outline to suggest itself. Try brain-storming. Jot down everything on a topic that occurs to you. Don't be critical at this
15 stage. Capitalize on those free associations, those creative if unformed ideas, those many images that float to the surface. Don't be inhibited. Don't say, "Oh, that won't

work." *Put it down*. Later, after you have
20 poured forth all those ideas, organize your jottings. Decide what belongs and what doesn't. Form the related ideas into a helpful outline.
   Letting your mind roam freely is excel-
25 lent procedure for any creative project. It is especially useful in writing.

The author's primary purpose in this passage is to _____ .

(A) extol the critical faculties in writing
(B) introduce Bergen Evans as a useful guide
(C) stress that writer's block is a trivial problem
(D) suggest a sound pre-writing technique
(E) recommend self-criticism in preparing to write

Answer to Trial Test

(D) Since the selection deals exclusively with the activity *before* writing, the word *pre-writing* provides an immediate clue. The author plays down the critical faculties and self-criticism at the pre-writing stage. (A) and (E) are incorrect. Evans is introduced to make an opening point, but the purpose goes beyond Evans. (B) is incorrect. Phrases like *paralyze the will* and *freeze determination* suggest that writer's block is not trivial.

Look at a typical question and then analyze the possible answers.

Problem

The explosive growth of racquetball as a sport is traceable in part to an increased interest in physical fitness. Instead of engaging in sedentary pursuits, many people have
5 learned to enjoy the demanding activity of jogging, bodybuilding, and other fitness sports. While it is true that racquetball enthusiasts have been lured away from tennis, handball, squash, and other related activi-
10 ties, the racquetball ranks have also been swelled by newcomers to strenuous physical activity.

What is the appeal of this relatively new sport? The key word is *action*. Racquetball
15 is played inside a box, an enclosed court with six playing surfaces: the four walls, the floor, and the ceiling. A close relative to squash or four-wall handball, racquetball is a flurry of incredibly swift action. Even be-
20 ginners soon learn to hit the ball at speeds exceeding 80 miles an hour. Split-second decisions require reflexes that astound spectators. The ball ricochets off all surfaces with apparently little rhyme or reason, but com-
25 petent players swoop balls out of corners, hit balls falling to within a few inches off the floor, and "kill" a smash without possibility of return. Quickness of response is the heart of the game.

30 Why has racquetball won converts from other sports? It requires little equipment: a sturdy racquet, a ball, and, desirably, protective eye covering. It requires relatively little time for a thorough workout. Busy peo-
35 ple can squeeze in an exciting match during a lunch hour. It requires only one opponent for a rousing game. Racquetball seems to be an idea whose time has come.

The primary purpose of the passage appears to be _____ .

(A) a comparison of squash and racquetball
(B) an explanation of racquetball's recent popularity
(C) a plea for physical fitness
(D) promotion of racquetball as a spectator sport
(E) condemnation of sedentary pursuits

_____

Strategy

The key to this question is the word *primary*. While it is true, for example, that the selection contains an implied plea for physical fitness, this thrust is not the primary purpose of the passage. We can eliminate (C). We can also eliminate (E), for though the author apparently approves of physical activity as opposed to sedentary pursuits, this point is by no means the primary purpose. Squash and racquetball come into comparison slightly, since some squash players have turned to racquetball, but this is a minor detail. Similarly, the appeal of racquetball to spectators takes up a sentence. We can thus reject (A) and (D). The remaining possibility, (B), is clearly the answer. The expression *explosive growth* in the opening sentence is a clue to the emphasis in the selection. This question might have been rephrased as one testing generalization.

A good title for this selection is . . . Racquetball—A Popular New Sport.

Time Out for Review

Try your skill. The passage below is followed by questions based on its content. Use the preceding example to help you find the right answers.

In too many performances of *Hamlet*, Polonius is depicted as a doddering old man, tottering shakily on the edge of senility. In productions like these, Polonius is often
5 played strictly for laughs. His advice to Laertes, though not out of keeping for a typical courtier, is ridiculed by the player's exaggerated infirmity of speech and decrepitude of action. His advice to Ophelia, though
10 reasonable in the context of the times, is made to seem arbitrarily absurd. His admitted garrulity is overemphasized, and his interference in the action is made the work of a clown.
15 Unfortunately for Polonius, there is some justification for laughing at his expense now and then. Hamlet derides Polonius at every opportunity, drawing a laugh from the courtier's eagerness to please at any cost. The
20 King often wishes Polonius would get to the point in breaking important news or giving advice on matters concerning Hamlet. Even the generally kindly Queen says at one time, "More matter with less art." Yet these
25 points are not decisive in any full appraisal of Polonius.
Despite the audience's occasional laughter at Polonius's expense, certain facts remain indisputably true. Till his death Polon-
30 ius remains a respected member of the court. Throughout the play he has been assigned positions of respect. The King seems to value Polonius's judgment and advice. Though Polonius's advice has proved faulty, the King
35 does not object when Polonius volunteers to spy on Hamlet and his mother. Then in her room, the Queen takes Polonius's ill-fated advice to "be round" with Hamlet. That proves to be the wrong tack.
40 Polonius meets his fate on an errand he interprets as serving his king, and his death precipitates the final tragedy. Polonius is not a nonentity, not a character provided for comic relief. He is not a pitiful dotard. He
45 supplies some of the humor, to be sure, but a sound case can be made for playing him as a reasonably typical courtier—not a mental or spiritual giant, but at least a respectable and generally honored member of the court
50 at Elsinore.

1. The author's primary purpose in this passage is to _____ .
   (A) suggest Hamlet's unfairness toward Polonius
   (B) criticize a little-tried interpretation of the part of Polonius
   (C) recommend playing Polonius with respect
   (D) suggest Shakespeare's uncertainty about the characterization of Polonius
   (E) recommend playing Polonius with relieved seriousness

   1 ___

2. The purpose of paragraph 2 is to _____ .
   (A) concede that Polonius can be laughed at
   (B) criticize the Queen's hypocrisy toward Polonius
   (C) suggest that a courtier should occasionally disagree with the King
   (D) present some of Polonius's strongest character traits
   (E) imply that Polonius is second to Hamlet in importance

   2 ___

3. The meaning of the quotation "More matter with less art" can probably be expressed as _____ .
   (A) "Come to the point."
   (B) "Start from the beginning."
   (C) "Speak more slowly."
   (D) "Repeat your last sentence."
   (E) "Don't breathe a word of this to anyone."

   3 ___

4. The advice to "be round" with Hamlet proved to be _____ .
   (A) generally sound
   (B) thoughtlessly blunt
   (C) ill-advised
   (D) well-planned
   (E) immediately disregarded

   4 ___

5. The author's attitude toward Polonius is generally _____.
   (A) bitter
   (B) puzzled
   (C) favorable
   (D) unpredictable
   (E) indifferent

   5 ___

6. According to the selection, which of the following adjectives may reasonably be applied to Polonius? _____.
   I. cruel
   II. long-winded
   III. senile
   IV. loyal
   V. brilliant
   (A) II only
   (B) III only
   (C) V only
   (D) I, II, and V
   (E) II and IV

   6 ___

7. The author points out typical errors in the portrayal of Polonius in lines _____.
   (A) 1–5
   (B) 30–35
   (C) 36–40
   (D) 41–45
   (E) 46–50

   7 ___

8. The death of Polonius is _____.
   (A) not explained in the selection
   (B) well merited
   (C) by order of the King
   (D) sometimes played for laughs
   (E) not unexpected

   8 ___

9. Which of the following titles best summarizes the content of the passage?
   (A) Hamlet and Polonius—A Study in Contrasts
   (B) Polonius—An Often-Misunderstood Character
   (C) The Dangers of Meddling
   (D) The Courtier's Role in *Hamlet*
   (E) Minor Characters with Major Impacts

   9 ___

SUMMARY PART 3

Understanding the Author's Role: Evaluating the Author's Purpose

Determining the author's purpose calls for a special kind of inference. Some questions require you to discover the purpose of the passage as a whole. Others require you to identify the purpose of a portion of the selection, perhaps a single sentence. When in doubt, use the process of elimination to isolate the correct answer.

PART 4

Evaluating the Author's Style

The author's purpose influences the tone of a passage. His attitude affects his purpose. All three are interrelated: purpose, tone, attitude. A fourth element belongs with this group: the author's style. SAT questions sometimes ask you to evaluate an author's style. Questions about style may be general or specific.

Note the difference in phraseology between the following two question types:

1. The style of the passage can best be described as . . .

   This general question can be followed by single-adjective alternatives like *light*, *argumentative*, or *wordy*.

2. Which of the following best describes the author's technique in this passage?

   This more specific question can be followed by more extended phrases like *trying to justify the use of force in certain circumstances*.

Since an author's technique is an ingredient in his special style, both questions ask you to appraise the author's effectiveness and the special flavor of his writing.

Trial Test

Take the following trial test to evaluate your skill.

When a forest is ravaged by fire, cut down to make way for a parking lot, or harvested for timber, there is the esthetic loss of something beautiful. A complete ecosys-
5 tem is destroyed, and the habitats of forest creatures are laid waste. There is an even more serious long-range problem, however: the effect upon the balance of oxygen and carbon dioxide in the atmosphere. On the
10 one hand, the ever-expanding use of fossil fuels has liberated into the atmosphere tremendous quantities of carbon dioxide. On the other hand, deforestation has reduced the vegetation needed to recycle the carbon
15 dioxide, store the carbon, and release essential oxygen for the world's living things. Too much release of stored carbon can also potentially raise the temperature of the atmosphere through the ''greenhouse effect.''

20 Forest vegetation stores 90% of the carbon held in terrestrial ecosystems. In eastern North America there has been some improvement in recent years through reforestation. But gains in the temperate zone have
25 been offset by losses in the tropics. Wholesale destruction of tropical forests is the greatest single threat, since most of the world's arboreal vegetation is found in the vast forest of the Amazon and other tropical
30 areas. Global awareness of the problem is needed to provide a basis for sound management of forests, the crucial agents in the carbon cycle.

The style of this passage can best be described as: _____ .

(A) self-conscious   (D) repetitious
(B) lyrical   (E) frivolous
(C) expository

_____

Answer to Trial Test

(*C*) This is a down-to-earth explanation of the importance of trees in the carbon cycle. It is strictly *expository*. It is too serious for (*E*), too objective for (*A*), too matter of fact for (*B*). There is no indication of repetition (*D*).

Look at a typical question and then analyze the possible answers.

Problem

Saving money takes odd forms. Comparison shoppers visit half a dozen supermarkets, save a total of $1.73, and spend $1.48 for gasoline. Anglers spend a fortune
5 on fishing gear, bait, boat charges—and catch three small flounders. Writers save odd pieces of string, worn rubber bands, rusty paper clips—and then throw out the lot at one time. Coupon clippers save 30¢ by buy-
10 ing a product when an equally good competing product can be bought for 50¢ less without a coupon. Amateur carpenters buy cheap nuts, bolts, and screws and find them stripping under pressure. Is all this econo-
15 mizing foolish? Not at all.

The comparison shopper has enjoyed the challenge and the pursuit. The angler has had a day on the water getting sunburned and happy. The writer has eased his soul, cleaned
20 the slate, and stimulated his genius to start again. The coupon clipper has had the satisfaction of getting "something for nothing." As for the amateur carpenter—well eventually he is going to call in a profes-
25 sional anyway. For his sake and the sake of his homestead, the sooner the better.

1. The style of this passage can best be described as _____.
   (A) serious but astute
   (B) light and cheerful
   (C) perceptive and rhetorical
   (D) critical and unfavorable
   (E) argumentative but good natured

   1 ___

2. The passage "For his sake and the sake of his homestead, the sooner the better" can best be described as _____.
   (A) humorous   (D) coarse
   (B) bitter   (E) rigid
   (C) calculated

   2 ___

3. "Something for nothing" is put in quotation marks because _____.
   (A) it suggests the purchaser's buying fantasies
   (B) these are the actual words used in the advertising
   (C) this is an actual quotation by the purchaser
   (D) the quotation is literally true
   (E) the writer believes the purchase is a bargain

   3 ___

Strategy

1. The topic, "saving money," is not taken seriously. The examples are light-hearted. The mock-serious explanation in paragraph 2 provides another clue to the answer. An expression like "getting sunburned and happy" suggests the writer is not really dealing with a subject seriously. Since the selection is not serious, (A) is incorrect. There is no real argument here: the purpose is to provide a chuckle. (E) is incorrect. *Rhetorical* eliminates (C). *Unfavorable* eliminates (D). (B), the remaining answer, is an accurate description.

2. The author looks upon the amateur carpenter with amused affection, but he doesn't have much faith in his ability. When he suggests calling in a professional "for his sake and the sake of his homestead," he is not serious. (A) is the answer.

3. There is no indication that anyone or anything specifically is being quoted. (B) and (C) are incorrect. If the saying were literally true, business would go out of business! (D) is incorrect. The writer's revelation that another product just as good could be bought for less proves he does not consider this purchase a bargain. The quotation marks suggest the buyer's dream is to get the best bargain for the money. The ultimate bargain is "something for nothing," a will-o'-the-wisp. (A) is the answer.

Time Out for Review

Try your skill. The passage below is followed by questions based on its content. Use the preceding example to help you find the right answers.

Our language is a magnificent achievement, but there are pitfalls built into it—snares that catch the unwary. One of the trickiest problems arises from the fact that
5 the structure of the language does not distinguish between *fact* and *opinion*. *Walter Payton is a member of the Chicago Bears* is a factual statement. *Walter Payton is the greatest runningback of all time* is a state-
10 ment of opinion. Both sentences *look* the same. Both sentences have the same grammatical structure: *subject*, *being verb*, *predicate nominative*. But the difference between the two statements is astronomical. Many of
15 the world's problems could be averted if all people—and especially those in positions of power—could recognize the difference and employ the difference honestly in their speeches.
20 There is an essential difference between a statement of fact and a statement of opinion. The former can be checked. The latter cannot. "This room is 20 × 24" is a factual statement. We can take out a ruler and check
25 the dimensions. We cannot check the statement "This room is cozy (dreary, small, large, impressive, depressing)."

What's wrong? We all have opinions and express them. There's nothing wrong with
30 having and stating opinions. The danger lies in confusing opinions with facts. If we make opinionated pronouncements and believe they are factual, we are muddying our thought processes and confusing our mes-
35 sages. If we read someone else's opinionated pronouncements and believe they are factual, we are clogging our brains with error.

Statements in factual form may be inaccurate, but at least they can be checked. That
40 room may actually be only 20 × 22. Statements in opinion form are neither *wrong* nor *right* in any test of truth. They are merely expressions of a point of view—interesting, perhaps, but not to be taken as Truth. State-
45 ments of opinion tend to tell us more about the speaker or writer than about the subject matter of the statement.

Learning to distinguish between fact and opinion is a test of linguistic sophistication and emotional maturity.

1. The author's style can best be described as _____.

   (A) impassive   (D) persuasive
   (B) sportive   (E) formal
   (C) ironic
                                    1 ___

2. Which of the following best describes the author's technique in this passage?
   (A) Emphasizing the essential weakness of the English language
   (B) Deriding the use of opinion to make any statement
   (C) Presenting a viewpoint without recommending any action
   (D) Using examples to make an important point
   (E) Minimizing the crucial difference between fact and opinion

                                    2 ___

3. From the selection we may infer that _____.

(A) it is worse to state an opinion than to make a factual statement, no matter how erroneous the latter may be
(B) to call a 20 × 24 room "large" is to make a factual statement
(C) most speakers intentionally use statements of opinion to mislead
(D) statements of fact and of opinion are sometimes difficult to tell apart
(E) a knowledge of grammar will guarantee the ability to distinguish between fact and opinion

3 ___

4. Which of the following sentences best expresses the central idea of the selection?

(A) "The danger lies in confusing opinions with facts."
(B) "The difference between the two statements is astronomical."
(C) "If we read someone else's opinionated pronouncements and believe they are factual, we are clogging our brains with error."
(D) "The former can be checked."
(E) "Both sentences have the same grammatical structure: *subject, being verb, predicate nominative.*"

4 ___

5. *Truth* is capitalized in line 44 because it represents _____.

(A) substantiated opinion
(B) verifiable fact
(C) fundamental reality
(D) modified skepticism
(E) idiosyncratic viewpoint

5 ___

6. The author's purpose in the last paragraph is to _____.

(A) provide another example of his basic thesis
(B) urge his readers to be on guard
(C) recommend further studies in semantic evaluation
(D) suggest overtly contesting the opinion of others
(E) reveal hitherto unsuspected similarities between fact and opinion

6 ___

7. From the passage it may be inferred that _____.

(A) statements of fact cannot tell us anything about the speaker or writer
(B) emotions play a larger role in expressions of opinion than in statements of fact
(C) speakers who avoid statements of opinion are the most respected debaters
(D) having a point of view is risky
(E) people in positions of power tend to rely heavily on factual arguments

7 ___

8. The writer obviously believes that _____.

(A) Walter Payton is the greatest runningback of all time
(B) the same room may be classified as *large* and *small*
(C) a ruler can settle all arguments of fact
(D) most people do indeed distinguish sharply between fact and opinion
(E) a viewpoint is different from an opinion

8 ___

SUMMARY PART 4

Understanding the Author's Role: Evaluating the Author's Style

If the style is the man, then writers put themselves into every page they write. When evaluating the author's style for an SAT question, read the passage through to get the flavor of it. If you are uncertain, read it again. Be on the lookout for certain clues: humorous contradictions, angry pronouncements, subtle suggestions.

Summary
Section IV: Understanding the Author's Role

The author's role reveals itself throughout an entire passage.

The *tone* and *attitude* can "be found in the overall impression created by the combination of descriptive and connotative words."

The *purpose* can be discovered by drawing an inference based upon the whole passage (unless, of course, a smaller portion is asked for).

The *style* reveals itself throughout the passage—in humorous touches, angered comments, criticisms, compliments, informal remarks, or formal statements.

The *tone*, *attitude*, *purpose*, and *style* are all ingredients calling for an examination of the flavor of the passage, the total impact.

PART 1   Evaluating the Author's Tone

A. Questions that ask about the author's tone provide answer choices of adjectives (*argumentative*, *ironic*, *reflective*, etc.) or sometimes nouns (*despair*, *indifference*, *sarcasm*, etc.)
B. Get an overall impression of the *whole* passage. Don't worry about details.
C. Think of words that describe its tone. Then choose the answer that best agrees with your description.
D. Most SAT passages are neutral in tone, but a few are not. If a question asks about the tone, it is probably *not* neutral.

PART 2   Evaluating the Author's Attitude

A. Questions ask for such attitudes as admiration, disdain, nostalgia, apathy, and skepticism.
B. Questions about attitude are often quite specific. They ask about the author's attitude *toward someone or something*.
C. Read the question and be sure you understand exactly whom or what it asks about.
D. Look for the persons or things asked for.
E. If you are unsure about specifics, reread the whole passage. Get a sense of the author's feeling toward the entire subject.

PART 3   Evaluating the Author's Purpose

A. Because the author's purpose usually is not stated, you must draw an inference based on the information, tone, and attitude in the passage.
B. Some questions ask about the purpose of the whole passage; others ask about a portion or a detail.
C. Read the question carefully. Be sure you understand what it asks about.
D. Reread what is asked about—the whole passage or a portion—to draw your inference about the purpose.

PART 4   Evaluating the Author's Style

A. Some questions about style are general; they ask for overall judgments of style, offering such word choices as *ironic*, *persuasive*, and *formal*.

B. Some questions about style are more specific; they ask for certain judgments of technique, offering detailed phrase choices such as *deriding the use of opinion to make any statement*.

C. Read the whole passage to get the flavor of it, the total impact. If you are unsure, reread it.

D. Look for evidence of humor, anger, cleverness, formality, persuasiveness, etc., to form your judgment.

Section V: Understanding Language in Action

PART 1

Evaluating the Author's Diction

SAT questions occasionally ask you to evaluate the use of an author's diction: its aptness or effectiveness. Words acquire special meanings in various contexts. A word's connotation (pages 41–46) is often determined by its neighbors on the printed page. We cannot tell what most words "mean" until they are used. *Old* means one thing when it applies to a joke and quite another when it applies to a person.

This aspect of words is tested in questions like these:

The word ... as used in line ... means ...
The narrator suggests that ... speaks of her husband as if he were ...
The word ... is meant to suggest ...

Note that the skill being tested is basically the same skill tested in "Clues from Context," pages 6–40. If you have mastered the material on those pages, you should do well with questions of meaning.

Trial Test

Take the trial test to review your skill.

California's Silicon Valley is creating a new language, and some people are objecting. Words like *input* and *interface* have already invaded the language but these are rel-
5   atively conservative additions. Some computer babble is like a foreign language. If people say, "I'm interrupt driven," they are complaining about their hectic schedule. If other people are labeled with a "read-only
10 memory," they are being charged with never learning anything, always saying the same thing over and over. A "gating event" is a turning point. "Bandwidth" is the amount of information exchanged in a conversation.

15   John A. Barry, columnist for *InfoWorld* magazine, attacks computer illiteracy as a failure to grasp the English language. Though change and growth are inevitable in language, Barry considers these linguistic
20 extravagances self-defeating and confusing. He feels that proliferation of such excesses can only serve to pollute the language.

The word *proliferation* as used in the last sentence means _____.

(A) approval
(B) reporting
(C) increase
(D) condemnation
(E) allocation

Answer to Trial Test

(*C*) Since John A. Barry is objecting to computer illiteracy, he would naturally object to any *increase*, since such increase would further pollute the language.

Look at a typical question and then analyze the possible answers.

Problem

The annals of our time are filled with horror stories, of beautiful rivers converted to sewers, of lakes destroyed by acid rain, of forests ruthlessly and thoughtlessly laid
5 waste. There are, fortunately, a growing number of success stories also, tales of people who rolled up their sleeves and refused to be defeated.

For some blasé city dwellers, there is
10 nothing novel under the sun, but New Yorkers have something new to cheer about. In the very backyard of New York City, in the shadow of skyscrapers and right next to busy Kennedy airport, a miracle has taken place.
15 Jamaica Bay Wildlife Refuge, covering 13,000 acres of marsh and woodland, is now a naturalist's paradise. It is home to more than 300 species of birds—nesting not far from the heart of the city.
20 The refuge did not come into existence overnight. Between World Wars I and II, Jamaica Bay became a disaster area, a dumping ground for sewage and industrial waste. It was an ecologist's nightmare. After
25 World War II the city took steps to clean up the mess. Dikes were built to create two freshwater ponds. Then, in 1953, Herbert Johnson, who was appointed superintendent of the new refuge, planned the gathering and
30 planting of the shrubs, trees, and grasses that make the area a haven for wildlife—for rare birds like the white pelican, the cinnamon teal, and the red-wing thrush.

35 Now a part of Gateway National Recreation Area, Jamaica Bay Wildlife Refuge has become a mecca for birdwatchers, an idyllic retreat for citizens overwhelmed by city tensions, and a model for other cities to emulate. It is unique. It is probably the "world's
40 only wildlife sanctuary reachable by subway."

1. The word *blasé* in the second paragraph is meant to suggest _____.
   (A) charm   (D) indifference
   (B) enthusiasm   (E) commitment
   (C) anger
                                    1 __

2. The word *idyllic* in the last paragraph means _____.
   (A) happy and peaceful
   (B) elusive and uncertain
   (C) calm but taut
   (D) spiritual and religious
   (E) slow and unchallenging
                                    2 __

3. The word *emulate* in the last paragraph adds to imitation the suggestion of _____.
   (A) failing   (D) planning
   (B) striving   (E) envying
   (C) studying
                                    3 __

Strategy

1. The phrase *nothing much new under the sun* suggests boredom. If *blasé* means "bored," then it suggests *indifference*, (*D*).
2. The contrast of the refuge with city noises and tensions provides the clue: *happy and peaceful*, (*A*).
3. The use of the word *model* suggests that other cities might try (*strive*) to imitate the refuge. (*B*) is correct.

Time Out for Review

Try your skill. The passage below is followed by questions based on its content. Use the preceding example to help you find the right answers.

"Nothing is the way we thought it was, and whatever we think we understand today will be changed to something else when looked at more closely tomorrow."

5   As we look outward from our island in the solar system, space probes and improved technology have changed our view of the cosmos we inhabit. As we direct our study inward, toward the very small, experimen-
10   tation in subatomic physics is changing our understanding of the microcosm. Now Lewis Thomas, author of the quotation above, suggests that biologists also are crossing a new threshold in their study of life forms. Until
15   recently, experts have held some hard-and-fast opinions about the conditions needed for life. Those opinions have now been turned upside down. We have discovered a set of creatures that violate all the rules about life
20   and life-support systems.

At the bottom of certain oceanic abysses, there are, from interior sources, chimneys that heat the sea water to temperatures exceeding 660 degrees Fahrenheit. We know
25   that water turns into steam at 212 degrees at sea level. At 660 degrees water remains a liquid only because it is under enormous pressure. Everything we thought we knew suggested that life could not survive in this
30   superheated water under 265 atmospheres of pressure. But it does.

In 1979, John Baross and some fellow oceanographers scooped up water from a depth of 2,600 meters and discovered living
35   bacteria flourishing in the superheated liquid. Later, Baross and Jody Deming of Johns Hopkins University proceeded to duplicate these extreme conditions and grow these incredible life forms. They were amazed to
40   discover that at 482 degrees Fahrenheit the bacteria increased a thousandfold in six hours. If "chilled" just below boiling, the bacteria would not grow at all.

Their joint discovery has opened up vast
45   new vistas. These bacteria produce methane, hydrogen, and carbon monoxide. There is a possibility these tiny creatures might play a role in long-range geologic change. They might become a valuable resource for a new
50   natural gas industry. Their enzymes might be useful in industrial processes that involve high temperatures and pressures.

When we think we have closed a door on one corridor of science, another door
55   swings wide open. Fixed ideas and closed minds have no place in science. The world is truly the home of miracles.

1. The word *microcosm* in line 11 means
   _____.
   (A) little world   (D) scientific
   (B) scientific   instrument
        method   (E) exploration
   (C) galaxy   1 ___

2. The word *abysses* in line 21 is meant to suggest _____.
   (A) extreme heat   (D) great depths
   (B) submarine   (E) submerged
        peaks   continents
   (C) underwater
        vegetation   2 ___

3. The word *chilled* in line 42 is enclosed in quotation marks because _____.
   (A) it is taken directly from Lewis Thomas' article
   (B) the writer intended to use a better word
   (C) the water was hot
   (D) Lewis Thomas disagrees with John Baross
   (E) the experiment was essentially inexact
                                        3 ___

4. One effect of putting water under great pressure is to _____.
   (A) prevent instruments from probing it
   (B) kill all life forms
   (C) change its subatomic structure
   (D) release enzymes useful for industry
   (E) prevent heated water from turning into steam
                                        4 ___

5. Which of the following best expresses the main idea of the selection?
   (A) Bacteria are remarkably adaptable organisms.
   (B) Baross and Deming are pioneers in an unexplored area.
   (C) Scientists must be ready to accept and explore new ideas.
   (D) The oceans may solve most of our problems.
   (E) Life can survive in inhospitable environments.

   5 ___

6. The passage suggests that _____.
   (A) we have barely scratched the surface of knowledge
   (B) oceanographers, as a group, are superior to physicists
   (C) life is certain to be found on the moon
   (D) there are no miracles in science
   (E) the various ice ages are attributable to the deep-sea bacteria

   6 ___

7. The author's purpose is to _____.
   (A) amuse and entertain while enlightening the reader
   (B) suggest a sense of wonder at recent discoveries
   (C) engage in a subtle debate over the value of "pure research"
   (D) discredit any experimentation that cannot be repeated
   (E) criticize biologists of the past

   7 ___

8. The bacteria grew a thousandfold at temperatures of _____.
   (A) 212 degrees   (D) 660 degrees
   (B) 265 degrees   (E) 2,650 degrees
   (C) 482 degrees

   8 ___

SUMMARY PART 1

Understanding Language in Action: Evaluating the Author's Diction

Questions about diction on the SAT rely heavily upon context (pages 6–40). When you answer such questions, carefully study the surrounding words. Use the various clues—contrast, pairing, signal words, direct explanation—to help you identify the correct alternative. All the words in a reading selection directly or indirectly affect the total context. Identifying one element in the fabric often requires understanding of the whole.

PART 2

Understanding Figurative Language

Your ability to interpret a figurative expression may be tested on the SAT. You will most likely be asked to identify the hidden comparison in a metaphor, but other figures of speech may also be tested.

This aspect of words is tested in a question like this:

The author uses the phrase *towering battlements* to describe . . .

In that particular question the *towering battlements* are skyscrapers. In another context they might apply to cliffs, tall trees, or castles.

Note that the skill being tested is basically the same skill tested in "Figurative Language," pages 47–52. If you have mastered the material on these pages, you should do well with questions involving figurative language.

Trial Test

Take the trial test to review your skills.

The victim explained from his hospital bed, "I had the right-of-way at the intersection."

Nearly half of all accidents occur at in-
5 tersections, especially intersections with traffic lights. Good preventive driving practice requires caution at all times. "Expect the worst" is one expert's advice. Writing in the *AAA* magazine, Deborah Allen says,
10 "Even if you think you have the right-of-way, don't assume that cross-traffic is going to stop for you. Check both ways to make sure the intersection is clear of both vehicles and pedestrians before you move out into it.
15 If you're approaching an intersection as the light turns green, take your foot off the gas pedal and be prepared to brake if necessary. Look first to the left and then to the right— *then to the left again*—to make sure the in-
20 tersection is clear." Whether you brake or accelerate depends upon the traffic pattern. If a lumbering juggernaut heads for you, accelerating and proper steering, rather than braking, may avert an accident. If you ex-
25 pect the worst, you'll be prepared.

The author uses the phrase "lumbering juggernaut" to mean a _____ .

(A) heavy vehicle   (D) construction
(B) speeding   truck
     ambulance   (E) trailer
(C) school bus

Answer to Trial Test

(*A*) *Lumbering* suggests slowness and bulk. *Juggernaut* suggests a force that crushes every object in its path. All the answers but (*A*) are too specific. *Juggernaut* doesn't specify truck, bus, trailer, or ambulance.

Look at the following typical question and then analyze the possible answers.

Problem

We left our houseboat and stepped into a shikara, that all-purpose floating store, post office, florist shop, supply vessel, water taxi, and suburban bus. Not unlike a Venetian
5 gondola, the shikara is easily and effectively maneuverable by one person, sometimes poling, sometimes paddling. Because power boats would pollute beautiful Dal Lake, the jewel of the Vale of Kashmir, the shikara
10 reigns supreme, darting back and forth across the surface with charm and grace.

Soon we left the open charms of Dal Lake for a tributary of the River Jhelum. A hand-operated lock regulates the water level of the
15 lake and prevents river pollutants from flowing back into the lake. Through narrow passageways lined with houseboats in every stage of repair and disrepair, we floated noiselessly along, observing the everyday
20 life of the Kashmiri, waving to happy children and nodding gravely to older members of the river community. Here was poverty but not ugliness. Beautiful pewter implements graced the shelves of even the poorest
25 houseboat. Washed clothes hung to dry from every home, no matter how modest.

After 45 minutes and another lock, we were carried into the broad expanse of the River Jhelum. Instead of simple houseboats,
30 tall multiple dwellings lined the river on both sides. A five-story apartment house, at a Pisa-like angle, clung to the hillside with Kashmiri tenacity. Old and decrepit, this aged skeleton still housed families glad for
35 some shelter in a crowded land. By contrast, the crumbling palace of a former maharajah, a ghostly sepulcher, showed no signs of life.

The vitality of the Kashmiri, their will to survive, is epitomized in the river and the
40 vitality along the river banks. If life is a river, each Kashmiri has a shikara to carry him along.

1. The "suburban bus" in the first sentence is _____ .
   (A) a front-wheel-drive vehicle
   (B) an official car
   (C) a boat
   (D) a tractor
   (E) a houseboat

   1 ___

2. The "skeleton" referred to in the third paragraph is _____ .
   (A) a former palace
   (B) a sinking houseboat
   (C) a condominium
   (D) a temple
   (E) an apartment house

   2 ___

3. The phrase "ghostly sepulcher" in the third paragraph suggests _____ .
   (A) lifelessness
   (B) a supernatural tale
   (C) plague
   (D) limited vitality
   (E) a legend

   3 ___

4. The expression "Pisa-like angle" suggests that the house _____ .
   (A) has collapsed
   (B) is basically sound
   (C) has a holy aura
   (D) is leaning
   (E) is being rebuilt

   4 ___

5. The shikara in the last sentence is _____ .
   (A) a gondola
   (B) a native ferry
   (C) a canoe
   (D) a government steamship
   (E) not a boat

   5 ___

Strategy

1. Like the five other functions, *suburban* bus is a function of the shikara. (*C*) is the correct answer.
2. The context tells us this "aged skeleton" still housed families. It is clearly the apartment house, (*E*).
3. *Ghostly sepulcher* is contrasted with the lively apartment house, with all its people and vitality. It does not have even limited vitality, (*D*). (*A*), *lifeless-ness*, is correct.
4. One of Pisa's claims to fame is the Leaning Tower. If the angle is Pisa-like, the building is leaning, (*D*).
5. The meaning of boat and river shifts here. Life is compared with a river. Then shikara must refer to the strength each Kashmiri has to carry him along that difficult river. In any event, shikara does not mean a boat here. (*E*), *not a boat*, is correct.

Time Out for Review

Try your skill. The passage below is followed by questions based on its content. Use the preceding examples to help you find the right answers.

The Extraordinary is easy. And the more extraordinary the Extraordinary is, the easier it is: "easy" in the sense that we can almost always recognize it .... The Extraordinary
5 does not let you shrug your shoulders and walk away.

But the Ordinary is a much harder case. In the first place, by making itself so notice-able—it is around us all the time—the Or-
10 dinary has got itself in a bad fix with us: we hardly ever notice it. The Ordinary, simply by *being* so ordinary, tends to make us ig-norant or neglectful; when something does not insist on being noticed, when we aren't
15 grabbed by the collar or struck on the skull by a presence or an event, we take for granted the very things that most deserve our gratitude.

And this is the chief vein and deepest
20 point concerning the Ordinary: that it *does* deserve our gratitude. The Ordinary lets us live out our humanity; it doesn't scare us, it doesn't excite us, it doesn't distract us .... Ordinariness can be defined as a breathing-
25 space: the breathing-space between getting born and dying, perhaps, or else the breath-ing-space between rapture and rapture; or,

more usually, the breathing-space between one disaster and the next. Ordinariness is
30 sometimes the *status quo*, sometimes the slow, unseen movement of a subtle but ine-luctable cycle, like a ride on the hour hand of the clock; in any case the Ordinary is above all *what is expected*.
35 And what is expected is not often thought of as a gift.

1. The author uses the phrase "struck on the skull" in line 15 to mean

   _____.

   (A) seriously injured
   (B) mildly irritated
   (C) overwhelmed
   (D) physically confronted
   (E) overlooked

   1 ___

2. A "breathing-space between rapture and rapture" in line 27 could be described as

   _____.

   (A) an uneventful period
   (B) a preparation for excitement
   (C) a reliving of an exciting past
   (D) an unsuspected tension
   (E) a crucial training regimen

   2 ___

3. The important characteristics of "a ride on the hour hand of a clock" in line 32 is that it is _____.
   - (A) slow and boring
   - (B) depressingly time-consuming
   - (C) subtle but unavoidable
   - (D) characterized by staccato leaps
   - (E) not always welcome

     3 ___

4. This selection is basically _____.
   - (A) a snide comment on pretense
   - (B) an attack on boredom
   - (C) a praise of the predictable
   - (D) an exposé of the "average"
   - (E) a paean to excitement

     4 ___

5. The author thinks that we take too much for granted those things that are _____.
   - (A) noticeable
   - (B) ordinary
   - (C) critical
   - (D) cyclical
   - (E) unexpected

     5 ___

6. Ordinariness may be _____.
   - (A) cyclical or unchanging
   - (B) cyclical and unexpected
   - (C) cyclical and upsetting
   - (D) unchanging or revolutionary
   - (E) unexpected or rapturous

     6 ___

7. The author implies that you can shrug your shoulders and walk away from _____.
   - (A) the Extraordinary
   - (B) the rapturous
   - (C) the unexpected
   - (D) the Ordinary
   - (E) the neglectful

     7 ___

SUMMARY PART 2

Understanding Language in Action: Understanding Figurative Language

Someone once called figurative language "it is what it isn't." Figurative expressions always mean more than they seem to say. Get behind the author's literal language and see if the author is making a subtle comparison. Figurative language is a kind of poetry. You need to use your imagination for best results.

PART 3

Evaluating Degree and Exclusion

Sometimes the phraseology of SAT questions requires a reversal of familiar techniques. Questions of this type are usually phrased as follows:

1. With which of the following statements would the author be LEAST likely to agree?
2. In the passage, the author exhibits all of the following attitudes toward the surroundings EXCEPT . . . .
3. It can be inferred from the passage that all of the following might explain why the author describes the EARTH as "presumably lifeless" (line ---) EXCEPT . . . .

These questions are the reverse of most questions. Ordinarily you are asked to choose the main idea or the most likely statement. In question 1 you do the opposite. You choose the *least* likely statement. Similarly, questions like 2 or 3 list a majority of items that are included and ask you to choose the one that is *not* included. These test many skills already touched upon, even though the phraseology is different.

Trial Test

Take the trial test to evaluate your skill.

When an insect army marches on trees, the old warriors are not without their own defenses. Scientists once thought that insect populations were controlled only by the
5 weather and by natural predators, like birds. New findings, however, show that trees and other plants are not passive victims. They fight back with an arsenal of deadly chemicals to thwart the insect hordes. What is even
10 more amazing is that trees under siege may warn their neighbors to get ready to fight!

Apparently when insects begin to ravage a tree, the tree sends poisonous chemicals into its leaves to discourage or kill the in-
15 vader. What is more, the tree sets off a silent alarm. An airborne chemical from the in-

fested tree is carried to neighboring trees. Forewarned, the neighboring trees increase the concentration of chemicals in *their* leaves
20 to protect themselves from the rampaging horde.

Different plants create different chemicals. A short-lived wildflower often has extremely powerful toxins ready to repel any
25 insect invader before it strikes. Since it has little time to grow and reproduce, it cannot waste any time. Long-lived trees, on the other hand, have a more elaborate strategy. Some of their chemicals merely interfere
30 with an insect's digestion. Others are more deadly. In the continuing battle between insect and plant life, the stationary, exposed plants are not entirely defenseless, even without man's intervention.

1. With which of the following statements would the author be LEAST likely to agree?
   (A) Without man's help, the great forests of the Northeast would be almost entirely denuded.
   (B) Insects avoid plants with toxic chemicals as their first line of defense.
   (C) In some way or other, trees transmit crucial messages to other trees.
   (D) Insect populations are not entirely controlled by birds and weather.
   (E) Plants vary in their ability to fight infestation.

   1 ___

2. In the struggle against insect infestations, the author mentions all of the following defenses EXCEPT _____ .
   (A) chemicals that interfere with digestion
   (B) powerful toxins
   (C) messages from one tree to another
   (D) other insects
   (E) concentration of chemicals

   2 ___

Answers to Trial Test

1. (A) Since trees do not depend on birds and weather for their defense, we can eliminate (D). If the tree's chemicals "discourage or kill the invader," we can eliminate (B), since the author clearly agrees. Trees and wildflowers handle insect infestations in different ways. We can eliminate (E). "Warn their neighbors" tells us the author agrees with (C). That leaves (A). Since trees have defenses independent of man, the author would disagree with (A). Therefore (A) is the right answer.

2. (D) The items mentioned in (A), (B), (C), and (E) are specifically mentioned in the selection. Therefore these alternatives can be discarded. Nowhere in the selection are other insects mentioned as a check on insect growth. (D) is correct.

Look at a typical question and then analyze the possible answers.

Problem

There is nothing more alone in the universe than man. He is alone because he has the intellectual capacity to know that he is separated by a vast gulf of social memory
5 and experiment from the lives of his animal associates. He has entered into the strange world of history, of social and intellectual change, while his brothers of the field and forest remain subject to the invisible laws of
10 biological evolution. Animals are molded by natural forces they do not comprehend. To their minds there is no past and no future. There is only the everlasting present of a single generation—its trails in the forest, its
15 hidden pathways of the air and in the sea.

Man, by contrast, is alone with the knowledge of his history until the day of his death. When we were children we wanted to talk to animals and struggled to understand
20 why this was impossible. Slowly we gave up the attempt as we grew into the solitary world of human adulthood; the rabbit was left on the lawn, the dog was relegated to his kennel. Only in acts of inarticulate compassion,
25 in rare and hidden moments of communion with nature, does man briefly escape his solitary destiny. Frequently in science fiction he dreams of worlds with creatures whose communicative power is the equivalent of
30 his own.

1. With which of the following statements would the author be LEAST likely to agree?
   - (A) In reality, children would like a closer communion with animals.
   - (B) Man's solitary destiny is sometimes escaped, but only for brief moments.
   - (C) Animals intuitively understand more than does man.
   - (D) Social and intellectual change has molded man.
   - (E) Science fiction may be a kind of wish fulfillment.

   1 ___

2. All the following are mentioned as characteristic of man EXCEPT _____.
   - (A) social memory
   - (B) living completely in the present
   - (C) knowledge of history
   - (D) hidden moments of communion
   - (E) acts of compassion

   2 ___

Strategy

1. Man's peculiar and unique destiny is awareness—of past and future. The first sentence in the second paragraph specifically says that man is *alone*. The animals cannot share his experience. (*C*), which gives animals a greater awareness, is in contradiction to the sense of the passage. (*C*) is correct.

2. Animals, rather than man, are able to live in *the everlasting present of a single generation*. (*B*) is correct.

Time Out for Review

Try your skill. The passage below is followed by questions based on its content.

Few manifestations of natural forces are as terrifying as the tsunami, the tidal wave that begins as a disturbance in the sea because of an earthquake and ends as a dev-
5 astating wall of water inundating an unprotected shore. As the tsunami strikes the shore, it may exceed 100 feet in height. Its power and destructiveness are awesome. A tsunami arising from the explosion of the
10 volcano Krakatoa, west of Java, killed more than 36,000 people 100 years ago. In 1896, on the northeast coast of Honshu in Japan, a tsunami killed more than 27,000 people. Modern detection and warning systems have
15 greatly reduced the loss of life from these deadly waves, but as recently as 1983 a tsunami raised havoc on the northwest coast of Honshu. Human error delayed the warning and many children lost their lives.
20 Some readers picture tsunamis as towers of water, rushing across the surface of the ocean, causing ships to rise and fall a hundred feet in a few seconds. Nothing could be further from the truth. Storm waves may
25 indeed rise to mountainous heights at sea and toss ships about like corks. Not tsunamis. If a tsunami passes beneath a boat in the open ocean, the passengers may be unaware of the gentle rise and fall of water, so slight it
30 seems. These mild swells become deadly as the tsunami approaches land. The ocean becomes shallower. Friction builds up. The sea bottom near shore is exposed as the tsunami seems to draw in its breath before striking.
35 Fish and other sea creatures flop about on the hitherto unexposed sea bottom. Then the tsunami strikes with devastating effect, crushing buildings near shore, tossing about ships in the harbor, washing out to sea any
40 curious, unlucky bystanders.

The basic difference between a tsunami and other sea waves is in the length of the wave, between crest and crest. Tsunamis, generated by a displacement in the land be-
45 neath the sea, have extraordinarily long wavelengths. William Van Dorn of the Scripps Institution of Oceanography in La Jolla, California, says, "A big wave is gen-

erated when you move a big piece of real
50 estate perhaps the size of Indiana a couple
of meters.'' This tremendous displacement
causes a huge bulge on the water that races
out in all directions. These waves may move
out with jet-plane speeds—as high as 600
55 m.p.h. Since the Pacific area is marked by
geologic instability, most tsunamis occur in
that area, with Japan particularly vulnerable
to their deadly arrival.

These seismic sea waves appropriately
60 have the Japanese name, *tsunami*; Japan, located on the Ring of Fire, is particularly vulnerable. The Pacific is encircled by a zone
of earthquake and volcanic activity. Seismic
activities anywhere in the vast area may have
65 consequences thousands of miles away.

There have been destructive tsunamis in
other areas, however. About 1450 B.C. the
volcano on the island of Thera in the Aegean
Sea exploded. The resulting tsunami seri-
70 ously crippled the Minoan civilization. More
than 3000 years later, a catastrophic earthquake struck Lisbon, on November 1, 1755.
The resulting waves and earthquakes killed
60,000 people.
75 The Pacific Tsunami Warning Center in
Hawaii monitors potential tsunami activity
and sends out warnings of the impending arrival of a tsunami, along with its strength
and probable arrival time. These warnings
80 do not prevent destruction of property but
they do save lives.

1. With which of the following statements
would the author be LEAST likely to
agree?
(A) The tsunami can have severe
economic and social effects.
(B) A tsunami is immediately
recognizable at the point of origin
because of the great height of water
generated above it.
(C) The excitement of watching a tsunami
approach a shore outweighs any slight
danger attendant upon the
observation.
(D) Tsunamis are quite different from
storm waves, both in origin and in
appearances.
(E) An area with much volcanic activity
is more likely to generate a tsunami
than a more stable area.

1 ___

2. All of the following are characteristic of
the tsunami EXCEPT _____.
(A) tie-in with earthquakes
(B) great height at the shore
(C) slow speed of dispersal
(D) shallow height at sea
(E) prevalence in the Pacific area

2 ___

3. In the grip of a storm, ships are compared
with _____.
(A) walls   (D) crushed
(B) sea creatures   buildings
(C) corks   (E) mild swells

3 ___

4. The best example of figurative language is
the expression _____.
(A) earthquake   (D) warning
zone   systems
(B) deadly waves   (E) unprotected
(C) Ring of Fire   shore

4 ___

5. The author uses the phrase ''draw in its
breath'' to mean _____.
(A) pull water away from the shore
(B) send jets of water forward
(C) completely squander its strength
(D) generate a strong wind
(E) meet resistance on the beach

5 ___

6. The author uses the phrase ''seismic activ-
ities'' to indicate _____.
(A) waves   (D) detection
(B) wavelengths   (E) earthquakes
(C) friction   6 ___

7. Which of the following titles best summa-
rizes the content of this passage?
(A) Earthquakes: The Unexpected Enemy
(B) The Ring of Fire
(C) The Killer Waves
(D) Detecting Tsunamis
(E) Nature at Its Deadliest

7 ___

8. If faced by an approaching tsunami on the open sea, the best procedure for a ship's captain to protect his ship is to _____.
   (A) turn the prow of the ship into the wave
   (B) steam in the same direction as the tsunami
   (C) alert all passengers to stand by for lifeboat drill
   (D) radio for help as a precautionary measure
   (E) take no unusual steps

8 ____

SUMMARY PART 3

Understanding Language in Action: Evaluating Degree and Exclusion

Least and *except* questions are merely variations of questions already discussed and tested. A *least* question calls for the opposite of a main idea. An *except* question asks you to identify a missing item. The key to success with these questions is reading the directions carefully.

Summary
Section V: Understanding Language in Action

How the author uses language is a legitimate testing area for the SAT. When asked to supply a meaning for a word in a reading passage, examine the context carefully. The question will not ordinarily ask for a strict dictionary definition. It will ask you to consider how the word is being used in the text selection (Connotation and Denotation, page 43). It may also ask you to consider whether or not there are figurative meanings concealed in the text (pages 47–52). When reading LEAST and EXCEPT questions, be especially careful.

Review these strategies for understanding language in action as you prepare for the SAT.

PART 1   Evaluating the Author's Diction

A. Questions on diction ask about the meaning and usage of specific words in the context of a passage.
B. Deciding on a word's meaning is the same skill as using context clues.
C. Read at least the whole sentence to decide on a word meaning.
D. Use your "Clues from Context" (pages 6–40): the entire sentence, pairing, direct explanation, comparison, contrast, sequence, signal words.

PART 2   Understanding Figurative Language

A. Giving the meaning for a figurative expression is the same skill explained in "Figurative Language" (pages 47–52).
B. Most such questions ask for the meaning of a metaphor, such as *lumbering juggernaut* for a *heavy vehicle*.
C. Find the expression and read at least the whole sentence in which it occurs. Then decide on the meaning.
D. Use your knowledge of "Figurative Language": metaphor, simile, personification, metonymy, synecdoche, hyperbole, understatement, irony.

PART 3   Evaluating Degree and Exclusion

A. "Least" and "except" questions are the reverse of most SAT questions.
B. A "least" question asks for a statement with which the author would be *least* likely to agree.
C. An "except" question presents information or statements, all of which the author would agree with *except* one.
D. Read "least" or "except" questions *very* carefully. Remember, they are the reverse of most questions.
E. Check back through the passage for information as needed.

Section VI: Looking Beyond the Passage

PART 1

Predicting Outcomes

SAT questions occasionally ask you to take a step beyond the selection, to predict what will happen next. The required skill is an extension of drawing an inference—with one difference. Instead of inferring something about an idea or event in the selection, you must decide what the future consequences of an idea or event will be.

Questions of this type may be phrased as follows:

1. The final statement in the passage suggests which of the following outcomes?
2. Which of the following is likely to happen next?

Though the answer is not spelled out in the reading selection, there are clues to help you. If an anxious lawyer candidate receives notice he or she has passed the bar exam, his or her likely reaction is exuberance. Read between the lines and take one step further. Though other answers may be possible, the most probable answer is the one to choose.

Trial Test

Take the trial test to evaluate your skill.

Ted glanced across the net at his opponent, Frank Gilbert, number one seed in the tournament. Coolly waiting for Ted to serve, Frank danced lightly on his toes and smiled.
5 Through dogged determination, Ted had stayed close in this final match and had kept the score respectable. But having lost the first set, 6-3, and dropped behind, 5-1, in the second set, Ted knew that the match was
10 nearly over.
Frank was living up to his reputation as a hard hitter with control and finesse. With a backhand as good as his forehand, Frank moved to either side easily to return the balls
15 with grace and authority. In desperation Ted had tried lobbing over the head of his opponent, but Frank reached up and showed an overhead shot as strong as his forehand.

Ted searched his memory for advice from
20 friends and coaches. "When in trouble, change your game. Whatever you've been doing—drop it. Do something different. Instead of angling your shots, hit back toward your opponent's belt buckle. What have you
25 got to lose?"
Ted served. Frank returned the ball with apparent ease. The rally continued. Then Ted tried a drop shot from midcourt. It was a beauty, falling two feet from the net. Frank
30 rushed in, scooped it up and gently lobbed the ball over Ted's head. The first point went to Frank. Ted served to Frank's backhand. The ball came back to Ted's forehand. "I've got to change," thought Ted as he moved
35 toward the ball.

1. The final statement in the passage suggests which of the following outcomes?

(A) Ted hits a smashing drive to Frank's backhand.

(B) Ted tries a deep lob over Frank's head.

(C) Frank unexpectedly rushes the net.

(D) Ted hits the ball directly at Frank.

(E) Ted glances up into the stands and gets a secret signal from his coach.

1 ___

2. Which of the following suggests the most probable outcome of the tennis match?

(A) Ted turns the match around and wins in three sets.

(B) After Frank has won in two sets, the two boys shake hands.

(C) After losing in two sets, Ted refuses to shake hands with Frank.

(D) Ted wins the second set, but Frank comes back to win the third.

(E) In exasperation, Ted walks off the court and defaults.

2 ___

Answers to Trial Test

1. (D) The only advice that has not yet been tried is hitting the ball back to the opponent, at "the belt buckle." The backhand strategy has failed. (A) is incorrect. Frank has killed overheads. (B) is incorrect. There is no discernible reason for Frank to rush the net. (C) is incorrect. No mention has been made of the coach's presence, but more important: Ted is moving toward the ball. He has no time to look up into the stands. (E) is incorrect.

2. (B) There is no logical reason to suppose that Ted can turn the match around at this point. Though turnabouts sometimes occur, the law of averages (except in fiction) tends to suggest otherwise. Ted is in trouble, only one game away from defeat. The logical outcome is (B). Thus we may eliminate (A) and (D).

Look at a typical question and then analyze the possible answers.

Problem

On a quiet St. Valentine's Day in 1981, 12-year-old Todd Domboski ran across his grandmother's yard in Centralia, Pennsylvania. Suddenly a 100-foot pit opened beneath his feet and he tumbled in. Fortunately a tree root broke his fall, and his cousin was able to pull him safely to the surface. This frightening episode symbolizes the troubles of Centralia, a once-prosperous mining town in the heart of some of the richest anthracite regions in the world.

Centralia has a devastating problem. Beneath the streets and houses of this community, a coal-fire has been burning for decades. No one knows just how long. Each year increases the danger as the fire spreads through rich coal seams and old mine tunnels.

Many efforts have been made to drown, smother, or in some other way contain the blaze, but every effort has failed. There is just not enough water for drowning it. There are too many natural vents to smother it. The fire could take a hundred years to burn out—or a thousand. It could spread to an additional 3,500 acres with potential for even greater havoc.

What have been the results of the fire thus far? Carbon monoxide seeps into houses, posing serious threats to health and life. Basement walls crack. Lawns sink several feet into the ground. Steam vents make the area seem like the thermal display of Yellowstone National Park.

Some residents have already left. Many
25 are reluctant to leave their homesteads, hoping against hope that the fire will burn itself
out. Most, however, have reached the conclusion that the situation is hopeless and are
asking the federal government for financial
30 assistance in relocating. The financial burden would be enormous, and officials are
seeking solutions that would not harm the
residents.

In Calamity Hollow, Pennsylvania, a
35 smaller mine fire turned out to be a blessing.
A new technique called *controlled burning*
did not attack the fire, attempting fruitlessly
to put it out. Instead this innovation used the
underground fire to produce natural energy
40 in this huge natural furnace. Controlled
burning can actually produce heat and electricity at a profit.

There are two additional advantages to
controlled burning. First, it utilizes coal that
45 would otherwise be wasted. Even an abandoned mine retains at least half its coal. Secondly, by fanning the flames this method
could end mine fires much sooner than they
would die out on their own.

50 The history of humankind is filled with
disasters that turned out to have many beneficial results. War, the ultimate horror, has
accelerated medical and surgical improvements. Citywide fires have encouraged in-
55 habitants to rebuild—and improve. To be
sure, no one recommends encouraging disasters so that we might be tested and thus
make far-reaching discoveries. But sometimes misfortunes may open doors to new
60 achievements.

1. Which of the following suggests the most
   probable outcome of the Centralia problem?
   (A) Most former inhabitants will be
       encouraged to return.
   (B) Profit from controlled burning will
       finance the relocation of Centralians.
   (C) Controlled burning will be found to
       be impractical for Centralia.
   (D) The government will make one last
       concerted attempt to put the
       underground fire out.
   (E) The Centralia fire will influence the
       price of coal on the open market.

   1 ___

2. The future of controlled burning as a solu-
   tion to underground fires can best be de-
   scribed as _____.
   (A) dubious   (D) uneconomical
   (B) hopeless   (E) unpopular
   (C) encouraging   2 ___

Strategy

1. Since all efforts at putting out the fire have failed miserably, it is unlikely
   the government will try again. (*D*) is incorrect. For the same reasons, it is
   unlikely that most inhabitants will return. (*A*) is incorrect. There is no
   indication that this fire in a small area of the United States could influence
   the price of coal. (*E*) is incorrect. There is no suggestion that the controlled
   burnout technique would not be successful in Centralia. Its inclusion in this
   excerpt clearly suggests it is a likely solution for the Centralia problem.
   (*C*) is incorrect. Since the selection mentions the profit from controlled
   burning, (*B*) is the most likely answer.
2. The excerpt is clearly enthusiastic about the future of controlled burning.
   The two advantages listed are specific clues. (*C*) is the most likely answer.

Time Out for Review

Try your skill. The passage below is followed by questions based on its content. Use the preceding example to help you find the right answer.

Half a billion books have been published since Gutenberg printed his first Bible. Each year about 30,000 books are published in America alone. Each year about the same
5 number go out of print. Thousands and thousands and thousands of books! What happens to them?

Most books disappear from public notice within a few years. They are stored in dusty
10 attics, damp basements, and back rooms. They are discarded in paper drives. They find their way to church fairs, old bookstores, and library book sales. The bright promise of their publication fades, and they land in
15 ignominious heaps on the tables of discount dealers, sold at a fraction of their publication price.

Many are physically destroyed. Fire and flood take a heavy toll. The deterioration of
20 cheap paper consigns many to the dustheap prematurely. A great many titles disappear utterly.

Despite the hazards of existence, many titles do survive in odd and unusual places.
25 There are some clever book detectives who make their living hunting up wanted out-of-print books and selling them at a high enough markup to provide a living. These bookfinders are ingenious, resourceful, persistent, and
30 often lucky!

Donald Dryfoos is a successful book detective. As he describes his business, "One, you find the people who want to find books; two, you find the books." Both steps require
35 time and effort.

Dryfoos has built up a list of regular customers. Some are individuals. Some are publishers. Some are other booksellers. When he is given a title to find, he checks his own
40 stock and then goes hunting elsewhere. He makes no charge for the search, but the price he gets for the book must cover his expenses. Profits from individual sale are not tremendous, but the thrill of the search keeps Dry-
45 foos ever on the trail.

What kind of people send out lists of books they want to find? Dryfoos calls them *uncategorizable*. They're all different. They all want different books. A bookstore spe-
50 cializing in bestsellers sells hundreds of copies of the same book. "To me that would be boring," insists Dryfoos.

Although customers vary, there are a few discernible trends. One group seeks books
55 with happy childhood associations. These people want their children or grandchildren to share their remembered joys. Another group specializes in medicine, science, music, or another field. These people want to
60 build up a specialized library, sometimes to provide a bibliography for a doctoral degree. Still another group has discovered an author, like Dorothy Miles Disney, whose works strike a responsive chord. These people will
65 buy anything by the favorite author.

Dryfoos has extensive sources beyond his own stock. Like all bookfinders, he frequents book fairs, hastily checking the books donated by retirees, house redesigners, peo-
70 ple moving out of state, legatees who don't want to be bothered with the impedimenta of an uncle's life. The competition between bookfinders is keen, and the pace is swift.

He has frequented the stores of all his
75 competitors and knows where many titles can be found. He confesses, "I can't remember what I had for breakfast, but I remember the location of those books." As he says, it's a lot of fun just to meander through book-
80 stores, even though it cannot provide a reasonable financial result for time spent.

Dryfoos has also built up contacts with many book suppliers throughout the country—bookstores and private libraries. Deal-
85 ers who specialize in a particular field send him their catalogs. The magazine *AB Bookman's Weekly* provides advertising space for dealers on the prowl for certain titles.

How successful is the search? "We find
90 very close to exactly 50 percent of the books we look for," says Dryfoos. If the book is to be found, it will probably be located within six weeks. As time goes on, hope dims, though occasionally a book will un-
95 expectedly turn up late in the search.

A true book detective is a lover of books. The same amount of skill, intelligence, and persistence when applied in another field might bring more lucrative results. But a true book lover picks up a book with affection, understanding, and anticipation. Every book is a key to a world beyond its pages.

1. If Donald Dryfoos found a book requested by one of his clients, he would probably _____.

   (A) send it out immediately to the customer
   (B) send the customer a description of the book's condition, together with its price
   (C) arrange to have the book cleaned up and rebound if it were discovered in imperfect condition
   (D) keep it temporarily for himself and the next customer, while looking for another copy of the book
   (E) contact another customer to set up a competitive bidding situation

   1 ___

2. All the following are mentioned as book-finding methods EXCEPT _____.

   (A) attending book fairs
   (B) tapping competitors' stocks
   (C) advertising in a magazine
   (D) getting in touch with private libraries
   (E) dealing directly with the original publishers

   2 ___

3. The word *ignominious* in the second paragraph is meant to suggest the _____.

   (A) author's crushed hope
   (B) publisher's anger
   (C) bookfinder's irritation
   (D) editor's embarrassment
   (E) advertiser's loss of revenue

   3 ___

4. The primary purpose of the passage appears to be to _____.

   (A) explain
   (B) amuse
   (C) persuade
   (D) irritate
   (E) challenge

   4 ___

5. The word *uncategorizable* (seventh paragraph) is applied to _____.

   (A) remaindered books
   (B) professional magazines
   (C) buyers of used books
   (D) bookfinders
   (E) book fair sponsors

   5 ___

6. Dorothy Miles Disney is mentioned as an author _____.

   (A) of children's books
   (B) of professional books
   (C) in demand
   (D) for candidates of doctoral degrees
   (E) who is never remaindered

   6 ___

7. From this selection we may infer that _____.

   (A) more books are published in science than in literature
   (B) book dealers never cooperate with each other
   (C) Dryfoos stays in his business primarily for monetary reasons
   (D) many books in recent years have been printed on rapidly deteriorating paper
   (E) there are no original Gutenberg Bibles in existence

   7 ___

8. The legatees in the ninth paragraph may best be characterized as _____.

   (A) prudent
   (B) cruel
   (C) antagonistic
   (D) disloyal
   (E) impatient

   8 ___

9. Which of the following best expresses the main idea of the passage?

   (A) Publishers are missing out on a profitable sideline.
   (B) Finding specific old books is an almost hopeless task.
   (C) Book detectives, on average, are wealthy individuals.
   (D) Looking for out-of-print books can be an exciting search.
   (E) Library book fairs are excellent sources for wanted books.

   9 ___

SUMMARY PART 1

Looking Beyond the Passage: Predicting Outcomes

When asked to predict outcomes, read the passage carefully for clues that point the way to future activity. Your answer should be consistent with the elements in the passage. It should reasonably be inferred from the salient points in the selection itself. Keep in mind that though all suggested answers may be possible, you will be asked to choose the most probable.

PART 2

Providing an Application

Another skill that takes you beyond the passage itself is providing applications of ideas in the reading passage. Like predicting outcomes, this skill requires that you carefully analyze the content of the passage and then take a step beyond. From a general principle in the passage, you might be asked to make a specific application. If, for example, the selection discussed the advantages of speed reading as a general skill, you might be asked to decide whether a light novel, an editorial, a math textbook, an article on quantum physics, or a legal contract should be read rapidly.

Here, for example, are two application questions taken directly from the SAT.

1. According to the information in the passage, an artist inspired by the basic principles of African art would most likely have produced which of the following?
2. The author believes that an ''ordinary'' person (lines 10 and 29) would be most likely to agree with which of the following statements about art?

Trial Test

Take the trial test to evaluate your skill.

Logical reasoning is usually classified as one of two kinds: inductive and deductive. People use both types often without knowing their names. Inductive reasoning proceeds
5 from the particular to the general. Deductive reasoning proceeds from the general to the particular.

Children begin using a kind of inductive reasoning at an early age. A child may touch
10 a hot radiator on a number of occasions and conclude that all radiators are hot. He has reasoned from the particular experiences— touching radiators—to the generalization—all radiators are hot. Though the conclusion may
15 be faulty because of insufficient and uncharacteristic examples, the process is still inductive.

Deductive reasoning proceeds in reverse. A child may be told by a parent not to touch
20 radiators because radiators are hot. Then he may test the generalization by touching a radiator. If the generalization is sound, the specific examples should follow. In this example, the generalization is unsound because
25 it is incomplete. Radiators are hot only at certain times. The example demonstrates the method, however.

Inductive reasoning is commonly used in science. On the basis of observation and ex-
30 periment, general principles or laws may be derived. These conclusions are subject to review as additional information becomes available, but they serve as useful guides in the meantime.

35 Deductive reasoning is commonly used in argumentation and persuasion. From a presumably accepted generalization, debaters derive arguments in favor of their positions. If the statement that smoking is harm-
40 ful to health is accepted, an editorial writer can plead for more restrictions on smoking in public places. Deductive arguments can often be put in the form of syllogisms, with major and minor premises and conclusions.

45 Both forms of reasoning are useful. Once their limitations are understood, they provide useful tools for handling the problems of everyday living.

According to the information in the passage, which of the following would be an example of deductive reasoning?

(A) A visitor to Mexico tastes several dishes with jalapeño peppers and decides that such dishes are too hot for his taste.

(B) On Saturday afternoon in a small city on his route, a traveler looks in vain for an open hardware store. He concludes stores in this city close Saturday afternoons.

(C) A chocolate enthusiast finds that he gets a headache after every bout of chocolate indulgence. He decides to give up chocolate because he may be allergic to it.

(D) Because Labrador retrievers have the reputation of being good with children, a father buys one for his young family.

(E) After finding a dozen strawberries in the basket utterly tasteless despite their luscious appearance, a cook throws away the rest of the box.

Answer to Trial Test

(*D*) The father starts with a generalization—that Labrador retrievers are good with children—and then concludes that a certain Labrador will be good for his children. If put in the form of a syllogism, the argument would look like this:

Major premise — Labrador retrievers are good for children.
Minor premise — This dog is a Labrador.
Conclusion   — This Labrador will be good with my children.

The other arguments are all inductive, drawing conclusions from a series of incidents.

Look at a typical question and then analyze the possible answers.

Problem

If wheels are the most efficient form of land transport ever invented by human beings, why did nature not develop creatures with some kind of wheels instead of feet,
5 paddles, or flippers? The question is not so frivolous as it sounds. Nature anticipated the invention of the submarine, glider, airplane, and jet-propelled vehicles. Why not wheels?

Some animals use their whole bodies as
10 wheels. The pangolin of Southeast Asia curls into a ball and rolls down steep hills to avoid predators. Rolling spiders and somersaulting shrimps use the principle of the wheel. Even rolling plants, like the western tumbleweed,
15 demonstrate the wheel in action. But none of these has wheels in place of appendages.

Some writers conjecture that the joint problem proved an insuperable obstacle for the development of a living wheel. A rotat-
20 ing joint of living tissue might be a biological impossibility. Other writers dispute this explanation, pointing out that nature has devised unbelievably sophisticated solutions to all kinds of problems. These scientists be-
25 lieve nature did not provide wheeled animals for sound reasons of survival.

Michael LaBarbera of the University of Chicago has suggested three reasons why animals are better off without wheels. As a pre-
30 face, he pointed out that human beings use wheels only under special conditions, for longer rather than shorter trips.

First, wheels are efficient only on hard surfaces. The heavier the wheeled vehicle,
35 the more difficult it is to move on a soft surface. The use of oversized tires reduces the problem but does not eliminate it.

Secondly, wheels are not too useful when confronted with vertical obstructions. A
40 wheeled vehicle with a rigid chassis cannot climb a curb higher than half the wheel radius.

Finally, wheels do not permit quick turning in a space cluttered with obstacles. Nor
45 can wheeled vehicles turn efficiently in a small space. The switchbacks on mountain roads, for example, test the limits of the maneuverability of wheeled vehicles.

The efficiency of the wheel under certain
50 conditions is more than offset by its inefficiency under other conditions. Certainly, under suitable conditions the wheel is incredibly more efficient than walking or running. In the Boston Marathon a wheelchair athlete
55 finished the course 22 minutes faster than the best runner. The bicycle, a common example of a wheeled vehicle, is 15 times as efficient as a running dog.

When conditions are right, the wheel is
60 indeed unexcelled for quick, clean, efficient locomotion. But since conditions are rarely "right" in the animal's natural domain, "wheeled animals" are an unlikely development in the scheme of things.

1. According to the point of view of the passage, which of the following statements is most likely true?
   (A) If the earth's surface were relatively flat and hard, creatures with wheels might have evolved.
   (B) The form of the wheel does not appear anywhere in natural design.
   (C) The adaptability of living tissue is severely limited.
   (D) Wheels would be particularly useful in woodlands.
   (E) The principle of jet propulsion in animals is quite different from the principle of jet propulsion in aviation.

   1 ___

2. With which of the following statements would the writer of this passage agree?
   (A) Wheeled prey animals would more easily escape their predators than four-footed ones.
   (B) Camels are more efficient in deserts than bicycles.
   (C) Any speculation about wheeled animals is a ridiculous waste of time.
   (D) Roller skates will eventually be used almost universally to save time and energy during shopping.
   (E) It is difficult to understand why animals have not developed wheels for locomotion.

   2 ___

Strategy

1. Since the passage emphasizes the adaptability of animals, it suggests three reasons why wheels were not developed. A surface relatively flat and hard would have removed the three obstacles. Theoretically, then, wheeled animals might have developed. (A) is correct. The passage says the form of the wheel appears in ways other than as appendages. Therefore, (B) is incorrect. The passage emphasizes the adaptability of living tissue. (C) is incorrect. Since woodland surfaces are not flat and hard, (D) is incorrect. Though the fuels are different, animals and man both use the same principle of jet propulsion. (E) is incorrect.

2. Since soft surfaces are difficult for wheeled vehicles, (B) is correct. Since prey animals do not live in conditions suitable for wheels, (A) is incorrect. The entire passage is devoted to speculation about wheeled animals. (C) is incorrect. There is no indication that roller skates will take over for legs

during short walking trips. The passage emphasizes the value of wheels for longer trips, not shorter ones. (*D*) is incorrect. Since the passage gives three reasons why animals have not developed wheels, (*E*) is incorrect.

Time Out for Review

Try your skill. The passage below is followed by questions based on its content.

Jules Verne is credited with anticipating many technological and scientific achievements of the 20th century, but 400 years earlier another prophet foresaw the world of the future with even more uncanny accuracy.
5 Verne embodied his prophecies in a series of enchanting science-fiction novels. Leonardo da Vinci sketched his prophetic visions in great detail. His sketches are so clear and informative that working models have been
10 constructed. A traveling IBM exhibit encourages young people to turn cranks, pull levers, and push buttons to demonstrate mechanically how brilliant were the conceptions of this artist-scientist-inventor.
15 Leonardo's notebooks contain the fruits of his fertile imagination. Written in tiny but accurate lefthanded mirror writing, the notebooks are filled with sketches of innovations,
20 creative ideas, inventions, and improvements of already existing devices. Designs for air conditioners, two-level highways for pedestrians and vehicles, parachutes, and rotating hoists poured from his inventive brain.
25 Leonardo devised an airplane that modern engineers say is technically sound. He defined a key aerodynamic principle 200 years before Newton. He foresaw the helicopter and devised an aerial screw to lift it.
30 His analysis of gears anticipated their use in modern-day machines. He even designed the first mechanical car.
He was a truly scientific mapmaker, devising an instrument for measuring the radius
35 of the earth accurately to within a few miles—all of this while Columbus was making his voyage of discovery to the New World. He invented a printing press that could be run by one man, a vast improve-
40 ment over the more cumbersome Gutenberg press. He devised a tank for warfare centuries before the British unveiled the first tank on the Western Front in World War I.
What kept all his inventions from revolutionizing world technology? He was too soon. His genius outstripped the facilities of

his time. He needed a compact power unit
5 and a metal hard enough for his needs. Though these were far in the future, his free-ranging mind had an impact on progress to come.
His studies in other branches of science
10 were far-ranging and perceptive. He described ring patterns of trees as a key to their growth. He systematically and individually pursued scientific studies of anatomy—of plants and the human body. He became in-
15 terested in the laws of optics. He studied meteorology and geology.
The breadth and the depth of Leonardo's genius are emphasized by his success in non-scientific areas. He was an artist of renown,
20 painter of the "Mona Lisa," "The Last Supper," "Virgin and Child with St. Anne," and other masterpieces. He had a powerful impact on the young Raphael and Michelangelo. Sometimes his paintings suggest the
25 fusion of his scientific and artistic interests.
This restless genius, turning from one field to another and interpreting the world with unimpaired vision, is the prototype of that many-faceted personality sometimes
30 called "Renaissance Man."

1. Which of the following persons most closely approaches the "Renaissance Man" qualities of Leonardo as outlined in the passage?
   (A) H. G. Wells, who wrote science fiction dealing with time machines and interplanetary travel
   (B) Emily Dickinson, who wrote poems of outstanding sensitivity from her self-imposed isolation
   (C) Samuel F. B. Morse, who was a painter of great renown before pioneering work in electric telegraphy
   (D) Ludwig van Beethoven, whose musical achievements were a triumph over deafness
   (E) Claude Monet, whose paintings helped to launch the Impressionist movement in art

1 ___

2. All the following inventions of Leonardo were mentioned in the selection EXCEPT _____.

   (A) parachute
   (B) two-level highway
   (C) mechanical car
   (D) machine gun
   (E) printing press

   2 ____

3. The word *cumbersome* (fourth paragraph) suggests _____ .

   (A) inefficiency
   (B) speed
   (C) plodding effectiveness
   (D) compactness
   (E) streamlining

   3 ____

4. The author's attitude toward Leonardo is one of _____ .

   (A) skepticism
   (B) envy
   (C) disbelief
   (D) awe
   (E) acceptance

   4 ____

5. For which of the following reasons did the writer mention Jules Verne?

   (A) Jules Verne is the best prophet of the future in all of history.
   (B) The popular mind associates Jules Verne with prophecy, but Leonardo is more deserving of the reputation.
   (C) Jules Verne and Leonardo were essentially alike as personalities.
   (D) Both Jules Verne and Leonardo were painters as well as prophets.
   (E) Leonardo's time machine anticipated Jules Verne's by four centuries.

   5 ____

6. From this passage we may infer that _____.

   (A) Leonardo at first accepted the idea of a flat earth but later rejected it.
   (B) Leonardo provided Columbus with a map for his first voyage to the New World.
   (C) Working models can teach mechanical principles more effectively than can mere sketches.

   (D) Jules Verne consulted the notebooks of Leonardo before beginning a novel.
   (E) Leonardo's airplane could not have flown, even with modern energy sources and materials.

   6 ____

7. Which of the following titles best summarizes the content of the passage?

   (A) Science in the 15th Century
   (B) Jules Verne and Leonardo da Vinci: A Study in Contrasts
   (C) Leonardo as a Key Renaissance Painter
   (D) Leonardo da Vinci: Renaissance Man
   (E) Unrecognized Genius: A Study in Failure

   7 ____

8. In the fourth paragraph Columbus is mentioned for which of the following reasons?

   (A) Leonardo measured the size of the earth while some people (though not Columbus) still believed in the flat-earth theory.
   (B) Columbus as an active adventurer, physically exploring, is contrasted favorably with Leonardo as an armchair scientist.
   (C) Columbus probably had worked closely with Leonardo in determining his strategy for exploring the New World.
   (D) Neither Columbus nor Leonardo could possibly anticipate the profound results of the opening up of the New World.
   (E) Columbus and Leonardo were both Italians, citizens of regions in social and political ferment.

   8 ____

SUMMARY PART 2

Looking Beyond the Passage: Providing an Application

Though providing applications requires you to go beyond the facts and statements in the passage, you will find in the passage sufficient hints and clues to guide you in your selection. The extraordinary virtuosity of Leonardo in the preceding passage provides clues for the application question, as well as for other questions.

Summary
Section VI: Looking Beyond the Passage

Predicting outcomes and providing applications are further extensions of one major skill: *drawing inferences*.

The inferences analyzed in this section are more specialized and often more challenging because they ask you to bring experience to bear on the answers. In one form or another, you have been predicting outcomes and providing applications all your life. In this section you will put those experiences and skills to work.

Review these strategies for looking beyond the passage when you are preparing for the SAT.

PART 1 Predicting Outcomes

A. Predicting an outcome is drawing an inference about a *probable* event based on information in the selection.
B. Look for clues that suggest what may happen in the future. (Sometimes you must "read between the lines.")
C. Many answers may be *possible*. Choose the most *probable* one.
D. Remember, information *in the passage* (not information you already know) should lead you to your answer.

PART 2 Providing an Application

A. Providing an application is predicting a specific outcome. It is another special kind of inference.
B. Look for clues in the passage that can suggest the application.
C. Choose the most probable (not just possible) application.
D. Although you must move beyond the passage for the application, the reasons for it are in the passage itself.

PRACTICE TESTS

How well have you developed skill in extracting the meaning from reading passages? Take the following practice tests for additional drill.

A.

Geometry is taught in the later grades. It is concerned in part with questions of spatial measurements. If I draw such a line and another such line, how far apart will their end
5 points be? How many square inches are there in a rectangle 4 inches long and 8 inches wide? Geometry is also concerned with aspects of space that have a strong aesthetic appeal or a surprise element. For example,
10 it tells us that in any parallelogram whatsoever, the diagonals bisect one another; in any triangle whatsoever, the three medians intersect in a common point. It teaches us that a floor can be tiled with equilateral triangles
15 or hexagons, but not with regular pentagons.

But geometry, if taught according to the arrangement laid out by Euclid in 300 B.C., has another vitally significant aspect. This is its presentation as a deductive science. Be-
20 ginning with a number of elementary ideas which are assumed to be self-evident, and on the basis of a few definite rules of mathematical and logical manipulation, Euclidean geometry builds up a fabric of deduc-
25 tions of increasing complexity.

What is stressed in the teaching of elementary geometry is not only the spatial or visual aspect of the subject but the methodology wherein hypothesis leads to conclu-
30 sion. This deductive process is known as *proof*. Euclidean geometry is the first example of a formalized deductive system and has become the model for all such systems. Geometry has been the great practice field
35 for logical thinking, and the study of geometry has been held (rightly or wrongly) to provide the student with a basic training in such thinking.

1. Which of the following titles best summarizes the content of the passage?
   (A) Geometry, the Queen of Sciences
   (B) The Two Major Aspects of Geometry
   (C) Deduction, the Heart of Euclidean Geometry
   (D) The Methodology of Geometric Triangulation
   (E) Geometry and the Reasoning Process

1 ___

2. The article suggests that real-life applications of geometry _____.
   (A) are misleading to amateur scholars
   (B) were surprisingly overlooked by Euclid in 300 B.C.
   (C) have nothing to do with the deductive process
   (D) are startling in their appropriateness
   (E) work for hexagons but not triangles

2 ___

3. Which of the following inferences may reasonably be drawn from the selection?
   (A) Arithmetic and geometry are two sides of the same process.
   (B) The author believes that geometry provides students excellent training in thinking.
   (C) A floor may be tiled with regular pentagons.
   (D) Euclid was an innovative giant but a flawed philosopher.
   (E) The diagonals of any four-sided figure bisect each other.

3 ___

4. Proof requires that _____.
   (A) a hypothesis lead to a conclusion
   (B) spatial aspects of a subject be submitted to scrutiny
   (C) random sampling truly represent the whole
   (D) the process have a strong aesthetic element
   (E) logical manipulation lead to increasing complexity

4 ___

5. The tone of the selection as a whole can best be described as _____.
   (A) skeptical   (D) explanatory
   (B) aggressive   (E) inspirational
   (C) ironic

5 ___

B.

Eta Carinae is an unusual star embedded in a cloud of luminous gas (the Keyhole Nebula), and astronomers have had difficulty classifying it. Is it a slow nova or a super-
5 nova? Explosive stars usually show a sharp rise in brilliance and then fade slowly over time, but Eta Carinae was bright for over 100 years before it flashed its record brilliance in 1843. During this peak, Eta Cari-
10 nae was the second brightest star in the sky— Sirius held on to its title even then. But while Sirius was a mere 9 light-years away, Eta Carinae was over 6,000 light-years away from our solar system. The 1843 star flash
15 has been estimated at several million times more luminous than the sun—perhaps as much as 4 million times—making Eta Carinae the most brilliant and luminous star ever recorded. If it did at any point equal 4 mil-
20 lion suns, it could have been observed through a powerful telescope (such as the 200-inch Mount Palomar reflector) from over 450 million light-years away, almost twice the distance to the Andromeda Galaxy.

25 What price glory? Just 25 years later, in 1868, this tremendous star was no longer visible to the human eye. Some astronomers believe the Eta Carinae exploded, leaving only its remnants expanding throughout the
30 thick gas and dust of the Keyhole Nebula. It would seem that the brighter they are, the sooner they fizzle.

1. The author apparently feels that _____.
   (A) Eta Carinae is the brightest star in the Andromeda Galaxy
   (B) for watchers from earth, Sirius has long been the brightest star
   (C) Eta Carinae is a slow nova rather than a supernova
   (D) a thousand years ago Eta Carinae was the second brightest star
   (E) sharp-eyed observers can today see the remains of Eta Carinae

1 ___

2. The Keyhole Nebula is actually _____.
   (A) an explosive star in rapid expansion
   (B) another name for the Andromeda Galaxy
   (C) a brilliant, luminous star
   (D) a cloud of luminous gas
   (E) a constellation

2 ___

3. At its brightest point Eta Carinae _____.
   (A) was observed by the Mount Palomar reflector
   (B) was millions of times brighter than the sun
   (C) retained that record brightness for over 100 years
   (D) was often confused with Sirius
   (E) was overlooked by most serious astronomers

3 ___

4. The distance to the Andromeda Galaxy is probably about _____.
   (A) 9 light-years
   (B) 6,000 light-years
   (C) 250 million light-years
   (D) 450 million light-years
   (E) the same as the distance to the Keyhole Nebula

4 ___

5. The last sentence in the passage is a paraphrase of what familiar expression?
   (A) The bigger they come, the harder they fall.
   (B) Pride goeth before a fall.
   (C) We have loved the stars too fondly to be fearful of the night.
   (D) Even a small star shines in the darkness.
   (E) Empty barrels make the most noise.

5 ___

C.

The planet itself is a sojourner in airless space, a wet ball flung across nowhere. The few objects in the universe scatter. The coherence of matter dwindles and crumbles to-
5　ward stillness. I have read, and repeated, that our solar system as a whole is careering through space toward a point east of Hercules. Now I wonder: what could that possibly mean, east of Hercules? Isn't space
10　curved? When we get "there," how will our course change, and why? Will we slide down the universe's inside arc like mud slung at a wall? Or what sort of welcoming shore is this east of Hercules? Surely we don't anchor
15　there, and disembark, and sweep into dinner with our host. Does someone cry, "Last stop, last stop"? At any rate, east of Hercules, like east of Eden, isn't a place to call home. It is a course without direction; it is
20　"out." And we are cast.

1. According to the writer of this passage the earth _____ .

    (A) has destination and a mission in space
    (B) is inextricably linked with every object in the universe
    (C) will slide down the universe's inside arc
    (D) is a homeless wanderer in space
    (E) will come to rest east of Hercules

    1 ___

2. As used in the selection, *careering* means _____ .

    (A) vibrating　　(D) sliding
    (B) speeding　　(E) anticipating
    (C) pulsating　　　　　　　2 ___

3. The tone of the passage can best be described as _____ .

    (A) perky and optimistic
    (B) coldly logical
    (C) assured and happy
    (D) vigorously antiscientific
    (E) wryly humorous

    3 ___

4. The author's appraisal of the future of earth is _____ .

    (A) confident　　(D) angry
    (B) sad　　　　(E) imitative
    (C) hopeful　　　　　　　4 ___

5. The expression "a wet ball flung across nowhere" is meant to suggest _____ .

    (A) hilarity　　　(D) purpose
    (B) condescension　(E) courage
    (C) insignificance

    5 ___

D.

The recovery of copper from the drainage water of mines was probably a widespread practice in the Mediterranean basin as early as 1000 B.C. Although such mining
5　operations are difficult to document, it is known that the leaching of copper on a large scale was well established at the Río Tinto mines in Spain by the 18th century. What none of the miners engaged in this traditional
10　method of mineral extraction realized until about 25 years ago is that bacteria take an active part in the leaching process. They help to convert the copper into a water-soluble form that can be carried off by the leach
15　water. Today bacteria are being deliberately exploited to recover millions of pounds of copper from billions of tons of low-grade ore. Copper obtained in this way accounts for more than 10 percent of the total U.S.
20　production. In recent years bacterial leaching has also been applied to the recovery of another nonferrous metal: uranium.

Recent progress in the genetic manipulation of microorganisms for industrial pur-
25　poses promises to revitalize not only the bacterial leaching of metal-bearing ores but also the microbiological treatment of metal-contaminated waste water. The enthusiasm of the microbiologists working on the devel-
30　opment of the new "biomining" techniques is matched by a need in the minerals industry to find alternatives to conventional methods of mining, ore processing and waste-water treatment. The need arises from recent trends
35　in the industry: the continued depletion of high-grade mineral resources, the resulting tendency for mining to be extended deeper underground, the growing awareness of environmental problems associated with the
40　smelting of sulfide minerals and the burning of sulfur-rich fossil fuels and the rising cost of the prodigious amounts of energy required in the conventional recovery methods. The current methods will surely prevail for many
45　years to come, but biological processes are generally less energy-intensive and less polluting than most nonbiological technology in mining ore processing, and waste-water treatment is likely to become increasingly
50　important.

1. Which of the following best describes the main idea of the passage?
    (A) Copper obtained from drainage water is superior to that directly mined.
    (B) Microbiologists decry the exploitation of genetics for industrial purposes.
    (C) The role of biological technology in mining and related areas is growing.
    (D) Waste-water treatment is undergoing major changes in technology.
    (E) Biological processes tend to be more polluting than nonbiological ones.

    1 ___

2. *Biomining* is put in quotation marks because _____ .
    (A) biomining is an unnatural procedure
    (B) it should really be *bioleaching*
    (C) it is a newly coined word
    (D) no scientist believes in its efficacy
    (E) the word was first used in the 18th century and revived

    2 ___

3. The recovery of copper from the waste water of mines _____ .
    (A) began in the Río Tinto mines of Spain
    (B) is an attractive plan but a will-o'-the-wisp in practice
    (C) relies basically on sulfur-rich fossil fuels during the processing
    (D) probably goes back 3,000 years
    (E) accounts for most copper produced in the United States

    3 ___

4. The passage admits which of the following are being exploited in the copper-recovery process?
    (A) miners
    (B) waste-water processors
    (C) microbiologists
    (D) bacteria
    (E) biochemical engineers

    4 ___

5. The leaching process is apparently most economically feasible with _____ .
    (A) low-grade ore
    (B) sulfide minerals
    (C) burning of fossil fuels
    (D) rich veins of ore
    (E) agriculture

    5 ___

6. All the following are mentioned as stimulating the need for biomining EXCEPT _____ .
    (A) depletion of high-grade mineral resources
    (B) environmental problems
    (C) intensive foreign competition
    (D) need for ever deeper mining
    (E) energy considerations

    6 ___

7. Microorganisms are playing a greater role in industrial technology as a result of _____ .
    (A) presidential decree
    (B) historical study
    (C) genetic manipulation
    (D) innovation by Spanish miners
    (E) underground exploration

    7 ___

8. As used in the passage, *leaching* refers to _____ .
    (A) bleaching discolored elements
    (B) chemically destroying pollutants
    (C) smelting sulfide minerals
    (D) separating components
    (E) depleting high-grade mineral resources

    8 ___

READING DIAGNOSTIC TESTS

Now you have an opportunity to practice the reading skills and strategies you have been using. First take Part A of the test. Allow yourself 20 minutes. Check your answers and go over the analysis for each of the 15 items. Note your incorrect answers. The page numbers in the Answer and Analysis section will tell you where to turn in this book for additional help and strategy review.

Next take Part B of the test. See how your score compares with Part A. Study the reference pages for those items that you did not answer correctly or were not sure of the answer.

Find your weaknesses well in advance of the SAT testing date so that you will have ample time to work on the types of test items that you find most difficult. Remember you are building your personal power to take the SAT with confidence.

Reading Diagnostic Test — A

PART 1   Reading Comprehension (1–10)

Each passage below is followed by questions based on its content. Answer all questions following a passage on the basis of what is *stated* or *implied* in that passage.

The traditional Arab proposed, in the traditional way, to run down Cheops, cross the eighth of a mile of sand intervening between it and the tall pyramid of Cephren, ascend
5 to Cephren's summit and return to us on the top of Cheops—all in nine minutes by the watch, and the whole service to be rendered for a single dollar. In the first flush of irritation, I said let the Arab and his exploits go
10 to the mischief. But stay. The upper third of Cephren was coated with dress marble, smooth as glass. A blessed thought entered my brain. He must infallibly break his neck. Close the contract with dispatch, I said, and
15 let him go. He started. We watched. He went bounding down the vast broadside, spring after spring, like an ibex. He grew smaller and smaller till he became a bobbing pygmy, away down toward the bottom—then dis-
20 appeared. We turned and peered over the other side—forty seconds—eighty seconds— a hundred—happiness, he is dead already?— two minutes—and a quarter—"There he goes!" Too true—it was too true. He was
25 very small, now. Gradually, but surely, he overcame the level ground. He began to spring and climb again. Up, up, up—at last he reached the smooth coating—now for it.

But he clung to it with toes and fingers, like
30 a fly. He crawled this way and that—away to the right, slanting upward—away to the left, still slanting upward—and stood at last, a black peg on the summit, and waved his pygmy scarf! Then he crept downward to the
35 raw steps again, then picked up his agile heels and flew. We lost him presently. But presently again we saw him under us, mounting with undiminished energy. Shortly he bounded into our midst with a gallant war-
40 whoop. Time, eight minutes, forty-one seconds. He had won. His bones were intact. It was a failure. I reflected. I said to myself, he is tired, and must grow dizzy. I will risk another dollar on him.

45 He started again. Made the trip again. Slipped on the smooth coating—I almost had him. But an infamous crevice saved him. He was with us once more—perfectly sound. Time, eight minutes, forty-six seconds.

50 I said to Dan, "Lend me a dollar—I can beat this game, yet."

Worse and worse. He won again. Time, eight minutes, forty-eight seconds. I was out of all patience now. I was desperate. Money
55 was no longer of any consequence. I said,

"Sirrah, I will give you a hundred dollars to jump off this pyramid head first. If you do not like the terms, name your bet. I scorn to stand on expenses now. I will stay right here
60 and risk money on you as long as Dan has got a cent."

1. The purpose of the author is to _____.
   (A) horrify   (D) persuade
   (B) enlighten   (E) preach
   (C) entertain
                                    1 ___

2. Dan is probably playing the role of _____.
   (A) knowledgeable go-between
   (B) skilled interpreter
   (C) angry friend
   (D) weary athlete
   (E) unwilling banker
                                    2 ___

3. What is likely to happen next?
   (A) The climber agrees to jump off the pyramid.
   (B) The author grumpily gives up his plan to win the bet.
   (C) Dan says he hasn't enjoyed himself so much in years.
   (D) The author is arrested by police for encouraging a criminal act.
   (E) The author determines to outdo the climber by performing the feat himself.
                                    3 ___

4. The *black peg* on the summit is actually _____.
   (A) the apex of the pyramid
   (B) a pygmy scarf
   (C) an ibex
   (D) the climber
   (E) the author
                                    4 ___

5. The author of the selection can best be characterized as _____.
   (A) humorously irascible
   (B) benevolently charitable
   (C) singlemindedly serious
   (D) unrelievedly vicious
   (E) unashamedly greedy
                                    5 ___

Anyone who has sincerely tried to describe some genuine experience exactly, no matter how small and insignificant it may have been, to someone who did not share
5 that experience with some degree of similarity, probably became keenly aware of the discrepancy between experience and words. And yet, the problems of knowing and understanding others—and, to some extent,
10 ourselves—centers around the relationship of language to reality or experience. The problem with using language to talk about and represent knowledge of the world is that the structure of language does not correspond to
15 the structure of reality. Although it seems obvious that a word itself is not the same as the object to which it refers, this type of structural difference is commonly forgotten. Such structural differences are simple in
20 themselves, but can be critically important to each of us in our daily lives, as well as to the scientist in her or his pursuit of scientific knowledge. Simple examples of these structural differences include such facts as:
25 1) there is not one word for each object, 2) the same word refers to many different things, and 3) many words can be used to describe any single aspect of one thing.

Another discrepancy between language
30 and reality centers around the "process nature" of reality. Language, used in a certain way, can give the impression that reality itself is static. While we cannot do without generalizations, classes, categories, and
35 names, we should realize that things change; generalizations are not always dependable or useful; classifications should not become rigid. To different degrees, we are all guilty of identifying the generalization, category,
40 or name with the object it describes and in doing so, we limit our own experiences and decrease our effectiveness in dealing with the real world.

Korzybski uses the analogy of a map's
45 relation to the territory it depicts to describe the relation of language to reality. His point is that the usefulness of a map depends precisely on the degree to which it corresponds to the territory. As differences arise between
50 the map and the territory, we must quickly be able to separate the two of them and recognize that it is the map that needs changing.

6. Which of the following titles best summarizes the content of the passage?
   (A) Words, Not Things
   (B) Limiting Our Experiences
   (C) Problems of Understanding Others
   (D) Differences Between Language and Reality
   (E) Korzybski: Language Pioneer

   6 ___

7. Which of the following pairings is most accurate?
   (A) language—territory
   (B) map—reality
   (C) language—map
   (D) map—territory
   (E) territory—categories

   7 ___

8. The "process nature" of reality can best be characterized as _____ .
   (A) static   (D) generalizing
   (B) changing   (E) dependable
   (C) analogous
                       8 ___

9. A map is valuable if _____ .
   (A) it corresponds to the territory
   (B) its language is creative
   (C) it is not static
   (D) it is scientifically explainable
   (E) it clarifies the discrepancies in language

   9 ___

10. The author points out that generalizations _____ .
    (A) are avoidable
    (B) describe reality accurately
    (C) are constantly changing
    (D) cannot be described in words
    (E) are essential

    10 ___

PART 2   Sentence Completion (11-15)

Select the word or set of words that *best* completes each of the following sentences. Write the letter for your choice.

11. When it is time to return home after achieving --- in medicine, some students from Third World countries ---.
    (A) miracles . . boast
    (B) prominence . . experiment
    (C) control . . question
    (D) competence . . balk
    (E) serenity . . quarrel

    11 ___

12. For 240 challenging days a year Japanese children have a much more --- schooling than do their American ---.
    (A) diluted . . colleagues
    (B) imaginative . . correspondents
    (C) imitative . . associates
    (D) spontaneous . . adherents
    (E) intensive . . counterparts

    12 ___

13. By the merest --- Denning attempts to --- the impressive philosophical structure outlined by his rival.
    (A) quibble . . topple
    (B) insinuation . . tout
    (C) flattery . . rationalize
    (D) hesitation . . justify
    (E) exposition . . deplete

    13 ___

14. Like many modern athletes, --- athletes in ancient Greek Olympic games --- their success.
    (A) harried . . envied
    (B) triumphant . . exploited
    (C) participating . . contemplated
    (D) canny . . squandered
    (E) lackluster . . belittled

    14 ___

15. --- communication with a pet dog or cat is often excellent ---
    (A) Casual . . strategy
    (B) Tactile . . therapy
    (C) Verbal . . psychology
    (D) Repetitive . . mimicry
    (E) Intuitive . . discipline

    15 ___

Reading Diagnostic Test — A

PART 1 Reading Comprehension (1–10)

Though the entire book is preparation for this section, pages 214–303 are especially helpful. Again, specific cross-references to pages in the text will enable you to find the help you need in reviewing for the SAT.

1. (C) The episode is reported in utter seriousness, but the outrageousness of the events tells us the author's purpose (266–269) is to entertain (C). Exaggeration, like its opposite, understatement, is often employed as a humorous device. The author's apparent hope to get the native killed is obvious exaggeration of a mild anoyance at the native's persistence.

2. (E) This question requires us to draw an inference (229–241). Though we are not told so directly, we can reasonably assume that Dan is being bothered for a silly whim. "As long as Dan has got a cent" suggests that Dan will not relish being relieved of all his money. The answer is (E).

3. (B) This question requires us to look beyond the passage and predict outcomes (291–296). It also calls for an inference. Choices (A) and (E) are absurd. There is no suggestion the police are involved (D). Dan hasn't said a word (C). Elimination brings us to (B), the most likely result.

4. (D) Finding details in the passages is a commonly tested skill (242–255). The sentence beginning "He crawled" clearly identifies the peg as the climber (D).

5. (A) The author's attitude (261–265) is humorously irascible (A). Note that *irascible* is related to *irate*. The other alternatives are unsuitable.

6. (D) Since the passage contrasts language and reality, the best title is (D) (222–223). (A) makes no statement about the contents of the passage or the relationship between words and things. (B) is too narrow. (C) is too broad. (E) is a detail.

7. (C) Korzybski uses an analogy that might be represented as follows:

map : territory :: language : reality

Thus *map* corresponds to *language* and *territory* to *reality*. The correct pairing is *language* and *map* (C). Two skills are involved here: finding details (242–255) and drawing inferences (229–241).

8. (B) This question requires analyzing the author's use of language (277–290). The first two sentences of paragraph two contrast the "process nature of reality" with the static impression sometimes given by language. If reality is not *static*, it must be *changing* (B).

9.   The passage says, "The usefulness of a map depends precisely on the degree to which it corresponds to the territory." Spotting this sentence (242–255) tells us (A) is the best choice.

10. (E) The passage flatly says, "We cannot do without generalizations." (242–255). Therefore (E) is correct.

PART 2   Sentence Completion (11–15)

11. (D) The sentence as a whole provides the clues (7–12). The answers are keyed to the clause "When it is time to return home." The best choice is (D). Students achieve competence and then balk at returning. The phrasing suggests that the students are expected to return home to provide services in their homeland. That expectation is frustrated. The other choices fail to catch this point.

12. (E) A comparison is suggested between the schooling of Japanese schoolchildren and American schoolchildren (22–25). Students are paired (13–16) to sharpen the comparison. If Japanese schoolchildren go to school "240 challenging days a year," we may infer that their training is harder—more *intensive* (E). The other choices do not concern themselves with that inference.

13. (A) Contrast provides the essential clue (26–29). *Merest* conflicts with *impressive*. The word modified by *merest* must contrast with *impressive*. *Quibble*, a "trivial objection," provides that contrast (A). If you are uncertain about *quibble*, you can still get the right answer by concentrating upon the second word in the pair. *Impressive philosophical structure* calls for a strong negative word in the blank. *Topple* meets the need. A strong structure can be *toppled*. The other choices make little sense.

14. (B) The answer relies upon comparison (22–25). Modern and ancient athletes are compared. *Triumphant* (B) best fits the sense for the first slot and *exploited* best fits the sense for the second. In the other choices, one or both words are unsuitable.

15. (B) This is a sentence in which all five first choices fit the first slot and all five second choices fit the second slot. But only one *pair* fits. *Casual*, for example, would fit with *communication*, but *strategy*, the other word in the pair, doesn't make sense in the completed sentence. On the other hand, *strategy* might fit in the second slot, but the completed sentence would need a word other than *casual* to make good sense. The context of the sentence (6–40) requires the words in (B). If *tactile* is unfamiliar, remember the *tact* root (99), meaning "touch."

Now that you have taken Part A and have read the analysis of the correct answers, try your skill at Part B. Again, at the end, correct answers will be analyzed for you, with cross-references to the pages which cover the skills being tested.

Taking both parts of the test may provide help in revealing areas where you are particularly strong as well as areas where you need special attention.

Reading Comprehension (1–15)

Each passage below is followed by questions based on its content. Answer all questions following a passage on the basis of what is *stated* or *implied* in that passage.

The character of the prince who now as-cended the throne of England and became lord of Normandy, Anjou, Touraine, and Maine, claimant to Brittany and heir to
5 Queen Eleanor's Aquitaine, was already well known. Richard had embodied the virtues which men admire in the lion, but there is no animal in nature that combines the con-tradictory qualities of John. He united the
10 ruthlessness of a hardened warrior with the craft and sublety of a Machiavellian. Al-though from time to time he gave way to furious rages, in which "his eyes darted fire and his countenance became livid," his
15 cruelties were conceived and executed with a cold, inhuman intelligence. Monkish chroniclers have emphasized his violence, greed, malice, treachery, and lust. But other records show that he was often judicious,
20 always extremely capable, and on occasions even generous. He possessed an original and inquiring mind, and to the end of his life treasured his library of books. In him the restless energy of the Plantagenet race was
25 raised to a furious pitch of instability. A French writer, it is true, has tried to throw the sombre cloak of madness over his moral deformities, but a study of his actions shows John gifted with a deep and persistent sa-
30 gacity, of patience and artifice, and with an unshakable resolve, which he fulfilled, to maintain himself upon the throne while the breath was in his body. The difficulties with which he contended, on the whole with re-
35 markable success, deserve cool and attentive study. Moreover, when the long tally is added it will be seen that the British nation and the English-speaking world owe far more to the vices of John than to the labours of
40 virtuous sovereigns; for it was through the union of many forces against him that the most famous milestone of our rights and freedom was in fact set up.

1. The selection focuses its major attention upon _____ .
   (A) the virtues of Richard
   (B) the progeny of Queen Eleanor
   (C) the energy of the Plantagenets
   (D) the contradictory nature of John
   (E) the deviousness of the Normans

   1 ___

2. Which of the following pairs of adjectives may be applied to John?
   (A) gentle and mad
   (B) cruel and intelligent
   (C) handsome and ruthless
   (D) patient and weak
   (E) greedy and stupid

   2 ___

3. Monkish chroniclers _____ .
   (A) tended to report John's worst qualities
   (B) glorified John
   (C) praised him for supporting freedom
   (D) called him a *Machiavellian*
   (E) commented on his fine library

   3 ___

4. A generalization that may be drawn from the passage is that _____ .
   (A) you can't tell a book by its cover
   (B) violence begets violence
   (C) evil actions may bring good results
   (D) restless energy leads to virtuous action
   (E) the concept of kingship is obsolete

   4 ___

Kentucky-born John Stark was fifty-eight years old when he first heard Joplin play the piece that was the patrons' favorite at Se-dalia's Maple Leaf Club. Disregarding
5 warnings that no market existed for black composers' works, Stark agreed to have Jo-plin's piece printed and to sell it in his music store. Published in September 1899, "Maple Leaf Rag" did not sell well at first. But it
10 gained popularity in the fall of 1900, boosted by the sudden eruption of a national ragtime craze. Stark and his son moved to St. Louis, where they printed ten thousand copies of Joplin's piece on a small hand press and hung
15 up a sign reading "John Stark and Son, Mu-sic Publishers." Orders for "Maple Leaf Rag" came in from all over the country. Stark hired a staff, exchanged his work clothes for a business suit, and prepared to
20 face life as a successful publisher. Soon he had a fine house in St. Louis and a thriving business whose principal product was the works of a previously unknown composer named Scott Joplin.
25   Joplin followed Stark to St. Louis in 1901. He bought a house there, equipped it with a piano, and settled down to his chosen work of serious composing. The composi-tions that Joplin produced in the next ten
30 years are still remembered as classics of rag-time. They were appealing pieces with flow-ing melodies, intricate syncopations, and ex-pressive themes. They bore such names as "The Entertainer," "Peacherine Rag,"
35 "The Easy Winners," "Elite Syncopa-tions," and "The Strenuous Life." He also wrote songs, marches, waltzes, and an ele-gant tango called "Solace." For several years, he appeared on vaudeville stages,
40 billed as "King of Ragtime Composers—Author of 'Maple Leaf Rag.'" But his am-bitions transcended the confines of popular dance and show music. He longed to adapt the rhythms of ragtime to more ambitious
45 musical forms, to show that characteristic black syncopation was capable of expressing enduring musical ideas.

5. Which of the following titles best summa-rizes the content of the passage?
(A) John Stark, Entrepreneur
(B) St. Louis, Home of Ragtime
(C) The Problems of Music Publishing
(D) Famous Composers of Ragtime
(E) The King of Ragtime

5 ___

6. "Maple Leaf Rag" took its name from
_____.
(A) a club in Sedalia
(B) a sign in John Clark's office
(C) Canada
(D) a tree in Joplin's garden
(E) a previous composition

6 ___

7. All the following types of musical compo-sition are mentioned in the passage EX-CEPT _____.
(A) waltz   (D) opera
(B) tango   (E) song
(C) march   7 ___

8. Scott Joplin had to earn his living as
_____.
(A) an assistant to John Stark
(B) a dance instructor
(C) a vaudeville entertainer
(D) a printer
(E) a distributor of his own work

8 ___

On a global basis, it has been estimated that the annual net loss of soil from cropland is some 23 billion tons in excess of soil for-mation. As world population expands, de-
5 mand for food and fiber expands. Driven by economic and social pressures, more of the world's marginal cropland is put to the plow each year—only to be abandoned as soils are depleted after a short period of production.
10 Mining of the world's arable soils is an on-going and accelerating process, the inevita-ble consequences of which must be obvious to any thinking person. It may come to pass that sustaining this nation's food and fiber-
15 producing capacity may become our most potent deterrent to international conflict.
   To blame farmers for abandoning well-known soil-conservation practices is akin to denouncing one who is drowning for futilely
20 clutching at straws. In far too many cases, the farmer is fighting for survival; when he is reduced to choosing between bankruptcy now or later, his choice is obvious. Long-term conservation practices suffer under the
25 harsh demands of economic survival. But there are others who are farming the subsidy/tax-incentives system for a quick profit at the expense of family farmers, consumers, and taxpayers alike.

9. As used in the selection *marginal* is equivalent to _____ .

   (A) bordering   (D) terminal
   (B) arable   (E) poor
   (C) desert

   9 ___

10. The author uses the phrase "futilely clutching at straws" to suggest _____ .

   (A) promising survival strategies
   (B) measures of desperation
   (C) short-term ineffectiveness, long-term success
   (D) taking advantage of the incentives system
   (E) compromises with reality

   10 ___

11. A major deterrent to global war may be America's _____ .

   (A) new, improved mining techniques
   (B) food-producing capacity
   (C) intelligent use of tax incentives
   (D) current treatment of farm problems
   (E) arsenal of military might

   11 ___

      In 1644, the Manchus, a tribal people on the northeastern frontier of the Ming empire, captured Peking, overthrew the Ming and established the Ch'ing dynasty, which lasted
5 until the founding of the Chinese Republic in 1911. Under the K'ang-hsi emperor (reigned 1662–1722), the early Ch'ing world was one of reconstruction after late Ming fragmentation. Orthodox painters aimed to
10 recapture the former glories of traditional painting by studying and copying ancient models. By infusing old conventions with renewed energy, painters attempted to achieve a true correspondence *(ho)* to ancient
15 models. On the other hand, some artists scorned the new orthodox conservatism. The so-called individualist masters often painted in a free, emotion-filled calligraphic manner. Because of their loyalty to the fallen Ming
20 dynasty, they expressed a strong sense of dislocation and alienation in their works. Avoiding the rationalism and methodology of the orthodox painters, the individualists preferred to derive their art directly from na-
25 ture and to express it through more personal artistic means.

12. Which of the following is the best characterization of the K'ang-hsi emperor?

   (A) He was the last of the Ming emperors; with him the Ming dynasty ended.
   (B) He was a painter who mastered the calligraphic style.
   (C) He was the spiritual forerunner of the Chinese republic.
   (D) He was an early emperor of the Ch'ing dynasty.
   (E) He was a master of the emotion-filled calligraphic manner.

   12 ___

13. Those who "preferred to derive their art directly from nature" are described in the selection as _____ .

   (A) orthodox painters and new conservatives
   (B) a tribal people on the frontier of the Ming empire
   (C) concentrating on the correspondence *(ho)* to ancient models
   (D) former warriors forced to become artists in peacetime
   (E) alienated because of loyalty to the Ming empire

   13 ___

14. The primary purpose of the passage appears to be to _____ .

   (A) compare the Ch'ing paintings unfavorably with those of the Ming
   (B) explain the failure of the 17th century artists to paint from nature
   (C) explain the two major schools of painting in the Ch'ing period
   (D) show how orthodox painters expressed nature through personal means
   (E) slyly suggest the inferior simplicity of Ming paintings

   14 ___

15. Toward the end of the Ming dynasty the "former glories of traditional painting" were _____ .

   (A) fragmented   (D) forgotten
   (B) overthrown   (E) improved
   (C) despised

   15 ___

ANSWERS AND ANALYSIS

Reading Diagnostic Test — B

Reading Comprehension (1–15)

Though the entire book is preparation for this section, pages 214–303 are especially helpful. Again, specific cross-references to pages in the text will enable you to find the help you need in reviewing for the SAT.

1. (D) The word *major* tells us we must draw a generalization (214–216) from the passage. Richard (A) is touched briefly. Queen Eleanor (B) is a detail. Energy (C) is one side of the Plantagenets. The deviousness of the Normans (E) is not in the passage. The contradictory personality of John is emphasized throughout—for example, his rages and his cold intelligence, his greed and his generosity. The best choice is (D).

2. (B) A passage may require us to seek out details (242–255) in the passage, as here. John's cruelty is mentioned ("cruelties were conceived"), as is his intelligence ("a cold, inhuman intelligence"). (B) is clearly the correct choice. John was not gentle (A), weak (D), or stupid (E). He is not called handsome (C) in the passage.

3. (A) This passage requires us to spot a detail (242–255) and then draw an inference (229–231). We read that "monkish chroniclers have emphasized his violence, greed, malice, treachery, and lust." We reasonably infer that these are "John's worst qualities" (A). None of the other choices can be justified by the passage. They either state the opposite (B) or make a point not mentioned in the passage at all (C), (D), (E).

4. (C) The point of the selection is summarized in the last sentence: "The English-speaking world owe(s) far more to the vices of John than to the labours of virtuous sovereigns." This says the same essentially as (C). Finding generalizations (214–216) often requires the candidate to draw inferences (230–241) as well.

5. (E) A title (222–223) must cover the subject, being neither too broad nor too narrow. The subject of the passage is not John Stark (A) but Scott Joplin. Stark is mentioned only as he plays a role in Joplin's life. (B) is too narrow. (C) is too broad—and partly off the subject. (D) is inaccurate. Other composers are not mentioned. (E) is the correct choice.

6. (A) The answer, a detail in the selection (242–255), is found in the opening sentence. The song was named after the Maple Leaf Club, where it was played (A).

7. (D) Questions with *except* (285–289) reverse the usual challenge. Check off items actually mentioned in the selection. The one left is the answer. "He also wrote *songs*, *marches*, *waltzes*, and an elegant *tango*." *Operas* are not mentioned by name in the passage.

8. (C) An actual detail (242–255) in the passage provides the answer: "For several years, he appeared on vaudeville stages." The correct choice is (C).

9. (E) Questions sometimes test your ability to define a word in context (6–40, 277–290), as here. *Marginal* cropland is plowed but quickly abandoned because of soil depletion. We may reasonably infer (229–241) that such soil is poor. (E) is the correct choice. Note that *margin* usually means *border*. *Bordering* for *marginal* is an enticing choice, but it doesn't fit here.

10. (B) Questions sometimes test figurative language (281–284). Since straws are insubstantial and clutching at them quite ineffectual, we may assume that (B) is the correct choice.

11. (B) This is the key sentence: "Sustaining this nation's food and fiber-producing capacity may become our most potent deterrent to international conflict." This suggests that the world may need America for food to survive (B). This detail (242–255) is there in the text. The other alternatives are inaccurate, opposed, or even not mentioned. Though you might be of the opinion that (E) is a reasonable answer, you cannot choose it, for it is nowhere mentioned in the selection.

12. (D) Dates are provided: 1644 for the overthrow of the Ming dynasty; 1662–1722 for the reign of K'ang-hsie. We may infer (229–241) from the details (242–255) that (D) is the correct choice. (A) is flatly incorrect. There is no justification for any of the other choices.

13. (E) The last sentence of the paragraph identifies those who "preferred to derive their art directly from nature" as individualists. The previous sentence tells us these same painters "expressed a strong sense of dislocation and alienation in their works." Once again selecting details (242–255) and then drawing the proper inference (230–241) suggest that (E) is the correct choice.

14. (C) Identifying the main purpose of the author (266–269) is akin to finding the main idea (217–221). Let's evaluate each choice in turn. There is no attempt to glorify one school of painting at the expense of another. The author is quite neutral and objective. Therefore (A) is incorrect. There is no suggestion that "17th century artists" failed to paint from nature. Eliminate (B). (C) expresses the central purpose of the author: to explain rather than criticize or take sides. (C) is correct. The individualists rather than the orthodox painters expressed nature through personal means. Eliminate (D). As we have already seen in (A), the author is not taking sides. Eliminate (E).

15. (A) Sentence 2 supplies the key phrase: "after late Ming fragmentation." Spotting this detail (242–255) enables us to infer that (A) is the correct choice. The "early Ch'ing world" occurred right after the fall of the Ming dynasty. At this time orthodox painters aimed to recapture the "former glories of traditional painting." Thus we may infer that toward the end Ming art had been fragmented.

DIVISION C

Facsimile Tests

A Strategy for the Facsimile Tests

■ You have come a long way and are ready for the moment of truth. The tests that follow approximate the SAT you will be taking, but they are practice tests only.

■ Before you begin, be sure you have the appropriate amount of time to spend on the test. Try to approximate test conditions as much as possible.

■ Have a watch with you to check your timing. Don't spend too much time on any one question. If you waste time on a question, you may not reach questions that are easy for you. If you have trouble with a question, go right on. If you have time later, come back and try again.

■ Read the questions carefully. Following directions is an important part of the test.

■ If you are unsure of an answer, don't panic. You won't know all the answers, but do the best you can. By now you have discovered that you have unexpected resources if you stay calm and build upon what you already know.

■ You will find complete explanations for the correct answers for Facsimile Tests 1, 2, and 3 beginning on page 391. This will help you analyze your responses. Correct answers only are given for Tests 4 and 5. The reference before each item tells you where to look in this book for help.

FACSIMILE TEST 1

Section 1

PART 1

For each question in this section, choose the best answer and write the letter on the line at the right.

Each question below consists of a word in capital letters, followed by five lettered words. Choose the word that is most nearly *opposite* in meaning to the word in capital letters. Since some of the questions require you to distinguish fine shades of meaning, consider all the choices before deciding which is best.

EXAMPLE

GOOD:

(A) sour   (D) hot
(B) bad   (E) ugly
(C) red
                                    __B__

74–76   1. INVARIABLE:

(A) unstable   (D) literal
(B) confusing   (E) habitual
(C) absolute
                                    1 ___

96   2. EJECT:

(A) disbar   (D) assign
(B) provide   (E) admit
(C) indicate
                                    2 ___

120–121   3. MONOCHROME:

(A) photographic
(B) multicolored
(C) cosmic
(D) single-minded
(E) strange
                                    3 ___

69–73   4. BOLSTER:

(A) repeat   (D) undercut
(B) announce   (E) apprehend
(C) control
                                    4 ___

87   5. DIVULGE:

(A) annul   (D) separate
(B) conceal   (E) flail
(C) array
                                    5 ___

47–52   6. FROSTY:

(A) chilly   (D) deadly
(B) friendly   (E) rainy
(C) flagrant
                                    6 ___

69–73   7. DEXTERITY:

(A) clumsiness (D) interest
(B) genius   (E) bashfulness
(C) skill
                                    7 ___

95   8. NULLIFY:

(A) verify   (D) abide
(B) debunk   (E) abandon
(C) implement
                                    8 ___

74–76   9. FRETFUL:

(A) fearful   (D) tranquil
(B) meaningless (E) worried
(C) powerless
                                    9 ___

77–78   10. MERCURIAL:

(A) poisonous   (D) eloquent
(B) swift   (E) constant
(C) metallic
                                    10 ___

74–76   11. DIVERGENT:

(A) similar   (D) remote
(B) atrocious   (E) complacent
(C) partial
                                    11 ___

47 12. LAGGARD:
    (A) stubborn   (D) swift
    (B) beautiful   (E) fierce
    (C) timeless

12 ___

69–73 13. SPLEEN:
    (A) universality   (D) indirection
    (B) esophagus   (E) kindliness
    (C) curiosity

13 ___

87, 94 14. ANTECEDENT:
    (A) grammatical
    (B) consequent
    (C) foreordained
    (D) postponed
    (E) predisposed

14 ___

132–133 15. BELITTLE:
    (A) repress   (D) alarm
    (B) scorn   (E) cohere
    (C) praise

15 ___

PART 2

Each sentence below has one or two blanks, each blank indicating that something has been omitted. Beneath the sentence are five lettered words or sets of words. Choose the word or set of words that *best* fits the meaning of the sentence as a whole.

EXAMPLE

Although its publicity has been ---, the film itself is intelligent, well-acted, handsomely produced, and altogether ---.
    (A) tasteless . . respectable
    (B) extensive . . moderate
    (C) sophisticated . . spectacular
    (D) risque . . crude
    (E) perfect . . spectacular

A

26–29 16. The arbitrator remained --- despite efforts of the press to anticipate his decision.
    (A) sluggish
    (B) prejudiced
    (C) irritated
    (D) insensitive
    (E) noncommittal

16 ___

6–12 17. If a patient's hospital room has a window overlooking a scenic stand of trees, --- tends to be ---.
    (A) boredom . . manifest
    (B) interest . . dispersed
    (C) convalescence . . inflexible
    (D) recuperation . . accelerated
    (E) mobility . . minimal

17 ___

17–21 18. Some endangered creatures may survive by transfer of populations, --- species in areas where they no longer occur.
    (A) commemorating
    (B) reestablishing
    (C) studying
    (D) uniting
    (E) popularizing

18 ___

30–33 19. Denny's --- behavior may lead him from the conventional to the --- in a few brief moments.
    (A) erratic . . outrageous
    (B) smooth . . uninspired
    (C) snobbish . . orthodox
    (D) atrocious . . solicitous
    (E) consistent . . theatrical

19 ___

17–21 20. Newborn infants are little Buddhas, observing life with --- glances and impressive ---.
    (A) inattentive . . comprehension
    (B) compassionate . . condescension
    (C) penetrating . . equanimity
    (D) competent . . indifference
    (E) stolen . . magnanimity

20 ___

Each passage below is followed by questions based on its content. Answer all questions on the basis of what is *stated* or *implied* in that passage.

One evening, about the turn of the century, after a weekend shoot in Scotland, a dozen guests sat around a dinner table discussing human monsters, famous murders,
5 and unsolved crimes. One of the guests, Dr. Joseph Bell, the eminent surgeon and medical instructor, had the others wide-eyed with his deductive acrobatics.

"The trouble with most people," he said,
10 "is that they see, but do not observe. Any really good detective ought to be able to tell, before a stranger has fairly sat down, his occupation, habits and past history through rapid observation and deduction. Glance at
15 a man and you find his nationality written on his face, his means of livelihood on his hands, and the rest of his story in his gait, mannerisms, tattoo marks, watch chain ornaments, shoe laces and in the lint adhering
20 to his clothes."

The guests were fascinated but skeptical. One challenged Dr. Bell to give an example of applied observation. Happily, Dr. Bell obliged.

25 "A patient walked into the room where I was instructing the students, and his case seemed to be a very simple one. I was talking about what was wrong with him. 'Of course, gentlemen,' I happened to say, 'he
30 has been a soldier in a Highland regiment, and probably a bandsman.' I pointed out the swagger in his walk, suggestive of the Highland piper; while his shortness told me that if he had been a soldier, it was probably as
35 a bandsman. But the man insisted he was nothing but a shoemaker and had never been in the army in his life. This was rather a floorer, but being absolutely certain, I told two of the strongest clerks to remove the
40 man to a side room and strip him.

"Under his left breast I instantly detected a little blue D branded on his skin. He was an army deserter. That was how they used to mark them in the Crimean days. You can
45 understand his evasion. However, this proved my first observation correct. He confessed having played in the band of a Highland regiment in the war against the Russians. It was really elementary, gentlemen."

50 Most of the guests were impressed. But one listener chidingly remarked: "Why, Dr. Bell might almost be Sherlock Holmes."

To which Dr. Bell snapped: "My dear sir, I *am* Sherlock Holmes."

229-241 21. The two qualities most closely associated with Dr. Bell were _____.

(A) egotism and irritability
(B) industry and conjecture
(C) athleticism and skill in surgery
(D) observation and deduction
(E) suggestibility and fairness

21 ___

242-254 22. Dr. Bell assumed the patient had been a soldier in a Highland regiment because of the patient's _____.

(A) shoes
(B) tattoo
(C) watch chain ornaments
(D) mannerisms
(E) walk

22 ___

242-254 23. Which of the following is correctly paired according to the selection?

(A) Dr. Bell . . famous writer
(B) Crimean days . . war against the Russians
(C) Sherlock Holmes . . Highland piper
(D) unsolved crimes . . surgeon
(E) skepticism . . deduction

23 ___

277-280 24. As used in the selection *swagger* suggests _____.

(A) modesty and humility
(B) simplicity and friendliness
(C) arrogance and pomposity
(D) fascination and criminality
(E) strength and openness

24 ___

25. The author's attitude toward Dr. Joseph Bell is one of _____ .

(A) obvious admiration
(B) studied irony
(C) indirect disparagment
(D) subtle criticism
(E) uncritical adulation

25 ____

During his residence in London, the accomplished Prince Florizel of Bohemia gained the affection of all classes by the seduction of his manner and by a well-considered generosity. He was a remarkable man even by what was known of him; and that was but a small part of what he actually did. Although of a placid temper in ordinary circumstances, and accustomed to take the world with as much philosophy as any ploughman, the Prince of Bohemia was not without a taste for ways of life more adventurous and eccentric than that to which he was destined by his birth. Now and then, when he fell into a low humour, when there was no laughable play to witness in any of the London theatres, and when the season of the year was unsuitable to those field sports in which he excelled all competitors, he would summon his confidant and Master of the Horse, Colonel Geraldine, and bid him prepare himself against an evening ramble. The Master of the Horse was a young officer of a brave and even temerarious disposition. He greeted the news with delight, and hastened to make ready. Long practice and a varied acquaintance of life had given him a singular faculty in disguise; he could adapt not only his face and bearing, but his voice and almost his thoughts, to those of any rank, character, or nation; and in this way he diverted attention from the Prince, and sometimes gained admission for the pair into strange societies. The civil authorities were never taken into the secret of these adventures; the imperturbable courage of the men and the ready invention and chivalrous devotion to each other had brought them through a score of dangerous passes; and they grew in confidence as time went on.

One evening in March they were driven by a sharp fall of sleet into an Oyster Bar in the immediate neighborhood of Leicester Square. Colonel Geraldine was dressed and painted to represent a person connected with the Press in reduced circumstances; while the Prince had, as usual, travestied his appearance by the addition of false whiskers and a pair of large adhesive eyebrows. These lent him a shaggy and weather-beaten air, which, for one of his urbanity, formed the most impenetrable disguise. Thus equipped, the commander and his satellite sipped their brandy and soda in security.

26. Which of the following best decribes the main idea of the selection?

(A) Prince Florizel is well liked by his friends and associates.
(B) Disguise is a deceitful, disagreeable device with little justification for its use.
(C) The Prince of Bohemia is basically an industrious, hardworking individual.
(D) The Prince and the Colonel seek new adventures and unusual experiences.
(E) Colonel Geraldine is the motivator of the disguised friends.

26 ____

27. As used in the selection *in reduced circumstances* means _____ .

(A) on a restricted assignment
(B) in a state of uncertainty
(C) attached to a newspaper
(D) in a shabby suit
(E) somewhat low in money

27 ____

28. Lines 12–13 suggest that the Prince's personality is _____ .

(A) essentially agreeable and loving
(B) complex and somewhat contradictory
(C) unruffled and consistent
(D) predictable but interesting
(E) unpleasant if superficially charming

28 ____

277-280 29. The context suggests that *temerarious* (line 24) probably means _____.

(A) rash and daring
(B) impatient and nasty
(C) reserved and thoughtful
(D) proud but shy
(E) rebellious and cruel

29 ___

291-296 30. Which of the following is likely to happen next?

(A) The Colonel is greeted by an old, forgotten friend.
(B) The Prince tires of the masquerade and returns home.
(C) The Prince and the Colonel have an unusual adventure.
(D) The disguised pair are unmasked by the press.
(E) The storm gets worse, and the men find lodgings.

30 ___

PART 4

Select the word or set of words that *best* complete each of the following sentences.

6-12 31. --- changes in basic swimming strokes have created new world records and made --- many previous swim techniques.

(A) Unexpected . . . ridiculous
(B) Subtle . . obsolete
(C) Extreme . . significant
(D) Mechanical . . dramatic
(E) Trivial . . valuable

31 ___

17-21 32. The radio signals were ---, with --- static that scrambled the message.

(A) intermittent . . disruptive
(B) melodic . . harmonious
(C) unanticipated . . frivolous
(D) clear . . isolated
(E) unbroken . . raucous

32 ___

6-12 33. Nowhere else in the United States, during the next decade, are as many --- species facing possible --- as in the Hawaiian Islands.

(A) exotic . . misinterpretation
(B) desert . . scrutiny
(C) poisonous . . mismanagement
(D) alpine . . stabilization
(E) native . . extinction

33 ___

26-29 34. Though *abnormality* is a frightening word, some --- from normal are ---, not harmful.

(A) quotations . . curious
(B) abstractions . . medicinal
(C) deviations . . benign
(D) condensations . . concise
(E) fluctuations . . provocative

34 ___

17-21 35. Americans have been accused of being ---, wasteful of their --- resources.

(A) indigent . . plentiful
(B) unconventional . . natural
(C) disillusioned . . subterranean
(D) profligate . . irreplaceable
(E) uncooperative . . aquatic

35 ___

PART 5

Each question below consists of a related pair of words followed by five lettered pairs of words. Select the lettered pair that *best* expresses a relationship similar to that expressed in the original pair.

EXAMPLE

YAWN : BOREDOM ::

(A) anger : madness
(B) dream : sleep
(C) smile : amusement
(D) face : expression
(E) impatience : rebellion

<u>C</u>

182–183 36. INFLUENCE: : DOMINA-
TION ::

(A) admiration : worship
(B) budget : plan
(C) subscriber : underwriter
(D) blossom : flower
(E) cooperation : sabotage

36 ___

174–175 37. MANUSCRIPT : EDIT ::

(A) lemonade : consume
(B) evidence : destroy
(C) account : audit
(D) peruse : newspaper
(E) dress : injury

37 ___

166–167 38. EXCESS : SCANT ::

(A) actor : incompetent
(B) true : hallucination
(C) deterioration : worse
(D) delegation : authorized
(E) delirium : logical

38 ___

172,175 39. CHISEL : CARPENTRY ::

(A) chain : bicycle
(B) mainsail : schooner
(C) scale : weight
(D) blowtorch : welding
(E) music : tuning fork

39 ___

187 40. SWAN : CYGNET ::

(A) fawn : deer
(B) goose : gosling
(C) goose : gander
(D) sheep : kid
(E) antelope : cub

40 ___

178–180 41. THERAPIST : REHABILITA-
TION ::

(A) direction : pilot
(B) physicist : atom
(C) lumberjack : cabinetmaking
(D) pharmacist : diagnosis
(E) jester : entertainment

41 ___

170–171 42. EXPOSURE : CHILL ::

(A) impertinence : flippancy
(B) obstruction : frustration
(C) abandonment : solidarity
(D) thrift : poverty
(E) frivolity : irritability

42 ___

168, 171 43. ELUDE : CUNNING ::

(A) embezzle : upright
(B) discriminating : criticize
(C) beautify : wealthy
(D) fumble : clumsy
(E) stubborn : endure

43 ___

185 44. OUNCES : GOLD ::

(A) apples : bushels
(B) gallons : fuel oil
(C) carats : diamonds
(D) miles : yards
(E) grain : elevator

44 ___

177, 180 45. LIBRETTIST : OPERA ::

(A) circus : clown
(B) angler : regatta
(C) mountaineer : rock face
(D) ornithologist : aquarium
(E) museum : curator

45 ___

Section 2

PART 1

For each question in this section, choose the best answer and write the letter on the line at the right.

Each question below consists of a word in capital letters, followed by five lettered words. Choose the word that is most nearly *opposite* in meaning to the word in capital letters. Since some of the questions require you to distinguish fine shades of meaning, consider all the choices before deciding which is best.

EXAMPLE

GOOD:
- (A) sour
- (B) bad
- (C) red
- (D) hot
- (E) ugly

    B

87 1. SUBSERVIENT:
- (A) supercilious
- (B) aggressive
- (C) tranquil
- (D) melodramatic
- (E) ambiguous

1 ___

47, 74 2. INCLINATION:
- (A) derivation
- (B) eclipse
- (C) reservation
- (D) dislike
- (E) infatuation

2 ___

118 3. EUPHORIA:
- (A) disapprobation
- (B) exaltation
- (C) dormancy
- (D) discretion
- (E) misery

3 ___

74-76 4. MONUMENTAL:
- (A) diminutive
- (B) marble
- (C) two-dimensional
- (D) commemorative
- (E) abstract

4 ___

89 5. OMNISCIENT:
- (A) alert
- (B) ignorant
- (C) negligent
- (D) indecisive
- (E) provocative

5 ___

41-48 6. HAUNT:
- (A) frequent
- (B) shock
- (C) dawdle
- (D) shun
- (E) dream

6 ___

69-73 7. CARDINAL:
- (A) irreligious
- (B) mammalian
- (C) humorous
- (D) numerous
- (E) unimportant

7 ___

74-76 8. DISADVANTAGEOUS:
- (A) squalid
- (B) beneficial
- (C) affable
- (D) detrimental
- (E) neutral

8 ___

74-76 9. LETHARGY:
- (A) indifference
- (B) hate
- (C) vigor
- (D) squeamishness
- (E) fulfillment

9 ___

41-46 10. CAGEY:
- (A) naive
- (B) unfettered
- (C) clownish
- (D) squeamish
- (E) sparse

10 ___

PART 2

Each sentence below has one or two blanks, each blank indicating that something has been omitted. Beneath the sentence are five lettered words or sets of words. Choose the word or set of words that *best* fits the meaning of the sentence as a whole.

EXAMPLE

Although its publicity has been ---, the film itself is intelligent, well-acted, handsomely produced, and altogether ---.

(A) tasteless. . respectable
(B) extensive . . moderate
(C) sophisticated . . amateur
(D) risqué . . crude
(E) perfect . . spectacular

A

26–29 11. Although some ecosystems are --- and able to adjust, others are too --- to survive much tampering.

(A) dependable . . . accommodating
(B) resilient . . . fragile
(C) prodigal . . . incompetent
(D) inflammable . . arid
(E) inexhaustible . . self-contained

11 ___

6–12 12. Formerly accepted --- of the proper roles of men and women have --- the fate of the mastodon and the sabre-toothed tiger.

(A) stereotypes . . experienced
(B) assignments . . retold
(C) depictions . . broadcast
(D) critiques . . elucidated
(E) reprimands . . analyzed

12 ___

26–29 13. In his autobiography Simenon does not spare himself, recounting his --- failures as well as his many --- successes.

(A) incredible . . undeserved
(B) tolerable . . . conspicuous
(C) ludicrous . . peevish
(D) personal . . professional
(E) cinematic . . ecclesiastical

13 ___

30–33 14. As the favorable election results poured from the television screen, the candidate went from quiet --- to expressive ---.

(A) uneasiness . . . contentment
(B) curiosity . . concern
(C) statement . . exaggeration
(D) confusion . . preeminence
(E) pleasure . . jubilation

14 ___

6–12 15. In the --- view of some critics, the only --- goal of television is not to inform or even entertain but to sell goods.

(A) positive . . overlooked
(B) jaundiced . . unrealized
(C) cynical . . serious
(D) tiresome . . illusory
(E) blatant . . unacknowledged

15 ___

PART 3

Each question below consists of a related pair of words, followed by five lettered pairs of words. Select the lettered pair that *best* expresses a relationship similar to that expressed in the original pair.

EXAMPLE

YAWN : BOREDOM::

(A) dream : sleep
(B) anger : madness
(C) smile : amusement
(D) face : expression
(E) impatience : rebellion

C

173, 175 16. PAMPHLET : TOME::

(A) turnip : radish
(B) oration : election
(C) butterfly : caterpillar
(D) hill : mountain
(E) shout : cry

16 ___

181, 186 17. HIBERNATION : INACTIVITY::

(A) disorder : entropy
(B) devastation : ruin
(C) deterioration : growth
(D) embargo : trade
(E) bafflement : tardiness

17 ___

176, 180 18. DISCIPLE : FOLLOWS::

(A) amphibian : slides
(B) cries : infant
(C) candidate : votes
(D) courier : writes
(E) trustee : administers

18 ___

169, 171 19. MOUTHPIECE : OBOE::

(A) clock : cape
(B) cannon : ammunition
(C) eyepiece : telescope
(D) warp : woof
(E) drill : bit

19 ___

184, 186 20. PATHOLOGY : SICKNESS::

(A) paleontology : fossils
(B) psychology : education
(C) archaeology : plant life
(D) geology : gasoline
(E) psychiatry : medicine

20 ___

179–180 21. ARTIST : PALETTE::

(A) conductor : baton
(B) saber : fencer
(C) soldier : boot
(D) typewriter : stenographer
(E) nurseryman : cradle

21 ___

183, 186 22. STEAK : BROIL::

(A) baste : turkey
(B) lawn : mow
(C) book : overlook
(D) roll : call
(E) neurotic : calm

22 ___

174–175 23. FABLE : STORY::

(A) factor : teacher
(B) sale : fair
(C) charter : mortgage
(D) senator : legislator
(E) wholesaler : retailer

23 ___

170–171 24. CASKET : JEWEL::

(A) doctrine : philosophy
(B) page : cover
(C) vase : flower
(D) water : kettle
(E) receptacle : ticket

24 ___

177, 180 25. NEUTRALITY : MEDIATOR::

(A) humor : physician
(B) fairness : pitcher
(C) hero : courage
(D) horse : patience
(E) skill : athlete

25 ___

PART 4

Each passage is followed by questions based on its content. Answer all questions following a passage on the basis of what is *stated* or *implied* in that passage.

Though the words *classical* and *roman-tic*, then, have acquired an almost technical meaning, in application to certain developments of German and French taste, yet this
5 is but one variation of an old opposition, which may be traced from the very beginning of the formation of European art and literature. From the first formation of anything like a standard of taste in these things,
10 the restless curiosity of their more eager lovers necessarily made itself felt, in the craving for new motives, new subjects of interest, new modifications of style. Hence, the opposition between the classicists and the ro-
15 manticists—between the adherents, in the culture of beauty, of the principles of liberty, and authority, respectively—of strength and order.

266-269 26. The author's primary purpose in this passage is to _____ .
(A) explore the meaning of the words *classical* and *romantic*
(B) set in opposition German and French taste in art and literature
(C) study how new modifications of style serve to sharpen understanding of old oppositions
(D) evaluate the motivation of German and French artists
(E) demonstrate that classicism and romanticism are basically the same

26 ___

277-280 27. In the passage the phrase *in the culture of beauty* applies to
_____ .
(A) romanticists only
(B) classicists and romanticists
(C) classicists only
(D) French and German critics only
(E) the beginnings of European art and literature

27 ___

232-234 28. With which of the following statements would the author probably agree?
(A) The supposed opposition between classicists and romanticists is superficial, masking a similarity of technique and purpose.
(B) French and German artists were pioneers in setting up standards of taste in art and literature.
(C) In the formation of art and literature, standards of taste are essential.
(D) The craving for new motives is essentially a barren impulse, robbing art and literature of beauty and stability.
(E) Restless curiosity outweighs all other elements in seeking the sources of beauty in art.

28 ___

It is said that one of the notions the Japanese have about the fox—a semi-sacred animal with them—is that, if you chance to see one crossing your path in the morning, all that comes before your vision on that day will be illusion. As an illustration of this belief it is related that a Japanese who witnessed the eruption of Krakatoa, when the heavens were covered with blackness and kindled with intermitting flashes and the earth shaken by the detonations, and when all others, thinking the end of the world had come, were swooning with extreme fear, viewed it without a tremor as a very sublime but illusory spectacle. For on that very morning he had seen a fox cross his path.

A somewhat similar effect is produced on our minds if we have what may be called a sense of historical time—a consciousness of the transitoriness of most things human—if we see institutions and works as the branches on a pine or larch, which fail and die and fall away successively while the tree itself lives forever, and if we measure their duration not by our own swift years but by the life of nations and races of men. It is, I imagine, a sense capable of cultivation, and enables us to look upon many of man's doings that would otherwise vex and pain us, and, as some say, destroy all the pleasure of our lives, not exactly as an illusion, as if we were Japanese and had seen a fox in the morning, but at all events in what we call a philosophic spirit.

229-241 29. The attitude of the Japanese man toward the eruption of Krakatoa can best be described as _____.
(A) foolhardy   (D) deluded
(B) angry   (E) terrified
(C) involved

29 ___

229-241 30. The lesson of the "fox in the morning" is to _____.
(A) mistrust the evidence of the senses
(B) face tragedy with indifference
(C) relish the destruction of institutions
(D) rebel against the blows of fate
(E) develop a philosophic calm

30 ___

277-280 31. As used in the passage, *transitoriness* suggests _____.
(A) preciousness
(B) variability
(C) magnificence
(D) permanence
(E) brevity

31 ___

229-241 32. A person who followed the advice in this selection would most likely _____.
(A) look at all human actions with equanimity and calm
(B) make a close study of human institutions for the lessons they teach
(C) seek natural spectacles as guides for the human spirit
(D) compare the Japanese superstition of the fox with Western beliefs
(E) try to get Japanese to give over the crippling illusion of the fox

32 ___

238-240 33. In the passage the branches on a pine or larch are compared with _____.
(A) the swift years of mankind
(B) the Japanese belief in the serenity of the spirit
(C) human institutions
(D) the tree itself
(E) the life of nations and races of men

33 ___

A basic structural design underlies every kind of writing. The writer will in part follow this design, in part deviate from it, according to his skill, his needs, and the unexpected events that accompany the act of composition. Writing, to be effective, must follow closely the thoughts of the writer, but not necessarily in the order in which those thoughts occur. This calls for a scheme of procedure. In some cases the best design is no design, as with a love letter, which is simply an outpouring, or with a casual essay, which is a ramble. But in most cases plan-

ning must be a deliberate prelude to writing.
15 The first principle of composition, therefore,
is to foresee or determine the shape of what
is to come and pursue that shape.

A sonnet is built on a fourteen-line frame,
each line containing five feet. Hence, the
20 sonneteer knows exactly where he is headed,
although he may not know how to get there.
Most forms of composition are less clearly
defined, more flexible, but all have skeletons
to which the writer will bring the flesh and
25 the blood. The more clearly he perceives the
shape, the better are his chances of success.

221-223 34. Which of the following titles best
summarizes the content of the pas-
sage?
(A) The Joys of Extemporaneous
Writing
(B) Skeletons in the Writing
Closet
(C) Form vs. Substance in Com-
position
(D) Planning: A Major Writing
Ingredient
(E) The Act of Composition

34 ___

229-241 35. With which of the following statements would the author of the passage probably disagree?
(A) The sonnet's restrictions
guide the sonneteer.
(B) Every kind of writing requires a deliberate plan.
(C) Design underlies writing,
even if it is not apparent.
(D) Most other writing is less rig-
idly controlled than the sonnet.
(E) In good writing the writer's
thoughts are carefully organized.

35 ___

270-274 36. The author's style may best be char-
acterized as _____ .
(A) flowery but informative
(B) straightforward and unpreten-
tious
(C) colloquial and artificial
(D) pointed and elegant
(E) learned and dramatic

36 ___

Planning the garden takes place, as all
the handbooks advise, long before the frost
is out of the ground, preferably on a night
recalling Keats's "Eve of St. Agnes," with
5 hail lashing the windows. The dependents
reverently produce the latest seed catalogue
and succumb to mass hypnosis. "Look at
those radishes—two feet long!" everyone
marvels. "We could have them, too, if that
10 lazy slug didn't curl up in the hammock all
day." A list of staples is speedily drawn up:
Brussels sprouts the size of a rugby, eggplant
like captive balloons, and yams. Granny
loves corn fritters; a half acre is allotted to
15 Golden Bantam. The children need a pumpkin for Halloween, and let's have plenty of
beets, we can make our own lump sugar.
Then someone discovers the hybrids—the
onion crossed with a pepper or a new vanilla-
20 flavored turnip that plays the "St. James Infirmary Blues." When the envelope is finally
sealed, the savings account is a whited
sepulcher and all we need is a forty-mule
team to haul the order from the depot.
25 The moment the trees are in bud and the
soil is ready to be worked, I generally come
down with a crippling muscular complaint
as yet unclassified by science. Suffering un-
told agonies, I nonetheless have myself
30 wheeled to the sideline and coach a small,
gnarled man of seventy in the preparation of
the seedbed. The division of labor works out
perfectly; he spades, pulverizes and rakes
the ground, while I call out encouragement
35 and dock his pay whenever he straightens up
to light his pipe. The relationship is an ideal
one, and I know he will never leave me as
long as the chain remains fastened to his leg.

256-260 37. The tone of the passage can best be described as _____ .
(A) ill natured and vitriolic
(B) confidential and ingratiating
(C) good-naturedly cynical
(D) fretfully condescending
(E) intimate and dispassionate

37 ___

266-269 38. The thrust of the writer's humor is directed at _____ .
(A) Granny and the children
(B) the gardener
(C) the garden handbooks
(D) himself
(E) the impractical plans for the garden

38 ___

256-260 39. The "crippling muscular complaint" can best be characterized as _____ .
(A) painful but not serious
(B) totally disabling
(C) caused by grueling effort
(D) mentioned for sympathy
(E) completely imaginary

39 ___

281-284 40. The last sentence in the first paragraph suggests that _____ .
(A) the writer has spent a fortune on too many seeds
(B) transportation to the writer's rural home is chancy at best
(C) the seeds are destined to die before they germinate
(D) the author seals the envelope without including payment
(E) the order, when received, proves to be incorrect

40 ___

FACSIMILE TEST 2

Section 1

PART 1

For each question in this section, choose the best answer and write the letter on the line at the right.

Each question below consists of a word in capital letters, followed by five lettered words. Choose the word that is most nearly *opposite* in meaning to the word in capital letters. Since some of the questions require you to distinguish fine shades of meaning, consider all the choices before deciding which is best.

69–73 1. ORAL:
    (A) rapid   (D) phonetic
    (B) verbal   (E) secret
    (C) written   1 ____

69–73 2. SAVOR:
    (A) favor   (D) undo
    (B) enjoy   (E) loathe
    (C) discharge   2 ____

47 3. BOTTLENECK:
    (A) relaxation   (D) foundation
    (B) impasse   (E) toehold
    (C) groundwork   3 ____

122 4. CRYPTIC:
    (A) hidden   (D) varied
    (B) grave   (E) obvious
    (C) technological   4 ____

132 5. MISSHAPEN:
    (A) fortunate   (D) ill-fated
    (B) symmetrical   (E) blessed
    (C) vague   5 ____

69–73 6. QUAINT:
    (A) customary   (D) spectacular
    (B) colorful   (E) proportionate
    (C) foreign   6 ____

140 7. SERFDOM:
    (A) freedom   (D) officialdom
    (B) martyrdom   (E) colonialism
    (C) wisdom   7 ____

89 8. OMNIPOTENT:
    (A) omniscient   (D) unwavering
    (B) many-sided   (E) underfed
    (C) weak   8 ____

125 9. KALEIDOSCOPIC:
    (A) premature   (D) visual
    (B) drab   (E) telescopic
    (C) combative   9 ____

74–76 10. INDISPUTABLE:
    (A) permanent   (D) paramount
    (B) unlovable   (E) doubtful
    (C) unequaled   10 ____

69–74 11. OVERCAST:
    (A) windy   (D) stormy
    (B) sunny   (E) depleted
    (C) underestimated   11 ____

41, 46 12. SAUCY:
    (A) flippant   (D) irrepressible
    (B) tasty   (E) dominant
    (C) shy   12 ____

77–81 13. SPARTAN:
    (A) permissive   (D) abrupt
    (B) quiet   (E) frugal
    (C) courageous   13 ____

69–73 14. ALLEGIANCE:
    (A) loyalty   (D) infidelity
    (B) support   (E) salutation
    (C) inattentiveness   14 ____

105 15. ALLEVIATE:
- (A) weigh
- (B) gladden
- (C) arouse
- (D) intend
- (E) aggravate

15 ___

PART 2

Select the word or set of words that *best* completes each of the following sentences.

6-12 16. First --- in 1865 by a group of French Republicans, Liberty was finally unveiled in New York Harbor in 1886.
- (A) advertised
- (B) completed
- (C) photographed
- (D) engineered
- (E) conceived

16 ___

13-16 17. The great horned owl, one of the most efficient and --- of all ---, occasionally kills more prey than it can eat.
- (A) docile . . birds
- (B) casual . . fliers
- (C) inept . . hunters
- (D) ruthless . . predators
- (E) amusing . . parents

17 ___

34-38 18. The dependence of public television upon public contributions for --- is a sad but --- fact of life.
- (A) expansion . . harrowing
- (B) survival . . inescapable
- (C) news . . humdrum
- (D) ratings . . captivating
- (E) audiences . . general

18 ___

17-21 19. The --- celebration of the Metropolitan Opera recalled a hundred years of great artists, innovative directors, and --- designers.
- (A) centennial . . creative
- (B) showy . . headstrong
- (C) recent . . inept
- (D) halfhearted . . indifferent
- (E) biennial . . avant-garde

19 ___

30-33 20. As the day wore on, New Delhi, at first uncomfortably warm, became --- hot and ---.
- (A) somewhat . . annoying
- (B) cloudlessly . . quiet
- (C) unbearably . . stifling
- (D) unexpectedly . . torrential
- (E) sleepily . . cheery

20 ___

PART 3

Each passage on the next page is followed by questions based on its content. Answer all questions following a passage on the basis of what is *stated* or *implied* in that passage.

"Rosemary, may I come in?" It was Philip.

"Of course."

He came in. "Oh, I'm sorry," he said, and stopped and stared.

"It's quite all right," said Rosemary smiling. "This is my friend, Miss —"

"Smith, madam," said the languid figure, who was strangely still and unafraid.

"Smith," said Rosemary. "We are going to have a little talk."

"Oh, yes," said Philip. "Quite," and his eye caught sight of the coat and hat on the floor. He came over to the fire and turned his back to it. "It's a beastly afternoon," he said curiously, still looking at that listless figure, looking at its hands and boots, and then at Rosemary again.

"Yes, isn't it?" said Rosemary enthusiastically. "Vile."

Philip smiled his charming smile. "As a matter of fact," said he, "I wanted you to come into the library for a moment. Would you? Will Miss Smith excuse us?"

The big eyes were raised to him but Rosemary answered for her. "Of course she will." And they went out of the room together.

"I say," said Philip, when they were alone. "Explain. Who is she? What does it all mean?"

Rosemary, laughing, leaned against the door and said: "I picked her up in Curzon Street. Really. She's a real pick-up. She asked me for the price of a cup of tea, and I brought her home with me."

"But what on earth are you going to do with her?" cried Philip.

"Be nice to her," said Rosemary quickly. "Be frightfully nice to her. Look after her. I don't know how. We haven't talked yet. But show her—treat her—make her feel—"

"My darling girl," said Philip, "you're quite mad, you know. It simply can't be done."

"I knew you'd say that," retorted Rosemary. "Why not? I want to. Isn't that a reason? And besides, one's always reading about these things. I decided—"

"But," said Philip slowly, and he cut the end of a cigar, "she's so astonishingly pretty."

"Pretty?" Rosemary was so surprised that she blushed. "Do you think so? I—I hadn't thought about it."

"Good Lord!" Philip struck a match. "She's absolutely lovely. Look again, my child. I was bowled over when I came into your room just now. However . . . I think you're making a ghastly mistake. Sorry, darling, if I'm crude and all that. But let me know if Miss Smith is going to dine with us in time for me to look up *The Milliner's Gazette*."

"You absurd creature!" said Rosemary, and she went out of the library, but not back to her bedroom. She went to her writing-room and sat down at her desk. Pretty! Absolutely lovely! Bowled over! Her heart beat like a heavy bell. Pretty! Lovely! She drew her cheque book towards her. But no, cheques would be no use, of course. She opened a drawer and took out five pound notes, looked at them, put two back, and holding the three squeezed in her hand, she went back to her bedroom.

266–269 21. The author's primary purpose in this passage is to _____ .

(A) expose Philip as a cruel cynic
(B) analyze, through conversation alone, the character of Rosemary
(C) suggest some of the dangers in old relationships
(D) reveal aspects of a bitter class struggle
(E) show how some people recognize beauty where others are blind

21 ___

277–280 22. The word *languid* in line 8 is meant to suggest _____ .

(A) Miss Smith's fatigue
(B) Rosemary's lack of perception
(C) Philip's curiosity
(D) Philip and Rosemary's essential malice
(E) repressed anger

22 ___

229-241 23. Rosemary's purpose in bringing the stranger home was to _____ .
   (A) make a friend of Miss Smith
   (B) provide a dinner guest
   (C) indulge a whim
   (D) understand a person from another class
   (E) make amends for a previous slight

23 ____

291-296 24. Which of the following is likely to happen next?
   (A) Philip leaves in an angry mood.
   (B) Miss Smith speaks at length with Philip.
   (C) Philip and Rosemary take Miss Smith to dinner.
   (D) Philip and Rosemary argue about Miss Smith's presence.
   (E) Rosemary sends Miss Smith away promptly.

24 ____

281-284 25. The sentence "Her heart beat like a heavy bell" suggests that Rosemary
   (A) has a physical weakness
   (B) finds she is running low on funds
   (C) is about to scream at Miss Smith
   (D) is jealous
   (E) realizes some money has been stolen

25 ____

There are, we fear, a number of people who regard Falstaff as a worthless fellow, and who would refrain (if they could) from laughing at his jests. These people do not
5 understand his claim to grateful and affectionate regard. He did more to produce that mental condition of which laughter is the expression than any man who ever lived. But for the cheering presence of him and men
10 like him, this vale of tears would be a more terrible dwelling-place than it is. In short, Falstaff has done an immense deal to alleviate misery and promote positive happiness. What more can be said of your heroes and
15 philanthropists?

It is, perhaps, characteristic of this commercial age that benevolence should be always associated, if not considered synonymous, with the giving of money. But this is
20 clearly mistaken, for we have to consider what effect the money given produces on the minds and bodies of human beings. Sir Richard Whittington was an eminently benevolent man, and spent his money freely for the
25 good of his fellow-citizens. . . . This is well. Let the sick and the poor, who enjoy his hospitality and receive his doles, bless his memory. But how much wider and further-reaching is the influence of Falstaff!
30 Those who enjoy his good things are not only the poor and the sick, but all who speak the English language. Nay, more; translation has made him the inheritance of the world, and the benefactor of the entire human race.
35 It may be, however, that some other nations fail fully to understand and appreciate the mirth and the character of the man. A Dr. G. G. Gervinus, of Heidelberg, has written, in the German language, a heavy work
40 on Shakespeare, in which he attacks Falstaff in a very solemn and determined manner and particularly charges him with selfishness and want of conscience. We are inclined to set down this malignant attack to envy. Falstaff
45 is the author and cause of universal laughter. Dr. Gervinus will never be the cause of anything universal; but, so far as his influence extends, he produces headaches. It is probably a painful sense of this contrast that
50 goads on the author of headaches to attack the author of laughter.

217-220 26. Which of the following best describes the main idea of the selection?
   (A) German criticism is biased and confusing, with limited sensibility.
   (B) Falstaff is a major contribution to the literature of laughter.
   (C) Falstaff is, far and away, Shakespeare's greatest character.
   (D) Philanthropy can never be associated with Falstaff.
   (E) Translations of Shakespeare can never do justice to his majestic verse.

26 ____

261–265 27. The author's attitude toward G. G. Gervinus is one of _____ .

(A) uncritical acceptance
(B) partial disagreement
(C) unrelieved scorn
(D) solemn appreciation
(E) unfair denunciation

27 ____

229–241 28. The "author of headaches" is none other than _____ .

(A) Shakespeare
(B) Falstaff
(C) Richard Whittington
(D) G. G. Gervinus
(E) "the author of laughter"

28 ____

232–234 29. With which of the following statements would the author agree?

(A) The gift of laughter can be greater than the gift of money.
(B) The sick and the poor alone can truly appreciate Falstaff.
(C) Life should never be characterized as a "vale of tears."
(D) Enjoyment of Shakespeare is unfortunately limited to those who speak English.
(E) Falstaff, though charming, is basically a worthless fellow.

29 ____

277–280 30. The author uses *a painful sense of this contrast* to suggest _____ .

(A) frankness   (D) awe
(B) injustice   (E) envy
(C) universality

30 ____

PART 4

Select the word or set of words that *best* completes each of the following sentences.

26–29 31. Although a bottom quark has a lifetime of only 1.5 trillionths of a second, this period is much --- than scientists had anticipated.

(A) shorter   (D) less
(B) longer   important
(C) more   (E) more
     dramatic   informative

31 ____

6–12 32. Improvements in --- and transportation have converted the entire world into a --- village.

(A) housing . . leaderless
(B) finance . . modern
(C) negotiation . . noisy
(D) individuality . . disorganized
(E) communication . . global

32 ____

26–29 33. Because of the tremendous potential for good or ill, recent progress in the field of genetic engineering has raised both --- and --- for the future.

(A) hopes . . fears
(B) challenges . . disappointments
(C) energy . . concern
(D) faith . . disbelief
(E) concerns . . anxieties

33 ____

26–29 34. At the antique car rally an ancient Franklin began slowly and --- then accelerated and --- by the judges' stand, to the delight of all spectators.

(A) grotesquely . . wheezed
(B) steadily . . inched
(C) noisily . . crept
(D) uncertainly . . whizzed
(E) sadly . . went

34 ____

34–38 35. Contrary to common beliefs about the effectiveness of a loud, ––– voice, young children are more likely to obey if they are directed in a ––– voice.

(A) discreet . . low
(B) sensitive . . colorless
(C) authoritative . . soft
(D) piercing . . high
(E) pleasing . . wavering

35 ___

PART 5

Each question below consists of a related pair of words, followed by five lettered pairs of words. Select the lettered pair that *best* expresses a relationship similar to that expressed in the original pair.

EXAMPLE

YAWN : BOREDOM ::

(A) dream : sleep
(B) anger : madness
(C) smile : amusement
(D) face : expression
(E) impatience : rebellion

C

176, 180 36. PEDIATRICIAN : CHILD ::

(A) ophthalmologist : eyes
(B) neurologist : criminals
(C) radiologist : mass media
(D) geologist : novas
(E) philosopher : sculpture

36 ___

182, 186 37. PAIN : AGONY ::

(A) drowsiness : laziness
(B) exploration : ramble
(C) industry : weakness
(D) plenty : adequacy
(E) fun : hilarity

37 ___

170–171 38. SUGAR : CANISTER ::

(A) barrel : oil
(B) table : dishes
(C) pig : sty
(D) horse : racetrack
(E) sheep : shepherd

38 ___

177–180 39. PHILANTHROPIST : GENER-OSITY ::

(A) nomad : stability
(B) knight : chivalry
(C) computer : programmer
(D) hockey : puck
(E) despot : amnesty

39 ___

181, 186 40. NEGLIGENCE : LAX ::

(A) leisure : energetic
(B) density : repetitive
(C) coincidence : skeptical
(D) novelty : fresh
(E) guile : candid

40 ___

185–186 41. TIME : MILLENNIA ::

(A) work : salary
(B) pain : aches
(C) distance : light-years
(D) weight : liters
(E) joys : laughter

41 ___

179–180 42. SCULPTOR : CHISEL ::

(A) carpenter : square
(B) wrench : plumber
(C) pilot : airplane
(D) surveyor : mortgage
(E) lawyer : automobile

42 ___

166, 171 43. HARMLESS : SCOUNDREL ::

    (A) ingenious : milliner
    (B) brilliant : moron
    (C) agent : condescending
    (D) literate : editor
    (E) studious : scholar

43 ___

174–175 44. FLOWER : SNAPDRAGON ::

    (A) flounder : perch
    (B) bread : doughnut
    (C) collie : spaniel
    (D) oak : elm
    (E) mineral : iron

44 ___

174–175 45. ENGRAVE : PLATE ::

    (A) purchase : presentation
    (B) strike : clock
    (C) find : excuses
    (D) bind : book
    (E) try : plan

45 ___

Section 2

PART 1

For each question in this section, choose the best answer and write the letter on the line at the right.

Each question below consists of a word in capital letters, followed by five lettered words. Choose the word that is most nearly *opposite* in meaning to the word in capital letters. Since some of the questions require you to distinguish fine shades of meaning, consider all the choices before deciding which is best.

EXAMPLE

GOOD:
- (A) sour
- (B) bad
- (C) red
- (D) hot
- (E) ugly

B

69–73   1. ACQUIT:
- (A) disentangle
- (B) criticize
- (C) pass judgment
- (D) convict
- (E) revolve

1 ___

87, 97   2. APPREHEND:
- (A) release
- (B) understand
- (C) misinform
- (D) comply
- (E) prevent

2 ___

118   3. HYPERCRITICAL:
- (A) insincere
- (B) insecure
- (C) scrupulous
- (D) undemanding
- (E) unwary

3 ___

77, 81   4. TITANIC:
- (A) ungodly
- (B) small
- (C) quiet
- (D) slipshod
- (E) moderate

4 ___

74–76   5. INSATIABLE:
- (A) pleasurable
- (B) satisfactory
- (C) pliable
- (D) believable
- (E) satisfied

5 ___

41, 46   6. DOWN:
- (A) feather
- (B) oblique
- (C) cheerful
- (D) fretful
- (E) around

6 ___

69–73   7. NOTORIOUS:
- (A) infamous
- (B) celebrated
- (C) offensive
- (D) flawed
- (E) respectable

7 ___

69–73   8. FLAUNT:
- (A) flout
- (B) conceal
- (C) flatter
- (D) obey
- (E) corrupt

8 ___

74–76   9. INEXHAUSTIBLE:
- (A) renewable
- (B) puny
- (C) barren
- (D) powerful
- (E) marketable

9 ___

132 10. MISGIVING:
- (A) assurance
- (B) acceptance
- (C) indecisiveness
- (D) modesty
- (E) generosity

10 ___

ENGLISH FOR THE COLLEGE BOARDS

PART 2

Select the word or set of words that *best* completes each of the following sentences.

22-25 11. Initial reserve soon disappeared, and the gathering of bird-watchers soon became as --- as a congregation of first-graders on the school playground.

(A) dignified   (D) subtle
(B) exuberant   (E) impressive
(C) mischievous

11 ___

30-33 12. The more the insect tried to disentangle itself from the spider's web, the more --- it became.

(A) wary   (D) angry
(B) formidable   (E) enmeshed
(C) careless

12 ___

26-29 13. Although most people consider cities --- wildlife, birds and even mammals --- in even the most unlikely urban areas.

(A) favorable toward . . thrive
(B) devoid of . . deteriorate
(C) receptive toward . . appear
(D) alien to . . . abound
(E) unconcerned with . . dart

13 ___

6-12 14. The book *The Evening Stars* presents a history of television's evening news programs, with --- those news anchors who came to --- the news.

(A) disregard for . . lead
(B) minor attention to . . enjoy
(C) description of . . study
(D) emphasis upon . . dominate
(E) affection for . . represent

14 ___

30-33 15. Plentiful and crystal clear at its source, the Arkansas River becomes less and less --- as it flows east, finally disappearing on the --- Kansas plains.

(A) abundant . . dry
(B) powerful . . fruitful
(C) beautiful . . moisture-laden
(D) polluted . . unplowed
(E) available . . hilly

15 ___

PART 3

Each question below consists of a related pair of words or phrases, followed by five lettered pairs of words or phrases. Select the lettered pair that *best* expresses a relationship similar to that expressed in the original pair.

168, 171 16. HIGH : AERIE::

(A) puzzling : dishonesty
(B) faithful : heretic
(C) exaggerated : caricature
(D) timid : swashbuckler
(E) picturesque : idol

16 ___

177-180 17. SHIP : NAVIGATOR::

(A) angler : lake
(B) stage : actor
(C) bookkeeper : studio
(D) office : puppeteer
(E) fire engine : nurse

17 ___

170-171 18. GERMINATE : GROWTH::
  (A) chuckle : humor
  (B) drop : chair
  (C) try : failure
  (D) harden : brittleness
  (E) combine : mixture

18 ____

169, 171 19. SOLAR SYSTEM : EARTH::
  (A) nebula : galaxy
  (B) comet : meteor
  (C) planet : satellite
  (D) sun : sunspots
  (E) asteroid : moon

19 ____

183, 186 20. AGRICULTURE : WEATHER::
  (A) prices : demand
  (B) wool : sheep
  (C) enthusiasm : lubrication
  (D) sincerity : radiation
  (E) wealth : formality

20 ____

178, 180 21. PIONEER : TRAILBLAZING::
  (A) typesetter : authorship
  (B) novelist : censure
  (C) pirate : theft
  (D) flight : fugitive
  (E) usher : entertainment

21 ____

172, 175 22. INCONVENIENCE : CALAMITY::
  (A) colorless : dull
  (B) fear : terror
  (C) fault : blame
  (D) diplomacy : tact
  (E) hysteria : reassurance

22 ____

184, 186 23. ETYMOLOGY : DERIVATIONS::
  (A) archaeology : rivers
  (B) entomology : primates
  (C) cosmology : decoration
  (D) ornithology : birds
  (E) analogy : argumentation

23 ____

174-175 24. ROD : FISHING::
  (A) ski : bobsledding
  (B) football : volleyball
  (C) javelin : shot put
  (D) sailing : oar
  (E) bow : archery

24 ____

173, 175 25. YEAR : DECADE::
  (A) comma : period
  (B) sapling : tree
  (C) hawk : falcon
  (D) anniversary : party
  (E) university : college

25 ____

PART 4

Each passage below is followed by questions based on its content. Answer all questions following a passage on the basis of what is *stated* or *implied* in the passage.

In the long run, though, the future of the infant clock industry lay with the bourgeoisie—originally and literally the residents of the *bourgs* (in colloquial American English, the *burgs*). Along with the crown, indeed in alliance with it, the town was the great beneficiary of the agricultural and commercial expansion of the high Middle Ages (eleventh to fourteenth centuries). Sleepy villages were becoming busy marketplaces; administrative centers and points of transshipment and exchange were growing into nodes of wholesale and retail trade and craft industry. The more successful residents of these new cities quickly came to constitute a new elite, an urban patriciate possessed of great wealth and a sense of power and self-esteem that rivaled that of the older landed elite. They were able, further, by shrewd cooperation with the crown and the construction of an urban military base, to win substantial autonomy for their municipalities, which were organized by collective agreement among the residents and by contractual arrangement with or concession from higher authority into self-administering communes. These had

their own fiscal resources, so that when mechanical clocks appeared on the scene, the
cities of western and Mediterranean Europe
30 could afford to build them as complements
to or successors to the cathedrals—a symbol
of a new secular dignity and power and a
contribution to the general welfare.

Why the general welfare? Because, just
35 like the monastery, the city needed to know
the time even before the mechanical clock
became available. Here, too, necessity was
the mother of invention.

217-220 26. Which of the following expresses
the main idea of the passage?
(A) Sleepy villages fostered the
rise of the bourgeoisie.
(B) Mediterranean Europe put
clocks on cathedrals for prestige purposes.
(C) The history of clocks was
shaped largely by the dwellers in cities.
(D) The alliance of the church
and the nobility made clocks
a needed commodity.
(E) The older elite made the cities prosperous.

26 ___

229-241 27. The ''new elite'' (line 15)
(A) lived in palatial mansions in
the country
(B) cooperated closely with the
older landed elite
(C) ordered mechanical clocks
from cottage industries near
the cities
(D) possessed wealth and a sense
of power
(E) had only meager fiscal resources

27 ___

281-284 28. As used here in a figurative sense,
the crown refers to _____ .
(A) landed gentry
(B) displaced royalty
(C) the power of the old elite
(D) local representatives of gov-
ernment
(E) the king and his government

28 ___

277-280 29. As used in this selection *nodes* (line
13) means _____ .
(A) centering points
(B) examples
(C) models
(D) representatives
(E) agents

29 ___

285-289 30. With which of the following statements would the author probably
NOT agree?
(A) Clocks are essential for the
growth of an industrial and
commercial society.
(B) During the late Middle Ages
clocks performed an almost
exclusively decorative function.
(C) The bourgeoisie were able to
secure a great deal of freedom for their municipalities.
(D) Great agricultural and commercial expansion took place
during the high Middle Ages.
(E) The town, rather than the village, became more important
as the high Middle Ages
rolled on.

30 ___

Despite the amazing recent progress of
computer technology, and the popular media
portrayal of intelligent robots, the kind of
humanoid robot found in science-fiction
5 movies is a long way off. Every human infant can do three things that no computer is
yet able to do—recognize a face, understand
a natural language and walk on two legs.
After two decades of robotics research, the
10 experts have concluded that making a robot
is considerably more complicated than simply linking together a television camera, a
microphone speaker, a mechanical hand and
a portable computer and then putting the
15 whole assemblage on wheels. In addition to
visual, locomotive and manipulation abilities, robots must also be capable of planning,
problem-solving and decision-making if they
are to mimic even the most rudimentary hu-
20 man skills.

Even tasks as elementary as piling boxes
on top of one another or pushing a crate off
a platform require highly sophisticated soft-
ware systems. Take the matter of vision. If

25 a computer is to recognize objects in a visual
scene, it must have some advance knowledge about the objects it's seeing.

266-269 31. The purpose of the author seems to
be to _____ .
(A) glorify the robot at the expense of man
(B) pay special tribute to the skill
of a newborn infant
(C) emphasize some of the limitations of robots
(D) recommend the use of a computer in every home
(E) commend the popular media
for the explanation of robotics

31 ___

285-289 32. For imitating human skills, all the
following are mentioned as neces-
sary EXCEPT _____ .
(A) visual skill
(B) planning
(C) locomotive skills
(D) arithmetic calculations
(E) manipulation abilities

32 ___

246-249 33. Which of the following statements
may be accurately derived from the
selection?
I. The typical science-fiction robot is
not yet available.
II. After 20 years of research, scien-
tists have acquired a new humility
about humanoid robots.
III. A child is very efficient in a task
requiring patience and repetition.
IV. Though a robot cannot yet under-
stand a natural language, it is able
to recognize a face.
V. The best robots are put on wheels.
(A) I, III, and V
(B) II and IV
(C) IV and V
(D) I, II, and III
(E) I and II

33 ___

Boston was another Edinburgh, with
marked variations of its own. It resembled
Edinburgh in many ways, as New England
resembled Scotland. The bitter climate and
5 the hard soil, the ice, the granite and the
Calvinism, yielding to more gracious forms
of faith, the common schools, the thrifty
farmer-folk, the coastline, with its ports and
sailors' customs, the abundant lakes and
10 mountains, the geological aspects of the region, all suggested the land of Sir Walter
Scott, as well as the adjacent land of Wordsworth, whose bareness and simplicity, together with his loftiness and depth—proofs,
15 as Hazlitt said, that his work was written in
a mountainous country—commended him to
the young New England mind; and if, in this
mind, there was something cold and hard
that recalled the ice and the granite, there
20 were reserves of feeling and perception that
were to find expression in the years to come.
A well-known Scottish traveller remarked of
Boston, "I could scarcely believe I was not
in Scotland." One found there, as in Edin-
25 burgh, the same wealth, similarly earned,
the same regard for manners and decorum,
the same respect for learning, the same religious point of view, alike in its antecedents
and in its liberal modifications, the same
30 scrupulous conscientiousness, the same
punctiliousness and the same pride, even the
same prudence. One found the same exac-
tions in matters of taste, the same aristocratic
prepossessions and the same democratic
35 feeling underneath them. The golden calf the
Bostonians worshiped was a mere pygmy, as
Dickens said, a generation later, beside the
giant effigies one found in the other American cities.

221-223 34. Which of the following titles best
summarizes the content of the pas-
sage?
(A) Boston: The Edinburgh of
New England
(B) The Effect of Environment on
Culture
(C) Boston, City of Ice and Gran-
ite
(D) A Tale of Two Cities
(E) The People of Boston

34 ___

229-241 35. New Englanders liked to read Wordsworth because _____.

(A) his flowery poetry contrasted with the New England scene

(B) they recognized in him a kindred spirit

(C) Sir Walter Scott had recommended him

(D) Wordsworth composed his verse in the mountains

(E) Wordsworth became associated in their minds with Edinburgh

35 ___

238-240 36. The "reserves of feeling and perception" (line 20) _____.

(A) contrasted with the ice and granite of the New England mind

(B) proved to the Scottish traveller that Boston was not as interesting as Edinburgh

(C) contradicted Hazlitt's comments about Boston

(D) showed that Bostonians were democrats as well as aristocrats

(E) were locked inside, never to play a role in Boston's future

36 ___

232-234 37. The meaning of the last sentence may be summarized in this way.

(A) Dickens considered the qualities of Boston more objectionable than those of other cities.

(B) Though Bostonians were interested in money, other American cities far outdid them in this respect.

(C) Bostonians worshiped a pagan idol while keeping a proper pretense for the world.

(D) A small calf symbolized the great wealth that Boston had amassed in a generation.

(E) Bostonians favored freedom of worship perhaps more than any other city in America.

37 ___

The truest and most profound observations on intelligence have in the past been made by the poets and, in recent times, by story writers. They have been keen observers and recorders and reckoned freely with the emotions and sentiments. Most philosophers, on the other hand, have exhibited a grotesque ignorance of man's life and have built up systems that are elaborate and imposing, but quite unrelated to actual human affairs. They have almost consistently neglected the actual process of thought and have set the mind off as something apart to be studied by itself. But no such mind, exempt from bodily processes, animal impulses, savage traditions, infantile impressions, conventional reactions, and traditional knowledge, ever existed, even in the case of the most abstract of metaphysicians. Kant entitled his great work *A Critique of Pure Reason.* But to the modern student of mind pure reason seems as mythical as the pure gold, transparent as glass, with which the celestial city is paved.

We do not think enough about thinking, and much of our confusion is the result of current illusions in regard to it. Let us forget for the moment any impressions we may have derived from the philosophers, and see what seems to happen in ourselves. The first thing that we notice is that our thought moves with such incredible rapidity that it is almost impossible to arrest any specimen of it long enough to have a look at it. When we are offered a penny for our thoughts, we always find that we have recently had so many things in mind that we can easily make a selection which will not compromise us too nakedly. On inspection we shall find that even if we are not downright ashamed of a great part of our spontaneous thinking, it is far too intimate, personal, ignoble, or trivial to permit us to reveal more than a small part of it. I believe this must be true of everyone. We do not, of course, know what goes on in other people's heads. They tell us very little and we tell them very little. The spigot of speech, rarely fully opened, could never emit more than driblets of the ever-renewed hogshead of thought. We find it hard to believe that other people's thoughts are as silly as our own, but they probably are.

38. The author apparently believes that _____ .

(A) thought is essentially a direct, logical process

(B) thinking should be divorced from emotions and sentiments

(C) Kant named his book *A Critique of Pure Reason* as a witty jest

(D) a mind is a pure abstraction, unpolluted by extraneous impulses

(E) poets do more real thinking that philosophers

38 ___

39. "The pure gold, transparent as glass" is compared with _____ .

(A) the paving in the celestial city

(B) the mind of the philosopher

(C) pure reason

(D) the effects of savage traditions and infantile impressions

(E) the writings of Kant

39 ___

40. According to the author, most of our thoughts are _____ .

(A) motivated by greed

(B) directed toward positive goals

(C) significant but personal

(D) haphazard and fleeting

(E) readily apparent to our friends

40 ___

FACSIMILE TEST 3

Section 1

PART 1

For each question in this section, choose the best answer and write the letter on the line at the right.

Each question below consists of a word in capital letters, followed by five lettered words or phrases. Choose the word that is most nearly *opposite* in meaning to the word in capital letters. Since some of the questions require you to distinguish fine shades of meaning, consider all the choices before deciding which is best.

69–73 1. BAN:

    (A) allow   (D) enclose

    (B) control   (E) deter

    (C) deflect   1 ___

132 2. OFFHAND:

    (A) casual   (D) extreme

    (B) backward   (E) callous

    (C) prepared   2 ___

41, 46 3. SULKY:

    (A) comely   (D) lackluster

    (B) smooth   (E) cheerful

    (C) irritable   3 ___

74–76 4. IMPRESSIONABLE:

    (A) naive   (D) shy

    (B) vigorous   (E) indifferent

    (C) excitable   4 ___

95 5. DORMANT:

    (A) biting   (D) active

    (B) colorful   (E) drowsy

    (C) repressed   5 ___

69–73 6. ADAMANT:

    (A) brilliant   (D) yielding

    (B) hard   (E) apparent

    (C) laudatory   6 ___

87, 95 7. PROFUSION:

    (A) confusion   (D) scarcity

    (B) discipline   (E) complexity

    (C) support   7 ___

123 8. HETEROGENEOUS:

    (A) well   (D) sullen

        distributed   (E) obscure

    (B) identical

    (C) unclassified   8 ___

47 9. HONEYED:

    (A) syrupy

    (B) tasty

    (C) defrauded

    (D) blameworthy

    (E) biting   9 ___

105 10. DIMINUTIVE:

    (A) amiable   (D) musical

    (B) huge   (E) fierce

    (C) capable   10 ___

69–73 11. DEBONAIR:

    (A) defiant   (D) swanky

    (B) carefree   (E) enclosed

    (C) coarse   11 ___

47 12. COMEDOWN:

    (A) achievement

    (B) despair

    (C) laughter

    (D) assent

    (E) advertisement   12 ___

87, 96 13. PROJECT:

    (A) instill   (D) impel

    (B) compress   (E) retrain

    (C) retract   13 ___

74-76 14. AROMATIC:
    (A) spicy   (D) salty
    (B) offensive   (E) damp
    (C) fresh

14 ___

77-81 15. JOVIAL:
    (A) glum
    (B) merry
    (C) downtrodden
    (D) polished
    (E) critical

15 ___

PART 2

Each sentence below has one or two blanks, each blank indicating that something has been omitted. Beneath the sentence are five lettered words or sets of words. Choose the word or set of words that *best* fits the meaning of the sentence as a whole.

26-29 16. The --- heat at midday was briefly relieved by a thunderstorm, but a short time later the temperatures again began to climb.
    (A) anticipated   (D) dappled
    (B) moderate   (E) oppressive
    (C) timely

16 ___

26-29 17. Though playwrights can usually manage a good first act, by the middle of the last act, --- often replaces ---.
    (A) consternation . . contemplation
    (B) desperation . . inspiration
    (C) deliberation . . commendation
    (D) cancellation . . alteration
    (E) stagnation . . disorganization

17 ___

6-12 18. The --- of many coastal plains and moors for housing and other development has --- many fine ecological habitats.
    (A) inaccessibility . . uncovered
    (B) analysis . . displayed
    (C) suitability . . doomed
    (D) advertisement . . enhanced
    (E) exclusion . . emphasized

18 ___

26-29 19. On our Spaceship, Earth, recycling is not a --- to be --- but a necessity to guide our actions.
    (A) concept . . followed
    (B) plant . . adapted
    (C) dream . . fantasized
    (D) luxury . . indulged
    (E) discipline . . fostered

19 ___

22-25 20. Like an airplane in a steep power dive, the falcon --- down upon the --- sparrows and captured a terrified victim.
    (A) swooped . . scattering
    (B) lunged . . assembled
    (C) flew . . disinterested
    (D) looked . . sluggish
    (E) circled . . courageous

20 ___

PART 3

Each passage below is followed by questions based on its content. Answer all questions following a passage on the basis of what is *stated* or *implied* in that passage.

Seated before a roast or a fowl, Gant began a heavy clangor on his steel and carving knife, distributing thereafter Gargantuan portions to each plate. Eugene feasted from
5 a high chair by his father's side, filled his distending belly until it was drumtight, and was permitted to stop eating by his watchful sire only when his stomach was impregnable to the heavy prod of Gant's big finger.
10 "There's a soft place there," he would roar, and he would cover the scoured plate of his infant son with another heavy slab of beef. That their machinery withstood this hammerhanded treatment was a tribute to
15 their vitality and Eliza's cookery.
Gant ate ravenously and without caution. He was immoderately fond of fish, and he invariably choked upon a bone while eating it. This happened hundreds of times, but each
20 time he would look up suddenly with a howl of agony and terror, groaning and crying out strongly while a half-dozen hands pounded violently on his back.
"Merciful God!" he would gasp finally,
25 "I thought I was done for that time."
"I'll vow, Mr. Gant," Eliza was vexed. "Why on earth don't you watch what you're doing? If you didn't eat so fast you wouldn't always get choked."
30 The children, staring, but relieved, settled slowly back in their places.

217-220 21. The chief focus of the passage is on which of the following?
(A) Describing a typical meal in a middle-class family
(B) Portraying the character of Gant
(C) Sermonizing on the dangers of eating rapidly
(D) Praising moderation in all things
(E) Suggesting that a roast is a better meat than fish

21 ____

229-241 22. Of Gant it might reasonably be said that _____.
(A) he was a devoted father and husband
(B) he believed in moderation in all things
(C) he was cruel to Eliza
(D) he didn't learn from experience
(E) he was careful not to make the children nervous

22 ____

242-255 23. Gant prodded Eugene's belly to _____.
(A) make sure Eugene was completely stuffed
(B) keep the baby awake
(C) irritate Eliza
(D) keep the children in line
(E) show his favoritism for the youngest child

23 ____

261-265 24. The author's attitude toward Gant's table behavior is one of _____.
(A) awe
(B) endorsement
(C) fury
(D) envy
(E) disapproval

24 ____

277-280 25. As used in this selection, *Gargantuan* (line 3) means _____.
(A) modest   (D) tasty
(B) thrifty   (E) rationed
(C) huge   25 ____

Man alone, of all creatures, is faced with the problem of deciding his own future because of the peculiar and unique survival mechanism he has developed, his symbol-using capacity. Through it he controls and molds and changes his environment to a degree not approached by any animal. It is the one characteristic that clearly distinguishes him from all other forms of life. It is his most powerful tool and weapon, both useful and dangerous to himself and to others.

Through the use of symbols he does something no other creature can do: he can transmit knowledge from generation to generation. He alone does not have to start each generation from scratch. He alone can use the knowledge accumulated in the past, learn in the present, and transmit to the future. He stands on the shoulders of the dead to peer into the future. Think of the vast numbers of speculations, observations, experiments, learnings by millions of men over thousands of years, the arduous, repeated trials and errors, the grand insights of geniuses which, transmitted through symbols, enable a young student to span the learning of centuries and write upon a blackboard the simple, beautiful, elegant equation, $E = mc^2$. Because we are able to span time through the use of symbols, Korzybski called this our "time-binding" ability and man the "time-binding" form of life.

Research to date indicates that all men belong to one species and all have the same time-binding potential, rooted in the enormous elaboration and development of his cerebral cortex and in the neurological structures associated with it. No one group, *as a group*, is inherently superior or inferior to any other. On a statistical basis we expect to find relatively the same percentage of sub-average, average, and above-average in each ethnic group. Superiority in knowledge, technical development, and arts, is presumed to be due to environmental and cultural conditions and not to any heritable superiority in neurological structure.

221-223 26. Which of the following titles best summarizes the content of the passage?
(A) Symbols vs. Reality
(B) Our Time-Binding Ability
(C) Man vs. Animal
(D) The Theories of Korzybski
(E) Deciding the Future

26 ____

242-255 27. The equation $E = mc^2$ is cited as dependent upon _____ .
(A) an incredible breakthrough by Korzybski
(B) the achievements of ethnic groups
(C) a young student at the blackboard
(D) a lucky accident by a researcher of genius
(E) the accumulated wisdom of the ages

27 ____

281-284 28. Which of the following most effectively used *figurative language* to make the author's point?
(A) "It is the one characteristic that clearly distinguishes him from all other forms of life."
(B) "He alone can use the knowledge accumulated in the past."
(C) "He stands on the shoulders of the dead to peer into the future."
(D) "No one group, *as a group*, is inherently superior or inferior to any other."
(E) "On a statistical basis we expect to find relatively the same percentage of sub-average, average, and above-average in each ethnic group."

28 ____

246-249 29. Which of the following statements may be accurately derived from the selection?

I. Man's control of his environment is traceable to his time-binding ability.

II. As a group, no group is basically more intelligent than any other.

III. Animals can transmit knowledge from generation to generation.

IV. Symbols are intimately connected with time binding.

V. The cerebral cortex is strongly developed in most animals.

(A) I, II, V   (D) III, V
(B) I, III, IV   (E) all
(C) I, II, IV

29 _____

229-231 30. A good definition of *time binding* is _____ .

(A) controlling time through the use of symbols
(B) trusting that time will solve problems
(C) putting past ages into categories for study
(D) a time awareness shared by man and the higher animals
(E) trying to predict the future in terms of the past

30 _____

PART 4

Select the word or set of words that *best* completes the following.

26-29 31. Though perpetual motion has long been classified as an impossible dream, --- inventors still try to patent machines that are supposed to run forever.

(A) informed   (D) candid
(B) callous   (E) undaunted
(C) biased

31 _____

6-12 32. In an attempt to stop the --- filibuster, some senators mapped strategy to --- the cloture rule.

(A) interminable . . enforce
(B) amusing . . dramatize
(C) unexpected . . discuss
(D) simple . . research
(E) enlightening . . evaluate

32 _____

6-12 33. The ranger explained, to our ---, that there is no typical "sled dog," that many breeds have proved suitable for the --- demands of exertion in temperatures below zero.

(A) consternation . . delicate
(B) horror . . occasional
(C) surprise . . rigorous
(D) amusement . . unfair
(E) satisfaction . . expected

33 _____

26-29 34. Events in the Olympics are not ---, for many events once popular have been dropped and, ---, many new events have been added.

(A) dull . . certainly
(B) controlled . . surprisingly
(C) changeable . . similarly
(D) unvarying . . conversely
(E) historical . . advantageously

34 _____

6-12 35. Tour groups in the South Pacific --- seem to find that explorer Captain James Cook --- them, whether the scene is Hawaii, Tahiti, or New Caledonia.

(A) doggedly . . outdid
(B) inevitably . . preceded
(C) breathlessly . . foresaw
(D) irritably . . missed
(E) complacently . . avoided

35 _____

PART 5

Each question below consists of a related pair of words followed by five lettered pairs of words. Select the lettered pair that *best* expresses a relationship similar to that expressed in the original pair.

181, 186 36. STEAM : SCALD::

(A) mist : reveal
(B) telescope : photograph
(C) ice : chill
(D) waterfall : display
(E) tree : leaf

36 ___

166, 171 37. EXCESSIVE : SCARCITY::

(A) cruel : joy
(B) energetic : fatigue
(C) curious : vigor
(D) numerous : quantity
(E) serious : play

37 ___

179–180 38. AERIALIST : TRAPEZE::

(A) makeup : clown
(B) score : singer
(C) jogger : routine
(D) circus : ringmaster
(E) pathfinder : compass

38 ___

170–171 39. TRIP : STUMBLE::

(A) weep : shout
(B) dominate : befriend
(C) try : err
(D) amuse : laugh
(E) eject : recall

39 ___

185–186 40. FOOT-POUND : WORK::

(A) kilowatt-hour : electricity
(B) land : acre
(C) dollar : gold
(D) sigh : sadness
(E) pound : liquid

40 ___

183, 186 41. WEED : GARDEN::

(A) trim : hedge
(B) describe : scene
(C) enjoy : concert
(D) soar : sailplane
(E) add : numbers

41 ___

166, 171 42. NURTURE : SUPPORTIVE::

(A) object : rude
(B) save : frugal
(C) fret : funny
(D) judge : argumentative
(E) reprimand : sorrowful

42 ___

177, 180 43. ARBITER : IMPARTIALITY::

(A) angler : ingenuity
(B) gardener : diversity
(C) artist : creativity
(D) hunter : compassion
(E) musician : serenity

43 ___

166, 171 44. MALICE : HUMANE::

(A) crusade : evangelical
(B) health : painstaking
(C) accord : agreeable
(D) accident : incidental
(E) farce : serious

44 ___

174–175 45. MOON : TIDES::

(A) pen : pencil
(B) dog : kennel
(C) friend : acquaintance
(D) weather : crops
(E) telephone : message

45 ___

Section 2

PART 1

For each question in this section, choose the best answer and write the letter on the line at the right.

Each question below consists of a word in capital letters, followed by five lettered words. Choose the word that is most nearly *opposite* in meaning to the word in capital letters. Since some of the questions require you to distinguish fine shades of meaning, consider all the choices before deciding which is best.

123 1. DYNAMIC:
  (A) electronic   (D) aroused
  (B) energetic   (E) feeble
  (C) mechanical
  1 ___

47 2. GLARING:
  (A) glowing   (D) daring
  (B) unseen   (E) offensive
  (C) obvious
  2 ___

132 3. FORBADE:
  (A) authorized
  (B) dissented
  (C) told in advance
  (D) argued
  (E) preferred
  3 ___

74–76 4. UNIMPAIRED:
  (A) doubled   (D) injured
  (B) unique   (E) improved
  (C) unmatched
  4 ___

107 5. VACUOUS:
  (A) heavy   (D) evil
  (B) full   (E) exhausted
  (C) exalted
  5 ___

69–73 6. ARID:
  (A) understated   (D) fruitful
  (B) afflicted   (E) sandy
  (C) fundamental
  6 ___

69–73 7. INSOLENT:
  (A) lazy
  (B) contemptuous
  (C) courteous
  (D) sensitive
  (E) cutting
  7 ___

41–46 8. HACKNEYED:
  (A) trite   (D) handwritten
  (B) ample   (E) creative
  (C) complete
  8 ___

87, 99 9. INVINCIBLE:
  (A) vulnerable   (D) portable
  (B) manageable   (E) comparable
  (C) tolerable
  9 ___

87 10. DILATE:
  (A) draw   (D) digress
  (B) contract   (E) apply
  (C) expand
  10 ___

PART 2

Each sentence below has one or two blanks, each blank indicating that something has been omitted. Beneath the sentence are five lettered words or sets of words. Choose the word or set of words that *best* fits the meaning of the sentence as a whole.

13–16 11. Many tennis experts suggest that the difference between the greats in tennis and the nearly greats is more a matter of ––– and single-mindedness of purpose rather than raw ability.

(A) talent
(B) dexterity
(C) egotism
(D) concentration
(E) guile

11 ___

6–12 12. Looking like something out of –––, a new X-ray machine can explore the body from every angle without making ––– and putting a scalpel to the patient.

(A) mystery stories . . an enquiry
(B) science fiction . . an incision
(C) motion pictures . . a fuss
(D) westerns . . a diagnosis
(E) fantasy . . a disturbance

12 ___

26–29 13. ––– gas furnaces may run at 65 percent efficiency or less, but a ––– breakthrough now offers furnaces with efficiency ratings of 96 percent or more.

(A) Conventional . . technological
(B) Rejected . . former
(C) Natural . . modest
(D) Ancient . . well-documented
(E) Unpopular . . costly

13 ___

34–38 14. The vice-presidency is widely considered a do-nothing office with little or no –––; yet there is never a shortage of applicants for that ––– lowly position.

(A) money . . truly
(B) regrets . . apparently
(C) clout . . disgracefully
(D) reward . . historically
(E) prestige . . supposedly

14 ___

26–29 15. The All-Star game is a ––– affair, offering the opportunity of making a great play and becoming a hero or committing a serious error and becoming an object of –––.

(A) breathless . . wonderment
(B) typical . . scorn
(C) one-shot . . criticism
(D) well-publicized . . analysis
(E) nightmare . . approval

15 ___

PART 3

Each question on the next page consists of a related pair of words, followed by five lettered pairs of words. Select the lettered pair that *best* expresses a relationship similar to that expressed in the original pair

188, 186 16. UTOPIA : PERFECTION ::
  (A) anesthesia : activity
  (B) uproar : noise
  (C) impudence : attention
  (D) contract : contribution
  (E) authority : commendation

16 ____

166, 171 17. INFINITY : BOUNDLESS ::
  (A) emotion : satisfying
  (B) gullibility : credulous
  (C) distinction : similarity
  (D) aptness : dexterity
  (E) deviation : repetition

17 ____

176, 180 18. SOOTHSAYER : FORETELLS ::
  (A) whimpers : puppy
  (B) soloist : animates
  (C) accountant : calculates
  (D) amateur : personifies
  (E) welder : glows

18 ____

170–171 19. FILE : CORRESPONDENCE ::
  (A) drawer : desk
  (B) stream : brook
  (C) book : concept
  (D) closet : clothing
  (E) room : window

19 ____

174–175 20. BEAGLE : DOG ::
  (A) sapphire : gem
  (B) cheetah : leopard
  (C) salamander : snake
  (D) beech : oak
  (E) insect : spider

20 ____

166, 171 21. PSEUDONYM : AUTHENTIC ::
  (A) flicker : flame
  (B) deliberation : reasonable
  (C) writer : anonymity
  (D) delay : punctual
  (E) measure : proportional

21 ____

178, 180 22. APPRENTICE : LEARN ::
  (A) penitent : rejoice
  (B) humanitarian : observe
  (C) devotee : fear
  (D) blackguard : reclaim
  (E) charlatan : deceive

22 ____

166, 171 23. BLASÉ : APATHY ::
  (A) lacking : deficiency
  (B) defense : armored
  (C) convex : microscopic
  (D) argumentative : conundrum
  (E) pagan : religious

23 ____

172, 175 24. NICK : GOUGE ::
  (A) niche : chip
  (B) crater : lava
  (C) dislike : detest
  (D) lethal : deadly
  (E) correction : fact

24 ____

169, 171 25. SUBHEAD : OUTLINE ::
  (A) song : recitation
  (B) lamp : light
  (C) clock : chime
  (D) lion : paw
  (E) sole : shoe

25 ____

PART 4

Each passage on the next page is followed by questions based on its content. Answer all questions following a passage on the basis of what is *stated* or *implied* in that passage.

And if extraterrestrial civilizations have visited Earth and have, on principle, left us to develop freely and undisturbed, might they have visited Earth so recently that human
5 beings had come into existence and were aware of them?

All cultures, after all, have tales of beings with supernormal powers who created and guided human beings in primitive days and
10 who taught them various aspects of technology. Can such tales of gods have arisen from the dim memory of visits of extraterrestrials to Earth in ages not too long past? Instead of life having been seeded on the planet from
15 outer space, could technology have been planted here? Might the extraterrestrials not merely have allowed civilization to develop here, but actually helped it?

It is an intriguing thought, but there is
20 no evidence in its favor that is in the least convincing.

Certainly, human beings need no visitors from outer space in order to be inspired to create legends. Elaborate legends with only
25 the dimmest kernels of truth have been based on such people as Alexander the Great and Charlemagne, who were completely human actors in the historical drama.

For that matter, even a fictional character
30 such as Sherlock Holmes has been invested with life and reality by millions over the world, and an endless flood of tales is still invented concerning him.

Secondly, the thought that any form of
35 technology sprang up suddenly in human history, or that any artifact was too complex for the humans of the time, so that the intervention of a more sophisticated culture must be assumed is about as surely wrong
40 as anything can be.

This dramatic supposition has received its most recent reincarnation in the books of Eric von Däniken. He finds all sorts of ancient works either too enormous (like the
45 pyramids of Egypt) or too mysterious (like markings in the sands of Peru) to be of human manufacture.

Archeologists, however, are quite convinced that even the pyramids could be built
50 with not more than the techniques available in 2500 B.C., plus human ingenuity and muscle. It is a mistake to believe that the ancients were not every bit as intelligent as we. Their technology was more primitive, but their
55 brains were not.

261–265 26. The author's attitude toward the possibility of visitors from outer space can best be characterized as _____.

(A) excitedly positive
(B) quietly skeptical
(C) paradoxically contradictory
(D) generally receptive
(E) unexpectedly indifferent

26 ___

229–241 27. Stories about Alexander the Great and Charlemagne demonstrate _____.

(A) a completely fictional source
(B) the gullibility of Eric von Däniken
(C) a tie-in with visits by extraterrestrials
(D) the influence of primitive technology
(E) the legend-making abilities of human beings

27 ___

246–249 28. Which of the following statements may be accurately derived from the selection?

I. Though supposedly a fictional character, Sherlock Holmes actually existed.
II. The great pyramids of Egypt could have been created by people with the technology of the times.
III. The belief in extraterrestrial visitors springs from motivating yearnings in all cultures.
IV. Though slight, the evidence for visits by extraterrestrials in recent years is convincing.
V. The ancients had qualities modern people do not have, but their intelligence was not as great as ours.

(A) I, III, V   (D) I, IV
(B) II, IV, V   (E) II only
(C) II, III

28 ___

29. The passage suggests that _____.
   (A) persons reporting UFO's are frauds and their motives are suspect
   (B) extraterrestrials probably visited the earth in distant ages
   (C) archaeologists are incorrect in suggesting how the pyramids were built
   (D) technological advances did not spring up suddenly throughout history
   (E) the markings in the sands of Peru are too mysterious to suggest a human origin

29 ____

The history of puns is a long one. Punning was very much in vogue, for example, during the 16th, 17th, and 18th centuries in England. In *The Spectator*, Addison, in
5 sketching the history of puns from the time of Aristotle, said that a pun "is a conceit arising from the use of two words that agree in sound but not in sense."

In *The Life of Samuel Johnson*, Boswell
10 quotes his mentor as saying, "I think no innocent species of wit or pleasantry should be suppressed and that a good pun may be admitted among the smaller excellencies of lively conversation."
15 Dr. Johnson himself is credited with several puns. Shakespeare's plays abound with them. In the Bard's time, the pun was a literary device not always intended to be humorous. Lady Macbeth says of murdered
20 Duncan, "If he do bleed, I'll gild the faces of the grooms withal; for it must seem their guilt."

An industrious Britisher, Dr. F. A. Bather, F.R.S., delivered a paper on Shake-
25 speare at the Wimbledon Public Library in 1923 in which he expressed reverence for the man who had such a command over language that he could perpetrate ten hundred and sixty-two puns. (We, in turn, must re-
30 vere Dr. Bather; he not only counted the puns, he cataloged and classified them by types!)

Nor were puns a pervasive element in Elizabethan literature alone. Through such
35 writers as Addison, and Swift (disguised as "Tom Pun-sibi"), we can look back to puns in the Pentateuch, in the great dramas of the Greeks, in Cicero and Virgil. German, French and Italian texts exist on the subject.
40 In Japanese poetry, noted the enthusiastic Dr. Bather, "word play and similar artifices are among the most admired ornaments." The Romans even had a word for pun-making: *paronomasia*.
45 From this, I give you a new word with which to conjure: *paronomania*. I suspect that it is a growingly common affliction. In the early stages, you are the life of the party. In the later stages, you don't get invited.

30. Which of the following best expresses the main idea of the passage?
   (A) Puns have had a long and, on the whole, respectable history.
   (B) Shakespeare was a good and inveterate punster.
   (C) Good punsters are the life of the party, welcome everywhere.
   (D) Puns had their greatest moments during the Elizabethan period in England.
   (E) Samuel Johnson praised punning and welcomed its use.

30 ____

31. According to Dr. F. A. Bather, Shakespeare _____.
   (A) created more than a thousand puns
   (B) learned the art of punning from the Pentateuch
   (C) had Macbeth make a pun during the murder scene
   (D) was a writer who deserved uncritical admiration
   (E) was avidly read by German, French, and Italian writers

31 ____

229-241 32. The last line of the passage suggests
that _____ .
- (A) Most people do not have a sense of humor.
- (B) Too much of a good thing is not good.
- (C) Partygoing is a boring activity.
- (D) People dislike the name *paronomania*.
- (E) Though dying out nearly everywhere, punning still has its adherents.

32 ____

285-289 33. In the passage a pun is called each of the following EXCEPT _____ .
- (A) smaller excellency
- (B) word play
- (C) *paronomasia*
- (D) literary device
- (E) an unclassifiable type

33 ____

There is no better example of the natural
perversity of Englishmen than their treatment of Henry VI. Not satisfied with depos-
ing him twice over they sought to have him
5 canonized. Few things enhance a man's reputation more than his wanton murder. It may
seem a meagre reward for a lifetime of pro-
bity to be battered to death in the Tower, but
such was the fate of this saintly simpleton.
10 At least his martyrdom dimmed the memory
of the fiascos of his reign.
   Government in the fifteenth century was
centered on the Sovereign, so whether a
kingdom flourished or declined depended on
15 its ruler. The qualities demanded of crowned
heads were so exacting that they often eluded
hereditary lotteries. Henry V, however, was
richly endowed with the necessary attributes
of his office: a commanding presence, a
20 shrewd judgment, a resolute nature, and
martial ardour. His sudden death from dys-
entery while campaigning in France in 1422,
when he was still young enough to have
known nothing of failure, left him a legend-
25 ary reputation by which his son was judged
and found wanting.
   No man could be less like his father than
Henry VI. Even his virtues were such as to
disqualify him from wearing the Crown.
30 Henry possessed in good measure the instincts of the cloister but lacked the heroic

qualities of the battlefield. The Tudors in-
geniously struggled to justify his shortcom-
ings in the hope of securing his canonization.
35 But the myth of the holy innocent would have
astonished Henry's contemporaries, who had
no illusions about his regal defects. A
Dutchman living at Ely suggested that a
sheep would be more appropriate than a ship
40 on coins of the realm. The Abbot of St. Albans, writing from personal knowledge, dismissed Henry as his "Mother's stupid offspring" who was too "half-witted" to
manage affairs of state. The ruthless world
45 of intrigue presided over by Louis XI, the
Borgias, and Vlad the Impaler, was no place
for innocents abroad. In such company it is
hardly surprising that Henry was powerless
to prevent the dissolution of the French Em-
50 pire his father had bequeathed him.

217-220 34. Which of the following best ex-
presses the main idea?
- (A) The legendary prowess of Henry V has secured him an honored spot in English history.
- (B) The English have sometimes misunderstood and mistreated their royalty.
- (C) The saintly qualities of Henry VI have richly entitled him to a canonization that has so far eluded him.
- (D) Fifteenth century kings were largely figureheads ruled by intriguing courtiers.
- (E) As monarch, Henry VI was a disastrous failure in an age of intrigue and violence.

34 ____

242-255 35. Which of the following are INCOR-
RECTLY matched?
- (A) "saintly simpleton"—Henry VI
- (B) "commanding presence"—Henry V
- (C) "innocent abroad"—Louis XI
- (D) "world of intrigue"—Borgias
- (E) "natural perversity"—En-glishmen

35 ____

229-241 36. The passage implies that _____.
  (A) the manner of Henry VI's death made his failures seem less grievous
  (B) Henry VI inherited his father's martial ardor but not his skill
  (C) the blood runs thin in the fourth and fifth generations
  (D) Henry VI was essentially a dissolute monarch with a passion for pleasure
  (E) the bias of the Abbot of St. Albans was based on hearsay, not personal knowledge

36 _____

281-284 37. Which of the following best summarizes the meaning of "hereditary lotteries"?
  (A) An instinct for gambling seems inborn in some people.
  (B) Basing a kingship upon inherited qualities is a gamble.
  (C) The inheritance of acquired characteristics is unproven.
  (D) Chance plays a minor role in inheritance.
  (E) Some English kings have been chosen by chance rather than design.

37 _____

The most important single invention within the whole complex of inventions which we today call the computer is undoubtedly the transistor. Electronic tubes
5   made the first high-speed processing possible, and the stored program led the way to the possibility of computer intelligence, but the transistor outranks them all. To appreciate its significance we need to dive once
10 again into detail.
  Tubes rely for their amplifying power on a heater electrode which pumps electrons through a vacuum. This electrode is a device which has to be shaped and manufactured
15 out of metal, and it becomes inoperative if it is reduced beyond a certain size. In any case, if it gets too small it cannot produce enough heat to activate the electrons. The transistor, in contrast, relies for its actions
20 on particular structures of a minute size which form inside silicon crystals, and these

can act as very powerful electronic amplifiers. Thus one can have a "solid state" amplifier based on a tiny fragment of silicon,
25 and a very substantial reduction in the size of the functioning unit of a computer becomes possible—indeed the very first transistorized devices occupied less than a hundredth of the space of an old-fashioned tube.
30 But there is another bonus. Because they do not rely on heat to drive their electrons along (transistor radios, as everyone knows, need no "warming up" period) they consume far less energy. They are also faster in opera-
35 tion, and much more reliable. With a bump which was heard around the world, the electronic tube hit the scrap heap.

281-284 38. The "bump which was heard around the world" was _____.
  (A) the sound of the electronic tube being destroyed
  (B) a jubilant broadcast using new techniques
  (C) a transistor literally exploding an electronic tube
  (D) the figurative replacement of an older substance by a newer
  (E) the first atomic explosion in Los Alamos

38 _____

285-289 39. All the following are mentioned as examples of the superiority of transistors to electronic tubes EXCEPT _____.
  (A) size
  (B) speed of operation
  (C) solid state
  (D) reliability
  (E) cost

39 _____

242-255 40. According to the selection, powerful electronic amplification takes place _____.
  (A) inside silicon crystals
  (B) more effectively in a vacuum tube than in a transistor
  (C) by highly modified electrodes
  (D) inside the electron, at subatomic levels
  (E) with high-speed processing

40 _____

FACSIMILE TEST 4

Section 1

PART 1

For each question in this section, choose the best answer and write the letter on the line at the right.

Each question below consists of a word in capital letters, followed by five lettered words or phrases. Choose the word or phrase that is most nearly *opposite* in meaning to the word in capital letters. Since some of the questions require you to distinguish fine shades of meaning, consider all the choices before deciding which is best.

69–73 1. DWINDLE:
    (A) ease
    (B) work successfully
    (C) outperform
    (D) increase
    (E) liquefy

    1 ___

69–73 2. ACCELERATE:
    (A) sadden   (D) slow
    (B) arouse   (E) inflate
    (C) accommodate   2 ___

74–76 3. IMPROBABILITY:
    (A) uncertainty
    (B) likelihood
    (C) approval
    (D) impossibility
    (E) impregnability

    3 ___

74–76 4. OCCASIONAL:
    (A) memorable   (D) opportune
    (B) unsteady   (E) frequent
    (C) nonparticipating   4 ___

118 5. EULOGY:
    (A) condemnation
    (B) paradox
    (C) distemper
    (D) performance
    (E) pride

    5 ___

77–81 6. GARGANTUAN:
    (A) tiny   (D) many-sided
    (B) precise   (E) heavy
    (C) quiet   6 ___

74–76 7. INFLAME:
    (A) burn   (D) consume
    (B) calm   (E) repair
    (C) erode   7 ___

69–73 8. ANNUL:
    (A) harden   (D) expel
    (B) heat   (E) deplete
    (C) renew   8 ___

74–76 9. VENTURESOME:
    (A) placid   (D) wearisome
    (B) awesome   (E) timid
    (C) lacking   9 ___

69–73 10. RESOLUTION:
    (A) determination
    (B) anger
    (C) combination
    (D) complication
    (E) perturbation

    10 ___

PART 2

Each sentence below has one or two blanks, each blank indicating that something has been omitted. Beneath the sentence are five lettered words or sets of words. Choose the word or set of words that *best* fits the meaning of the sentence.

30–33 11. Strenuous exercise can be --- and sometimes ---, especially for those in the middle years and later.
  (A) easygoing . . overwhelming
  (B) physical . . unpleasant
  (C) addictive . . excessive
  (D) habitual . . occasional
  (E) comical . . austere

11 ___

13–16 12. In the desert a severe storm fifty miles away may cause --- flooding, drowning --- travelers.
  (A) deep . . arrogant
  (B) surprising . . eastern
  (C) alpine . . mountain-climbing
  (D) catastrophic . . unwary
  (E) monumental . . lackadaisical

12 ___

30–33 13. At first --- by the British escalation of taxation, the American colonists became indignant and then --- to the point of rebellion.
  (A) irked . . enraged
  (B) amused . . motivated
  (C) compelled . . irritated
  (D) unmoved . . enlivened
  (E) untouched . . nudged

13 ___

26–29 14. Although the --- of many a Renaissance painting is a portrait, the artist managed to insert a lovely landscape into the ---.
  (A) foreground . . framework
  (B) description . . setting
  (C) basis . . altarpiece
  (D) ground . . border
  (E) subject . . background

14 ___

13–16 15. When asked about his stand on the civil rights issue, the shrewd candidate --- and then ---, leaving considerable doubt as to his real position.
  (A) stammered . . shouted
  (B) hesitated . . equivocated
  (C) rose . . explained
  (D) sighed . . babbled
  (E) shouted . . apologized

15 ___

PART 3

Each question below consists of a related pair of words or phrases, followed by five lettered pairs of words or phrases. Select the lettered pair that *best* expresses a relationship similar to that expressed in the original pair.

177, 180 16. COACH : ATHLETE::
  (A) criminal : victim
  (B) teacher : student
  (C) hunter : angler
  (D) writer : editor
  (E) child : doll

16 ___

173–174 17. STREAM : RIVER::
  (A) bridge : span
  (B) automobile : motorcycle
  (C) pamphlet : correspondence
  (D) highway : road
  (E) sapling : tree

17 ___

183, 186 18. LOOM : WEAVING::
    (A) engraving : stylus
    (B) parallel bar : gymnasium
    (C) quarterback : football
    (D) easel : painting
    (E) swimming : pool

               18 ____

166, 171 19. INVOLUNTARY : PREMEDI-
           TATION::
    (A) exaggerated : understatement
    (B) fundamental : reality
    (C) critical : review
    (D) circumstantial : evidence
    (E) circular : hole

               19 ____

183, 186 20. MILLER : GRAIN::
    (A) jogger : track
    (B) chef : menu
    (C) baker : dough
    (D) veterinarian : kennel
    (E) umpire : baseball

               20 ____

168, 171 21. NUPTIAL : WEDDING::
    (A) obvious : nuance
    (B) everlasting : eternity
    (C) legacy : contribution
    (D) civil : disrespect
    (E) beauty : attractive

               21 ____

168, 171 22. AROUSE : INFLAME::
    (A) interfere : promote
    (B) flinch : trifle
    (C) bulge : bubble
    (D) jar : jolt
    (E) acquit : denounce

               22 ____

181, 186 23. CANDLE : LIGHT::
    (A) physique : stature
    (B) magic : charm
    (C) countersign : password
    (D) sword : saber
    (E) perfume : scent

               23 ____

170–171 24. VASE : BUD::
    (A) crate : orange
    (B) barrel : basket
    (C) seed : sunflower
    (D) band : wedding
    (E) ailment : cure

               24 ____

166, 171 25. GARRULOUS : SILENCE::
    (A) simultaneous : different
    (B) inflatable : mute
    (C) infirm : strength
    (D) deliberate : composure
    (E) heedful : attention

               25 ____

PART 4

Each passage below is followed by questions based on its content. Answer all questions on the basis of what is *stated* or *implied* in that passage.

If the essence of history is the memory of things said and done, then it is obvious that every normal person, Mr. Everyman, knows some history. Of course we do what
5 we can to conceal this invidious truth. Assuming a professional manner, we say that so-and-so knows no history, when we mean no more than that he failed to pass the examinations set for a higher degree; and sim-
10 ple-minded persons, undergraduates and others, taken in by academic classifications of knowledge, think they know no history because they have never taken a course in history in college, or have never read Gib-
15 bon's *Decline and Fall of the Roman Empire*. No doubt the academic convention has its uses, but it is one of the superficial accretions that must be stripped off if we would understand history reduced to its lowest
20 terms. Mr. Everyman, as well as you and I, remembers things said and done, and must do so at every waking moment. Suppose Mr. Everyman to have awakened this morning unable to remember anything said or done.
25 He would be a lost soul indeed. This has happened, this sudden loss of all historical knowledge. But normally it does not happen.

Normally the memory of Mr. Everyman, when he awakens in the morning, reaches

30 out into the country of the past and of distant places and instantaneously recreates his little world of endeavor, pulls together as it were things said and done in his yesterdays, and coordinates them with his present percep-

35 tions and with things to be said and done in his tomorrows. Without this historical knowledge, this memory of things said and done, his today would be aimless and his tomorrow without significance.

266-269 26. The major purpose of the passage is to _____ .
(A) suggest Gibbon as a prerequisite for every historian
(B) show that a knowledge of history is universal
(C) put history into a special category of human knowledge
(D) emphasize that Mr. Everyman is more frequently wrong than right
(E) provide a humorous description of a day in the life of a historian

26 ____

232-234 27. "History reduced to its lowest terms" is _____ .
(A) a subject taken by undergraduates
(B) the proud boast of Mr. Everyman
(C) passing examinations
(D) remembering even commonplace events
(E) an academic convention

27 ____

229-241 28. Another name for a "sudden loss of all historical knowledge" is _____.
(A) perception
(B) falsification
(C) regret
(D) feebleness
(E) amnesia

28 ____

232-234 29. When Mr. Everyman "recreates his little world of endeavor" every morning, he is also _____ .
(A) risking an aimless today and a tomorrow without significance
(B) becoming, for a moment at least, a lost soul
(C) providing continuity between past and future
(D) subtly rejecting all historical knowledge
(E) coordinating irrelevant materials for no apparent purpose

29 ____

When Agatha Christie died in January 1976, she was undoubtedly the most famous detective story writer in the world. In Britain alone all of her most popular titles sold in

5 millions; in the United States they were almost equally successful; and in every European country her name was a household word. Her fame even extended to the heart of the Soviet bloc: an edition of some books

10 published in Moscow sold out immediately.

The personality behind the creation of Hercule Poirot and Miss Marple was that of a shy and in most ways very conventional middle-class English lady. Agatha Mary

15 Clarissa Miller was born in the Devonshire seaside resort of Torquay in 1890, the third child of a well-to-do American father and a mother who was markedly sensitive and aesthetically perceptive. In her charming auto-

20 biography Agatha gives very clear sketches of them both, her father an idle but agreeable man, her mother almost clairvoyant at times, and a person who saw life and people in colors that "were always slightly at variance

25 with reality." Perhaps this is the quality she passed on most directly to Agatha, the romantic tendency to see everything a little bigger than life-size, to be fascinated by the mysterious and strange, and to weave stories

30 that explained the strangeness.

There was nothing unusual about Agatha Miller's childhood, except that she never went to school. She was taught at home by her mother, and at times by governesses, and

35 evolved elaborate games that she played by herself, games in which one can perhaps see

the germ of the intricate plots she evolved in later years. In adolescence, like other young girls of her class and time, she went to dances
40 (never unaccompanied, because "you did not go to a dance alone with a young man") where she found difficulty in managing her programme so that she danced with the right young man. She flirted, had proposals, and
45 in 1914 married dashing Archie Christie, who became one of the first pilots in the Royal Flying Corps during World War I.

Agatha worked in a hospital and eventually found herself an assistant in the dis-
50 pensary. There she conceived the idea of writing a detective story, something she had been challenged to do a year or two earlier by her elder sister Madge. Since she was surrounded by poisons, what more natural
55 than that this should be a poisoning case. What kind of plot should it be? "The whole point of a *good* detective story was that it must be somebody obvious but at the same time, for some reason, you would then find
60 that it was *not* obvious, that he could not possibly have done it." Readers of her first detective story, *The Mysterious Affair at Styles*, will remember that this is just what happens in the book.

285-289 30. From the description provided in the passage, which of the following words is the LEAST appropriate to describe Agatha Christie?

(A) bored   (D) conventional
(B) shy   (E) literary
(C) romantic   30 ___

242-255 31. Agatha Christie was motivated to try her hand at detective stories _____.

(A) because of a challenge from her husband
(B) through a suggestion by her sister
(C) so that she could bring Hercule Poirot to life
(D) to exorcise the ghosts of an unhappy childhood
(E) to while away the time at Torquay

31 ___

277-280 32. Use of the word *even* in sentence 3 suggests that _____.

(A) one might not expect Soviet readers to be Christie fans
(B) Agatha Christie sold as many copies in Moscow as in New York
(C) her fame, though considerable in Russia, was not extensive
(D) writers from the middle class were forbidden to visit Russia
(E) though Christie sold in Russia, she was never popular in Czechoslovakia

32 ___

Those who speak of the various "ages" of man, such as the Age of Belief, the Age of Discovery, the Age of Reason, the Atomic Age, and so forth, may be responsible for
5 the nonsensical belief, widely held today, that mankind has become sophisticated, that we are less superstitious than the species used to be, less susceptible to hoaxes and irrational fears; that our minds, in short, are far
10 from the primitive.

Perhaps the matter can never be fully resolved, since a scientific poll cannot be taken of the human being of other ages to learn just how superstitious he was. Certainly
15 some of his superstitions have been exploded by modern science, and certainly there are hundreds of thousands of people today, able to read, who can be aware of such exposés. But we accept new superstitions as we dis-
20 card old ones; intellectual development does not necessarily reform our mental behavior and habits even when we know better. A scientist may develop a most complicated computer, and still toss some salt over his
25 left shoulder if he spills it at the table, or walk around a black cat, or refuse the third light on a match, or whatever it is he harbors in the way of superstitious hangover. For, no matter how far advanced our intellectual
30 development, we still have no control over the autonomic nervous system: we cannot prevent the hair from "standing on end" when we are suddenly frightened in the dark.

So, while we have every right to point
35 out the nonsense which man accepts, and indeed by which he directs his life, we would

do well to temper our merriment with the realization that at bottom our own thinking is just as solidly based upon the primitive mentality as was that of the serf, the ancient Roman, or the tribesman in awe of the Umbundu chant. As the French philosopher Lévy-Bruhl put it: "Dans tout esprit humain, quel qu'en soît le développement intellectuel, subsiste un fond indéracinable de mentalité primitive." (In all human kind, whatever its intellectual attainments, an ineradicable basis exists of primitive mentality.) And Nilsson said: "Primitive mentality is a fairly good description of the mental behavior of most people today except in their technical or consciously intellectual activities."

217–220 33. Which of the following best describes the main idea of the passage?

(A) The mind of modern man is far from the primitive.

(B) The Atomic Age is the latest in a list of famous "ages."

(C) The autonomic nervous system sometimes makes our hair stand on end.

(D) For all their sophistication, people today have their primitive superstitions.

(E) Lévy-Bruhl and Nilsson share a particular point of view.

33 ___

229–241 34. A scientist who tosses some salt over the left shoulder _____ .

(A) is prudently playing it safe, "just in case"

(B) is consciously pointing out to others the weakness of superstition

(C) demonstrates the point of view of Lévy-Bruhl

(D) shows a greater sophistication than the primitive tribesman

(E) becomes the immediate butt of all his or her colleagues

34 ___

285–289 35. All the following are mentioned as examples of superstition or primitive mentality EXCEPT _____ .

(A) walking around a black cat

(B) being in awe of the Umbundu chant

(C) refusing the third light on a match

(D) throwing salt over the left shoulder

(E) breaking a mirror and worrying about bad luck

35 ___

229–241 36. From the passage it may be inferred that _____ .

(A) wide reading automatically protests against superstition

(B) Lévy-Bruhl overstates his case for primitive mentality

(C) in many ways modern thinking is comparable to that of the ancient Roman

(D) science is reluctant to undermine long-held convictions

(E) we can congratulate ourselves on being immune from Nilsson's criticism

36 ___

Agee's struggle from childhood to the grave was essentially with himself. The gifted, white Anglo-Saxon Protestant charmer had every door opened for him. His precocious literary talent was recognized at St. Andrew's, Phillips Exeter Academy, and Harvard, and poor grades were never allowed to impede his progress. At a time when the majority of graduates were unemployed, Agee went straight from Cambridge to Henry Luce's newly created business magazine, *Fortune*, that haven for liberal journalists on the 50th floor of the Chrysler Building. (Was there ever a journal that allowed its staff such freedom to bite the editor's hand and mock its readers' ethos?) During his 18 years with Luce he had the opportunity to accompany Walker Evans to live among Alabama sharecroppers in 1936, the experience that produced "Let Us Now Praise Famous Men," while the anonymous movie reviews he wrote for *Time* subsidized the signed film columns he contributed to *The Nation*.

25   In Hollywood, after he quit *Time* in 1948, he was sympathetically treated by a variety of producers. Indeed, the shining thread running through an often murky story is the continual presence of kindly advisers,
30 long-suffering employers, considerate colleagues, loving friends, and forgiving women, wherever the willful, childlike Agee went.

    Of course he entertained his friends with
35 an endless flow of intoxicating and intoxicated conversation. He was generous with his time, money and sympathy. He served his employers well, frequently too well, giving more than they needed. He invariably
40 provided *Time* with book reviews three times the requisite length. On his way to deliver the manuscript of ''Let Us Now Praise Famous Men'' to his desperate publishers in 1939, he stopped on the approach to Man-
45 hattan and headed back to his decrepit New Jersey retreat for a further year's revisions. He ruined his chance of getting a Guggenheim Fellowship in 1937 by putting up an eloquent, 20-page list of over 50 projects in-
50 stead of modestly asking for a grant to complete ''Famous Men.''

224-227 37. Which of the following summaries best sums up Agee's life?
- (A) He fulfilled the promise of his early years and succeeded in all activities.
- (B) He never had a chance, unfairly treated as he was by friends and colleagues.
- (C) He met every commitment, every deadline on time.
- (D) His life was confusing, contradictory, paradoxical.
- (E) His rise from poverty to wealth, from obscurity to fame, was a rags-to-riches story.

37 ____

229-241 38. The publishers (paragraph 3) were desperate because _____.
- (A) the manuscript was overdue
- (B) they had paid Agee an advance
- (C) he submitted his manuscript to *Time* instead
- (D) he chose a Guggenheim Fellowship instead
- (E) the manuscript was three times the suggested length

38 ____

242-255 39. ''Let Us Now Praise Famous Men'' _____.
- (A) was converted into a screenplay by Agee
- (B) first appeared in *The Nation*
- (C) was written after a break with Henry Luce
- (D) first appeared serialized in *Fortune* magazine
- (E) deals with Alabama sharecroppers

39 ____

277-280 40. In the context of the passage, the adjectives *willful, childlike* suggest that Agee was _____.
- (A) charming, entertaining, predictable
- (B) likable, naive, immature
- (C) loving, forgiving, considerate
- (D) strong, stubborn, brutal
- (E) critical, bitter, unfriendly

40 ____

Section 2

PART 1

For each question in this section, choose the best answer and write the letter on the line at the right.

Each question below consists of a word in capital letters, followed by five lettered words or phrases. Choose the word that is most nearly *opposite* in meaning to the word in capital letters. Since some of the questions require you to distinguish fine shades of meaning, consider all the choices before deciding which is best.

47 1. BRISTLY:
   (A) belligerent
   (B) hairy
   (C) placid
   (D) narrow
   (E) conventional

   1 ____

132 2. UNDERMINE:
   (A) allocate
   (B) plow
   (C) strengthen
   (D) overstate
   (E) superimpose

   2 ____

87, 96 3. REGRESS:
   (A) invite   (D) consume
   (B) withdraw   (E) advance
   (C) dislocate

   3 ____

74–76 4. INTERCHANGEABLE:
   (A) unique
   (B) variable
   (C) unstable
   (D) multicolored
   (E) adaptable

   4 ____

69–73 5. EXODUS:
   (A) genesis   (D) intermission
   (B) entrance   (E) advance
   (C) quiet period

   5 ____

117 6. ANTISEPTIC:
   (A) prolific
   (B) harmless
   (C) unsophisticated
   (D) poisonous
   (E) medical

   6 ____

47 7. RATTLE:
   (A) shake   (D) chant
   (B) compress   (E) annoy
   (C) comfort

   7 ____

74–76 8. LAGGARD:
   (A) punctual   (D) intense
   (B) untamed   (E) docile
   (C) powerful

   8 ____

77–81 9. CHIMERICAL:
   (A) humorous   (D) mild
   (B) implausible (E) practical
   (C) tragic

   9 ____

141 10. CONVALESCENT:
   (A) medicinal   (D) therapeutic
   (B) worsening   (E) fractured
   (C) healing

   10 ____

69–73 11. CELEBRATED:
   (A) renowned   (D) lionized
   (B) unknown   (E) announced
   (C) sad

   11 ____

95, 138 12. LIQUEFY:
(A) pasteurize   (D) combine
(B) pave   (E) solidify
(C) dissolve
                            12 ___

87 13. DISPASSIONATE:
(A) even-   (D) partial
    tempered   (E) weary
(B) involved
(C) customary
                            13 ___

69–73 14. SECRETE:
(A) disclose   (D) deliver
(B) flood   (E) mislay
(C) oppose
                            14 ___

87, 143 15. DEHUMANIZE:
(A) ignore   (D) civilize
(B) tantalize   (E) make
(C) degrade   bestial
                            15 ___

PART 2

Each sentence below has one or two blanks, each blank indicating that something has been omitted. Beneath the sentence are five lettered words or sets of words. Choose the word or set of words that *best* fits the meaning of the sentence.

13-16 16. Though never accepted by society and the military, Eva Peron, wife of Argentinian president Juan Peron, won --- and emotional support from the masses of people.
(A) contempt
(B) interest
(C) adoration
(D) appeasement
(E) acquaintanceship
                            16 ___

26–29 17. Exhausted but not ---, the climbers gazed at the peak of Everest and resolved to make a run for the --- the next day.
(A) elated . . camp
(B) defeated . . summit
(C) incapacitated . . slope
(D) foolish . . sanctuary
(E) indifferent . . flag
                            17 ___

34–38 18. The continuing success of "Radio Reader" on National Public Radio proves --- that even adults like to be read to, if the material is ---.
(A) humorously . . outrageous
(B) paradoxically . . personal
(C) vigorously . . abstruse
(D) conclusively . . interesting
(E) brilliantly . . prerecorded
                            18 ___

13-16 19. Believing that the story of Jason and the Golden Fleece has a basis in historical fact, a British author duplicated the voyage of the *Argo*, using a --- of a Bronze Age boat for the ---.
(A) replica . . venture
(B) representative . . trip
(C) photograph . . routing
(D) pilot . . production
(E) hull . . safari
                            19 ___

26–29 20. Casey Stengel, whose --- prose often concealed a great deal of baseball sense, found new ways of making a simple idea ---.
(A) brilliant . . crystal clear
(B) recorded . . emphatic
(C) straightforward . . incomprehensible
(D) vigorous . . unimportant
(E) tortured . . complicated
                            20 ___

PART 3

Each passage below is followed by questions based on its content. Answer all questions following a passage on the basis of what is *stated* or *implied* in that passage.

I was on the point of slinking off, to think how I had best proceed, when there came out of the house a lady with a handkerchief tied over her cap, and a pair of gardening
5 gloves on her hands, wearing a gardening-pocket like a toll-man's apron, and carrying a great knife. I knew her immediately to be Miss Betsey, for she came stalking out of the house exactly as my poor mother had so
10 often described her stalking up our garden at Blunderstone Rookery.

"Go away!" said Miss Betsey, shaking her head, and making a distant chop in the air with her knife. "Go along! No boys
15 here!"

I watched her, with my heart at my lips, as she marched to a corner of her garden, and stopped to dig up some little root there. Then, without a scrap of courage, but with
20 a great deal of desperation, I went softly in and stood beside her, touching her with my finger.

"If you please, ma'am," I began.

She started and looked up.

25 "If you please, aunt."

"Eh?" exclaimed Miss Betsey, in a tone of amazement I had never heard approached.

"If you please, aunt, I am your nephew."

30 "Oh, Lord!" said my aunt. And sat flat down in the garden path.

"I am David Copperfield, of Blunderstone, in Suffolk—where you came, on the night when I was born, and saw my dear
35 mamma. I have been very unhappy since she died. I have been slighted, and taught nothing, and thrown upon myself, and put to work not fit for me. It made me run away to you. I was robbed at first setting out, and
40 have walked all the way, and have never slept in a bed since I began the journey." Here my self support gave way all at once; and with a movement of my hands intended to show her my ragged state, and call it to
45 witness that I had suffered something, I broke into a passion of crying, which I suppose had been pent up within me all the week.

My aunt, with every sort of expression but wonder discharged from her counte-
50 nance, sat on the gravel staring at me, until I began to cry; when she got up in a great hurry, collared me, and took me into the parlour. Her first proceeding there was to unlock a tall press, bring out several bottles,
55 and pour some of the contents of each into my mouth. I think they must have been taken out at random, for I am sure I tasted aniseed water, anchovy sauce, and salad dressing. When she had administered these restora-
60 tives, as I was still quite hysterical, and unable to control my sobs, she put me on the sofa, with a shawl under my head, and the handkerchief from her own head under my feet, lest I should sully the cover; and then,
65 sitting herself down behind the green fan or screen I have already mentioned, so that I could not see her face, ejaculated at intervals, "Mercy on us!" letting those exclamations off like minute-guns.

221-223 21. Which of the following titles best summarizes the content of the passage?

(A) David meets Miss Betsey
(B) A Sad Story
(C) How I Traveled from Blunderstone to Miss Betsey's
(D) The Practical Uses of Hysteria
(E) Blood Is Thicker Than Water

21 ___

229-241 22. The expression "Mercy on us" is meant to suggest Miss Betsey's _____ .

(A) sense of humor
(B) deeply religious nature
(C) control of the unexpected situation
(D) love for her newly arrived nephew
(E) agitation

22 ___

266–269 23. The author's mention of "aniseed water, anchovy sauce, and salad dressing" is intended to _____ .

(A) suggest Miss Betsey's basic indifference
(B) add a touch of humor
(C) reveal the manners and mores of the time
(D) show how David would react to an unusual drink
(E) display a mastery of prose rhythms

23 ____

229–241 24. The passage implies that _____ .

(A) David is a cruel boy, about to take advantage of a relative
(B) Miss Betsey is, at best, an inefficient gardener
(C) Miss Betsey is not really disturbed by David's arrival
(D) Miss Betsey has a prejudice against boys
(E) David's hysteria is feigned

24 ____

229–241 25. From her actions we may infer that Miss Betsey

(A) despised David immediately and intensely
(B) felt a house should be lived in, not preserved as a museum piece
(C) was gruff but not unkind
(D) kept in close communication with David's mother
(E) welcomed the newcomer without reservations

25 ____

At noon white wings sailed over the sand dunes and a snowy egret swung down long black legs. The bird alighted at the margin of a pond that lay, half encircled by marsh, between the eastern end of the dunes and the inlet beach. The pond was called Mullet Pond, a name given to it years before when it had been larger and mullet had sometimes come into it from the sea. Every day the small white heron came to fish the pond, seeking the killifish and other minnows that darted in its shallows. Sometimes, too, he found the young of larger fishes, for the highest tides of each month cut through the beach on the ocean side and brought in fish from the sea.

The pond slept in noonday quiet. Against the green of the marsh grass the heron was a snow-white figure on slim black stilts, tense and motionless. Not a ripple nor the shadow of a ripple passed beneath his sharp eyes. Then eight pale minnows swam single file above the muddy bottom, and eight black shadows moved beneath them.

With a snakelike contortion of its neck, the heron jabbed violently, but missed the leader of the solemn little parade of fish. The minnows scattered in sudden panic as the clear water was churned to muddy chaos by the feet of the heron, who darted one way and another, skipping and flapping his wings in excitement. In spite of his efforts, he captured only one of the minnows.

The heron had been fishing for an hour and the sanderlings, sandpipers, and plovers had been sleeping for three hours when a boat's bottom grated on the sound beach near the point. Two men jumped out into the water and made ready to drag a haul seine through the shallows on the rising tide. The heron lifted his head and listened. Through the fringe of sea oats on the sound side of the pond he saw a man walking down the beach toward the inlet. Alarmed, he thrust his feet hard against the mud and with a flapping of wings took off over the dunes toward the heron rookery in the cedar thickets a mile away. Some of the shore birds ran twittering across the beach toward the sea. Already the terns were milling about overhead in a noisy cloud, like hundreds of scraps of paper flung to the wind. The sanderlings took flight and crossed the point, wheeling and turning almost as one bird, and passed down the ocean beach about a mile.

The ghost crab, still at his hunting of beach fleas, was alarmed by the turmoil of birds overhead, by the many racing shadows that sped over the sand. By now he was far from his own burrow. When he saw the fisherman walking across the beach he dashed into the surf, preferring this refuge to flight. But a large channel bass was lurking near by, and in a twinkling the crab was seized and eaten. Later in the same day, the bass was attacked by sharks and what was left of it was cast up by the tide onto the sand. There the beach fleas, scavengers of the shore, swarmed over it and devoured it.

238–240 26. The flying terns are compared with
_____ .

    (A) alarmed herons
    (B) wheeling sanderlings
    (C) scraps of paper
    (D) twittering shore birds
    (E) noisy clouds

                               26 ___

266–269 27. The author's purpose in introducing the episode of the ghost crab is to
_____ .

    (A) show how the food chain operates
    (B) deplore the arrival of the fisherman
    (C) demonstrate the courage of this lowly creature
    (D) contrast its behavior with that of the heron
    (E) suggest the voraciousness of the channel bass

                               27 ___

232–234 28. The last sentence in the passage provides an example of _____ .

    (A) humor
    (B) simile
    (C) personification
    (D) irony
    (E) heroism

                               28 ___

229–241 29. From the passage we may infer that
_____ .

    (A) killifish are not minnows
    (B) the name *Mullet Pond* is no longer an accurate description
    (C) the heron is rarely disturbed by the arrival of man
    (D) plovers do not rest during the day
    (E) the heron perches on tall black posts

                               29 ___

250–254 30. The *eight black shadows* belong to
_____ .

    (A) terns   (D) ghost crabs
    (B) herons   (E) minnows
    (C) egrets

                               30 ___

PART 4

Select the word or set of words that *best* completes each of the following sentences.

17–21 31. In *Puzzles from Other Worlds*, the author-wizard Martin Gardner provides --- brainteasers, with one puzzle leading to another and another, all written in --- prose that carries the reader effortlessly along.

    (A) numerous . . adequate
    (B) several . . flowery
    (C) challenging . . spritely
    (D) repetitive . . pedestrian
    (E) transparent . . humdrum

                               31 ___

6–12 32. The --- rain of tropical rain forests may deprive the soil of precious nutrients and leave it ecologically --- for other uses.

    (A) constant . . unsuitable
    (B) warm . . overheated
    (C) occasional . . arid
    (D) well-publicized . . ready
    (E) moisture-laden . . accommodating

                               32 ___

26-29 33. --- old Boston belies its reputation as a --- city, for it surprisingly celebrates Bastille Day, on July 14, with dancing and feasting on Marlborough Street.

   (A) Unruffled . . backwoods
   (B) Wily . . New England
   (C) Flighty . . down-to-earth
   (D) Exuberant . . tempestuous
   (E) Staid . . proper

                                    33 ___

26-29 34. The golden tan, now a --- symbol suggesting affluence and a carefree life-style, once was --- avoided by all Victorian ladies.

   (A) familiar . . seldom
   (B) cheerful . . sullenly
   (C) variable . . unintentionally
   (D) prestige . . earnestly
   (E) hard-won . . unconsciously

                                    34 ___

22-25 35. To the --- visitors, the dome of the Taj Mahal, like a silver bowl floating on a shadowy sea, had an --- glow in the moonlight.

   (A) casual . . incandescent
   (B) awestruck . . otherworldly
   (C) numerous . . ineffectual
   (D) critical . . obscure
   (E) assembled . . unimaginable

                                    35 ___

PART 5

Each question below consists of a related pair of words followed by five lettered pairs of words. Select the lettered pair that *best* expresses a relationship similar to that expressed in the original pair.

181, 186 36. MARATHON : ENDURANCE::

   (A) track : field
   (B) gardening : strength
   (C) nightmare : dream
   (D) fever : temperature
   (E) impetuosity : patience

                                    36 ___

166, 171 37. ALARM : TERRIFY::

   (A) revive : alert
   (B) scatter : clutter
   (C) look : see
   (D) reveal : disclose
   (E) reprimand : denounce

                                    37 ___

177, 180 38. NOMAD : WANDERING::

   (A) laborer : humor
   (B) invalid : health
   (C) gymnast : curiosity
   (D) surgeon : dexterity
   (E) peasant : wealth

                                    38 ___

181, 186 39. HEAT : CONVECTION::

   (A) freeze : cold
   (B) loss : anxiety
   (C) thermometer : degrees
   (D) oration : rebuttal
   (E) poison : antidote

                                    39 ___

166, 171 40. AMAZE : ASTONISHMENT::
    (A) designate : veto
    (B) interfere : interchange
    (C) merge : coalition
    (D) intensify : inspire
    (E) entwine : weave

          40 ___

174-175 41. BUS : VEHICLE::
    (A) squash : spinach
    (B) child : infant
    (C) time : tide
    (D) waterfall : canyon
    (E) hammer : tool

          41 ___

183, 186 42. CHESS : KNIGHT::
    (A) swimming : diving
    (B) croquet : mallet
    (C) gold : fairway
    (D) football : goalposts
    (E) softball : pitcher

          42 ___

173, 175 43. ATOM : MOLECULE::
    (A) neutron : atom
    (B) cell : nucleus
    (C) electron : kilowatt
    (D) amoeba : protozoa
    (E) yard : inch

          43 ___

183, 186 44. SPECULATION : RISK::
    (A) compromise : conciliation
    (B) travel : research
    (C) communication : telephone
    (D) skiing : skis
    (E) reading : pamphlet

          44 ___

177-178 45. WIZARD : MAGIC
    (A) embezzler : money
    (B) computer program-
        mer : calculator
    (C) linguist : language
    (D) dreamer : confusion
    (E) cyclist : handlebars

          45 ___

FACSIMILE TEST 5

Section 1

PART 1

For each question in this section, choose the best answer and write the letter on the line at the right.

Each question below consists of a word in capital letters, followed by five lettered words. Choose the word that is most nearly *opposite* in meaning to the word in capital letters. Since some of the questions require you to distinguish fine shades of meaning, consider all the choices before deciding which is best.

41–46   1. BUSTLE:

(A) noise
(B) haste
(C) disappointment
(D) repose
(E) excitement

1 ___

69–73   2. SMUG:

(A) unobscured   (D) snappy
(B) envious   (E) humble
(C) righteous

2 ___

87   3. DISPASSIONATE:

(A) impartial   (D) unexcitable
(B) passable   (E) valiant
(C) emotional

3 ___

88   4. IMMOBILE:

(A) improbable
(B) irritable
(C) transportable
(D) essential
(E) fixed

4 ___

123   5. HOMOGENEOUS:

(A) duplicate   (D) alienated
(B) mixed   (E) equivalent
(C) unmanly

5 ___

132   6. OVERACT:

(A) react   (D) underplay
(B) understate   (E) abide
(C) subordinate

6 ___

87   7. DECIPHERABLE:

(A) puzzling
(B) clear
(C) comprehensible
(D) decisive
(E) manageable

7 ___

41–46   8. FLIGHTY:

(A) fidgety
(B) aerial
(C) subterranean
(D) wiry
(E) stable

8 ___

41–46   9. SEEDY:

(A) mineral   (D) corrupt
(B) dapper   (E) infertile
(C) slovenly

9 ___

74–76   10. INERADICABLE:

(A) soiled   (D) possible
(B) staunch   (E) comfortable
(C) removable

10 ___

ENGLISH FOR THE COLLEGE BOARDS

PART 2

Each sentence below has one or two blanks, each blank indicating that something has been omitted. Beneath the sentence are five lettered words or sets of words. Choose the word or set of words that *best* fits the meaning of the sentence as a whole.

17-21 11. Brad knocks over glasses and bumps into things with the cheerful --- of a month-old puppy.

(A) vigor
(B) premeditation
(C) friendliness
(D) malice
(E) clumsiness

11 ____

13-16 12. It is a hard fact of economics that some of the most boring, ---, repetitive jobs bring the lowest financial ---.

(A) tedious . . remuneration
(B) challenging . . reward
(C) unnecessary . . recognition
(D) weary . . productivity
(E) life-threatening . . contracts

12 ____

26-29 13. Within the borders of Nepal are some of the highest mountains in the world, but the southern portion of the country contains the Terai, a --- region of swamps, forests, and cultivable land.

(A) barren   (D) friendly
(B) low-lying   (E) historic
(C) steep

13 ____

13-16 14. Because the field of computers encourages creative ---, many young computer wizards have made significant --- and have become millionaires.

(A) duplication . . contributions
(B) experimentation . . failures
(C) imitation . . modifications
(D) innovation . . breakthroughs
(E) communication . . miniatures

14 ____

17-21 15. When there is stiff competition, airlines offer all kinds of bonuses and --- that --- passengers to choose one airline rather than another.

(A) tickets . . impel
(B) meals . . compel
(C) incentives . . induce
(D) awards . . allow
(E) theories . . provoke

15 ____

PART 3

Each question below consists of a related pair of words or phrases, followed by five lettered pairs of words or phrases. Select the lettered pair that *best* expresses a relationship similar to that expressed in the original pair.

181, 186 16. BRAZEN : BOLDNESS::

(A) brassy : iron
(B) freezing : heat
(C) breathless : patient
(D) cramped : congestion
(E) competitive : victory

16 ____

178, 180 17. SUPERVISES : DIRECTOR::

(A) swimmer : dives
(B) sketches : orator
(C) disrupts : troublemaker
(D) provokes : acquaintance
(E) recalls : astronaut

17 ____

166, 171 18. CHILDLIKE :
SOPHISTICATION ::
(A) tardy : punctuality
(B) purposeful : goal
(C) cowardly : foolishness
(D) critical : rebuke
(E) reliable : recompense

18 ___

183, 186 19. KITCHEN : COOKING::
(A) cabinetmaker : carpentry
(B) pebble : gardening
(C) barn : refrigeration
(D) office : weaving
(E) theater : acting

19 ___

166, 171 20. CAUSTIC : SOOTHE::
(A) hilarious : entertain
(B) greedy : share
(C) barbaric : frighten
(D) talkative : blabber
(E) generous : provide

20 ___

169, 171 21. FLOOR : ROOM::
(A) arm : leg
(B) orange : pit
(C) television : video recorder
(D) sole : shoe
(E) pot : frying pan

21 ___

183, 186 22. EQUATOR : EARTH::
(A) circumference : circle
(B) latitude : longitude
(C) degree : minute
(D) skin : pear
(E) pencil : eraser

22 ___

183, 186 23. DISCUS : SPORT::
(A) bow : arrow
(B) hoe : gardening
(C) baseball : catcher
(D) music : conductor
(E) hang gliding : sky diving

23 ___

174–175 24. GRAFT : TWIG::
(A) animal : train
(B) destroy : evidence
(C) assail : argument
(D) reserve : judgment
(E) plant : cuttings

24 ___

177, 180 25. PILGRIM : SHRINE::
(A) carnival : tent
(B) craftsman : museum
(C) bee : hive
(D) tailor : clothing
(E) merchant : wholesaler

25 ___

PART 4

Each passage below is followed by questions based on its content. Answer all questions following a passage on the basis of what is *stated* or *implied* in that passage.

Tension is probably the most widespread complaint that people bring to their physicians. It gives them headaches, backaches, elevated blood pressure. It keeps them awake
5 at night or tossing in unrestful sleep. It makes them inefficient at work and irritable at home. They take expensive pills and go on expensive vacations to get rid of their tension. The pills and the vacations work, to a
10 degree, about as well as the dieting for overweight. They win relief for a while, but the tension is always there, stealing back into muscles and nerves and tying body and mind into little knots.
15 Walking is the direct physiological answer to tension. Even a short brisk walk can drain away anger and anxiety, solve a problem, untangle the knots both physical and psychological. Walking as a regular part of
20 the day or week draws off tensions before they turn into headaches and insomnia that need pills, or backaches that take expensive orthopedic skills to relieve them.

Most people do not know that walking, commonplace ordinary walking, can perform these wonders for them. Or if they have been told, they do not believe it. Yet it is a relatively simple interaction of body and mind, psychosomatic and somatopsychic, which does not require a course in physiology to understand. The mechanisms by which walking restores and preserves muscular, nervous, and emotional health are a heritage as ancient as the first man.

266-269 26. The main purpose of the author is to _____ .
(A) set up a program for successful weight loss
(B) promote walking as a means to better health
(C) explain how muscles and nerves suffer from tension
(D) extol vacations as a welcome break from deadening routine
(E) excuse irritability caused by tension

26 ____

229-241 27. The passage suggests that _____.
(A) physicians do not practice what they preach
(B) the interaction of mind and body is a complicated area of study
(C) ancient man enjoyed the therapeutic values of walking
(D) tension is particularly prevalent among office workers
(E) unlike other problems, insomnia cannot be helped by walking

27 ____

261-265 28. The author's attitude toward dieting for overweight is one of _____.
(A) curiosity   (D) dismay
(B) approval   (E) skepticism
(C) probing
28 ____

John Dewey has emphasized, quite rightly, the fact that thought which does not ultimately guide action is incomplete. But the reverse of Dewey's dictum is likewise true. Action that does not, in turn, lead to reflection, is perhaps even more gravely incomplete. For one person who is lost so completely in reverie or abstract thought that he forfeits the capacity to act, there are now a hundred so closely committed to action or routine that they have lost the capacity for rational insight and contemplative reconstruction: therefore they have lost the very possibility of re-formation and self-direction. But it is only by constant reflection and evaluation that our life, in fact, becomes fully meaningful and purposeful. In addition, when we prolong the good moments, by holding the flavor of them on the tongue, we achieve a sense of completion and fulfillment that comes by no other method. This is one of the reasons perhaps for the deep inner joy and perpetually self-renewing life of the great painters. In the humblest life that has achieved the capacity for reflection—and in rural cultures the gift is still not unknown among simple people—the second living sweetens and deepens the first.

Now life is the only art that we are required to practice without preparation, and without being allowed the preliminary trials, the failures and botches, that are essential for the training of a mere beginner. In life, we must begin to give a public performance before we have acquired even a novice's skill; and often our moments of seeming mastery are upset by new demands, for which we have acquired no preparatory facility. Life is a score that we play at sight, not merely before we have divined the intentions of the composer, but even before we have mastered our instruments: even worse, a large part of the score has been only roughly indicated, and we must improvise the music for our particular instrument, over long passages. On these terms, the whole operation seems one of endless difficulty and frustration; and indeed, were it not for the fact that some of the passages have been played so often by our predecessors that, when we come to them, we seem to recall some of the score and can anticipate the natural sequence of the notes, we might often give up in sheer despair. The wonder is not that so much cacophony appears in our actual individual lives, but that there is any appearance of harmony and progression.

29. "Some of the passages . . . played so often by our predecessors" is a tribute to _____.

229-241

(A) innate flexibility
(B) cultural heritage
(C) musical abilities
(D) intuitive understanding
(E) our parent's love

29 ___

232-234 30. Which of the following is the best interpretation of lines 29–46?

(A) We face the problems of life afresh, without adequate training or preparation.
(B) Learning how to play a musical instrument helps in facing life's problems.
(C) Life is challenging but ultimately fulfilling.
(D) Life provides a script that we can understand if we keep our wits about us.
(E) Some people, good at sight-reading of musical scores, do better at solving life's problems than the average person.

30 ___

277-280 31. From the context we may infer that *cacophony* means _____.

(A) challenge
(B) despair
(C) discord
(D) individuality
(E) loud music

31 ___

217-220 32. The main point of the first paragraph is that _____.

(A) John Dewey was right in his perceptive observation about thought and action
(B) simple people tend to miss the joys of contemplation
(C) painting is recommended as excellent therapy
(D) reflection is essential, though often neglected
(E) most people are dreamers, not doers

32 ___

Peering into the moonless void, Columbus suddenly saw an eerie light ahead. Was it land? According to the turbulent Spanish historian Bartolomé de las Casas, the first to see land that night was Rodrigo de Triana, a sailor aboard *Pinta*. For our purposes it makes no difference who saw it first. The important point—generally agreed on—is that the Admiral did see a flickering light.

In his précis of *Historia de las Indias* las Casas wrote: "As the caravel *Pinta* was faster than the other two and ahead of the Admiral, she discovered the land and gave the signals that the Admiral had ordered. He who first saw the land was a sailor called Rodrigo de Triana, notwithstanding that the Admiral, at ten o'clock that evening, had seen a light. But the thing was so indistinct that he did not dare assert that it was land; nonetheless, he called Pedro Gutierrez, confidant of the King, and told him that he seemed to have seen a light, and that he should look too, which he did, and he saw it . . . . After the Admiral had spoken, this light was seen once or twice more; and it was like a bad waxen candle that rose up and went down, which few would have thought an indication of land; nonetheless the Admiral was certain of being close to it."

What could that mysterious light have been? An illusion? Samuel Eliot Morison, authority on Columbus and the lore of the sea, thought so. "Volumes have been written to explain what this light was or might have been. To a seaman it requires no explanation. It was an illusion, created by tense watchfulness. When uncertain of your exact position, and straining to make a night landfall, you are apt to see imaginary lights and flashes and to hear nonexistent bells and breakers."

217-220 33. The passage is principally concerned with _____.

(A) the achievement of Rodrigo de Triana
(B) protocol aboard the *Pinta*
(C) the reputation of Columbus for reliability
(D) the mysterious flickering light
(E) the accuracy of *Historia de las Indias*

33 ___

285-289 34. Which of the following is NOT true according to the passage?

(A) Columbus confided his hopes to Pedro Gutierrez.
(B) Rodrigo de Triana was mentioned by Bartolomé de las Casas.
(C) *The Admiral* is another designation for Columbus.
(D) Bartolomé de las Casas was a crewman on the *Pinta*.
(E) Samuel Eliot Morison knows the sea and its ways.

34 ____

229-241 35. From the passage we may infer that _____.

(A) a waxen candle provided the flickering light
(B) there was no flickering light
(C) de las Casas agrees with Samuel Eliot Morison
(D) Pedro Gutierrez disagreed with Columbus
(E) the *Pinta* was slower than the other ships in Columbus's little fleet

35 ____

It may be argued then that these are the three basic assumptions of tragedy: first, the dignity of man, second, the freedom of his will and his responsibility for the use which
5 he makes of that will, and third, the existence in the universe of a superhuman factor. It may be further suggested that, having made these assumptions, tragedy is fundamentally oriented towards the problem of
10 evil, either explicitly or implicitly. It faces squarely the fact of evil in the world, that there is misery in man's life, which is a life to be ended by the mystery of death. Sometimes tragedy grapples directly with the
15 problem as is the case in Aeschylus' *Prometheus Bound* and *Oresteia*. Perhaps it is because of their direct attack upon the essence of evil that these plays achieve a scale and universality never reached in Shake-
20 speare. Sometimes the orientation is more implicit, as it is in Euripides' *Hippolytus*, for example, or in *Hamlet*, or *Othello*, or *Oedipus the King*, or *The Bacchae*. The action of all these plays illustrates the working of
25 one aspect of evil or another, and provides

in a sense material out of which one can construct some terms upon which the fact of evil can be faced. Therefore, rather than maintain with Aristotle and Bradley that
30 tragedy occurs only in connection with a tragic hero and his "tragic flaw," it seems better to insist upon a wider scope, a genus which will include the Aristotelian type as one of its most important species, namely,
35 that tragedy makes the three assumptions with respect to man's life, and then places him over against the everlasting and eternally mysterious question of evil. Then and only then does tragedy arise, but it is im-
40 portant to note that this does not mean utter defeat for man, since the first assumption is that man's life is meaningful. That there is not utter defeat in true tragedy seems to be at the very core of Horatio's last lines of
45 farewell to Hamlet:

> Now cracks a noble heart. Good night, sweet prince,
> And flights of angels sing thee to thy rest.

50 And may it not be that there are those who seek to interpret life, make the three assumptions of the tragic, face the problem of evil, and call life a tragedy, but never a defeat?

217-220 36. The major subject of the passage is _____.

(A) Aristotle's analysis of Greek tragedy
(B) the problem of evil in tragedy
(C) tragic heroes and the "tragic flaw"
(D) the dignity of man
(E) the appeal of Greek tragedy

36 ____

285-289 37. With which of the following statements would the author probably DISAGREE?

(A) In some respects, Shakespeare is less universal than Greek tragedy.

(B) *Prometheus Bound* deals with the problem of misery in man's life.

(C) Horatio's farewell to Hamlet suggests a ray of hope.

(D) Though tragic, life is not a defeat.

(E) Aristotle's definitions of tragedy are complete and unassailable.

37 ___

285-289 38. All the following are mentioned as true ingredients of Greek tragedy EXCEPT _____.

(A) the freedom of will

(B) responsibility for the use of free will

(C) the malice of fate

(D) the superhuman factor

(E) the problem of evil

38 ___

229-241 39. It may be inferred that _____.

(A) tragedy helps teach man how to face evil

(B) Bradley was an inept critic of Greek tragedy

(C) true tragedy emphasizes the meaninglessness of life

(D) tragedy tends to sidestep at least one major problem of life

(E) Euripides' *Hippolytus* directly and obviously confronts the problem of evil

39 ___

242-255 40. The author of *Oedipus the King is* _____.

(A) Euripides   (D) Aristotle

(B) Aeschylus   (E) not

(C) Shakespeare   mentioned

40 ___

Section 2

PART 1

For each question in this section, choose the best answer and write the letter on the line at the right.

Each question below consists of a word in capital letters, followed by five lettered words or phrases. Choose the word or phrase that is most nearly *opposite* in meaning to the word in capital letters. Since some of the questions require you to distinguish fine shades of meaning, consider all the choices before deciding which is best.

41–46   1. PRIM:

    (A) proper
    (B) conceited
    (C) unconventional
    (D) prissy
    (E) fashionable

    1 ____

132   2. MISSHAPEN:

    (A) deformed   (D) gluttonous
    (B) irregular   (E) symmetrical
    (C) reserved

    2 ____

69–73   3. STRAIGHTFORWARD:

    (A) undeveloped
    (B) insincere
    (C) round
    (D) receding
    (E) direct

    3 ____

87, 99   4. PROTRACTED:

    (A) shortened   (D) attracted
    (B) subtracted   (E) inverted
    (C) rebuked

    4 ____

117, 125   5. ANONYMITY:

    (A) signature   (D) renown
    (B) multiplicity   (E) parity
    (C) health

    5 ____

77–81   6. MACHIAVELLIAN:

    (A) aloof   (D) downcast
    (B) cunning   (E) aboveboard
    (C) efficient

    6 ____

87   7. DISAVOW:

    (A) repudiate   (D) embrace
    (B) reject   (E) restrain
    (C) break away

    7 ____

87   8. DEFERENTIAL:

    (A) overbearing
    (B) similar
    (C) contemplative
    (D) nonessential
    (E) stressful

    8 ____

47   9. INIMICAL:

    (A) easily   (D) comparable
        imitated   (E) timid
    (B) distasteful
    (C) friendly

    9 ____

41–46   10. INHERENT:

    (A) sticky   (D) unsuitable
    (B) alien   (E) faultfinding
    (C) intrinsic

    10 ____

74–76   11. STRADDLE:

    (A) decide   (D) strike
    (B) limp   (E) stoop
    (C) fluctuate

    11 ____

41–46   12. FOOLHARDY:

    (A) reckless   (D) well
    (B) cautious   informed
    (C) wise   (E) weak

    12 ____

74-76 13. TARTNESS:

(A) saltiness   (D) weakness
(B) cleanliness   (E) smoothness
(C) cleverness

13 ___

41-46 14. FLIPPANT:

(A) unhappy   (D) pert
(B) unruffled   (E) proud
(C) serious

14 ___

74-76 15. IRRESPONSIBLE:

(A) recoverable   (D) accountable
(B) headlong   (E) unanswerable
(C) dishonorable

15 ___

PART 2

Each sentence below has one or two blanks, each blank indicating that something has been omitted. Beneath the sentence are five lettered words or sets of words. Choose the word or set of words that *best* fits the meaning of the sentence as a whole.

30-33 16. In the sad history of species extinction, the story of the great auk provides one of the most --- chapters.

(A) depressing   (D) agreeable
(B) rewarding   (E) awe-
(C) profound   inspiring

16 ___

6-12 17. Hal's cruel --- of his old friend Falstaff in *Henry IV*, *Part Two*, was --- in Hal's transformation from playboy to king.

(A) recognition . . understated
(B) promotion . . perplexing
(C) rejection . . inevitable
(D) ridicule . . ludicrous
(E) deliverance . . superficial

17 ___

30-33 18. Though an underdog at the Democratic convention in 1912, Woodrow Wilson --- held on through 46 ballots and --- won the nomination from a disappointed "Champ" Clark.

(A) nervously . . predictably
(B) cheerfully . . easily
(C) unintentionally . . casually
(D) doggedly . . finally
(E) unexpectedly . . dejectedly

18 ___

26-29 19. Despite the disappearance of the great mass magazines, specialized magazines in a --- variety of subjects and fields have testified to the --- of magazine publishing in America.

(A) limited . . decline
(B) bewildering . . vitality
(C) colorful . . perils
(D) nonexistent . . unimportance
(E) diminishing . . contraction

19 ___

30-33 20. In *Buddenbrooks* Thomas Mann shows how a merchant family's overemphasis upon --- values and appearances ultimately leads to disintegration and ---.

(A) unanticipated . . surprise
(B) inviolate . . indifference
(C) glamorous . . fulfillment
(D) spiritual . . disappointment
(E) material . . tragedy

20 ___

           ENGLISH FOR THE COLLEGE BOARDS

Each passage below is followed by questions based on its content. Answer all questions following a passage on the basis of what is *stated* or *implied* in that passage.

The importance of nonsense hardly can be overstated. The more clearly we experience something as "nonsense," the more clearly we are experiencing the boundaries
5 of our own self-imposed cognitive structures. "Nonsense" is that which does not fit into the prearranged patterns which we have superimposed on reality. There is no such thing as "nonsense" apart from a judgmen-
10 tal intellect which calls it that.

True artists and true physicists know that nonsense is only that which, viewed from our present point of view, is unintelligible. Nonsense is nonsense only when we have
15 not yet found that point of view from which it makes sense.

In general, physicists do not deal in nonsense. Most of them spend their professional lives thinking along well-established lines of
20 thought. Those scientists who establish the established lines of thought, however, are those who do not fear to venture boldly into nonsense, into that which any fool could have told them is clearly not so. This is the
25 mark of the creative mind; in fact, this *is* the creative process. It is characterized by a steadfast confidence that there exists a point of view from which the "nonsense" is not nonsense at all—in fact, from which it is
30 obvious.

In physics, as elsewhere, those who most have felt the exhilaration of the creative process are those who best have slipped the bonds of the known to venture far into the
35 unexplored territory which lies beyond the barrier of the obvious. This type of person has two characteristics. The first is a childlike ability to see the world as it is, and not as it appears according to what we know
40 about it. This is the moral of the (child's?) tale, "The Emperor's New Clothes." When the emperor rode naked through the streets, only a child proclaimed him to be without clothes, while the rest of his subjects forced
45 themselves to believe, because they had been told so, that he wore his finest new clothing.

The child in us is always naive, innocent in the simplistic sense. A Zen story tells of Nan-in, a Japanese master during the Meiji
50 era who received a university professor. The professor came to inquire about Zen. Nan-in served tea. He poured his visitor's cup full, and then kept on pouring. The professor watched the overflow until he no longer
55 could restrain himself.

"It is overfull. No more will go in!"

"Like this cup," Nan-in said, "you are full of your own opinions and speculations. How can I show you Zen unless you first
60 empty your cup?"

Our cup usually is filled to the brim with "the obvious," "common sense," and "the self-evident."

242-255 21. A good definition of *nonsense* as set forth in the passage is _____.

(A) inconsequential triviality, blown up out of proportion
(B) contradiction and confusion
(C) something that doesn't fit into accepted dogmas
(D) verbal wordplay in poor taste
(E) slapstick comedy and farcical interplay

21 ___

229-241 22. The author reserves his deepest admiration for _____.

(A) those who do the unappreciated drudgery of science
(B) artists who are, at the same time, physicists
(C) children, who come to the world without prejudice
(D) writers of nonsense verse and humorous prose
(E) scientists who venture into the unknown

22 ___

23. The anecdote about Nan-in suggests that _____ .

(A) Japanese masters are incurably eccentric
(B) the tea ceremony usually encourages deep philosophical thought
(C) the Meiji era was characterized by numbing of creativity
(D) people tend to have closed minds
(E) Nan-in was absentminded

23 ____

24. An application of "The Emperor's New Clothes" is that _____ .

(A) we should not blindly accept what we are told
(B) a knowledge of physics helps us see through lying
(C) Zen provides us a philosophy that cuts through hypocrisy
(D) we should accept reality when it is based upon consensus of opinions
(E) people should always listen to a little child

24 ____

25. In the expression "which any fool could have told them is clearly not so," *fool* is used to suggest _____ .

(A) a clear-seeing scientist
(B) a person saturated with conventional wisdom
(C) a man-in-the-street, without scientific qualifications
(D) a wise man pretending to be a simpleton
(E) a clown, superficially stupid but actually profound

25 ____

Once, from eastern ocean to western ocean, the land stretched away without names. Nameless headlands split the surf; nameless lakes reflected nameless moun-
5 tains; and nameless rivers flowed through nameless valleys into nameless bays.

Men came at last, tribe following tribe, speaking different languages and thinking different thoughts. According to their ways of
10 speech and thought they gave names, and in their generations laid their bones by the streams and hills they had named. But even when tribes and languages had vanished, some of those old names, reshaped, still live
15 in the speech of those who followed.

After many centuries a people calling themselves Americans held the land. They followed the ways of the English more than of any others, especially in their speech. Yet
20 they gathered together in their blood and in their manner of life something of all those who had lived in the land before them. Thus they took as a heritage many names of the past. Adding more names, they gave to their
25 children with every generation the heritage, richer than before.

A few hundred were great names, known to all Americans, of states and cities, mountains and rivers. But most of them were little
30 names, known only to those who lived near by, of ponds and swamps and creeks and hills, of townships and villages, of streets and ranches and plantations, of coves and gulches and meadows. These little names
35 arose by so many thousands that at last they were numbered by millions.

Thus the names lay thickly over the land, and the Americans spoke them, great and little, easily and carelessly—Virginia, Sus-
40 quehanna, Rio Grande, Deadman Creek, Sugarloaf Hill, Detroit, Wall Street—not thinking how they had come to be. Yet the names had grown out of the life, and the life-blood, of all those who had gone before. From the
45 names might be known how here one man hoped and struggled, how there another dreamed, or died, or sought fortune, and another joked, twisting an old name to make a new one—Providence and Battle Mountain,
50 Hardscrabble, Troy, Smackover, Maine, Elrio, Pasadena, Troublesome Creek, Cape Fear, Nashville, Lincoln County, Fourth Crossing.

In this heritage of names the Americans
55 were fortunate, for in general the names were good, and they were closely bound with the land itself and the adventures of the people. In older countries the story of the naming was lost in the ancient darkness. But in the
60 land between the two oceans much of the record could still be read—who gave the names and when, and even why one name was chosen rather than another.

217-220 26. Which of the following best describes the main idea of the passage?

    (A) American names recall the long, colorful history of the land.

    (B) Americans followed the English in culture as well as language.

    (C) Americans gave many names to formerly nameless mountains.

    (D) Names tell of dreams and hopes, sorrows and joys.

    (E) In general, names given to American lakes and mountains were good names.

    26 ____

242-255 27. When Americans came on the scene, they _____ .

    (A) tended to slight the heritage they received

    (B) concentrated on the "great names," known to all Americans

    (C) preserved much of the old heritage in names

    (D) settled first along the mountains and rivers

    (E) respected the religious significance of current names

    27 ____

229-241 28. From the passage we may infer that _____ .

    (A) Indian tribes had produced names that repelled newcomers

    (B) those who follow a disappearing culture retain many of the old names

    (C) *Detroit* is an Indian name with a French spelling

    (D) Indian tribes spoke a universal language before the Europeans came

    (E) European names are as colorful and accessible as American names

    28 ____

285-289 29. Each of the following is mentioned as a name in America EXCEPT _____ .

    (A) Troy   (D) Maine

    (B) Elrio   (E) Knoxville

    (C) Rio Grande

    29 ____

246-249 30. Which of the following statements may be accurately derived from the selection?

    I. Naming is affected by ways of thought and speech.

   II. Every generation adds its own names to the naming heritage.

   III. Men seek immortality by incorporating their own names into place names.

   IV. American names, though fascinating, tend to be obscure and difficult to explain.

   V. The name *Americans* was given to the new settlers by the displaced Indian tribes.

    (A) I, II, and III

    (B) II and IV

    (C) I and V

    (D) I and II

    (E) all five

    30 ____

PART 4

Select the word or set of words that *best* completes each of the following sentences.

22–25 31. Like expressing a taste for certain kinds of food, movie criticism tends to be ---, reflecting the --- and prejudices of the reviewer rather than absolute truths.

(A) objective . . faults
(B) petty . . profundities
(C) exaggerated . . anecdotes
(D) subjective . . whims
(E) deceptive . . pride

31 ___

17–21 32. Human --- is nowhere better demonstrated than in collectibles, for people will --- anything enthusiastically, from barbed wire to used oil rags.

(A) discretion . . purchase
(B) eccentricity . . hoard
(C) irritability . . trade
(D) envy . . peddle
(E) sensitivity . . advertise

32 ___

30–33 33. Martha's Vineyard, once a sleepy vacation spot for --- visitors, has now become a --- mecca for hordes of sun-worshiping tourists.

(A) myriad . . quiet
(B) impoverished . . weary
(C) discriminating . . bustling
(D) impetuous . . depressing
(E) curious . . pensive

33 ___

6–12 34. Fluctuating interest rates encourage a --- game involving borrowers and lenders, impelling some borrowers to take on disastrous obligations and putting some --- thrift organizations in peril.

(A) rational . . conservative
(B) lively . . well balanced
(C) stylish . . extraordinary
(D) sophisticated . . stubborn
(E) guessing . . imprudent

34 ___

26–29 35. Costa Rica, a country with more volcanoes per capita than any other nation, has, ---, a quiet political and social scene, reflecting the maturity and --- of its people.

(A) by contrast . . stability
(B) correspondingly . . uncertainty
(C) for example . . concern
(D) repressively . . alertness
(E) proudly . . excitability

35 ___

PART 5

Each question below consists of a related pair of words, followed by five lettered pairs of words. Select the lettered pair that *best* expresses a relationship similar to that expressed in the original pair.

170, 175 36. CHURN : BUTTER::
  (A) barber : hair
  (B) cultivation : flour
  (C) needle : thread
  (D) pot : stew
  (E) trap : mouse

36 ___

166, 171 37. LAVISH : STINGINESS::
  (A) positive : confidence
  (B) plentiful : profusion
  (C) evasive : stupidity
  (D) disorganized : comfort
  (E) rash : caution

37 ___

170, 175 38. CRADLE : INFANT::
  (A) pouch : knapsack
  (B) wallet : leather
  (C) pigeonhole : papers
  (D) bucket : pail
  (E) food : platter

38 ___

179-180 39. MASON : TROWEL::
  (A) clay : potter
  (B) whaler : harpoon
  (C) mechanic : automobile
  (D) meteorologist : weather
  (E) plasterer : wall

39 ___

185-186 40. MILLIMETER : CENTIMETER::
  (A) booklet : book
  (B) mansion : cottage
  (C) mile : kilometer
  (D) spider : beetle
  (E) liter : gram

40 ___

174-175 41. LILAC : SHRUB::
  (A) beagle : terrier
  (B) watch : timepiece
  (C) marigold : chrysanthemum
  (D) motorcycle : bus
  (E) color : blue

41 ___

178, 180 42. COMPETITOR : VICTORY::
  (A) diamond : facet
  (B) percussion : drum
  (C) shrine : pilgrim
  (D) trainer : athlete
  (E) prospector : gold

42 ___

173, 175 43. DOWNPOUR : DRIZZLE::
  (A) whisper : shout
  (B) fact : fiction
  (C) conflagration : glow
  (D) game : contest
  (E) carrot : motivation

43 ___

166, 171 44. DIVERSIFY : SIMILARITY::
  (A) admire : contempt
  (B) detrimental : harm
  (C) memorable : monument
  (D) verify : testify
  (E) offend : aggression

44 ___

172, 175 45. RAZOR : BEARD::
  (A) tree : pruning hook
  (B) fork : knife
  (C) pencil : inventory
  (D) bow : violin
  (E) lamp : illumination

45 ___

ANSWERS: TIME OUT FOR REVIEWS, REVIEW TESTS, AND PRACTICE TESTS

Page 11: Time Out for Review
1. B 2. D 3. A 4. C 5. D 6. A 7. E
8. C 9. B 10. B

Page 15: Time Out for Review
1. A 2. D 3. C 4. C 5. B 6. B 7. C
8. B 9. D 10. B

Page 20: Time Out for Review
1. A 2. D 3. A 4. B 5. C 6. E 7. B
8. B 9. A 10. C

Page 23: Time Out for Review
1. C 2. B 3. D 4. B 5. A 6. E 7. C
8. B 9. C 10. D

Page 28: Time Out for Review
1. C 2. A 3. D 4. B 5. C 6. D 7. C
8. D 9. A 10. B

Page 32: Time Out for Review
1. C 2. D 3. B 4. E 5. A 6. C 7. D
8. A 9. B 10. D

Page 37: Time Out for Review
1. B 2. C 3. D 4. A 5. B 6. E 7. B
8. D 9. C 10. C

Page 39: Time Out for Review
1. fortress
2. overcrowding
3. made poor
4. wearing away
5. timid
6. pierced
7. harsh
8. yellowish
9. soaked
10. noisy speech
11. hateful
12. poisonous
13. peculiarities
14. overelaborate
15. turned aside
16. deceit
17. excessive
18. nobody
19. punishment
20. equivalent

Page 45: Time Out for Review
1. B 2. B 3. D 4. D 5. A 6. E 7. B
8. C 9. B 10. D

Page 51: Time Out for Review
1. A 2. C 3. G 4. D 5. B 6. E 7. H
8. G 9. A 10. E

Page 57: Time Out for Review
A.
1. wholesome, sanitary, healthy
2. title, pseudonym, name
3. antiquated, olden, elderly
4. wound, damage, pain
5. pretty, beautiful, graceful
6. attained, won, earned
7. achievement, feat, performance
8. quarrel, feud, strife
9. shrill, boisterous, loud
10. grotesque, witty, comical

B.
1. gazed
2. stared
3. scanned
4. peered
5. observed
6. distinguished
7. surveyed
8. recognized
9. scrutinized
10. glowered

Page 65: Time Out for Review
A. 1. A 2. B 3. D 4. B 5. A 6. C
7. E 8. B 9. C 10. A

B.
1. persevere — synonym
2. evade — unrelated
3. qualify — unrelated
4. deficiency — synonym
5. abbreviate — synonym
6. embarrass — unrelated
7. uncouth — synonym
8. efficiency — unrelated
9. advise — unrelated
10. disagreement — synonym

C.
1. credulity — doubt
2. anguish — ease
3. often — seldom
4. respect — shame
5. deathless — mortal
6. arouse — restrain
7. enlarge — decrease
8. inescapable — unavoidable
9. peevish — easygoing
10. flat — uneven
11. broad — limited
12. majestic — ignoble
13. costly — worthless
14. interrogate — answer
15. recover — abandon
16. divide — combine
17. mettlesome — spiritless
18. yield — resist
19. loquacious — silent
20. appetizing — tasteless

Page 72: Time Out for Review
1. D 2. C 3. E 4. E 5. B 6. D 7. E
8. E 9. E 10. E

Page 76: Time Out for Review
1. (6) 2. (9) 3. (1) 4. (3)
5. (7) 6. (10) 7. (8)
8. (2) 9. (4) 10. (5)

Page 82: Review Test
1. C 2. D 3. B 4. E 5. E 6. B 7. D
8. B 9. D 10. A

Page 91: Time Out for Review

1. con	6. re	11. med	16. extra
2. inter	7. quadr	12. oct	17. circum
3. Pre	8. sub	13. in	18. du
4. dec	9. trans	14. de	19. pro
5. ad	10. vice	15. quint	20. super

Page 100: Time Out for Review

1. arbit	6. rid	11. tract	16. ora
2. prob	7. viv	12. pel	17. fac
3. sci	8. struct	13. cept	18. orn
4. clus	9. cred	14. mon	19. hib
5. aud	10. ora	15. tact	20. sent

Page 112: Time Out for Review
A. 1. C 2. C 3. B 4. D 5. E 6. B
7. A 8. C 9. A 10. B

B. Answers will vary.
This is a sample. Many other words are possible.

accede	defer	interrupt	prescribe
apprehend	dissolve	nonsense	prospect
antedate	extract	obtain	submerge
compel	extravert	perfect	supervise
contradict	insult	postpone	transgress

Page 128: Time Out for Review
A. 1. B 2. E 3. B 4. A 5. E 6. A
7. B 8. B 9. C 10. A

B. autonomic democracy neuralgia telephone
chiropodist geography photometer theology
cosmopolitan microscope

Page 135: Time Out for Review
1. B 2. E 3. D 4. B 5. A 6. A 7. A
8. C 9. D 10. A

Page 136: Time Out for Review

background	goldfish	railroad	sunstroke
dressmaker	handbook	sawmill	toothache
eyesight	homeless	seasickness	waterworks
footstep	lifeboat	skyrocket	workman
gateway	moonbeam	snowstorm	wristband

Page 146: Time Out for Review
1. B 2. A 3. E 4. D 5. C 6. A 7. E
8. D 9. B 10. E

Page 152: Time Out for Review
A. 1. D 2. C 3. E 4. A 5. D 6. A 7. B
8. E 9. C 10. B
B. 1. B 2. B 3. D 4. C 5. C 6. A 7. D
8. C 9. C 10. B 11. D 12. B 13. E
14. B 15. D 16. E 17. D 18. B 19. D
20. B

Page 159: Time Out for Review

1. doled	5. peer	8. venture
2. hale	6. conceit	9. guardian
3. sample	7. sprite	10. antiques
4. humane		

Page 161: Review Test
A. 1. C 2. A 3. E 4. B 5. A 6. B 7. A
8. C 9. C 10. B
B. 1. E 2. D 3. E 4. A 5. C 6. B 7. E
8. A 9. B 10. B

Page 171: Time Out for Review
1. A 2. D 3. E 4. E 5. A

Page 175: Time Out for Review
1. A 2. C 3. B 4. E 5. E

Page 180: Time Out for Reveiw
1. C 2. B 3. D 4. C 5. A

Page 185: Time Out for Review
1. E 2. A 3. C 4. E 5. C

Page 187: Time Out for Review
1. D 2. A 3. B 4. D 5. C

Page 188: Review Test
1. C 2. C 3. A 4. D 5. B 6. B 7. B
8. B 9. B 10. C

Page 216: Time Out for Review
1. D 2. C 3. C

Page 219: Time Out for Review
1. B 2. A

Page 223: Time Out for Review
1. E 2. B

Page 226: Time Out for Review
1. D 2. A 3. E

Page 231: Time Out for Review
1. C 2. A

Page 234: Time Out for Review
1. C 2. D 3. B 4. D

Page 237: Time Out for Review

1. D 2. A 3. C

Page 239: Time Out for Review

1. C 2. B 3. D 4. C

Page 244: Time Out for Review

1. E 2. A 3. D 4. A 5. A 6. E 7. B

Page 248: Time Out for Review

1. C 2. E 3. A 4. B 5. C

Page 253: Time Out for Review

1. C 2. C 3. E 4. C 5. E 6. A

Page 258: Time Out for Review

1. A 2. B 3. C 4. B 5. E 6. B 7. D
8. C 9. A

Page 263: Time Out for Review

1. E 2. B 3. C 4. B 5. B 6. D 7. A
8. E 9. A 10. C

Page 268: Time Out for Review

1. C 2. A 3. A 4. C 5. C 6. E 7. A
8. A 9. B

Page 272: Time Out for Review

1. D 2. D 3. D 4. A 5. C 6. B 7. B 8. B

Page 279: Time Out for Review

1. A 2. D 3. C 4. E 5. C 6. A 7. B 8. C

Page 282: Time Out for Review

1. C 2. A 3. C 4. C 5. B 6. A 7. D

Page 287: Time Out for Review

1. C 2. C 3. C 4. C 5. A 6. E 7. C 8. E

Page 294: Time Out for Review

1. B 2. E 3. A 4. A 5. C 6. C 7. D
8. E 9. D

Page 300: Time Out for Review

1. C 2. D 3. A 4. D 5. B 6. C 7. D 8. A

Page 304: Practice Tests

A. 1. E 2. D 3. B 4. A 5. D
B. 1. B 2. D 3. B 4. C 5. A
C. 1. D 2. B 3. E 4. C 5. C
D. 1. C 2. C 3. A 4. D 5. A
    6. C 7. C 8. D

ANSWERS TO FACSIMILE TEST 1
Section 1
(pages 320–332)

PART 1

1. INVARIABLE:
   (A) unstable   (D) literal
   (B) confusing   (E) habitual
   (C) absolute

   (*A*) **Invariable** means *unchanging, constant*. Therefore its opposite is *unstable*. *Habitual* is somewhat similar in meaning. The other alternatives are unrelated.

2. EJECT:
   (A) disbar   (D) assign
   (B) provide   (E) admit
   (C) indicate

   (*E*) **Eject** means *cast out*. Therefore its opposite is **admit**. *Disbar* is somewhat similar in meaning. The others are unrelated.

3. MONOCHROME:
   (A) photographic   (D) single-minded
   (B) multicolored   (E) strange
   (C) cosmic

   (*B*) **Monochrome** means of *one color*. Therefore its opposite is **multicolored.** *Monochrome* is sometimes mentioned in photographic work, but *photographic* is not an antonym. The other words are unrelated.

4. BOLSTER:
   (A) repeat   (D) undercut
   (B) announce   (E) apprehend
   (C) control

   (*D*) To **bolster** is to *boost*; therefore **undercut** is its opposite in meaning. The alternatives are neither synonyms nor related words.

5. DIVULGE:
   (A) annul   (D) separate
   (B) conceal   (E) flail
   (C) array

   (*B*) **Divulge** means *reveal*; therefore its opposite is **conceal.** The alternatives are unrelated.

6. FROSTY:
   (A) chilly   (D) deadly
   (B) friendly   (E) rainy
   (C) flagrant

   (*B*) **Frosty** may be used in a figurative sense meaning *unfriendly*. Therefore its opposite is **friendly.** *Chilly* is a synonym. *Rainy* is related in weather reports. The other words are unrelated.

7. DEXTERITY:
   (A) clumsiness   (D) interest
   (B) genius   (E) bashfulness
   (C) skill

   (*A*) **Dexterity** means *skill*. Therefore its opposite is **clumsiness.** *Skill* is a synonym. **Dexterity** is sometimes (but not always) allied with *genius*. *Bashfulness* and *interest* are unrelated.

8. NULLIFY:
   (A) verify   (D) abide
   (B) debunk   (E) abandon
   (C) implement

   (*C*) **Nullify** means *make void, annul*. Therefore its opposite is **implement;** *carry out. Verify* is slightly opposed in meaning but is not a true antonym. The other alternatives are unrelated.

9. FRETFUL:
   (A) fearful   (D) tranquil
   (B) meaningless   (E) worried
   (C) powerless

   (*D*) **Fretful** means *uneasy, worried*. Therefore its opposite is **tranquil.** *Fearful* and *worried* are synonyms. The other two are unrelated.

10. MERCURIAL:
    (A) poisonous   (D) eloquent
    (B) swift   (E) constant
    (C) metallic

    (*E*) **Mercurial** means *changeable, unpredictable*. Its opposite is **constant.** *Poisonous* and *metallic* refer to qualities of the element mercury, but are not related to *mercurial*. *Swift* is associated with the god Mercury. *Eloquent* is unrelated.

11. DIVERGENT:

(A) similar
(B) atrocious
(C) partial
(D) remote
(E) complacent

(A) To *diverge* is *to move in different directions.* **Divergent** therefore means *different.* Its opposite is **similar.** The alternatives are unrelated.

12. LAGGARD:

(A) stubborn
(B) beautiful
(C) timeless
(D) swift
(E) fierce

(D) The verb *lag* means *fall behind.* The adjective **laggard** means *falling behind.* Its opposite is **swift.** One may be *laggard* because he or she is *stubborn,* but the words are not opposite in meaning. The other words are unrelated.

13. SPLEEN:

(A) universality
(B) esophagus
(C) curiosity
(D) indirection
(E) kindliness

(E) **Spleen** means *bad temper,* from an old idea that this emotion is associated with the spleen, an organ in the body. Its opposite is **kindliness.** Esophagus is also an organ in the body, but the word is not opposite to *spleen.* The other alternatives are unrelated.

14. ANTECEDENT:

(A) grammatical
(B) consequent
(C) foreordained
(D) postponed
(E) predisposed

(B) **Antecedent** means *going before, preceding.* Its opposite is **consequent,** which means *following.* Since *antecedent* is a word used in grammar, *grammatical* is used here, but not as an antonym. *Foreordained* and *predisposed* both have a prefix meaning before, but they are not antonyms of *antecedent.* *Postponed* is tricky because it has the prefix *post,* which is opposed to *ante.* But the word is unrelated.

15. BELITTLE:

(A) repress
(B) scorn
(C) praise
(D) alarm
(E) cohere

(C) **Belittle** means *make small* or *unimportant.* Its opposite is **praise.** *Scorn* is a synonym. The other words are unrelated.

PART 2

16. The arbitrator remained --- despite efforts of the press to anticipate his decision.

(A) sluggish
(B) prejudiced
(C) irritated
(D) insensitive
(E) noncommittal

(E) If the arbitrator thwarted the efforts of the press to anticipate his decision, he didn't give things away. He was **noncommittal.**

17. If a patient's hospital room has a window overlooking a scenic stand of trees, --- tends to be ---.

(A) boredom . . manifest
(B) interest . . dispersed
(C) convalescence . . inflexible
(D) recuperation . . accelerated
(E) mobility . . minimal

(D) A favorable setting would hasten a person's recovery. Therefore his or her **recuperation** would be **accelerated.**

18. Some endangered creatures may survive by transfer of populations, --- species in areas where they no longer occur.

(A) commemorating
(B) reestablishing
(C) studying
(D) uniting
(E) popularizing

(B) If creatures are transferred to areas where they no longer occur, they are **reestablished** in the new area.

19. Denny's --- behavior may lead him from the conventional to the --- in a few brief moments.

(A) erratic . . outrageous
(B) smooth . . uninspired
(C) snobbish . . orthodox
(D) atrocious . . solicitous
(E) consistent . . theatrical

(A) The context tells us that *conventional* is being contrasted with another word. Both *theatrical* and **outrageous** provide such a contrast, but only **erratic** suitably completes the sentence. Though Denny's behavior may become *theatrical,* it would not then be *consistent.*

20. Newborn infants are like little Buddhas, observing life with --- glances and impressive ---.
    (A) inattentive . . comprehension
    (B) compassionate . . condescension
    (C) penetrating . . equanimity
    (D) competent . . indifference
    (E) stolen . . magnanimity

    (C) Newborn infants are obviously too young to show *comprehension, condescension* or *magnanimity*. Both **equanimity** and *indifference* are possible, but only **penetrating** suitably completes the sentence. A newborn infant could scarcely be called *competent*.

PART 3

21. The two qualities most closely associated with Dr. Bell were ---.
    (A) egotism and irritability
    (B) industry and conjecture
    (C) athleticism and skill in surgery
    (D) observation and deduction
    (E) suggestibility and fairness

    (D) The emphasis in the selection is on Dr. Bell's ability to observe closely and draw conclusions based on his observations. The alternatives are irrelevant.

22. Dr. Bell assumed the patient had been a soldier in a Highland regiment because of the patient's ---.
    (A) shoes   (D) mannerisms
    (B) tattoo   (E) walk
    (C) watch chain ornaments

    (E) Dr. Bell mentioned the swagger in the patient's **walk** as a clue to the man's association with the Highland regiment.

23. Which of the following is correctly paired according to the selection?
    (A) Dr. Bell --- famous writer
    (B) Crimean days --- war against the Russians
    (C) Sherlock Holmes --- Highland piper
    (D) unsolved crimes --- surgeon
    (E) skepticism --- deduction

    (B) **Crimean days** and the **war against the Russians** are linked in the third paragraph from the end. The other pairings are unsuitable.

24. As used in the selection *swagger* suggests _____.
    (A) modesty and humility
    (B) simplicity and friendliness
    (C) arrogance and pomposity
    (D) fascination and criminality
    (E) strength and openness

    (C) By a process of elimination, **arrogance and pomposity** is clearly the best answer. Those who play in marching bands always march with a certain pride and flair. The alternatives are unsuitable.

25. The author's attitude toward Dr. Joseph Bell is one of ---.
    (A) obvious admiration
    (B) studied irony
    (C) indirect disparagement
    (D) subtle criticism
    (E) uncritical adulation

    (A) The use of *wide-eyed* is a clue to the attitude of the guests, an attitude obviously shared by the writer, as he tells of some of Dr. Bell's exploits.

26. Which of the following best describes the main idea of the selection?
    (A) Prince Florizel is well liked by his friends and associates.
    (B) Disguise is a deceitful, disagreeable device with little justification for its use.
    (C) The Prince of Bohemia is basically an industrious, hard-working individual.
    (D) The Prince and the Colonel seek new adventures and unusual experiences.
    (E) Colonel Geraldine is the motivator of the disguised friends.

    (D) There are many clues to the main idea --- for example, the words *adventurous* and *eccentric, imperturbable courage, ready invention* and *chivalrous devotion*. Alternative (A) is at best a minor detail. (E) is false. (B) is nowhere implied here. (C) suggests boredom and avoidance of adventure.

27. As used in the selection *in reduced circumstances* means ---.
    (A) on a restricted assignment
    (B) in a state of uncertainty
    (C) attached to a newspaper
    (D) in a shabby suit
    (E) somewhat low in money

    (E) *Reduced circumstances* suggests a shortage of money.

28. Lines 12-13 suggest that the Prince's personality is ---.
    (A) essentially agreeable and loving
    (B) complex and somewhat contradictory
    (C) unruffled and consistent
    (D) predictable but interesting
    (E) unpleasant if superficially charming

    (B) The Prince had a "placid temper" and took life as it came, but he had a "taste for ways of life more adventurous and eccentric . . ." He is **complex** in his interests and **contradictory** in his mood swings.

29. The context suggests that *temerarious* (line 24) probably means ---.
    (A) rash and daring
    (B) impatient and nasty
    (C) reserved and thoughtful
    (D) proud but shy
    (E) rebellious and cruel

    (A) The word *brave* tells us much about Colonel Geraldine, but it is followed by "even temerarious disposition," which suggests that *temerarious* is a further extension of *brave*.

30. Which of the following is likely to happen next?
    (A) The Colonel is greeted by an old, forgotten friend.
    (B) The Prince tires of the masquerade and returns home.
    (C) The Prince and the Colonel have an unusual adventure.
    (D) The disguised pair are unmasked by the press.
    (E) The storm gets worse, and the men find lodgings.

    (C) The stage is set for something unusual to happen. The men are disguised. The weather is bad. The adventurers are in a strange place. There's certainly an adventure to come.

PART 4

Select the word or set of words that *best* completes each of the following sentences.

31. --- changes in basic swimming strokes have created new world records and made --- many previous swim techniques.
    (A) Unexpected . . ridiculous
    (B) Subtle . . obsolete
    (C) Extreme . . significant
    (D) Mechanical . . dramatic
    (E) Trivial . . valuable

(B) If new world records have come about because of changes in swimming strokes, then the correct pair must complete a positive statement. Only **subtle** and **obsolete** make sense in this context.

32. The radio signals were ---, with --- static that scrambled the message.
    (A) intermittent . . disruptive
    (B) melodic . . harmonious
    (C) unanticipated . . frivolous
    (D) clear . . isolated
    (E) unbroken . . raucous

    (A) If the signals are being scrambled, the static must be **disruptive.** The first word in the pair, **intermittent,** also fits perfectly into the sentence.

33. Nowhere else in the United States, during the next decade, are as many --- species facing possible --- as in the Hawaiian Islands.
    (A) exotic . . misinterpretation
    (B) desert . . scrutiny
    (C) poisonous . . mismanagement
    (D) alpine . . stabilization
    (E) native . . extinction

    (E) Though occasionally a word in a pair makes sense, only **native** and **extinction** both fit into the sentence. These are obviously correct, but an examination of all the other alternatives shows their unsuitability.

34. Though *abnormality* is a frightening word, some --- from the normal are ---, not harmful.
    (A) quotations . . curious
    (B) abstractions . . medicinal
    (C) deviations . . benign
    (D) condensations . . concise
    (E) fluctuations . . provocative

    (C) Be especially aware of function words that provide essential clues (pages 34–38). The word *though* tells us that a contrast is coming. We'd expect anything abnormal to be bad, but *though* tells us to expect the unexpected. Some **deviations** from abnormality may not be bad but **benign.**

35. Americans have been accused of being ---, wasteful of their --- resources.
    (A) indigent . . plentiful
    (B) unconventional . . natural
    (C) disillusioned . . subterranean
    (D) profligate . . irreplaceable
    (E) uncooperative . . aquatic

    (D) The key to the sentence is *wasteful*. We are most concerned about waste when resources cannot be replaced. **Profligate** means *wasteful*, but even if the word is unfamiliar to you, the second word of the pair will help you choose the right pair.

PART 5

36. INFLUENCE : DOMINATION ::
    (A) worship : admiration
    (B) budget : plan
    (C) subscriber : underwriter
    (D) blossom : flower
    (E) cooperation : sabotage

    (A) **Influence** is a lesser degree of **domination.** In the same way, **admiration** is a lesser form of **worship. (Q,** pages 182–183)

37. MANUSCRIPT : EDIT ::
    (A) lemonade : consume
    (B) evidence : destroy
    (C) account : audit
    (D) peruse : newspaper
    (E) dress : injury

    (C) A **manuscript** is **edited.** In the same way an **account** is **audited. (J,** page 174)

38. EXCESS : SCANT ::
    (A) actor : incompetent
    (B) true : hallucination
    (C) deterioration : worse
    (D) delegation : authorized
    (E) delirium : logical

    (E) Here we have a word and an opposed word. **(A,** page 166) **Excess** is opposed to **scant.**

39. CHISEL : CARPENTRY ::
    (A) chain : bicycle
    (B) mainsail : schooner
    (C) scale : weight
    (D) blowtorch : welding
    (E) music : tuning fork

    (D) A **chisel** is used in **carpentry (F,** page 172) In the same way a **blowtorch** is used in **welding.** All other pairs are related, but not in the same way. A *tuning fork* is used in *music,* but the terms are reversed.

40. SWAN : CYGNET ::
    (A) fawn : deer   (D) sheep : kid
    (B) goose : gosling   (E) antelope : cub
    (C) goose : gander

    (B) A **cygnet** is a **young swan. (W,** page 187) A **gosling** is a **young goose.** (A) is reversed. (C) differentiates between male and female. (D) and (E) have incorrect pairings of animals.

41. THERAPIST : REHABILITATION ::
    (A) direction : pilot
    (B) physicist : atom
    (C) lumberjack : cabinetmaking
    (D) pharmacist : diagnosis
    (E) jester : entertainment

    (E) The goal of a **therapist** is **rehabilitation. (N,** pages 178–179) The goal of a **jester** is **entertainment.**

42. EXPOSURE : CHILL ::
    (A) impertinence : flippancy
    (B) obstruction : frustration
    (C) abandonment : solidarity
    (D) thrift : poverty
    (E) frivolity : irritability

    (B) **Chill** is the result of **exposure. (D,** page 170) **Frustration** is the result of **obstruction.**

43. ELUDE : CUNNING ::
    (A) embezzle : upright
    (B) discriminating : criticize
    (C) beautify : wealthy
    (D) fumble : clumsy
    (E) stubborn : endure

    (D) To **elude,** you must be **cunning.** Though the words are of different parts of speech, they are related. **(B,** pages 168–169) To **fumble,** you must be **clumsy.** (E) is reversed.

44. OUNCES : GOLD ::
    (A) apples : bushels
    (B) fuel oil : gallons
    (C) carats : diamonds
    (D) miles : yards
    (E) grain : elevator

    (*C*) **Ounces** are units to measure **gold.** (**T,** page 185) **Carats** are units to measure **diamonds.**

45. LIBRETTIST : OPERA ::
    (A) circus : clown
    (B) angler : regatta
    (C) mountaineer : rock face
    (D) ornithologist : aquarium
    (E) museum : curator

    (*C*) A **librettist** is associated with the **opera.** (**M,** pages 177–178) A **mountaineer** is associated with the **rock face** of a mountain. (*A*) and (*E*) are reversed.

PART 1

1. SUBSERVIENT:
   (A) supercilious   (D) melodramatic
   (B) aggressive   (E) ambiguous
   (C) tranquil

   (B) **Subservient** means *being submissive, giving in to others*. Therefore its opposite is **aggressive**. *Supercilious* is somewhat opposed in meaning, but it lacks a suggestion of aggressiveness.

2. INCLINATION:
   (A) derivation   (D) dislike
   (B) eclipse   (E) infatuation
   (C) reservation

   (D) **Inclination** means *fondness, liking*. Its opposite is **dislike**. **Inclination** and *eclipse* are words used in astronomy, but they are unrelated. *Infatuation* is a strong synonym, not an antonym. The other two words, *derivation* and *reservation*, end in *ion*, as does *inclination*, but the three words are unrelated.

3. EUPHORIA:
   (A) disapprobation   (D) discretion
   (B) exaltation   (E) misery
   (C) dormancy

   (E) **Euphoria** is a *feeling of well-being*, of *elation*. Its opposite is **misery**. *Exaltation* is a synonym. The other words are unrelated.

4. MONUMENTAL:
   (A) diminutive   (D) commemorative
   (B) marble   (E) abstract
   (C) two-dimensional

   (A) **Monumental** means *huge, massive*. Its opposite is **diminutive**. Monuments may be made of *marble*; the words are not opposed in meaning. Monuments may also be *commemorative* in nature, but again the words *monumental* and *commemorative* are not antonyms. The other words are unrelated.

5. OMNISCIENT:
   (A) alert   (D) indecisive
   (B) ignorant   (E) provocative
   (C) negligent

   (B) **Omniscient** means *all-knowing*. Its opposite is **ignorant**.

6. HAUNT:
   (A) frequent   (D) shun
   (B) shock   (E) dream
   (C) dawdle

   (D) **Haunt** is *frequent*, to *appear and reappear*. Its opposite is **shun**. Note that *haunt* is used here as a verb

7. CARDINAL:
   (A) irreligious   (D) numerous
   (B) mammalian   (E) unimportant
   (C) humorous

   (E) **Cardinal** means *main, chief, important*. Its antonym is **unimportant**. *Irreligious* may mislead because a cardinal is a religious dignitary, but as an adjective *cardinal* does not, necessarily, have anything to do with religion. *Mammalian* may also mislead, since a bird is not a mammal, but *mammalian* and *cardinal* are not antonyms. The other words are unrelated.

8. DISADVANTAGEOUS:
   (A) squalid   (D) detrimental
   (B) beneficial   (E) neutral
   (C) affable

   (B) **Disadvantageous** means *unfavorable, harmful*. Its opposite is **beneficial**. *Detrimental* is a synonym. *Neutral* is between *disadvantageous* and *beneficial*. *Squalid* and *disadvantageous* are somewhat related, not antonyms. *Affable* is unrelated.

9. LETHARGY:
   (A) indifference   (D) squeamishness
   (B) hate   (E) fulfillment
   (C) vigor

   (C) **Lethargy** means *laziness, sluggishness*. Its opposite is **vigor**. *Indifference* may be associated with *lethargy*. The other words are unrelated.

10. CAGEY:
    (A) naive   (D) squeamish
    (B) unfettered   (E) sparse
    (C) clownish

    (A) **Cagey** means *wary, shrewd*. Its opposite is **naive**. The other words are unrelated.

PART 2

11. Although some ecosystems are --- and able to adjust, others are too --- to survive much tampering.
    - (A) dependable . . accommodating
    - (B) resilient . . fragile
    - (C) prodigal . . incompetent
    - (D) inflammable . . arid
    - (E) inexhaustible . . self-contained

    (*B*) **Dependable, resilient,** and **inexhaustible** could fill the first slot. Therefore the second word in the pair is crucial. If the ecosystems cannot survive much tampering, they must be **fragile**. Thus, even if *resilient* is a new word for you, the clues for choosing *resilient . . fragile* are easy to find.

12. Formerly accepted --- of the proper roles of men and women have --- the fate of the mastodon and the sabre-toothed tiger.
    - (A) stereotypes . . experienced
    - (B) assignments . . retold
    - (C) depictions . . broadcast
    - (D) critiques . . elucidated
    - (E) reprimands . . analyzed

    (*A*) Once again the second word in the pair is a major clue. Both the mastodon and the sabre-toothed tiger are extinct. A common idiom is *experience the fate*. **Experienced** fits the second slot nicely. **Stereotypes** fits into the first slot, and the modifiers *formerly accepted* makes the choice certain. The stereotypes are as extinct as the animals.

13. In his autobiography Simenon does not spare himself, recounting his --- failures as well as his many --- successes.
    - (A) incredible . . undeserved
    - (B) tolerable . . conspicuous
    - (C) ludicrous . . peevish
    - (D) personal . . professional
    - (E) cinematic . . ecclesiastical

    (*D*) The use of *as many as* suggests a contrast between Simenon's failures and successes. A process of elimination suggests that **personal** *failures* is being contrasted with **professional** *successes*. The other alternatives do not provide the needed contrast.

14. As the favorable election results poured from the television screen, the candidate went from quiet --- to expressive ---.
    - (A) uneasiness . . contentment
    - (B) curiosity . . concern
    - (C) statement . . exaggeration
    - (D) confusion . . preeminence
    - (E) pleasure . . jubilation

    (*E*) The context suggests a change in degree in the candidate's reactions. *Quiet* **pleasure** gives way to *expressive* **jubilation**. *Favorable* suggests that both words must be positive. The other alternatives all contain negative elements.

15. In the --- view of some critics, the only --- goal of television is not to inform or even entertain but to sell goods.
    - (A) positive . . overlooked
    - (B) jaundiced . . unrealized
    - (C) cynical . . serious
    - (D) tiresome . . illusory
    - (E) blatant . . unacknowledged

    (*C*) Since most proponents of television insist its primary purpose is to *inform* or *entertain*, the emphasis on *sell goods* is clearly a **cynical** reaction. The other alternatives make no sense or contain contradictions.

PART 3

16. PAMPHLET : TOME ::
    - (A) turnip : radish
    - (B) oration : election
    - (C) butterfly : caterpillar
    - (D) hill : mountain
    - (E) shout : cry

    (*D*) A **pamphlet** is smaller than a **tome**. In the same way a **hill** is smaller than a **mountain**. (**H**, pages 173–174) The other pairs are related to each other, but do not complete the analogy. A **turnip** and a **radish** are vegetables, but a turnip is not related to a radish in size. An **oration** may be used in **election** speeches. A **caterpillar** may become a **butterfly**. A **shout** and a **cry** are roughly synonymous. Only *hill : mountain* shows the proper relationship.

17. HIBERNATION : INACTIVITY ::
    (A) disorder : entropy
    (B) devastation : ruin
    (C) deterioration : growth
    (D) embargo : trade
    (E) bafflement : tardiness

    (B) **Inactivity** is a quality associated with **hibernation**. (**P**, page 181) In the same way **ruin** is associated with **devastation**. **Disorder** is associated with **entropy**, but the words are reversed.

18. DISCIPLE : FOLLOWS ::
    (A) amphibian : slides
    (B) cries : infant
    (C) candidate : votes
    (D) courier : writes
    (E) trustee : administers

    (E) A **disciple follows**. (**K**, page 176) In the same way a **trustee administers**. An **infant cries**, but the words are reversed. **Amphibians** may **slide**, but sliding is not their main feature or function. A **courier carries** messages and doesn't **write** them. **Candidate : votes** seems tricky at first, but the primary function of the candidate is to be elected.

19. MOUTHPIECE : OBOE ::
    (A) clock : cape
    (B) cannon : ammunition
    (C) eyepiece : telescope
    (D) warp : woof
    (E) drill : bit

    (C) A **mouthpiece** is part of an **oboe**. (**C**, page 169) In the same way an **eyepiece** is part of a **telescope**. The **bit** is part of a **drill**, but the words are reversed. **Ammunition** is inserted into a **cannon**, but it is not an essential part of a cannon. **Warp** and **woof** are threads used in weaving but their relationship to each other is complementary. The **warp** is not a smaller part of the **woof**.

20. PATHOLOGY : SICKNESS ::
    (A) paleontology : fossils
    (B) psychology : education
    (C) archaeology : plant life
    (D) geology : gasoline
    (E) psychiatry : medicine

    (A) **Pathology** is the study of **sickness**. (**S**, page 184) In the same way **paleontology** is the study of **fossils**. Words in the other pairs are associated, but not in the same way.

21. ARTIST : PALETTE ::
    (A) conductor : baton
    (B) saber : fencer
    (C) soldier : boot
    (D) typewriter : stenographer
    (E) nurseryman : cradle

    (A) An **artist** uses a **palette**. (**O**, page 179) In the same way a **conductor** uses a **baton**. The pairs in (B) and (D) are reversed. Besides, a **stenographer** may not use a **typewriter**. A **soldier** wears a **boot**, but doesn't use it as an *artist* uses a *palette*. The association of *nursery* and *child* accounts for the incorrect (E).

22. STEAK : BROIL ::
    (A) baste : turkey
    (B) lawn : mow
    (C) book : overlook
    (D) roll : call
    (E) neurotic : calm

    (B) A **steak** may be **broiled** (**R**, pages 183–184) in the same way a **lawn** may be **mowed**. The other alternatives are unacceptable. The **roll** may be **called**, but there is no physical action taking place. A **book** may be **overlooked**, but there is no physical change in book. A **neurotic** may be **calmed**, but such action is quite different from that in *broiling* and *mowing*. A **turkey** may be **basted**, but the words are reversed.

23. FABLE : STORY ::
    (A) factor : teacher
    (B) sale : fair
    (C) charter : mortgage
    (D) senator : legislator
    (E) wholesaler : retailer

    (D) **Fable** is a kind of **story**, but it is a more specific term. (**I**, page 174) In the same way **senator** is a kind of **legislator**, but it too is a more specific term.

24. CASKET : JEWEL ::
   (A) doctrine : philosophy
   (B) page : cover
   (C) vase : flower
   (D) water : kettle
   (E) receptacle : ticket

   (C) A **jewel** is kept in a **casket**. (E, page 170)
   In the same way a **flower** is kept in a **vase**.
   Water is kept in a *kettle*, but the words are
   reversed. The trickiest alternative is (*E*). A
   ticket may be kept in a *receptacle*, but *receptacle* is a general word that may contain
   hundreds of dissimilar items of all sizes. Besides, a *receptacle* is not a primary container
   for a *ticket*.

25. NEUTRALITY : MEDIATOR ::
   (A) humor : physician
   (B) fairness : pitcher
   (C) hero : courage
   (D) horse : patience
   (E) skill : athlete

   (*E*) **Neutrality** is the quality needed for a **mediator**. (L, page 177) In the same way, **skill**
   is the quality needed for an **athlete**. *Courage* is the quality needed for a *hero*, but the
   words are reversed. The other pairings suggest desirable qualities but not essential
   ones. *Humor* is not essential for a *physician*,
   though it might help!

PART 4

To benefit from the analysis of the reading questions and answers, be sure to go back to the original
reading selection to see how and why answers have
been derived. (Pages 329–331)

26. The author's primary purpose in this passage is
   to _____ .
   (A) explore the meaning of the words *classical*
   and *romantic*
   (B) set in opposition German and French taste
   in art and literature
   (C) study how new modifications of style
   serve to sharpen understanding of old oppositions
   (D) evaluate the motivation of German and
   French artists
   (E) demonstrate that classicism and romanticism are basically the same

   (*A*) The paragraph contrasts the various meanings of the words *classical* and *romantic*.
   Note especially that the opening sentence
   and the closing sentence both stress the contrast between the two terms being studied.
   (*B*) and (*C*) are details. (*D*) is irrelevant.
   (*E*) is downright incorrect.

27. In the passage the phrase *in the culture of beauty*
   applies to ---.
   (A) romanticists only
   (B) classicists and romanticists
   (C) classicists only
   (D) French and German critics only
   (E) the beginnings of European art and litera-
   ture

   (*B*) The adherents referred to in line 15 are both
   classicists and romanticists. Their philoso-
   phies differ, but they are both interested in
   beauty.

28. With which of the following statements would
   the author probably agree?
   (A) The supposed opposition between classicists and romanticists is superficial, masking a similarity of technique and purpose.
   (B) French and German artists were pioneers
   in setting up standards of taste in art and
   literature.
   (C) In the formation of art and literature standards of taste are essential.
   (D) The craving for new motives is essentially
   a barren impulse, robbing art and literature
   of beauty and stability.
   (E) Restless curiosity outweighs all other elements in seeking the sources of beauty in
   art.

   (*C*) The writer's reference to "the first formation of anything like a standard of taste in
   these things" suggests that he approves of
   such standards.

29. The attitude of the Japanese man toward the
   eruption of Krakatoa can best be described as
   ---.
   (A) foolhardy   (D) deluded
   (B) angry   (E) terrified
   (C) involved

   (*D*) Since the volcano *did* in fact erupt, the man
   was deceived, **deluded**.

30. The lesson of the "fox in the morning" is to ---.
    (A) mistrust the evidence of the senses
    (B) face tragedy with fear
    (C) relish the destruction of institutions
    (D) rebel against the blows of fate
    (E) develop a philosophic calm

    (*E*) The key to this answer is ". . . enables us to look upon many of man's doings that would otherwise vex and pain us." If we develop a "sense of historical time," we'll develop a **philosophic calm**.

31. As used in the passage, *transitoriness* suggests ---.
    (A) preciousness   (D) permanence
    (B) variability   (E) brevity
    (C) magnificence

    (*E*) The author's use of words like "fail and die and fall away successively," suggests that *transitoriness* means **brevity**. Most human things pass rapidly away.

32. A person who followed the advice in this selection would most likely ---.
    (A) look at all human actions with equanimity and calm
    (B) make a close study of human institutions for the lessons they teach
    (C) seek natural spectacles as guides for the human spirit
    (D) compare the Japanese superstition of the fox with western beliefs
    (E) try to get Japanese to give over the crippling illusion of the fox

    (*A*) This question is allied to 30. Often one question will tie into another, as here. The author suggests developing "a sense of historical time," calmly taking the long-range view.

33. In the passage the branches on a pine or larch are compared with ---.
    (A) the swift years of mankind
    (B) the Japanese belief in the serenity of the spirit
    (C) human institutions
    (D) the tree itself
    (E) the life of nations and races of men

    (*C*) The key lines, 21–22, make the comparison clear.

34. Which of the following titles best summarizes the content of the passage?
    (A) The Joys of Extemporaneous Writing
    (B) Skeletons in the Writing Closet
    (C) Form vs. Substance in Composition
    (D) Planning: A Major Writing Ingredient
    (E) The Act of Composition

    (*D*) The opening sentence provides the clue to the central theme: planning and design. (*A*) is mentioned only in connection with love letters. (*E*) is much too broad. The author does not make the contrast suggested in (*C*). (*B*) is off the topic.

35. With which of the following statements would the author of the passage probably disagree?
    (A) The sonnet's restrictions guide the sonneteer.
    (B) Every kind of writing requires a deliberate plan.
    (C) Design underlies writing, even if it is not apparent.
    (D) Most other writing is less rigidly controlled than the sonnet.
    (E) In good writing the writer's thoughts are carefully organized.

    (*B*) When the writer says, "In some cases the best design is no design," he clearly indicates that not all writing requires a deliberate plan.

36. The author's style may best be characterized as ---.
    (A) flowery but informative
    (B) straightforward and unpretentious
    (C) colloquial and artificial
    (D) pointed and elegant
    (E) learned and dramatic

    (*B*) The author states his thesis simply and then develops it directly. There is no padding, no attempt at flowery writing.

37. The tone of the passage can best be described as ---.
    (A) ill natured and vitriolic
    (B) confidential and ingratiating
    (C) good-naturedly cynical
    (D) fretfully condescending
    (E) intimate and dispassionate

    (*C*) The writer is poking fun at gardening mania, while showing his own methods for avoiding all the toil. In describing the outlandish claims of some seed catalogs, he is cynical, but he is **good-naturedly cynical**.

38. The thrust of the writer's humor is directed at ---.
    (A) Granny and the children
    (B) the gardener
    (C) the garden handbooks
    (D) himself
    (E) the impractical plans for the garden

    (D) Although the writer pokes fun at garden books, he is really using himself as the center of humor. We have a feeling that the *lazy slug* (lines 26–28) is none other than the writer. His ailment, unclassified by science, is pure laziness. The "untold agonies" are purely imaginary. This able-bodied man "wheeled to the side line" is contrasted with the hardworking old man. His directions are the extent of his work, unless we consider docking the man's pay as work! The chain fastened to the man's leg is the final exaggeration, all in fun.

39. The "crippling muscular complaints" can best be characterized as ---.
    (A) painful but not serious
    (B) totally disabling
    (C) caused by grueling effort
    (D) mentioned for sympathy
    (E) completely imaginary

    (E) Since that crippling complaint mysteriously begins when work is to start, we can assume it is **completely imaginary**.

40. The last sentence in the first paragraph suggests that ---.
    (A) the writer has spent a fortune on too many seeds
    (B) transportation to the writer's rural home is chancy at best
    (C) the seeds are destined to die before they germinate
    (D) the author seals the envelope without including payment
    (E) the order, when received, proves to be incorrect

    (A) Since "the savings account is a whited sepulcher," we can assume too much money was spent. If we need a "forty-mule team" just to haul the order from the depot, we can be sure that the family fortune is gone! The writer uses hyperbole (page 48) to make his humorous points.

PART 1

1. ORAL:
   - (A) rapid
   - (B) verbal
   - (C) written
   - (D) phonetic
   - (E) secret

   (C) **Oral** means *spoken*. Therefore its opposite is **written**. *Verbal* is a general word meaning *involving words*. In recent years it has come into use as a rough synonym for *oral*, but it is in no way an antonym. *Phonetic* transcription studies *oral* language, but *phonetic* is not an antonym of *oral*.

2. SAVOR:
   - (A) favor
   - (B) enjoy
   - (C) discharge
   - (D) undo
   - (E) loathe

   (E) **Savor** means *taste*, especially *taste with pleasure*. Its opposite is **loathe**.

3. BOTTLENECK:
   - (A) relaxation
   - (B) impasse
   - (C) groundwork
   - (D) foundation
   - (E) toehold

   (A) A **bottleneck** is a situation that restricts movement. Its opposite is **relaxation**. *Impasse* is a synonym.

4. CRYPTIC:
   - (A) hidden
   - (B) grave
   - (C) technological
   - (D) varied
   - (E) obvious

   (E) **Cryptic** means **hidden**, *obscure*. Its opposite is **obvious**. *Hidden* is a synonym.

5. MISSHAPEN:
   - (A) fortunate
   - (B) symmetrical
   - (C) vague
   - (D) ill-fated
   - (E) blessed

   (B) **Misshapen** means *deformed*. Its opposite is **symmetrical**. *Fortunate* is a tricky alternative. A *misshapen* person may be the opposite of *fortunate*, but *fortunate* is a much broader term, not an antonym.

6. QUAINT:
   - (A) customary
   - (B) colorful
   - (C) dull
   - (D) spectacular
   - (E) proportionate

   (A) A major definition of **quaint** is *odd, unusual*. In this sense its opposite is **customary**. *Colorful* is a synonym.

7. SERFDOM:
   - (A) freedom
   - (B) martyrdom
   - (C) wisdom
   - (D) officialdom
   - (E) colonialism

   (A) **Serfdom** is *bondage*. Its opposite is **freedom**. *Serfdom* has sometimes been charged against *colonialism*, but the words are not, in any event, antonyms.

8. OMNIPOTENT:
   - (A) omniscient
   - (B) many-sided
   - (C) weak
   - (D) unwavering
   - (E) underfed

   (C) **Omnipotent** means *all powerful*. Its opposite is **weak**. Don't be misled by the *omni* in *omniscient* or *many* in *many-sided*.

9. KALEIDOSCOPIC:
   - (A) premature
   - (B) drab
   - (C) combative
   - (D) visual
   - (E) telescopic

   (B) **Kaleidoscopic** means *producing beautiful images*. Its opposite is **drab**. *Visual* is a related word. *Telescopic* merely shares the Greek root *scop, to see*.

10. INDISPUTABLE:
    - (A) permanent
    - (B) unlovable
    - (C) unequaled
    - (D) paramount
    - (E) doubtful

    (E) **Indisputable** means *not able to be doubted, debated*. Its opposite is **doubtful**.

11. OVERCAST:
    - (A) windy
    - (B) sunny
    - (C) underestimated
    - (D) stormy
    - (E) depleted

    (B) **Overcast** means *clouded over*. Its opposite is **sunny**. An *overcast* day may be *windy*, or *stormy*; neither word is an antonym.

12. SAUCY:
    - (A) flippant
    - (B) tasty
    - (C) shy
    - (D) irrepressible
    - (E) dominant

    (C) **Saucy** means *bold, impertinent, impudent*. Its opposite is **shy**. A *saucy* person may well be *flippant* and *irrepressible*, but these words are not antonyms.

13. SPARTAN:
    (A) permissive   (D) abrupt
    (B) quiet   (E) frugal
    (C) courageous

    (A) **Spartan** means *disciplined*, especially *self-disciplined*. Its opposite is **permissive**.

14. ALLEGIANCE:
    (A) loyalty   (D) infidelity
    (B) support   (E) salutation
    (C) inattentiveness

    (D) **Allegiance** means *devotion*, **loyalty**. Its opposite is **infidelity**, *faithlessness*. *Loyalty* is a synonym. *Salutation* is included to mislead, since we *salute* the flag and pledge *allegiance*.

15. ALLEVIATE:
    (A) weigh   (D) intend
    (B) gladden   (E) aggravate
    (C) arouse

    (E) **Alleviate** means *relieve*, *lighten*. Its opposite is **aggravate**. Sometimes it helps to put the words in sentences like these:
    > The treatment *alleviated* the cold symptoms.
    > The treatment *aggravated* the cold symptoms.

    These paired sentences clearly show that the words are antonyms.

PART 2

16. First --- in 1865 by a group of French Republicans, Liberty was finally unveiled in New York Harbor in 1886.
    (A) advertised   (D) engineered
    (B) completed   (E) conceived
    (C) photographed

    (E) The difference in dates, *1865* and *1886*, suggests that the project took a long time. **Conceived** suggests the beginning of the project.

17. The great horned owl, one of the most efficient and --- of all ---, occasionally kills more prey than it can eat.
    (A) docile . . birds
    (B) casual . . fliers
    (C) inept . . hunters
    (D) ruthless . . predators
    (E) amusing . . parents

    (D) If the owl kills more prey than it can eat, it must be **ruthless**. When we try **predators** in the second slot, we find that it fits nicely. If you know only one word in the pair, you can often guess the pair correctly.

18. The dependence of public television upon public contributions for --- is a sad but --- fact of life.
    (A) expansion . . harrowing
    (B) survival . . inescapable
    (C) news . . humdrum
    (D) ratings . . captivating
    (E) audiences . . general

    (B) If we try every pair in the sentence, only **survival . . inescapable** makes sense. *Harrowing* is much too strong a word in (A). *Humdrum* in (C) makes little sense. *Captivating* is scarcely a word to be used with *fact* (D). *Public contributions* wouldn't bring *audiences* (E). *General* is a meaningless term.

19. The --- celebration of the Metropolitan Opera recalled a hundred years of great artists, innovative directors, and --- designers.
    (A) centennial . . creative
    (B) showy . . headstrong
    (C) recent . . inept
    (D) halfhearted . . indifferent
    (E) biennial . . avant-garde

    (A) The *hundred years* is a clue to **centennial** in the first slot. We need a positive word for the second slot, to go along with great and innovative. Only **creative** fits.

20. As the day wore on, New Delhi, at first uncomfortably warm, became --- hot and ---.
    (A) somewhat . . annoying
    (B) cloudlessly . . quiet
    (C) unbearably . . stifling
    (D) unexpectedly . . torrential
    (E) sleepily . . cheery

    (C) *Uncomfortably warm* suggests that matters grew worse. **Unbearably** hot and **stifling** complete the expected sequence.

PART 3

To benefit from the analysis of Part 3, be sure to go back to the original reading selection to see how and why answers have been derived. (Pages 334–336).

21. The author's primary purpose in this passage is to --- .
    - (A) expose Philip as a cruel cynic
    - (B) analyze, through conversation alone, the character of Rosemary
    - (C) suggest some of the dangers in old relationships
    - (D) reveal aspects of a bitter class struggle
    - (E) show how some people recognize beauty where others are blind

    (B) The focus of the selection is on Rosemary. Her motives are subtly analyzed purely by what she says and how she reacts to Philip's comments.

22. The word *languid* in line 8 is meant to suggest --- .
    - (A) Miss Smith's fatigue
    - (B) Rosemary's lack of perception
    - (C) Philip's curiosity
    - (D) Philip and Rosemary's essential malice
    - (E) repressed anger

    (A) There are at least three clues: the terrible weather, the request for a cup of tea, and the word *listless*. Miss Smith's weariness is contrasted with Rosemary's well-fed, well-taken-care-of perkiness.

23. Rosemary's purpose in bringing the stranger home was to --- .
    - (A) make a friend of Miss Smith
    - (B) provide a dinner guest
    - (C) indulge a whim
    - (D) understand a person from another class
    - (E) make amends for a previous slight

    (C) Rosemary is less interested in Miss Smith than in her own self-image as a kind and gentle benefactor. Her hasty dismissal of Miss Smith suggests that this kindness was a self-indulgent action.

24. Which of the following is likely to happen next?
    - (A) Philip leaves in an angry mood.
    - (B) Miss Smith speaks at length with Philip.
    - (C) Philip and Rosemary take Miss Smith to dinner.
    - (D) Philip and Rosemary argue about Miss Smith's presence.
    - (E) Rosemary sends Miss Smith away promptly.

    (E) When Rosemary takes the three pounds from a drawer, we know she is about to send Miss Smith away.

25. The sentence "Her heart beat like a heavy bell" suggests that Rosemary
    - (A) has a physical weakness
    - (B) finds she is running low on funds
    - (C) is about to scream at Miss Smith
    - (D) is jealous
    - (E) realizes some money has been stolen

    (D) Apparently Philip has seen through the motives for Rosemary's actions and has subtly put a stop to her self-indulgence. His comment that Miss Smith is *pretty*, *lovely*, and that he is *bowled over* ends the mockery by making Rosemary instantly jealous.

26. Which of the following best describes the main idea of the selection?
    - (A) German criticism is biased and confusing, with limited sensibility.
    - (B) Falstaff is a major contribution to the literature of laughter.
    - (C) Falstaff is, far and away, Shakespeare's greatest character.
    - (D) Philanthropy can never be associated with Falstaff.
    - (E) Translations of Shakespeare can never do justice to his majestic verse.

    (B) The association of Falstaff with laughter permeates every sentence in the selection. *(A)* and *(E)* may, in part, be inferred, but they are minor details. *(C)* is never discussed or implied *(D)* is irrelevant.

27. The author's attitude toward G. G. Gervinus is one of --- .
    - (A) uncritical acceptance
    - (B) partial disagreement
    - (C) unrelieved scorn
    - (D) solemn appreciation
    - (E) unfair denunciation

    (C) The words associated with Dr. Gervinus are *malignant*, *headaches*, *painful*. The author has little respect for the doctor's judgment.

28. The "author of headaches" is none other than ---.
    (A) Shakespeare
    (B) Falstaff
    (C) Richard Whittington
    (D) G. G. Gervinus
    (E) "the author of laughter"

    (D) The "author of headaches" (Gervinus) is contrasted with the "author of laughter" (Falstaff).

29. With which of the following statements would the author agree?
    (A) The gift of laughter can be greater than the gift of money.
    (B) The sick and the poor alone can truly appreciate Falstaff.
    (C) Life should never be characterized as a "vale of tears."
    (D) Enjoyment of Shakespeare is unfortunately limited to those who speak English.
    (E) Falstaff, though charming, is basically a worthless fellow.

    (A) The author thinks Falstaff's contribution is greater than that of the benevolent Richard Whittington. The remaining alternatives are opposed to ideas expressed in the selection.

30. The author uses *a painful sense of this contrast* to suggest ---.
    (A) frankness   (D) awe
    (B) injustice   (E) envy
    (C) universality

    (E) If Dr. Gervinus cannot equal Falstaff's universal appeal, then he will attack Falstaff out of pure envy.

PART 4

31. Although a bottom quark has a lifetime of only 1.5 trillionths of a second, this period is much --- than scientists had anticipated.
    (A) shorter
    (B) longer
    (C) more dramatic
    (D) less important
    (E) more informative

    (B) The clue lies in the important word *although*, which suggests a contrast. *Only 1.5 trillionths of a second* suggests an almost unimaginable brevity. The only contrasting word is **longer.**

32. Improvements in --- and transportation have converted the entire world into a --- village.
    (A) housing . . leaderless
    (B) finance . . modern
    (C) negotiation . . noisy
    (D) individuality . . disorganized
    (E) communication . . global

    (E) **Global** is clearly the word needed for the second *blank. Modern* is possible but less suitable. **Communication**, often paired with *transportation*, completes the sentence perfectly.

33. Because of the tremendous potential for good or ill, recent progress in the field of genetic engineering has raised both --- and --- for the future.
    (A) hopes . . fears
    (B) challenges . . disappointments
    (C) energy . . concern
    (D) faith . . disbelief
    (E) concerns . . anxieties

    (A) The use of *good or ill, both . . and* suggests we need contrasting words. Though there is a contrast suggested in (B) and (D), only (A) makes sense.

34. At the antique car rally an ancient Franklin began slowly and --- then accelerated and --- by the judges' stand, to the delight of all spectators.
    (A) grotesquely . . wheezed
    (B) steadily . . inched
    (C) noisily . . crept
    (D) uncertainly . . whizzed
    (E) sadly . . went

    (D) *Accelerated* makes nonsense of (A), (B), and (C). *Went* in (E) is too general. Besides, *sadly* makes no sense in the first blank.

35. Contrary to common beliefs about the effectiveness of a loud, --- voice, young children are more likely to obey if they are directed in a --- voice.
    (A) discreet . . low
    (B) sensitive . . colorless
    (C) authoritative . . soft
    (D) piercing . . high
    (E) pleasing . . wavering

    (C) *Contrary* tells us that a loud voice is not too effective. We need a rough synonym in the first blank and a contrasting word in the second. *Piercing* is a possibility in the first blank, but the needed contrast in the second blank is missing in *high*.

PART 5

36. PEDIATRICIAN : CHILD ::
    - (A) ophthalmologist : eyes
    - (B) neurologist : criminals
    - (C) radiologist : mass media
    - (D) geologist : novas
    - (E) philosopher : sculpture

    (A) A **pediatrician** acts upon or treats a **child**. In the same way an **opthalmologist** acts upon or treats **eyes**. (**K**, page 176) The alternatives show no meaningful relationships.

37. PAIN : AGONY ::
    - (A) drowsiness : laziness
    - (B) exploration : ramble
    - (C) industry : weakness
    - (D) plenty : adequacy
    - (E) fun : hilarity

    (E) **Pain** is a lesser degree of **agony**. In the same way **fun** is a lesser degree of **hilarity**. (**Q**, pages 182–183) Similar relationships occur in (B) and (D), but the words are reversed. (C) presents antonyms. *Drowsiness* and *laziness* are related but *drowsiness* is not a degree of *laziness*.

38. SUGAR : CANISTER ::
    - (A) barrel : oil
    - (B) table : dishes
    - (C) pig : sty
    - (D) horse : racetrack
    - (E) sheep : shepherd

    (C) **Sugar** is kept in a **canister**. In the same way **pigs** are kept in a **sty**. (**E**, page 170) *Oil* is kept in a *barrel*, but the words are reversed. *Dishes* may be placed on, not kept in, a *table*; in any event the words are reversed. A *horse* is kept in a *stable*, not a *racetrack*. *Sheep* and **shepherd** are associated in a different way altogether.

39. PHILANTHROPIST : GENEROSITY ::
    - (A) nomad : stability
    - (B) knight : chivalry
    - (C) computer : programmer
    - (D) hockey : puck
    - (E) despot : amnesty

    (B) The essential quality of a **philanthropist** is **generosity**. In the same way the essential quality of a **knight** is **chivalry**. (**L**, page 177) (A) and (E) show contrasted pairs. (C) and (D) are associated pairs, but they do not show the same relationship as does (B).

40. NEGLIGENCE : LAX ::
    - (A) leisure : energetic
    - (B) density : repetitive
    - (C) coincidence : skeptical
    - (D) novelty : fresh
    - (E) guide : candid

    (D) **Lax** is an adjective associated with **negligence**. In the same way, **fresh** is an adjective associated with **novelty**. (**P**, pages 181–182). (A) and (E) suggest opposite qualities. (B) and (C) are scarcely related.

41. TIME : MILLENNIA ::
    - (A) work : salary
    - (B) pain : aches
    - (C) distance : light-years
    - (D) weight : liters
    - (E) joys : laughter

    (C) **Millennia** is a measure of **time**. In the same way, **light-years** is a measure of **distance**. (**T**, page 185) **Liters** measures capacity not *weight*. Though *salary* is related to *work*, it is not a measure of work. (B) and (E) show pairs of related words . . . without any suggestion of measurement.

42. SCULPTOR : CHISEL ::
    - (A) carpenter : square
    - (B) wrench : plumber
    - (C) pilot : airplane
    - (D) surveyor : mortgage
    - (E) lawyer : automobile

    (A) A **sculptor** uses a **chisel** as an important tool in his or her work. In the same way a **carpenter** uses a **square**. (**O**, page 179) A *plumber* uses a *wrench* as an important tool, but the words are reversed. The other selections do not relate a tool and an artisan.

43. HARMLESS : SCOUNDREL ::
    - (A) ingenious : milliner
    - (B) brilliant : moron
    - (C) agent : condescending
    - (D) literate : editor
    - (E) studious : scholar

    (B) A **scoundrel** is not **harmless**. In the same way, a **moron** is not **brilliant**. (**A**, pages 166–167) The words are not antonyms because one word in each pair is a noun and one an adjective. But they do suggest opposition of essential qualities. (A), (D), and (E) suggest association rather than opposition. There is no clear relationship of any kind in (C).

44. FLOWER : SNAPDRAGON ::
    (A) flounder : perch
    (B) bread : doughnut
    (C) collie : spaniel
    (D) oak : elm
    (E) mineral : iron

    (*E*) **Snapdragon** is a more specific term than **flower**. In the same way, **iron** is a more specific term than **mineral**. (**I**, page 174) (*A*), (*C*), and (*D*) provide specific terms only. *Doughnut* is not a specific word for *bread*.

45. ENGRAVE : PLATE ::
    (A) purchase : presentation
    (B) strike : clock
    (C) find : excuses
    (D) bind : book
    (E) try : plan

    (*D*) To **engrave** is to perform some constructive action on a **plate**. In the same way, to **bind** is to perform some constructive action on a **book**. (**J**, page 174). While we may *try* a *plan*, we do not then perform the same kind of physical action as we do when we *engrave* a *plate* or *bind* a *book*. The other alternatives are still further afield.

ANSWERS TO FACSIMILE TEST 2
Section 2
(pages 340–346)

PART 1

1. ACQUIT:
   (A) disentangle (D) convict
   (B) criticize (E) revolve
   (C) pass judgment

   (D) **Acquit** means free of all charges. Therefore its opposite is **convict.** *Pass judgment* is a general term applied to *acquitting* or *convicting*. The other words are unrelated.

2. APPREHEND:
   (A) release (D) comply
   (B) understand (E) prevent
   (C) misinform

   (A) In one sense, **apprehend** means *arrest.* Therefore its opposite is **release.** In another sense *apprehend* means *understand.* (B) would therefore be a synonym, not an antonym.

3. HYPERCRITICAL:
   (A) insincere (D) undemanding
   (B) insecure (E) unwary
   (C) scrupulous

   (D) **Hypercritical** means *too critical.* (For consideration of the Greek prefix *hyper* see page 118). Therefore its opposite is **undemanding.** Don't confuse *hypercritical* with *hypocritical*: *insincere.*

4. TITANIC:
   (A) ungodly (D) slipshod
   (B) small (E) moderate
   (C) quiet

   (B) **Titanic** means *large, huge.* Therefore its opposite is **small.** Though the Titans were Greek gods, *titanic* and *ungodly* are not related.

5. INSATIABLE:
   (A) pleasurable (D) believable
   (B) satisfactory (E) satisfied
   (C) compliable

   (E) **Insatiable** means *unable to be satisfied.* Therefore its opposite is **satisfied.** *Satisfactory* has the same root as *insatiable* and *satisfied*, but its meaning is neither synonymous nor antonymous.

6. DOWN:
   (A) feather (D) fretful
   (B) oblique (E) around
   (C) cheerful

   (C) **Down** has many meanings. The task is to find a meaning that contrasts with the meaning of an alternative. Here *down* means *depressed* and its opposite is **cheerful.** (D) is a related word. (A) is a synonym in one sense. The others refer to directions, neither of which is an antonym.

7. NOTORIOUS:
   (A) infamous (D) flawed
   (B) celebrated (E) respectable
   (C) offensive

   (E) **Notorious** means famous, but in a negative sense. Therefore its opposite is **respectable.** (A) is a synonym. (B) is related in meaning, not an antonym.

8. FLAUNT:
   (A) flout (D) obey
   (B) conceal (E) corrupt
   (C) flatter

   (B) **Flaunt** means *publicly display.* Therefore its opposite is **conceal.** *Flaunt* and *flout* are sometimes confused. They are not antonyms.

9. INEXHAUSTIBLE:
   (A) renewable (D) powerful
   (B) puny (E) marketable
   (C) barren

   (A) **Inexhaustible** means *not able to be used up.* Therefore its opposite is **renewable.** The other words are unrelated.

10. MISGIVING:
    (A) assurance (D) modesty
    (B) acceptance (E) generosity
    (C) indecisiveness

    (A) **Misgiving** means *doubt, uncertainty.* Therefore its opposite is **assurance.** A *misgiving* may lead to *indecisiveness.* The words are not antonyms.

PART 2

11. Initial reserve soon disappeared, and the gathering of bird-watchers soon became as --- as a congregation of first-graders on the school playground.
    - (A) dignified
    - (B) exuberant
    - (C) mischievous
    - (D) subtle
    - (E) impressive

    (B) If the *initial reserve* disappeared, the missing word must suggest its opposite: **exuberant.** There is another clue: the activity of first-graders on a school playground.

12. The more the insect tried to disentangle itself from the spider's web, the more --- it became.
    - (A) wary
    - (B) formidable
    - (C) careless
    - (D) angry
    - (E) enmeshed

    (E) A contrast is suggested between *disentanglement* and the insect's entrapment. The contrasting word here is **enmeshed.**

13. Although most people consider cities --- wildlife, birds and even mammals --- in even the most unlikely urban areas.
    - (A) favorable toward . . thrive
    - (B) devoid of . . deteriorate
    - (C) receptive toward . . appear
    - (D) alien to . . abound
    - (E) unconcerned with . . dart

    (D) The word *unlikely* is an important clue. Both *thrive* and **abound** fit the second blank, but *although* suggests that *favorable toward* (A) does not fit the first blank. **Alien to** and **abound** complete the sentence logically.

14. The book *The Evening Stars* presents a history of television's evening news programs, with --- those news anchors who came to --- the news.
    - (A) disregard for . . lead
    - (B) minor attention to . . enjoy
    - (C) description of . . study
    - (D) emphasis upon . . dominate
    - (E) affection for . . represent

    (D) The title, with its key word *stars*, suggests that the book is dealing with the major news anchors. Therefore **dominate** fits perfectly into the second blank. **Emphasis upon** neatly completes the sentence.

15. Plentiful and crystal clear at its sources, the Arkansas River becomes less and less --- as it flows east, finally disappearing on the --- Kansas plains.

    - (A) abundant . . dry
    - (B) powerful . . fruitful
    - (C) beautiful . . moisture-laden
    - (D) polluted . . unplowed
    - (E) available . . hilly

    (A) The word *plentiful,* followed by *less and less* suggests that a contrast is called for. The essential word for the first blank is **abundant. Dry** perfectly completes the sentence.

PART 3

16. HIGH : AERIE ::
    - (A) puzzling : dishonesty
    - (B) faithful : heretic
    - (C) exaggerated : caricature
    - (D) timid : swashbuckler
    - (E) picturesque : idol

    (C) An **aerie** is **high.** In the same way, a **caricature** is **exaggerated. (B,** pages 168–169) In both pairs an essential quality is listed. Though an *idol* may be *picturesque,* picturesqueness is not an essential quality. In the same way *puzzling* is not essential to *dishonesty.* (*B*) and (*D*) show opposite qualities.

17. SHIP : NAVIGATOR ::
    - (A) angler : lake
    - (B) stage : actor
    - (C) bookkeeper : studio
    - (D) office : puppeteer
    - (E) fire engine : nurse

    (B) A **navigator** is associated with a **ship.** In the same way an **actor** is associated with a **stage. (M,** pages 177–178). An *angler* is associated with a *lake,* but the words are reversed.

18. GERMINATE : GROWTH ::
    - (A) chuckle : humor
    - (B) drop : chair
    - (C) try : failure
    - (D) harden : brittleness
    - (E) combine : mixture

    (E) To **germinate** is to lead to **growth.** In the same way to **combine** is to lead to a **mixture. (D,** page 170) The other alternatives do not show cause and effect.

19. SOLAR SYSTEM : EARTH ::
    (A) nebula : galaxy
    (B) comet : meteor
    (C) planet : satellite
    (D) sun : sunspots
    (E) asteroid : moon

    (D) The **earth** is a part of the **solar system.** In the same way **sunspots** are a part of the **sun.** (**C,** page 169). A *nebula* may be a *galaxy.* A *comet* and a *meteor* are different objects, as are *asteroid* and *moon.* A *satellite* may be attached to a *planet,* but it is not part of the planet.

20. AGRICULTURE : WEATHER ::
    (A) prices : demand
    (B) wool : sheep
    (C) enthusiasm : lubrication
    (D) sincerity : radiation
    (E) wealth : formality

    (A) **Agriculture** is affected by the **weather.** In the same way **prices** are affected by **demand.** (**R,** page 183) None of the other pairs show a similar relationship.

21. PIONEER : TRAILBLAZING ::
    (A) typesetter : authorship
    (B) novelist : censure
    (C) pirate : theft
    (D) flight : fugitive
    (E) usher : entertainment

    (C) A major purpose or activity of the **pioneer** is **trailblazing.** In the same way a major purpose or activity of a **pirate** is **theft.** (**N,** pages 178–179) An *usher* may be present at an *entertainment,* but his or her major activity is showing people to their seats. The words in (*D*) are reversed.

22. INCONVENIENCE : CALAMITY ::
    (A) colorless : dull
    (B) fear : terror
    (C) fault : blame
    (D) diplomacy : tact
    (E) hysteria : reassurance

    (B) **Inconvenience** shows a lesser degree of intensity than **calamity.** In the same way **fear** is a lesser form of **terror.** (**G,** page 173) None of the other pairs show a similar relationship.

23. ETYMOLOGY : DERIVATIONS ::
    (A) archaeology : rivers
    (B) entomology : primates
    (C) cosmology : decoration
    (D) ornithology : birds
    (E) analogy : argumentation

    (D) **Etymology** is the study of (word) **derivations.** In the same way **ornithology** is the study of **birds.** (**S,** page 184) *Entomology* is the study of *insects,* not *primates.*

24. ROD : FISHING ::
    (A) ski : bobsledding
    (B) football : volleyball
    (C) javelin : shot put
    (D) sailing : oar
    (E) bow : archery

    (E) A **rod** is used in **fishing.** In the same way a **bow** is used in **archery.** (**F,** page 172) (*A*), (*B*), and (*C*) deal with wholly different activities. An *oar* may be used in *sailing* if the wind drops down, but it is not essential to sailing. Besides, the words are reversed.

25. YEAR : DECADE ::
    (A) comma : period
    (B) sapling : tree
    (C) hawk : falcon
    (D) anniversary : party
    (E) university : college

    (B) A **year** is smaller than a **decade.** In the same way a **sapling** is smaller than a **tree.** (**H,** page 173) (*E*) might be a possibility, but the words are reversed.

PART 4

To benefit from the analysis of Part 4 be sure to go back to the original reading selection to see how and why answers have been derived. (Page 342).

26. Which of the following expresses the main idea of the passage?
    (A) Sleepy villages fostered the rise of the bourgeoisie.
    (B) Mediterranean Europe put clocks on cathedrals for prestige purposes.
    (C) The history of clocks was shaped largely by the dwellers in cities.
    (D) The alliance of the church and the nobility made clocks a needed commodity.
    (E) The older elite made the cities prosperous.

    (C) The first two sentences suggest the topic. The first sentence suggests that the clock industry was crucial to the bourgeoisie. The second sentence links *towns* to *bourgeoisie.* The sentences that follow elaborate on the importance of clocks to the cities and their leaders. The other alternatives are details.

27. The "new elite" (line 15)
    (A) lived in palatial mansions in the country
    (B) cooperated closely with the older landed elite
    (C) ordered mechanical clocks from cottage industries near the cities
    (D) possessed wealth and a sense of power
    (E) had only meager fiscal resources

    (D) The expression *possessed of great wealth and a sense of power* (line 16) identifies the answer to this question. There is no linkage with the other alternatives.

28. As used here in a figurative sense, *the crown* refers to _____ .
    (A) landed gentry
    (B) displaced royalty
    (C) the power of the old elite
    (D) local representatives of government
    (E) the king and his government

    (E) The *crown* as an expression identifying the king and his government is an example of metonymy (page 47). The word *crown* is itself an indication it refers to the king.

29. As used in this selection *nodes* (line 13) means ___.
    (A) centering points   (D) representatives
    (B) examples   (E) agents
    (C) models

    (A) The busy marketplaces, administrative centers, and exchange points suggest that *nodes* means *centering points*. The word *centers* is a most helpful clue.

30. With which of the following statements would the author probably NOT agree?
    (A) Clocks are essential for the growth of an industrial and commercial society.
    (B) During the late Middle Ages clocks performed an almost exclusively decorative function.
    (C) The bourgeoisie were able to secure a great deal of freedom for their municipalities.
    (D) Great agricultural and commercial expansion took place during the high Middle Ages.
    (E) The town, rather than the village, became more important as the high Middle Ages rolled on.

    (B) The author points out that clocks were functional, valuable as far more than mere decorations. The other alternatives are stated or implied. (Don't fail to see *NOT* in the question.)

31. The purpose of the author seems to be to ---.
    (A) glorify the robot at the expense of man
    (B) pay special tribute to the skill of a new-born infant
    (C) emphasize some of the limitations of robots
    (D) recommend the use of a computer in every home
    (E) commend the popular media for the explanation of robotics

    (C) The opening sentence makes the major point that robots have limitations, and succeeding sentences amplify that statement. (A) runs counter to the theme of the selection. (B) is a detail. (D) and (E) are irrelevant.

32. For imitating human skills, all the following are mentioned as necessary *EXCEPT* _____ .
    (A) visual skill
    (B) planning
    (C) locomotive skills
    (D) arithmetic calculations
    (E) manipulation abilities

    (D) (A), (C), and (E) are mentioned together in lines 15–16. Planning is mentioned in line 17. (D) is nowhere mentioned. (Don't miss *EXCEPT*.)

33. Which of the following statements may be accurately derived from the selection?
    I. The typical science-fiction robot is not yet available.
    II. After 20 years of research, scientists have acquired a new humility about humanoid robots.
    III. A child is very efficient in a task requiring patience and repetition.
    IV. Though a robot cannot yet understand a natural language, it is able to recognize a face.
    V. The best robots are put on wheels.
    (A) I, III, and V
    (B) II and IV
    (C) IV and V
    (D) I, II, and III
    (E) I and II

    (E) This is more difficult because it presents items in combination. The selection does not talk about a child's patience or efficiency in repetitive tasks (*III*). The selection flatly denies (*IV*). It makes no value judgments about (*V*). Only (*I*) and (*II*) may be derived from the selection.

34. Which of the following titles best summarizes the content of the passage?
    (A) Boston: The Edinburgh of New England
    (B) The Effect of Environment on Culture
    (C) Boston, City of Ice and Granite
    (D) A Tale of Two Cities
    (E) The People of Boston

    (A) The comparison of Boston and Edinburgh runs through the selection. The topic sentence, the first, tells the story. (B) and (D) are too broad. (C) is misleading. (E) is a detail.

35. New Englanders liked to read Wordsworth because ———.
    (A) his flowery poetry contrasted with the New England scene
    (B) they recognized in him a kindred spirit
    (C) Sir Walter Scott had recommended him
    (D) Wordsworth composed his verse in the mountains
    (E) Wordsworth became associated in their minds with Edinburgh

    (B) New Englanders liked Wordsworth's "bareness and simplicity, together with his loftiness and depth." These qualities are inferred as applying to New Englanders as well. The others are not mentioned.

36. The "reserves of feeling and perception" (line 20) ———.
    (A) contrasted with the ice and granite of the New England mind
    (B) proved to the Scottish traveller that Boston was not as interesting as Edinburgh
    (C) contradicted Hazlitt's comments about Boston
    (D) showed that Bostonians were democrats as well as aristocrats
    (E) were locked inside, never to play a role in Boston's future

    (A) Lines 15–21 clearly present two sides of the New England mind: the ice and the granite and the reserves of feeling and perception.

37. The meaning of the last sentence may be summarized in this way.
    (A) Dickens considered the qualities of Boston more objectionable than those of other cities.
    (B) Though Bostonians were interested in money, other American cities far outdid them in this respect.
    (C) Bostonians worshiped a pagan idol while keeping a proper pretense for the world.
    (D) A small calf symbolized the great wealth that Boston had amassed in a generation.

(E) Bostonians favored freedom of worship perhaps more than any other city in America.

    (B) The golden calf is a symbol of wealth. The Bostonian love of wealth paled (*pygmy*) beside the positive adulation (*giant*) of other American cities. Dickens praised Boston (A). (C) and (D) take the golden calf literally instead of figuratively. The comparison in (E) is nowhere made.

38. The author apparently believes that ———.
    (A) thought is essentially a direct, logical process
    (B) thinking should be divorced from emotions and sentiments
    (C) Kant named his book *A Critique of Pure Reason* as a witty jest
    (D) a mind is a pure abstraction, unpolluted by extraneous impulses
    (E) poets do more real thinking than philosophers

    (E) (A) and (D) contradict the point of the selection. (C) is nowhere suggested. The author doesn't take a position in (B).

39. "The pure gold, transparent as glass," is compared with ———.
    (A) the paving in the celestial city
    (B) the mind of the philosopher
    (C) pure reason
    (D) the effects of savage traditions and infantile impressions
    (E) the writings of Kant

    (C) The last sentence of paragraph one specifically says that pure reason is mythical, like "the pure gold, transparent as glass." The gold is part of the mythical pavement, not compared with it (A). The other selections merely take snatches of phrases from the selection without making the comparison.

40. According to the author, most of our thoughts are ———.
    (A) motivated by greed
    (B) directed toward positive goals
    (C) significant but personal
    (D) haphazard and fleeting
    (E) readily apparent to our friends

    (D) One clue to the answer is the expression *incredible rapidity* (line 32) and the sentence of which it is a part. The following sentences give examples of this flightiness and instability. Thoughts may be personal but not necessarily significant (C). (E) contradicts the meaning of the passage. (A) and (B) are nowhere implied.

ANSWERS TO FACSIMILE TEST 3
Section 1
(Pages 347–352)

PART 1

1. BAN:
   - (A) allow
   - (B) control
   - (C) deflect
   - (D) enclose
   - (E) deter

   (A) **Ban** means *prohibit*. Its opposite is **allow**. *Ban* is itself a word with negative connotation. The alternatives lack this connotation.

2. OFFHAND:
   - (A) casual
   - (B) backward
   - (C) prepared
   - (D) extreme
   - (E) callous

   (C) **Offhand** means *casual, without preparation*. Its opposite is **prepared**. The other words are unrelated.

3. SULKY:
   - (A) comely
   - (B) smooth
   - (C) irritable
   - (D) lackluster
   - (E) cheerful

   (E) **Sulky** means *sullen, bad-tempered*. Its opposite is **cheerful**. *Irritable* is a related word. The other words are unrelated.

4. IMPRESSIONABLE:
   - (A) naive
   - (B) vigorous
   - (C) excitable
   - (D) shy
   - (E) indifferent

   (E) **Impressionable** means *receptive, responsible*. Its opposite is **indifferent**. An *impressionable* person may be *shy* or *naive*, but the words are not antonyms.

5. DORMANT:
   - (A) biting
   - (B) colorful
   - (C) repressed
   - (D) active
   - (E) drowsy

   (D) **Dormant** means *inactive, sluggish*. Its opposite is **active**. *Drowsy* is a synonym. The anagram *mordant* means **biting**, but *dormant* and *biting* are unrelated.

6. ADAMANT:
   - (A) brilliant
   - (B) hard
   - (C) laudatory
   - (D) yielding
   - (E) apparent

   (D) **Adamant** means *unyielding, unbreakable*. Its opposite is **yielding**. *Hard* is a related word.

7. PROFUSION:
   - (A) confusion
   - (B) discipline
   - (C) support
   - (D) scarcity
   - (E) complexity

   (D) **Profusion** means *abundance, extravagance*. Its opposite is **scarcity**. *Confusion* sounds like *profusion* but is unrelated. (*Pro* and *con* are not opposite in this pair!)

8. HETEROGENEOUS:
   - (A) well distributed
   - (B) identical
   - (C) unclassified
   - (D) sullen
   - (E) obscure

   (B) **Heterogeneous** means *different, unlike*. Its opposite is **identical**. *Heterogeneous* groupings may be *well distributed*, but the words are not antonyms. The other words are unrelated.

9. HONEYED:
   - (A) syrupy
   - (B) tasty
   - (C) defrauded
   - (D) blameworthy
   - (E) biting

   (E) **Honeyed** means *soothing, sweet*. Its opposite is **biting**. *Syrupy* and *tasty* are somewhat related in sense but not antonyms of *honeyed*. The other words are unrelated.

10. DIMINUTIVE:
    - (A) amiable
    - (B) huge
    - (C) capable
    - (D) musical
    - (E) fierce

    (B) **Diminutive** means *small*. Its opposite is **huge**. *Diminuendo* is a word used in music, but *diminutive* is not related to *musical*.

11. DEBONAIR:
    - (A) defiant
    - (B) carefree
    - (C) coarse
    - (D) swanky
    - (E) enclosed

    (C) **Debonair** means *suave, polished*. Its opposite is **coarse**. *Carefree* and *swanky* are related words.

12. COMEDOWN:
    - (A) achievement
    - (B) despair
    - (C) laughter
    - (D) assent
    - (E) advertisement

    (A) **Comedown** is a *failure*, a *descent in rank or dignity*. Its opposite is **achievement**. A *comedown* may cause *despair*, but the words are not antonyms.

ENGLISH FOR THE COLLEGE BOARDS

13. PROJECT:
 (A) instill
 (B) compress
 (C) retract
 (D) impel
 (E) retrain

 (C) **Project** is here used as a verb meaning *stick out*, *protrude*. Since the alternatives are all verbs, you know that the *verb* use is called for. Its opposite is **retract**. In one sense of *project*, *instill* is related, but in no sense is it an antonym.

14. AROMATIC:
 (A) spicy
 (B) offensive
 (C) fresh
 (D) salty
 (E) damp

 (B) **Aromatic** means *fragrant*, *having a pleasing smell*. Its opposite is **offensive**. The other words are sometimes associated with *aromatic*, but none is an antonym.

15. JOVIAL:
 (A) glum
 (B) merry
 (C) downtrodden
 (D) polished
 (E) critical

 (A) **Jovial** means *cheerful*, *good-humored*. Its opposite is **glum**. *Merry* is a synonym.

PART 2

16. The --- heat at midday was briefly relieved by a thunderstorm, but a short time later the temperatures again began to climb.
 (A) anticipated
 (B) moderate
 (C) timely
 (D) dappled
 (E) oppressive

 (E) The key word is *relieved*, which suggests the heat must have been *uncomfortable*. The second clause supports the choice of **oppressive** in the blank.

17. Though playwrights can usually manage a good first act, by the middle of the last act, --- often replaces ---.
 (A) consternation . . contemplation
 (B) desperation . . inspiration
 (C) deliberation . . commendation
 (D) cancellation . . alteration
 (E) stagnation . . disorganization

 (B) *Though* tells us a contrast is called for between the good first act and the middle of the last act. The first word in the pair must be negative and the second positive. *Consternation* is a possibility for the first blank, but *contemplation* makes no sense. The only suitable pair is **desperation . . inspiration**.

18. The --- of many coastal plains and moors for housing and other development has --- many fine ecological habitats.
 (A) inaccessibility . . uncovered
 (B) analysis . . displayed
 (C) suitability . . doomed
 (D) advertisement . . enhanced
 (E) exclusion . . emphasized

 (C) The context suggests that ecological habitats are being threatened. The only suitable word for the second blank is **doomed**. **Suitability** fits nicely into the first blank.

19. On our spaceship, Earth, recycling is not a --- to be --- but a necessity to guide our actions.
 (A) concept . . followed
 (B) plan . . adapted
 (C) dream . . fantasized
 (D) luxury . . indulged
 (E) discipline . . fostered

 (D) *Not* tells us the first blank is opposed to *necessity*. The opposite of *necessity* is **luxury**. **Indulge** suitably completes the sentence.

20. Like an airplane in a steep power dive, the falcon --- down upon the --- sparrows and captured a terrified victim.
 (A) swooped . . scattering
 (B) lunged . . assembled
 (C) flew . . disinterested
 (D) looked . . sluggish
 (E) circled . . courageous

 (A) The falcon's action is compared to an airplane in a steep power dive. The verb that best expressed the comparison is **swooped**. **Scattering** suitably completes the sentence.

PART 3

To benefit from the analysis of Part 3 be sure to go back to the original reading selection to see how and why answers have been derived. (Page 349)

21. The chief focus of the passage is on which of the following?
    - (A) Describing a typical meal in a middle-class family
    - (B) Portraying the character of Gant
    - (C) Sermonizing on the dangers of eating rapidly
    - (D) Praising moderation in all things
    - (E) Suggesting that a roast is a better meal than fish

    (B) The unusual behavior of Gant is touched upon throughout the selection, as the family revolves about him. (A) is all wrong. (C) might be inferred, but it's not the main idea. (D) is much too broad. (E) is nowhere stated or implied.

22. Of Gant it might reasonably be said that ---.
    - (A) he was a devoted father and husband
    - (B) he believed in moderation in all things
    - (C) he was cruel to Eliza
    - (D) he didn't learn from experience
    - (E) he was careful not to make the children nervous

    (D) That he kept choking on a fish bone says little for his ability to learn from experience. In some respects he may have been a devoted father (A), but nothing is said about his credentials as a husband. He obviously didn't believe in moderation (D) and he did make the children nervous (E). (C) is not stated or implied.

23. Gant prodded Eugene's belly to ---.
    - (A) make sure Eugene was completely stuffed
    - (B) keep the baby awake
    - (C) irritate Eliza
    - (D) keep the children in line
    - (E) show his favoritism for the youngest child

    (A) *Impregnable to the heavy prod of Gant's big finger* (lines 8–9) tells us he wanted to make sure Eugene was stuffed.

24. The author's attitude toward Gant's table behavior is one of ---.
    - (A) awe   (D) envy
    - (B) endorsement   (E) disapproval
    - (C) fury

    (E) Since Gant was doing nothing to help self or family, the author clearly disapproves of

Gant's table behavior. (A) and (B) are incorrect. (C) is too strong. (D) is nowhere suggested.

25. As used in this selection, *Gargantuan* (line 3) means ---.
    - (A) modest   (D) tasty
    - (B) thrifty   (E) rationed
    - (C) huge

    (C) The portions had to be large to fill Eugene's distending belly. (A), (B), and (E) are opposed to the meaning of the selection. (D) is not related. *Gargantuan* is a word from a name.

26. Which of the following titles best summarizes the content of the passage?
    - (A) Symbols vs. Reality
    - (B) Our Time-Binding Ability
    - (C) Man vs. Animal
    - (D) The Theories of Korzybski
    - (E) Deciding the Future

    (B) The concept of time-binding permeates the passage. (A) is much too broad. (C) is a detail in a very minor sense. (D) is a minor detail. (E) is not touched upon.

27. The equation $E = mc^2$ is cited as dependent upon ----.
    - (A) an incredible breakthrough by Korzybski
    - (B) the achievement of ethnic groups
    - (C) a young student at the blackboard
    - (D) a lucky accident by a researcher of genius
    - (E) the accumulated wisdom of the ages

    (E) The sentence containing the equation (lines 20–28) emphasizes, the accumulated wisdom of the ages. The alternatives are off the topic.

28. Which of the following most effectively used *figurative language* to make the author's point?
    - (A) "It is the one characteristic that clearly distinguishes him from all other forms of life."
    - (B) "He alone can use the knowledge accumulated in the past."
    - (C) "He stands on the shoulders of the dead to peer into the future."
    - (D) "No one group, *as a group*, is inherently superior or inferior to any other."
    - (E) "On a statistical basis we expect to find relatively the same percentage of subaverage, and above-average in each ethnic group."

    (C) There are no *literal* dead shoulders to stand on. This is an example of *figurative* language. The other statements are quite literal.

29. Which of the following statements may be accurately derived from the selection?
   I. Man's control of his environment is traceable to his time-binding ability.
   II. As a group, no group is basically more intelligent than any other.
   III. Animals can transmit knowledge from generation to generation.
   IV. Symbols are intimately connected with time-binding.
   V. The cerebral cortex is strongly developed in most animals.
   (A) I, II, V (D) III, V
   (B) I, III, IV (E) all
   (C) I, II, IV

   (C) First decide which statements may be derived from the selection and then look at the alternatives. Alternative (I) is suggested at the beginning of the third paragraph (lines 33–38). Alternative (II) is flatly stated in the sentence beginning ''No one group . . .'' (lines 38–40). Alternative (III) is denied in the first paragraph. Alternative (IV) is covered in the last two sentences of the second paragraph. Alternative (V) is nowhere stated or implied. Thus, (I), (II), and (IV) may be derived from the selection.

30. A good definition of *time binding* is _____.
   (A) controlling time through the use of symbols
   (B) trusting that time will solve problems
   (C) putting past ages into categories for study
   (D) a time awareness shared by man and the higher animals
   (E) trying to predict the future in terms of the past

   (A) Again the last two sentences of the second paragraph provide the answer. The alternatives are general, fuzzy statements unrelated to, or contradicted by, the passage.

PART 4

31. Though perpetual motion has long been classified as an impossible dream, --- inventors still try to patent machines that are supposed to run forever.
   (A) informed (D) candid
   (B) callous (E) undaunted
   (C) biased

   (E) Perpetual motion is an impossible dream. *Though* tells us the inventors refuse to accept this truth. The only word that makes sense is **undaunted**. The inventors are not discouraged by the cold reality.

32. In an attempt to stop the --- filibuster, some senators mapped strategy to --- the cloture rule.
   (A) interminable . . enforce
   (B) amusing . . dramatize
   (C) unexpected . . discuss
   (D) simple . . research
   (E) enlightening . . evaluate

   (A) *Stop* tells us that the filibuster is unpopular. We need a negative word for the first blank. Only **interminable** fits. **Enforce** effectively completes the sentence. (C), with *unexpected* in the first blank, seems possible, but *discussing* a rule wouldn't stop the filibuster; so **discuss** doesn't fit.

33. The ranger explained, to our ---, that there is no typical ''sled dog,'' that many breeds have proved suitable for the --- demands of exertion in temperatures below zero.
   (A) consternation . . delicate
   (B) horror . . occasional
   (C) surprise . . rigorous
   (D) amusement . . unfair
   (E) satisfaction . . expected

   (C) The first word of each pair in (A) and (B) is much too strong. (D) and (E) make little sense. If there is no *typical* ''sled dog,'' we must have been surprised.

34. Events in the Olympics are not ---, for many events once popular have been dropped and, ---, many new events have been added.
   (A) dull . . certainly
   (B) controlled . . surprisingly
   (C) changeable . . similarly
   (D) unvarying . . conversely
   (E) historical . . advantageously

   (D) If events are being dropped and added, then the events are not unvarying. (C) presents an opposite meaning entirely.

35. Tour groups in the South Pacific --- seem to find that explorer Captain James Cook --- them, whether the scene is Hawaii, Tahiti, or New Caledonia.
   (A) doggedly . . outdid
   (B) inevitably . . preceded
   (C) breathlessly . . foresaw
   (D) irritably . . missed
   (E) complacently . . avoided

   (B) (C), (D), and (E) refer to emotional reactions out of place with the quiet tone of the sentence. Since Captain Cook was an explorer, not a tourist, *outdid* makes nonsense out of (A). Only **inevitably . . preceded** makes sense within the sentence.

PART 5

36. STEAM : SCALD ::
   (A) mist : reveal
   (B) telescope : photograph
   (C) ice : chill
   (D) waterfall : display
   (E) tree : leaf

   (*C*) **Steam scalds**. In the same way **ice chills**
   (**P**, page 181). A *mist* conceals, not *reveals*.
   A *telescope* may be used to *photograph* celestial bodies, but the photographing is not
   essentially connected with the telescope.

37. EXCESSIVE : SCARCITY ::
   (A) cruel : joy
   (B) energetic : fatigue
   (C) curious : vigor
   (D) numerous : quantity
   (E) serious : play

   (*B*) When something is **excessive**, there is no
   scarcity. In the same way, when someone
   is **energetic**, there is no **fatigue**. (**A**, pages
   166–167). Note that the two pairs contain
   opposed words, but they are not the same
   part of speech. **Excessive** and **energetic** are
   adjectives. **Scarcity** and **fatigue** are nouns.
   Play can be a very **serious** business, eliminating (*E*). In (*A*), *miserable* would be a
   better pairing than **cruel**.

38. AERIALIST : TRAPEZE ::
   (A) makeup : clown
   (B) score : singer
   (C) jogger : routine
   (D) circus : ringmaster
   (E) pathfinder : compass

   (*E*) The **aerialist** uses a **trapeze** in his or her major activity. In the same way, a **pathfinder**
   uses a **compass**. (**O**, page 179) A *clown* uses
   makeup, but the words are reversed, as are
   score : *singer*. A *jogger* may follow a *routine*, but he or she doesn't *use* a routine.

39. TRIP : STUMBLE ::
   (A) weep : shout
   (B) dominate : befriend
   (C) try : err
   (D) amuse : laugh
   (E) eject : recall

   (*D*) To **stumble** results from to **trip**. In the same
   way, to **laugh** results from to **amuse**. Cause
   and effect are suggested here. (**D**, page 170)
   (*E*) suggests opposites. There is no connection between *weep* and *shout*.

40. FOOT-POUND : WORK ::
   (A) kilowatt-hour : electricity
   (B) land : acre
   (C) dollar : gold
   (D) sigh : sadness
   (E) pound : liquid

   (*A*) **Foot-pound** is a measure of **work**. In the
   same way a **kilowatt-hour** is a measure of
   electricity. (**T**, page 185). *Acre* is a measure
   of *land*, but the words are reversed.

41. WEED : GARDEN::
   (A) trim : hedge
   (B) describe : scene
   (C) enjoy : concert
   (D) soar : sailplane
   (E) add : numbers

   (*A*) When we **weed** a **garden** or **trim** a **hedge**,
   we perform a physical action. (**R**, page 183)
   The hedge and the garden are physically
   changed by the activity. When we *describe*
   a *scene*, *enjoy* a *concert*, or *add numbers*,
   we are not performing the same kind of
   physical activity.

42. NURTURE : SUPPORTIVE ::
   (A) object : rude
   (B) save : frugal
   (C) fret : funny
   (D) judge : argumentative
   (E) reprimand : sorrowful

   (*B*) Those who **nurture** are **supportive**. In the
   same way those who **save** are **frugal**. (**B**,
   pages 168–169). The alternatives show relationships, but these are nonessential or
   negative relationships. Those who *object*
   may or may not be *rude*. Those who *fret* are
   not likely to be *funny*. Those who *judge*
   should be impartial, not *argumentative*.
   Those who *reprimand* may make others *sorrowful*.

43. ARBITER : IMPARTIALITY ::
   (A) angler : ingenuity
   (B) gardener : diversity
   (C) artist : creativity
   (D) hunter : compassion
   (E) musician : serenity

   (*C*) An essential quality of an **arbiter** is **impartiality**. In the same way an essential quality
   of an **artist** is **creativity**. (**L**, page 177) In
   the remaining alternatives, the qualities may
   be associated with the subjects, but the connection is not essential.

44. MALICE : HUMANE ::
   (A) crusade : evangelical
   (B) health : painstaking
   (C) accord : agreeable
   (D) accident : incidental
   (E) farce : serious

   (*E*) **Malice** is not **humane**. In the same way a **farce** is not **serious**. (**A**, pages 166–167). These are opposed words of different parts of speech. (*A*) and (*C*) show related words, not opposed.

45. MOON : TIDES ::
   (A) pen : pencil
   (B) dog : kennel
   (C) friend : acquaintance
   (D) weather : crops
   (E) telephone : message

   (*D*) The **moon** acts upon **tides**. In the same way **weather** acts upon **crops**. (**J**, page 174) The alternatives fail to show a similar relationship.

ANSWERS TO FACSIMILE TEST 3
Section 2
(Pages 353–359)

PART 1

1. DYNAMIC:
   (A) electronic
   (B) energetic
   (C) mechanical
   (D) aroused
   (E) feeble

   (E) **Dynamic** means *active, energetic*. Its opposite is **feeble.** *Energetic* is a synonym.

2. GLARING:
   (A) glowing
   (B) unseen
   (C) obvious
   (D) daring
   (E) offensive

   (B) **Glaring** means *very bright and obvious*. Its opposite is **unseen.** *Obvious* is a synonym.

3. FORBADE:
   (A) authorized
   (B) dissented
   (C) told in advance
   (D) argued
   (E) preferred

   (A) **Forbade** means *prohibited*. Its opposite is **authorized.** Don't be misled by *for*. The prefix *fore* (not *for*) means *in advance*.

4. UNIMPAIRED:
   (A) doubled
   (B) unique
   (C) unmatched
   (D) injured
   (E) improved

   (D) **Unimpaired** means *not damaged or injured*. Its opposite is **injured.** Don't be misled by the root *pair* and link it with *doubled*. Actually the *root* in *unimpaired* is not linked with *pair*, meaning *two*.

5. VACUOUS:
   (A) heavy
   (B) full
   (C) exalted
   (D) evil
   (E) exhausted

   (B) **Vacuous** means *empty*. Its opposite is **full.**

6. ARID:
   (A) understated
   (B) afflicted
   (C) fundamental
   (D) fruitful
   (E) sandy

   (D) **Arid** means *dry, unproductive*. Its opposite is **fruitful. Arid** soil is often *sandy*, but the words are not antonyms.

7. INSOLENT:
   (A) lazy
   (B) contemptuous
   (C) courteous
   (D) sensitive
   (E) cutting

   (C) **Insolent** means *overbearing, rude*. Its opposite is **courteous.** *Contemptuous* is a related word.

8. HACKNEYED:
   (A) trite
   (B) ample
   (C) complete
   (D) handwritten
   (E) creative

   (E) **Hackneyed** means *overused, trite, commonplace*. Its opposite is **creative.** *Trite* is a synonym.

9. INVINCIBLE:
   (A) vulnerable
   (B) manageable
   (C) tolerable
   (D) portable
   (E) comparable

   (A) **Invincible** means *unconquerable*. Its opposite is **vulnerable.**

10. DILATE:
    (A) draw
    (B) contract
    (C) expand
    (D) digress
    (E) apply

    (B) **Dilate** means *enlarge*. Its opposite is **contract.** *Expand* is a synonym.

PART 2

11. Many tennis experts suggest that the difference between the greats in tennis and the nearly greats is more a matter of --- and single-mindedness of purpose than raw ability.
    (A) talent
    (B) dexterity
    (C) egotism
    (D) concentration
    (E) guile

    (D) The context suggests a contrast between *raw ability* and another quality. That quality is here linked with *single-mindedness* of *purpose*. *Talent* and *dexterity* are too close to *raw ability*. *Guile* and *egotism* are irrelevant. The only word that fits is **concentration.**

12. Looking like something out of ---, a new X-ray machine can explore the body from every angle without making --- and putting a scalpel to the patient.
    (A) mystery stories . . an enquiry
    (B) science fiction . . an incision
    (C) motion pictures . . a fuss
    (D) westerns . . a diagnosis
    (E) fantasy . . a disturbance

    (B) "Putting a scalpel" suggests *cutting*, an **incision.** This new machine doesn't make an *incision.* Thus (B) is the correct answer. **Science fiction** fits neatly into the first blank.

13. --- gas furnaces may run at 65 percent efficiency or less, but a --- breakthrough now offers furnaces with efficiency ratings of 96 percent or more.
    (A) conventional . . technological
    (B) rejected . . former
    (C) natural . . modest
    (D) ancient . . well-documented
    (E) unpopular . . costly

    (A) *But* tells us a contrast is needed. *Breakthrough* contrasts with only one word, **conventional. Technological** perfectly completes the sentence.

14. The vice-presidency is widely considered a do-nothing office with little or no ---, yet there is never a shortage of applicants for that --- lowly position.
    (A) money . . truly
    (B) regrets . . apparently
    (C) clout . . disgracefully
    (D) reward . . historically
    (E) prestige . . supposedly

    (E) *Clout, reward,* and *prestige* all fit into the first blank, but only **supposedly** suitably completes the sentence. (D) is the closest alternative, but when there are two possibilities, be sure to pick the better.

15. The All-Star game is a --- affair, offering the opportunity of making a great play and becoming a hero or committing a serious error and becoming an object of ---.
    (A) breathless . . wonderment
    (B) typical . . scorn
    (C) one-shot . . criticism
    (D) well-publicized . . analysis
    (E) nightmare . . approval

    (C) The context suggests a contrast between *becoming a hero* and *becoming an object of* **criticism. Scorn** is too strong, and **typical** doesn't fit well into the first blank. Only (C) makes good sense.

PART 3

16. UTOPIA : PERFECTION ::
    (A) anesthesia : activity
    (B) uproar : noise
    (C) impudence : attention
    (D) contract : contribution
    (E) authority : commendation

    (B) The quality associated with **utopia** is **perfection.** In the same way the quality associated with **uproar** is **noise.** (P, page 181)

17. INFINITY : BOUNDLESS ::
    (A) emotion : satisfying
    (B) gullibility : credulous
    (C) distinction : similarity
    (D) aptness : dexterity
    (E) deviation : repetition

    (B) By definition **infinity** is **boundless.** In the same way **gullibility** is **credulous.** The words in the pairs are related words, though not of the same part of speech. (B, page 168) *Emotion* may or may not be *satisfying.* Beware : (D) presents related words, but these are synonyms, of the same part of speech.

18. SOOTHSAYER : FORETELLS ::
    (A) whimpers : puppy
    (B) soloist : animates
    (C) accountant : calculates
    (D) amateur : personifies
    (E) welder : glows

    (C) A **soothsayer foretells.** In the same way an **accountant calculates.** (K, page 176). A *puppy whimpers,* but the words are reversed.

19. FILE : CORRESPONDENCE ::
    (A) drawer : desk
    (B) stream : brook
    (C) book : concept
    (D) closet : clothing
    (E) room : window

    (D) **Correspondence** is kept in a **file.** In the same way **clothing** is kept in a **closet.** (E, page 170). The alternatives do not show the same relationship between container and thing contained.

20. BEAGLE : DOG ::
    (A) sapphire : gem
    (B) cheetah : leopard
    (C) salamander : snake
    (D) beech : oak
    (E) insect : spider

    (*A*) **Beagle** is a more specific term for **dog.** In the same way **sapphire** is a more specific term for **gem. (I,** page 174) (*B*) and (*D*) contain specific terms only. A *salamander* is not a *snake,* just as an *insect* is not a *spider.*

21. PSEUDONYM : AUTHENTIC ::
    (A) flicker : flame
    (B) deliberation : reasonable
    (C) writer : anonymity
    (D) delay : punctual
    (E) measure : proportional

    (*D*) A **pseudonym** is not **authentic.** In the same way **delay** is opposed to **punctual. (A,** pages 166–167). These are opposed words of different parts of speech. *Deliberation* may or may not be *reasonable.* A *measure* may or may not be *proportional.* In (*A*) and (*C*) both words are the same part of speech.

22. APPRENTICE : LEARN ::
    (A) penitent : rejoice
    (B) humanitarian : observe
    (C) devotee : fear
    (D) blackguard : reclaim
    (E) charlatan : deceive

    (*E*) The purpose of an **apprentice** is to **learn.** In the same way the purpose of a **charlatan** is to **deceive. (N,** pages 178–179) The other alternatives show possible casual relationships but not major purposes.

23. BLASE : APATHY ::
    (A) lacking : deficiency
    (B) defense : armored
    (C) convex : microscopic
    (D) argumentative : conundrum
    (E) pagan : religious

    (*A*) To be **blase** is characteristic of **apathy.** In the same way to be **lacking** is characteristic of **deficiency. (A,** pages 166–167) These are related words, but of different parts of speech. The other words show no meaningful associations.

24. NICK : GOUGE ::
    (A) niche : chip
    (B) crater : lava
    (C) dislike : detest
    (D) lethal : deadly
    (E) correction : fact

(*C*) **Nick** is a lesser form of **gouge.** In the same way **dislike** is a lesser form of **detest. (G,** pages 172–173) *Lava* pours from a *crater.* It is not a lesser form of *crater.*

25. SUBHEAD : OUTLINE ::
    (A) song : recitation
    (B) lamp : light
    (C) clock : chime
    (D) lion : paw
    (E) sole : shoe

    (*E*) A **subhead** is part of an **outline.** In the same way a **sole** is part of a **shoe. (C,** page 169) In (*D*) the words are reversed.

PART 4

To benefit from the analysis of Part 4 be sure to go back to the original reading selection to see how and why answers have been derived. (Pages 355–356).

26. The author's attitude toward the possibility of visitors from out of space can best be characterized as ---.
    (A) excitedly positive
    (B) quietly skeptical
    (C) paradoxically contradictory
    (D) generally receptive
    (E) unexpectedly indifferent

    (*B*) The words "no evidence in its favor that is in the least convincing" (lines 19–21) clearly indicate the author's attitude is **skeptical.**

27. Stories about Alexander the Great and Charlemagne demonstrate ---.
    (A) a completely fictional source
    (B) the gullibility of Eric von Daniken
    (C) a tie-in with visits by extraterrestrials
    (D) the influence of primitive technology
    (E) the legend-making abilities of human beings

    (*E*) The sentence beginning with "elaborate legends" (lines 24–28) makes the point that *human beings are prone to create legends.* The Sherlock Holmes example reinforces the point.

28. Which of the following statements may be accurately derived from the selection?
   I. Though supposedly a fictional character, Sherlock Holmes actually existed.
   II. The great pyramids in Egypt could have been created by people with the technology of the times.
   III. The belief in extraterrestrial visitors springs from motivating yearnings in all cultures.
   IV. Though slight, the evidence for visits by extraterrestrials in recent years is convincing.
   V. The ancients had qualities modern people do not have, but their intelligence was not as great as ours.
   (A) I, III, V
   (B) II, IV, V
   (C) II, III
   (D) I, IV
   (E) II only

   (C) Once again check each statement to see if it is derived from the selection. Alternative (*I*) is expressly denied. Alternative (*II*) is touched on in the last paragraph. Alternative (*III*) is implied in the second paragraph. The author disavows (*IV*). His last sentence denies (*V*). Only (*II*) and (*III*) may be derived.

29. The passage suggests that ---- .
   (A) persons reporting UFO's are frauds and their motives are suspect
   (B) extraterrestrials probably visited the earth in distant ages
   (C) archaeologists are incorrect in suggesting how the pyramids were built
   (D) technological advances did not spring up suddenly throughout history
   (E) the markings in the sands of Peru are too mysterious to suggest a human origin

   (D) The author disagrees with (*B*), (*C*), and (*E*). He doesn't call anyone a fraud (*A*). (*D*) is clearly stated in lines 34–40.

30. Which of the following best expresses the main idea of the passage?
   (A) Puns have had a long and, on the whole, respectable history.
   (B) Shakespeare was a good and inveterate punster.
   (C) Good punsters are the life of the party, welcome everywhere.
   (D) Puns had their greatest moments during the Elizabethan period in England
   (E) Samuel Johnson praised punning and welcomed its use.

   (*A*) Alternatives (*B*) through (*E*) are details. (*A*) is the central idea.

31. According to Dr. F. A. Bather, Shakespeare ____ .
   (A) created more than a thousand puns
   (B) learned the art of punning from the Pentateuch
   (C) had Macbeth make a pun during the murder scene
   (D) was a writer who deserved uncritical admiration
   (E) was avidly read by German, French, and Italian writers

   (*A*) "Ten hundred and sixty-two puns" (line 28) is "more than a thousand." (*B*) is nowhere suggested. Lady Macbeth, not Macbeth, made the pun (*C*). (*D*) and (*E*) are not stated or implied, though they may well be true. Always stick to the passage.

32. The last line of the passage suggests that ____ .
   (A) most people do not have a sense of humor
   (B) too much of a good thing is not good
   (C) partygoing is a boring activity
   (D) people dislike the name *Paronomania*
   (E) though dying out nearly everywhere, punning still has its adherents

   (*B*) "The later stages" suggests an excess. The alternatives are irrelevant.

33. In the passage a pun is called each of the following *EXCEPT* ____ .
   (A) smaller excellency
   (B) word play
   (C) *paronomasia*
   (D) literary device
   (E) an unclassifiable type

   (*E*) **Smaller excellencies** is attributed to Samuel Johnson (line 13). **Word play** is noted in Japanese poetry (line 41). *Paronomasia* is mentioned (line 44). **Literary device** is quoted in the reference to Shakespeare (line 17). Only **unclassifiable type** is nowhere mentioned.

34. Which of the following best expresses the main idea of the passage?
    (A) The legendary prowess of Henry V has secured him an honored spot in English history.
    (B) The English have sometimes misunderstood and mistreated their royalty.
    (C) The saintly qualities of Henry VI have richly entitled him to a canonization that has so far eluded him.
    (D) Fifteenth century kings were largely figureheads ruled by intriguing courtiers.
    (E) As monarch, Henry VI was a disastrous failure in an age of intrigue and violence.

    (E) (A) is a detail. (B) is a minor inference. (C) and (D) are contradicted in the selection. Only (E) expresses the central idea.

35. Which of the following are *INCORRECTLY* matched?
    (A) "saintly simpleton" – Henry VI
    (B) "commanding presence" – Henry V
    (C) "innocent abroad" – Louis XI
    (D) "world of intrigue" – Borgias
    (E) "natural perversity" – Englishmen

    (C) The "**innocent abroad**" is more correctly linked with Henry VI, not Louis XI.

36. The passages implies that ___.
    (A) the manner of Henry VI's death made his failures seem less grievous
    (B) Henry VI inherited his father's martial ardor but not his skill
    (C) blood runs thin in the fourth and fifth generations
    (D) Henry VI was essentially a dissolute monarch with a passion for pleasure
    (E) the bias of the Abbot of St. Albans was based on hearsay, not personal knowledge.

    (A) (B) is expressly denied. (C) is not mentioned. (D) is contradicted by the content. The Abbot was "writing from personal knowledge" (E). Sentences 2 and 3 suggest (A) is correct.

37. Which of the following best summarizes the meaning of "hereditary lotteries"?
    (A) An instinct for gambling seems inborn in some people.
    (B) Basing a kingship upon inherited qualities is a gamble.
    (C) The inheritance of acquired characteristics is unproven.
    (D) Chance plays a minor role in inheritance.
    (E) Some English kings have been chosen by chance rather than design.

    (B) "The hereditary lottery" brought a most unsuitable king to the throne, Henry VI. *Lottery* itself suggests **gamble.**

38. The "bump which was heard around the world" was ___.
    (A) the sound of the electronic tube being destroyed
    (B) a jubilant broadcast using new techniques
    (C) a transistor literally exploding an electronic tube
    (D) the figurative replacement of an older substance by a newer
    (E) the first atomic explosion in Los Alamos

    (D) The expression "The electronic tube hit the scrap heap" is another way of saying that the electronic tube became obsolete. No actual physical action is implied. This is a figurative expression.

39. All the following are mentioned as examples of the superiority of transistors to electronic tubes *EXCEPT* ___.
    (A) size
    (B) speed of operation
    (C) solid state
    (D) reliability
    (E) cost

    (E) Transistors are tiny (line 20). They are "faster in operation" (line 34). They are "solid state" (line 23). They are "much more reliable" (line 35). Only **cost** is not mentioned.

40. According to the selection, powerful electronic amplification takes place ___.
    (A) inside silicon crystals
    (B) more effectively in a vacuum tube than in a transistor
    (C) by highly modified electrodes
    (D) inside the electron, at subatomic levels
    (E) with high-speed processing

    (A) The answer is provided in "form inside silicon crystals" (line 2).

Answers to Facsimile Test 4
(Pages 360–373)

Section 1

Part 1

1. D 2. D 3. B 4. E 5. A 6. A 7. B
8. C 9. E 10. D

Part 2

11. C 12. D 13. A 14. E 15. B

Part 3

16. B 17. E 18. D 19. A 20. C 21. B
22. D 23. E 24. A 25. C

Part 4

26. B 27. D 28. E 29. C 30. A 31. B
32. A 33. D 34. C 35. E 36. C 37. D
38. A 39. E 40. B

Section 2

Part 1

1. C 2. C 3. E 4. A 5. B 6. D 7. C
8. A 9. E 10. B 11. B 12. E 13. D
14. A 15. D

Part 2

16. C 17. B 18. D 19. A 20. E

Part 3

21. A 22. E 23. B 24. D 25. C 26. C
27. A 28. D 29. B 30. E

Part 4

31. C 32. A 33. E 34. D 35. B

Part 5

36. D 37. E 38. D 39. B 40. C 41. E
42. B 43. A 44. A 45. C

Answers to Facsimile Test 5
(Pages 374–387)

Section 1

Part 1

1. D 2. E 3. C 4. C 5. B 6. D 7. A
8. E 9. B 10. C

Part 2

11. E 12. A 13. B 14. D 15. C

Part 3

16. D 17. C 18. A 19. E 20. B 21. D
22. A 23. B 24. E 25. C

Part 4

26. B 27. C 28. E 29. B 30. A 31. C
32. D 33. D 34. D 35. B 36. B 37. E
38. C 39. A 40. E

Section 2

Part 1

1. C 2. E 3. B 4. A 5. D 6. E 7. D
8. A 9. C 10. B 11. A 12. B 13. E
14. C 15. D

Part 2

16. A 17. C 18. D 19. B 20. E

Part 3

21. C 22. E 23. D 24. A 25. B 26. A
27. C 28. B 29. E 30. D

Part 4

31. D 32. B 33. C 34. E 35. A

Part 5

36. D 37. E 38. C 39. B 40. A 41. B
42. E 43. C 44. A 45. D

INDEX